H 10
H M19
E 95

Ethnicity, Identity, and History

Ethnicity, Identity, and History

Essays in Memory of Werner J. Cahnman

Edited by
Joseph B. Maier and Chaim I. Waxman

Transaction Books
New Brunswick (U.S.A.) and London (U.K.)

The editors gratefully acknowledge the support of the Cahnman family and the Midgard Foundation in the publication of this volume.

Library of Congress Catalog Number: 82–6928
ISBN: 0–87855–461–0 (cloth)
Printed in the United States of America

Library of Congress Cataloging in Publication Data
Main entry under title:

Ethnicity, identity, and history.
  Bibliography: p.
  Includes index.
  1. Sociology—Addresses, essays, lectures. 2. Cahnman, Werner Jacob, 1902–   — Addresses, essays, lectures. 3. Jews—United States—Addresses, essays, lectures. 4. United States—Ethnic relations —Addresses, essays, lectures. I. Cahnman, Werner Jacob, 1902–
II. Maier, Joseph, 1911–   . III. Waxman, Chaim Isaac.
HM19.E85   301   82–6928
ISBN 0–87855–461–0   AACR2

Contents

1.

Werner J. Cahnman: An Introduction to His Life and Work

Joseph B. Maier and Chaim I. Waxman

Many social scientists regard system-building as the chief mark of genuine scholarship. Werner Cahnman's achievement was of a different sort; it lay, above all, in his superb ability to sift from the multitude of data furnished by history and experience that which is significant, and to analyze it in such a way as to enhance our knowledge and understanding. His rich lifework, written in German and English, mirrored his fate as a wanderer between worlds and cultures and as a mediator between them. The chief purpose of this Introduction is to sketch the development of Cahnman's mind in the great maze of his writings.

Cahnman's specific talent, his sensitivity to the historically relevant and sociologically significant, can be observed throughout his life. In trying to discern stages of his development we may perhaps distinguish four periods. The first would naturally be his German period, the springtime of his life as a young intellectual becoming aware of the breaks and fissures in the German/Jewish symbiosis, on the one hand, and the decisive importance of the enduring forms of human existence, such as family and people, on the other. It comprises the thirteen years from 1914 — the year World War I began and he read Arthur Ruppin's *Juden der Gegenwart* — to 1926, when his first paper, "Judentum und Volksgemeinschaft," was published (*Der Morgen*, 1926). That paper exudes an uncommon freshness and flavor of commitment and enthusiasm. It deals, after all, with the life and death questions of an old and tried people, with what is truly their own, their habits, outlook, memories, traditions; in fine, their history both individual and collective.

Werner Jacob Cahnman was born in Munich on September 30, 1902, the first son of an old German Jewish family. His paternal and maternal families were quite different. His father was born in a village, Rheinbischofsheim, and so were almost all of his relatives. Their Judaism was rus-

1

tic and folksy, sentimentally attached to family and community, but without Jewish learning. Werner's maternal family, on the other hand, was almost entirely concentrated in Munich and Nuremberg. They belonged to the *haute bourgeoisie*, were real estate operators, bankers, industrialists and jurists, not retailers. Their sons and daughters were interested in art and music or literature and philosophy. *Kultur* was their religion. Julius Schuelein, the famous Munich painter, was Werner's uncle. They thought of themselves as "good Jews," but their Judaism was either declaratory or cast in a free-thinking vein. The Jewish heroes of Werner's mother were Spinoza and Mendelssohn; her religion had an ethical orientation; she rarely, if ever, attended services. Yet she respected her husband's adherence to traditional values, helped in her matter-of-fact way in the observance of the Friday Eve and Passover *Seder* rituals, but disregarded the dietary laws. "The main idea of my mother," Werner recalled in the 1970's, "was that everybody, but especially a Jew, should promote justice in the world. She died in Piaski, Poland, in unimaginably terrible circumstances and in a situation of utmost injustice."

While Werner was always nearer to the female line in his maternal as well as his paternal families, it is from his father that he inherited the perspective of participant observer, the emotional attachment to places of his youth, and Jewishness as a matter of unquestioned belongingness or *Gemeinschaft*. Father Cahnman had been deeply interested in all aspects of Jewish life. Several times vice-president and president of the Munich Loge in B'nai B'rith, not a Zionist nor any kind of ideologue, but what Werner called "an adherent of Jewish peoplehood," he was an inveterate story-teller. "Thanks to him," Werner explained in a "Methodological Note" to a typological study of "Village and Small Town Jews in Germany" (1974), "my memory reaches three or four generations back into the past. My father's sister, Clementine Kraemer, has fixed some of these stories in writing. Having inherited my father's historical enthusiasm, I have collected many family-related data since early youth, partly by consulting archives, but chiefly by interviewing older relatives." The house of his parents in Munich was a meeting place for notables of all persuasions. Zionism, socialism, and women's problems were frequently discussed. While Werner got thus exposed to a variety of Jewish and political viewpoints, he felt that, on the whole, the Jews of Munich were bourgeois liberals. The Judaism of most of them was satisfied with the fact as such. They were neither religiously, nor philosophically, nor politically (Zionist) oriented, though possibly kind and generous in giving money to those in need. When they said, "I do not deny being Jewish" — that was as far as they would go.

In this situation Werner decided, "I must be Jewish in a much more genuine sense and that the way of moving along that path was Jewish learning." The decision had nothing to do with disagreeable experiences in school. On the contrary, "my classmates liked me, but they were aware that I was Jewish and I was aware of their awareness." Strangely enough for a teenager, he began with an excursion into Jewish demography by reading one of the first and best studies of the time, to be sure, the above-mentioned *Juden der Gegenwart* by Arthur Ruppin. Thenceforth, facts and figures about baptism, intermarriage, nonmarriage, declining birth-rates and what they seemed to augur about Jewish continuity, became an abiding concern to him. He read Theodor Herzl's Zionist writings and Davis Trietsch's *Palaestina-Handbuch*, and soon knew all the early settlements by heart. There, he thought, the Jew could be entirely himself, a worker and a fighter, a Maccabean. But World War I interfered. "My German patriotism was aroused, the revolution and its aftermath were deeply disturbing and I could not imagine myself running away to the fabled East when my right to live in my country was contested." University studies in economics, history, political science, and sociology in Berlin and Munich led to a doctorate with a dissertation on Ricardo (1927) sponsored by Professor von Zwiedinek-Suedenhorst, the noted exponent of *Sozialpolitik* at the University of Munich, and to an ever more intensive absorption in Jewish learning and Jewish political activity. Werner read all there was of Baeck, Buber, Rosenzweig, Brod, Graetz, Dubnow, Achad Haam, Fleg, Beer-Hofmann, including Benno Jacob's *Das erste Buch der Tora*, Morris Rosenfeld's *Songs from the Ghetto* (in a German translation from Rosenfeld's Yiddish), as well as Stifter's *Abdias*, and the varied antisemitic and philosemitic literature of the time. Buber, who frequently came to Munich, was the great guide in those years. What he meant to him, Werner recorded later in *The Reconstructionist* (1965). His paper on "Judentum and Volksgemeinschaft" was only the first quintessential expression of what was to become a characteristic Cahnman combination of elements — romantic philosophy and historiography, political democracy, and Jewish ethnicity.

Cahnman's second period comprises what he has sometimes called his years as a "social worker." These included his time as research associate at the Berlin *Industrie- und Handelskammer* and the *Institut fuer Weltwirtschaft* at the University of Kiel (1928–29), the years as *Syndikus* for Bavaria of the *Centralverein deutscher Staatsbuerger juedischen Glaubens* (1930–34), and the years as *Dozent* at the *Juedisches Lehrhaus* and member of the *Kulturbund* in Munich, until his escape from Germany in 1939. The position of *Syndikus* at the *Centralverein*, the major defense organization of German Jewry, offered the greatest challenge in view of the dark storm clouds gathering on the political horizon. Men in their twenties were, as a rule, hardly considered mature and experienced enough to cope with the responsibilities of the job. When Werner was finally chosen, he accepted enthusiastically, attempting to calm the fears of his elders with the assurance that "at my age, Napoleon won the battle of Arcole." He knew, alas, that nothing of the kind was in store. The watchword of the day was first defense then survival, of German Jewry.

There is no need to write here in detail about Cahnman's work in the *Centralverein* and the six years he spent under Nazi rule. He described and analyzed the events of that time in two incisive papers, "Die Juden in Muenchen 1918–1943" (*Zeitschrift fuer Bayerische Landesgeschichte*, 1979), and "The Decline of the Munich Jewish Community, 1933–1938" (*Jewish Social Studies*, 1941). It must be left to a future historian to mine properly the riches of Werner's *Centralverein* files. There is no doubt, the work demanded real courage and energy on the part of leaders and followers alike. Werner came to appreciate the Jews in the antisemitic small towns of Franconia and Suebia (also in Regensburg, Straubing, Weiden, and Ingolstadt). He discovered in them, especially the Jewish teachers among them, a degree of sensitivity, patience, perseverance in adversity and Jewish loyalty which he could not find in the big city Jews of Munich, Augsburg, and Nuremberg. Two late sociological harvestings of that period he presented in "Role and Significance of the Jewish Artisan Class" (*The Jewish Journal of Sociology*, 1965) and "Village and Small Town Jews in Germany" (*Leo Baeck Yearbook*, 1974). The Berlin leadership, Werner felt, never fully comprehended what was happening in Bavaria, and "when the catastrophe was upon us, the initial attitude of incomprehension and vain hope gradually changed (after 1935, surely after 1938) into an urge to flee."

Cahnman could not share the hyperpatriotic position of the Jewish war veterans' organization because it was so utterly unrealistic and at times even callous and undignified. Unlike most other *Centralverein* leaders, he made common cause with the Zionists, the Zionist youth associations, and the *Ostjuden*, Jews of East European descent, who then constituted 25 percent of the Jews of Munich — now, in the 1980s, they are 85 percent. He met and taught them at the *Lehrhaus*, even as he was a fellow student with them in the Hebrew language courses and came to love Hebrew as a link "connecting us over the generations, something that binds and strengthens us." Werner published many papers, journal articles, and book reviews at that time, including a piece titled "Warum Hebraeisch lernen?" (*Frankfurter Israelitisches Gemeindeblatt*, 1937). Most of them are *oeuvres d'occasion*, reflecting the fact that he could no longer choose his topics as freely as before. He continued his work even after the *Centralverein* office was closed down and he was briefly thrown into the Munich police prison as "a leader of an illegal organization."

In the spring of 1937 Werner visited Palestine. "The sacredness of its soil could still be experienced," he said. He met many Jewish leaders. The

Arab riots lasted throughout his stay in the Holy Land. When he saw Judah Magnes, president of the Hebrew University, on Mount Scopus, he commented that, unlike others, he thought the unrest might last a long time. Magnes replied: "A *very* long time." Cahnman abandoned original plans of permanent settlement. He strongly felt that his place was still in Munich — "I had been a Jewish official, after all" — in order to help where help was needed. In a report to the non-Zionist members of the Jewish Agency, which he wrote after his return to his native city, Munich, he stressed two weak spots of the *Yishuv*: the lack of a post-medieval religious movement and the inability of many Jews to understand that they must share the land with the Arabs. He concluded by saying that "only deep anxiety for what we love can give us the strength to confront both raging hostility from the outside and blind partisanship in our own midst."

Werner was confident that his luck would not desert him and that he would be able to catch the right moment to leave Germany. That moment came when Hitler marched into Vienna. He was sure that World War II was now imminent. His number on the waiting list for an immigration visa to the USA would not be called so soon. He knew he could not wait for two or three more years. Fortunately, an elderly lady cousin in London underwrote his stay in England and Werner was able to emigrate in June 1939, just a few short weeks before the outbreak of the war. But first he had to go through the trials and tribulations of the concentration camp in Dachau, with torture and death ever before his very eyes. Werner's description of his two months in Dachau, November and December 1938, is still a moving document (*Chicago Jewish Forum*, 1964).

America opened an entirely new chapter in Werner Cahnman's life story. Before moving on to the American scene, however, a few words must be said about Austria, especially Vienna. There is, first, the obvious fact of Munich's geographical propinquity to the Austrian border. More importantly, Werner's principal teacher at the University of Munich, Professor von Zwiedineck, was an Austrian and hence sensitive to questions of nationality. Werner was in touch with Erich von Kahler, the noted humanist. In the *Centralverein*, he had been charged with maintaining contact with the Austrian sister organization, the *Oesterreichisch-Israelitische Union*. He had visited Vienna in 1932 to see his opposite numbers at the *Union* and some Catholic leaders, especially Eugen Kogon and Father Bichlmaier, even Professor Joseph Nadler. The decisive contacts, however, were established in 1937, when Werner went to Vienna illegally. On that occasion he met with a sizable number of Jewish religious leaders and scholars, Austrian Zionists *della prima hora*, and others closely connected with Jewish national movements.

Without the help of these men, Werner tells us in an unpublished manuscript, "My Relation to Jews and Judaism" (1979), "I could neither have started nor completed my researches into the reasons for the rise of the Jewish national movement in Austria which I centered around the person of Adolph Fischhof and his pamphlet, *Oesterreich und die Buergschaften seines Bestandes* (1869)." He had to delay work on these topics, he adds, for twenty turbulent and distressing years, until he received support from the "Conference on Material Claims against Germany" in the 1950's. He published four papers on Fischhof, two in English, two in German, which "clearly establish Fischhof as the fountainhead not only of federal thinking, but also of the Jewish national movement in Austria."

Work on another topic conceived at that time but completed much later — in three versions, the latest in 1969 — deals with "The Three Regions of German Jewry," showing that a unified and uniform German Jewry never existed. There was southwest German Jewry, northeast German Jewry, and the Jews of the Austrian-Bohemian region. Werner further assembled materials, which were never published, demonstrating from biographical data that German Jewry was a branch of Ashkenazic Jewry, not a separate entity.

Cahnman came to the United States in 1940. His first feeling on American soil was one of immense relief, of joy that he had succeeded in getting a spot on Noah's Ark to the land of freedom. The country's English origins were still alive, and not merely in the history books. The English past was then only beginning to recede, decade after decade, until the English heritage became what it is today — a mere component in the ethnic multiplicity of America. Werner's Americanization began almost immediately in a summer seminar for foreign scholars and teachers at the Brewster Free Academy, a Quaker institution in Wolfboro, New Hampshire. The guiding spirit of the seminar was Herbert A. Miller, "a wise old scholar" and long-time friend and colleague of Robert E. Park in the sociology department of the University of Chicago. He told the newcomers: "This is the land of the free and the home of the brave, where everybody can do as he likes — and if he doesn't, you make him. One must quickly learn to howl with the wolves. The pressure to conform is relentless. You are welcome, provided you do not object; if you do, you are not punished, you are merely ignored."

Werner tried all along not to surrender his liberty, but he paid a price. The University of Munich had certified him as *Doctor oeconomiae publicae*, something of a cross between an economist, economic historian, jurist, and political scientist, but Professor Miller evaluated his Jewish, Bavarian, German, Austrian, and near Eastern antecedents, as far as intellectual interests were concerned, in such a way as to define and designate him as a race and culture specialist in sociology. He recommended him as a "visiting Ph.D." to the Department of Sociology at the University of Chicago. In due course, "I became a Chicago sociologist," Werner recalled, "very near to Everett Hughes; through Redfield something of an anthropologist;

through Blumer something of a social psychologist," but chiefly indebted to Robert E. Park who "influenced my thinking very much." Without that particular association, he believed, a number of papers that still make exciting reading "could not have been written," among them "Mediterranean and Caribbean Regions: A Comparison in Race and Culture Contacts" (*Social Forces*, 1943), "Religion and Nationality" (*American Journal of Sociology*, 1944), "The Concept of *Raum* and the Theory of Regionalism" (*American Sociological Review*, 1944), "France in Algeria" (*Review of Politics*, 1945).

It was in Chicago, too, that Cahnman met Louis Wirth, one of the few and certainly the best known Jewish sociologist in the country at the time. Their common interest in things Jewish did not, however, make for a warm relationship between them, if for no other reason than their opposing perspectives on ethnicity in general, and Jewish ethnicity in particular. Werner maintained his strong survivalist perspective, projecting the survival of ethnic groups from both normative and empirical viewpoints. Wirth, on the other hand, insisted on a strong assimilationist outlook. He was, to be sure, very much interested in Jewish themes, but on the condition that the student demonstrate the inevitability of the absorption of the Jews, as of any other group, into the mainstream of the larger society. While their conflicting stance did not permit them to become friends, it allowed the development of a formal relationship. After Werner had spent several years as an instructor at Fisk and Atlanta Universities, Wirth even helped him get the position of research associate to Oscar Janowsky, director of the Jewish Community Center Study of the National Jewish Welfare Board. In a way, Werner wistfully remarked, "I was thus relegated to an (academic) backwater."

On the Jewish scene in America, meanwhile, Cahnman encountered pitfalls as well as compensations. From Munich he had brought with him two sets of data which he hoped to publish. One was the statistics on Jewish emigration from Munich 1933–39. In undertaking the study, his idea was to not let that Jewish community go under without a song, to retain a document of its existence. Salo W. Baron, Professor of Jewish History at Columbia University, accepted the paper immediately for the *Journal of Jewish Studies*, even as Werner never forgot that the great historian, himself of Austrian birth, had always been hospitable to Jewish refugee scholars. It was different with another paper, "Herzl and the Munich Jewish Community," which he had saved from the community's archives. Strangely enough, Zionist leaders were not interested. Even after Professor Guido Kisch, himself an immigrant, had published it in his *Historia Judaica*, the Zionist Organization of America took no notice of the story which elucidates an important chapter in the history of the Zionist movement.

There were some Jewish scholars whose friendship meant a great deal to

Werner in those trying years. He observed that, except Salo Baron, none held a university position of any importance. There was Joshua Bloch, the director of the Jewish section of the New York Public Library; there was Mark Wishnitzer, whose posthumous work on Jewish arts and crafts he helped publish; there was the latter's wife, Rachel Wishnitzer, the dean of Jewish art historians; there was Bernard Richards, one of the founders of the American Jewish Congress; there was Henry Hurwitz, the editor of the *Menorah Journal*, who published his sketch of a memorable meeting with Stefan Zweig in Salzburg. And there was Chaim Greenberg, the leader of the Labor Zionists and editor of the *Jewish Frontier*, who tactfully never asked him to join the party, but invited him, or had him invited through Ben Halpern, to the meetings of the journal's editorial board and published a number of his papers.

At the time, Cahnman felt actually closer to the *Hashomer Hatzair* than to the Labor Zionists, even as he opposed their antireligious attitude and was skeptical toward their Marxism. He liked their *Gemeinschaft* way of life, and in agreement with them, he supported the idea of a binational state in Palestine rather than the Biltmore Program. He was, in those years, perhaps more of a *Chovev Zion* than a political Zionist. In due course, Werner realized that the binational state was an illusion — the Arabs would never agree to it. There is no way back from the Jewish State, except catastrophe. In 1948, Chaim Greenberg involved him in the fight for the Partition Resolution of the United Nations. Werner was supposed to use his contacts with blacks. "I enlisted the initially wavering votes of Liberia and Haiti," he recalled, "which simple fact ensured victory." No doubt he enjoyed that "volunteer excursion into high politics."

Werner Cahnman did finally find his "home" in American Jewish life, when Rabbis Mordecai M. Kaplan and Eugene Kohn asked him to join the editorial board of *The Reconstructionist* magazine. To the end of his life, he faithfully cooperated in the work of the editorial board and published many thoughtful articles in the journal. It would be an exaggeration, though, to say that he was a thoroughly *kosher* Reconstructionist. For one, he did not share their William James–John Dewey tradition. He preferred his science and religion pure; he found no sense in a "scientific" religion and in a "natural" rather than supernatural God. His God was the God of *Nishmat kol chai* whom we can acknowledge, but never recognize. Werner did, however, agree with Kaplan's idea of "peoplehood." To Kaplan, Judaism is not a religion, like Presbyterianism or Lutheranism. The Jewish people have a religion. Said Werner, "We are a people, the land of Israel, which we love, is not the center, but the periphery; the Jewish people as a world-people, defines the center and holds it in place. That is the kind of Zionism I can accept." Thus his initially regionalistic and autonomistic thinking à la Fischhof got reformulated in an American setting.

In his fourth period it appeared that Cahnman "had it made" at last. That period comprises the close-to-twenty remaining years of his life: from the termination of his government service in the "Voice of America," through his teaching at Rutgers University and the New School for Social Research, his teaching at his old *alma mater* in Munich, his prominent participation in the work of the interdisciplinary faculty University Seminar on Content and Methods of the Social Sciences at Columbia, until his short trip to Kiel, the scene of his first scholarly position, to deliver the principal address on "Toennies und die Theorie des sozialen Wandels" at the Toennies Symposium of the University in the summer of 1980 (*Zeitschrift für Soziologie*, 1981).

Werner felt he had been "finally rescued for sociology, when Joseph Maier brought me to Rutgers University" in 1960, and he became a full Professor of Sociology. He was highly respected among all his colleagues, although he did not become part of the "inner circle" of that faculty either. For that he was too fastidious in his ideals and standards, too set in his customs and habits, too German, too Jewish, too much himself. He felt himself, as he was seen by others, to be a "stranger." It is no accident that he was time and again preoccupied with the conceptual clarification of the term "stranger," as used by Toennies, Brentano, and Simmel. Sociologically, a stranger is not merely a wanderer who comes today and leaves tomorrow, but who comes today and stays tomorrow. To Simmel, himself a German Jew, the Jews of Europe were the most striking example of the "stranger." Cahnman preferred the term "*Vermittler*" or "intermediary" for the stranger who stays, and he distinguished him sharply from the "pariah." To him, strangers are not "pariahs" nor are "pariahs" (in India) strangers. He uses the term "intermediary" not exclusively microsociologically in Simmel's sense, who refers to the *tertium gaudens* as an intermediary between two others, but rather macrosociologically in the sense of Toennies, that is, as a commercial and cultural intermediary within a social structure. The function of mediation has its two sides, Cahnman said: "On the one hand, the intermediary as an outsider is looked upon with suspicion; on the other, because he is an outsider, he is welcomed as a friend, a counsellor, an impartial judge. He is a neighbor, but he has the advantage of remoteness."

In the years of this last period, Werner Cahnman crossed the boundary for what had hitherto been his chosen areas within sociology. Although apparent in his earlier writings, there now emerged an even greater, one might say systematic, concern with the historical perspective in sociology. The appearance of his (and Alvin Boskoff's) *Sociology and History* (1964) has made a difference in American sociology. Through his own writings and as chairman of the Historical Sociology Section in the American Sociological Association, he has indeed marked the way of a new sociology that steers its course between the Scylla of rigid generalization and the Charybdis of sheer empiricism. He explained "Historical Sociology: What It Is and What It Is not" (1976) and showed that sophisticated use of comparative materials and typological devices is enormously helpful in producing work which is both sociologically oriented and historically relevant.

Allied to his efforts in historical sociology in these years was Werner's work as a Toennies scholar. True, to Charles Loomis belongs the credit for the translation into English of *Gemeinschaft und Gesellschaft*. With *Ferdinand Toennies: A New Evaluation* (1973), however, and *Ferdinand Toennies on Sociology: Pure, Applied and Empirical* (1971), which he co-edited with Rudolf Heberle, Toennies' son-in-law, Werner Cahnman has done more than any American scholar before and since to bring Toennies onto the center stage of sociological theory. For all the frequent use of the German terms *Gemeinschaft* and *Gesellschaft* and their frequently mistaken identification with Durkheim's "mechanical" and "organic" solidarity, Toennies had been virtually unknown in this country. As Everett Hughes told us recently: "American sociologists in following their self-appointed leaders have neglected all but a few European sociologists. Their favorites are Durkheim and Weber. They don't know anything about LePlay, Toennis, Simmel, and others a person could name. This has been our great weakness. The Chicago people took sociology where they found it. The majority of American sociologists, I fear, find it only at two or three shrines. Cahnman had the misfortune to go to the wrong shrine."

Even his work on ethnicity in general and Jewish ethnicity in particular came to occupy a distinct place on the American scene. That things are different now is in no little measure owed to him. His *Intermarriage and Jewish Life* (1963) was the first of a whole series of publications on a subject very much on the mind of Jews. A Jewish orientation is acknowledged in sociology. A vigorous minority of Jewish sociologists is organized in an Association for the sociological Study of Jewry, with its own organ, *Contemporary Jewry*, and Werner serving on its editorial board. His "Nature and Varieties of Ethnicity" (1980), the last essay to appear just before his death, is in more than one way a quintessential statement of his thought on the theme. It deals with ethnicity in different times, countries, and global regions, concluding with an astute assessment of ethnicity in a civilizational context.

At the very end, Werner was ready to branch out into deeper and more detailed studies in the major areas of his concern and competence. His papers on "Hobbes, Toennies and Vico" and "Schelling and the New Thinking in Judaism" are in print at this writing. There is an unfinished manuscript on the history of sociology; there are notes on a variety of research projects, memoranda and correspondence on past and planned activities of the "Rashi Association for the Preservation of Jewish Cultural Monuments in Europe," which he had tirelessly directed for several years. They confirm that he was busy on a host of old and new endeavors. At this point his life was cut short. He died of cancer in New York on September 27, 1980, leaving a devoted and loving wife, Gisella, who had shared his trials and triumphs since their early days in Chicago.

2.

Interaction Between Cultures:
Herder's *Volk* and Fichte's *Nation*

Louis Dumont

The remarks that follow are detached from a work in progress bearing on social thought in Germany from 1770 to 1830. They must be prefaced by a short and rough statement of the intention from which they spring and the approach that shapes them. The intention is to compare national subcultures within modern civilization, more precisely to compare nationally predominant systems of ideas and values, here called ideologies, taken as so many (equivalent) variants of modern ideology at large. Such comparison is made possible by its being located within a wider perspective where modern ideology itself is subjected to comparison with systems of the same order. Apart from the necessary distantiation or relativization, the wider research has produced a few conceptual tools that are brought to bear on the narrower subject matter. In actual fact, previous work has consisted simply of a bipolar comparison between the modern West and traditional India,[1] and the conceptual kit may be found very rudimentary, for it is made up essentially of two tools: the distinction between individualism and holism, and the concept of hierarchy or of "the hierarchical opposition."

I speak of "holism" when in a given society the primary value attaches to the society as a whole, and of "individualism" when it attaches to the human individual. When the individual is valued above all else, I write of him as the Individual. Although this distinction was, so to speak, forced upon me by the Indian study, and in the first place by the need inherent in a social-anthropological work bearing on Indian people for their values to be compared to our own, the distinction has another side, namely its parentage in (by definition Western modern) sociology. The immediate forebear is Toennies. As Werner Cahnman has put us in his debt most particularly by his work on Toennies, reviving his thought and drawing attention to his merits as one of the founders of sociology, it is apposite that I should here stress my indebtedness to Toennies. Retrospectively, it is clear that the hol-

13

ism/individualism distinction reproduces with some modification Toennies' distinction between *Gemeinschaft* and *Gesellschaft*, community and society. Cahnman has appropriately recalled the contrast and the controversy between Toennies and the early Durkheim of the *Division of Labour*.[2] The apparent inversion between Toennies' community/society and Durkheim's mechanical/organic (solidarity) is easily understood if one takes into account the difference in the level of consideration: the former author speaks of conscious aspects, representations of norm-concepts, what I call ideology; the latter states the results of external observation. As is often the case, there is between those two levels a kind of mirror effect, an inversion. From the point of view of the present study, the more important, more radical view is that of Toennies — the more so as it can accommodate in a subordinate position what amounts to Durkheim's qualification or reversal of it. But such a more complete view lies beyond our present purpose, which is limited to the ideological aspect. It is important to remark that Toennies's distinction is fed from German intellectual history, so to speak. It is well known that his *Gemeinschaft* is related to the view of Adam Müller, a romantic theoretician of the State from whom Othmar Spann derived his "universalism," i.e., what is called here holism. But more generally it can be said that Toennies perceived and expressed two antagonistic as well as complementary modes of thought that were first opposed and then again combined in German thought all through the nineteenth century. Toennies's eminence consists to my mind in the fact that he was able — he was perhaps the first to be able — again to analyze where others had wanted rather to unite or confound.

Toennies's distinction is I think extremely useful for comparative purposes. I hope to show this usefulness here, itself in a limited example, extracted from German intellectual history. But of course the example cannot be taken as really demonstrative, given what was said above about the German origin of the distinction itself. While my feeling is to have brought it back from India, it is true that when applying it to German thought I only refer it back, so to speak, to the climate from which it originally sprung. The truth is that India has only helped in sharpening the tool by including the dimension of the relative valuation of the two terms of the distinction in each case. It can be objected that in my practice I go too far in a direction opposed to Toennies's major interest. But I believe it is more a matter of emphasis than of opposition. While Toennies stressed the coexistence of the two modes in any, and especially in modern societies, he nevertheless recognized the steady increases of *Gesellschaft* — like formations in "late" societal development. I am content most of the time with characterizing modern society by the sole predominance of the individualist valuation. While contending that it is essential to do so for comparative purposes at the present stage, because most societies, or those to be considered, do actually very markedly subordinate one mode to the other and must be compared as unified wholes, I do admit that this sort of consideration is still very gross, that it represents only a first step, and that we should be able in the future to take into account at the same time the subordinate levels and describe their articulation. It will be readily seen that this can be done only in terms of values, i.e., of the hierarchy of levels, and not by simply juxtaposing items, i.e., situations or contexts and value orientations, as if they were of equal weight in the eyes of the protagonists themselves.

We are thus led to the second "tool" mentioned at the beginning, which I called hierarchy or "the hierarchical opposition." Unfortunately, space forbids my enlarging on this question as it would deserve. I shall briefly note a few fundamental points: (1) Hierarchy has principally nothing to do with political power although it is often found inextricably enmeshed in it. (2) Nor does hierarchy require a linear succession of terms or entities, although it can generate such chains. (3) It is most economically seen as a relation between *two* entities in which the one is super, the other subordinated. The relation of the two to a whole being explicitly or implicitly present; the most immediate case is when the first entity constitutes *the whole* in question while the second is *an element* of it (system and subsystem). (4) The hierarchical relation is best analyzed into two statements bearing on two ranked levels: on the superior level the two ranked entities are identical, or consubstantial; on the inferior level they are opposed as contrary, complementary or contradictory. Therefore I speak of the hierarchical relation as *the encompassing of the contrary.* Thus in the creation of man and woman in the first Book of Genesis, Eve is fashioned from a rib of Adam to signify that woman is encompassed in man, man being: (a) on the first level the representative of the human species as a whole, (b) on the second level the opposite of woman. Apart from the linguistic fact of man (or Adam) figuring on the two levels, the essential feature is that *the couple as a whole hierarchizes its components*, one should say unites them while recognizing their difference.[3]

Let me state the precise sense in which "comparison" is here understood. It has nothing to do with "cross-cultural" studies, for we do not assume to be in possession of universal categories in terms of which we could classify or compare all cultures. The paradigm of comparison is that which is present, explicitly or implicitly, in the work of the social anthropologist: he himself is rooted in one culture, and he studies another by bridging the gap between the two, empirically at first through participant observation, and then by a sustained effort at building up correspondences or equivalences between congeries of very disparate elements. The work is radical in the sense that the researcher puts in question his own presuppositions every time they block the way to understanding. As it is impossible to put in question everything at the same time the work is necessarily piecemeal, even though it is essential to look at every detail against the widest relevant background. It proceeds largely by trial and error, it aims at taking advantage of the particularities of the subject matter rather than at building according to a preconceived system. In that sense the work is unsystematic, although it takes advantage of some systematic aspects found in the discipline. All in all it is a matter of a bipolar comparison, radically empirical and relatively unsystematic, holistic in intention but piecemeal by necessity.

When I start "comparing" in that sense French and German social idologies, the situation is somewhat different. True, I am a native in one of the two subcultures in question, but instead of doing fieldwork in the other I resort to the study of written evidence, I read the literature. I believe I can do so because, in place of fieldwork, I have at my disposal a fulcrum outside these subcultures, namely the small conceptual kit that I, so to speak, brought back from India. It should be clear also that the comparison is primarily static, morphological. It is not dynamic, nor immediately concerned with interaction. Only it so happens that the comparison of forms leads in conclusion to surmising a certain interaction. I shall here for the sake of brevity anticipate the conclusion and present the case straightaway in terms of interaction.

The first point that requires notice is that our more or less national subcultures, although they do participate in the same modern culture, do not by any means communicate between themselves as immediately and easily as one might suppose, and as common sense does suppose, especially perhaps French common sense. Actually, as we shall see French common sense hardly recognizes at all the existence of different subcultures. Modern culture has a powerful universalist slant which leads to rejecting to other domains the differences when actually encountered. One speaks of different "national characters," and each European country uses stereotypes about neighboring countries which imply that the "cognitive map" is the same here and there, and the differences only a matter of behavioral idiosyncrasies. National subcultures are to some extent opaque to each other — thus France and Germany. That the conflicts and estrangement of the nineteenth and twentieth centuries do not result only from the confrontation of two national states, one older, the other younger, as shown by the dispute among historians about Alsace-Lorraine after 1870 and by the qualms of conscience and tortured re-examinations of several notable French Germanists-cum-philosophers around 1914. It is testified again by two outstanding witnesses, Heinrich Heine and Ernst Troeltsch, who have perceived, the former as the heir of romanticism, the latter as a historian and sociologist who had lived through the World War I, the distance between the two nationally predominant modes of thought and the difficulty of making them communicate.

Actually in the case of Troeltsch, the contrast is rather between the German and what he calls the "western" ideological make-up, British first and French only second. I am referring to a remarkable address which he gave on a solemn occasion in 1922, and which would be lost to us but for the judicious inclusion of a translation of it by Ernest Barker in his edition of Gierke in 1934, where it is intended as throwing light on the latter's German holism.[4] The traumatism of defeat has here sharpened Troeltsch's reflection, and in hindsight the text has a prophetic ring — as have also other German essays of the time. It interests us here for its lucid depiction of the gap between the two ideologies. For Troeltsch, the divergence is due to German innovation. While the West, Catholic or Calvinist, remained deeply in touch with stoic and christian individualism, modern Germany, essentially Lutheran, has developed a set of quite different representations. There are two stages. A period of ideological building up is followed by a period where the new ideology becomes adapted to the historical circumstances and acquires some of its least attractive features. The innovation is attributed to German romanticism taken obviously in a very wide sense, since beyond the romantics proper it extends not only to Herder but to Hegel and represents in the last analysis only an intensification of what was already present in classicism. We may thus understand by the term the movement of ideas which takes shape with the *Sturm und Drang* in the 1770s, culminates in the first decade of the nineteenth century and extends to the two following. In essence, it is "a new concept of individuality" that constitutes a "new principle of ethical and historical reality." Individuality is conceived "in a mystico-metaphysical manner as the every time particular incarnation of the divine spirit in individual persons and in superpersonal communities and organizations." Here is the principle of the contrast between the two mentalities:

> On the one side, an eternal, rational and divinely ordained system of Order, embracing both morality and law, (...) on the other, individual, living, and perpetually new incarnations of an historically creative Mind. Those who believe in an eternal and divine Law of Nature, the Equality of man, and a sense of Unity pervading mankind, and who find the essence of Humanity in these things, cannot but regard the German doctrine as a curious mixture of mysticism and brutality. Those who take an opposite view — who see in history an ever-moving stream, which throws up unique individualities as it moves, and is always shaping individual structures on the basis of a law which is always new — are bound to consider the west-European world of ideas as a world of cold rationalism and equalitarian atomism, a world of superficiality and Pharisaïsm (Barker's translation, *loc. cit.*, p. 204).

Troeltsch acknowledges the superiority of the German view regarding historical awareness, which amounts to a discovery of the historical dimension, the emancipation of subjective morality and the recognition of societies as wholes. At the same time he deplores the fact that, although German ideology is in the last analysis just as the western one based on the autonomy of personality, Germany has strayed away dangerously from stressing the value that should always encompass (*umschliessen*, p. 22) all others, namely the universal community of mankind and the rights of man as such, and he demands that it should be revived. We know that this necessary reunion has been delayed for a quarter century by renewed historical vicissitudes of which we may say as Troeltsch did of the previous ones that they resulted in "brutalising romanticism and romanticising cynicism." Perhaps the fact is an index of the immediate incompatibility of the two sets of values, while Troeltsch, in this official address, seems to suppose that surmounting the opposition is unproblematic. At any rate, he has clearly diagnosed the cleavage, and we must be thankful to him for it. He warrants the existence of a distinctive German variant of modern ideology, with whose beginnings, or an aspect of them, we are concerned here.

I shall focus on a major aspect of the historical interaction of French and German subcultures. Beginning in the eighteenth century and especially with the *Sturm und Drang* movement, and throughout the age of the French Revolution and of Napoleon's Empire, German culture exhibits, at the level of learned humanism, an unprecedented development. This development brings about on the one hand complete emancipation in relation to French culture, which previously dominated the scene to the extent of appearing coterminous with culture in general, or universally valid. On the other hand, the same development not only lays the basis of modern German ideology, but builds it up in its essential framework. I should add, but it is hardly necessary, that this same movement of thought has been of the first importance not only for Germany but for modern ideology — or culture — in general.

For this very reason, to present it as I just did is likely to arouse protests: it will be argued that the great philosophical systems are part of our universal patrimony and have nothing to do with national ideologies. Even if one admits that German thought was goaded on so to speak by French and English enlightenment and the French Revolution, one will hesitate to see in that thought itself the result of an interaction between national cultures. After all the French Revolution itself is more than a French phenomenon. It is part and parcel of modern culture at large. And perhaps I should make it clear that I do not propose to reduce German thought to the conditions of its genesis any more than the truth or value of a statement is reducible to the circumstances in which it was arrived at. Especially for the anthropologist a feature is no less universal for its being rooted in a particular tradition. In the main, however, the question is whether the proposed approach throws light on the matter, and the objections must give way if in the end the new perspective gives a better account of the data than the more habitual view.

In 1774, at the time of the short-lived *Sturm und Drang* movement, or German preromanticism, Herder, who is thirty years old, publishes "Another Philosophy of History" (*Auch eine Philosophie der Geschichte*). The title indicates a reply to Voltaire, and, while the philosophy of history it propounds is actually complex, the short book (it takes 110 pages in the edition of the complete works) is in essence an impassioned polemic against the Enlightenment with its platitudinous rationalism and its narrow conception of progress, and in the very first place against the hegemony of this universalist rationalism which despises all that is foreign to it and presumes to impose everywhere its senile refinement. Herder rehabilitates everything that the French and English eighteenth century rejected or ignored: the barbarous Middle Ages, ancient Egypt sacrificed to the glory of Greece, and very importantly, religion. Instead of history consisting in the accession of reason, a reason disembodied and everywhere identical to itself, Herder sees in history the contrasted interplay of individual cultures or cultural individuals each of which constitutes a specific human community or *Volk*, each embodying an aspect of general humanity in a unique and irreplaceable manner. The German *Volk* which carries the western christian culture is the modern example of the category. In the flow of history, there is not only simply progress (*Fortschritt*) but, within each of the two civilizational complexes, the ancient and the modern, what one may call a sucession of "forward strivings" or blossomings (*Fortgang, Fortstreben*), all "of equal necessity, equal originality, equal merit, equal happiness."[5]

All in all, in the face of the dominant universalism, Herder in 1774 asserts with ardor the diversity of cultures, each of which he extols in turn. He does not ignore the borrowings by one culture from another, always accompanied by a thorough modification of the borrowed element. He even notes fleetingly that each excellence is paid for by some shortcoming, so that all those perfections are unilateral or incomplete.

We may say that, by anticipation, the basis is laid here for a right of the cultures or "peoples" in contrast to the future Rights of Man. This implies a deep transformation in the definition of man: as opposed to the abstract individual, a representative of the human species, endowed with reason but stripped of all particularity, man for Herder is what he is, in all his modes of thinking, feeling and acting, by virtue of his belonging to a given cultural community. This view, as much else in Herder, is not absolutely new. One thinks in the first place of Rousseau, who parted with the *Encyclopédistes* precisely on this point, as a "citizen of Geneva" fully acknowledging the social nature of man, that is to say his belonging to a concrete society as a necessary condition of his education into a man.

We have before us here a fundamental difference in the conception of man. In the last analysis, either the fundamental value is attached to the

Individual, and we may speak in this sense of the "individualism" of Voltaire and the authors of the *Encyclopédie*, or the fundamental value is attached to the society or culture, to the collective being, and in that sense I shall speak of "holism" as emerging in Rousseau and in Herder. If as I believe the accession of individualism to predominance distinguishes modern culture from all others and at any rate from the other great civilizations, we face here, in the resurgence of a holistic aspect in modern culture, an important fact of history. Yet we must note an unprecedented novelty. In traditional holism, the society is exclusive, humankind coincides with the society formed by *us*, and strangers are devalued as being, at best, imperfect men. By the way, even modern patriotism is tinged with that feeling. On the contrary, with Herder all cultures are recognized as equal in principle. It should be clear that such an assertion is possible only because cultures are viewed as so many individuals, equal among themselves notwithstanding their difference: *cultures are individuals of a collective nature.* In other words Herder on the one hand discards individualism in favor of holism on the level of the elements, i.e., when he considers individual human beings, but on the other hand he uses the individualist principle by transferring it to the level of compounds, so to speak. That is when he considers collective entities that were until then unacknowledged or subordinated. It would be wrong therefore to see Herder as rejecting wholesale the individualist — mainly French — culture, for he accepts at the same time a major feature of it in order to assert against that very culture the existence and the value of German culture, and with it of all the others that have flourished in history. Therefore again, taken globally, Herder's reaction must be located *within* the modern value system. His holism must be seen as contained within the individualism which he fiercely attacks — and the circumstance may well account for the style of the book, that is, tense, screaming, almost panting.

Later, in the more serene climate of Weimar, Herder will attempt to reconcile universality and concreteness in his *Ideen* through the notion of *Humanität* which embodies the tension between the two poles and which, perhaps for this reason, he despairs of defining. The strident protest of the 1774 booklet is much clearer. It presents a momentous case of what anthropologists have called in our days acculturation.

It may be said in all rigor that Herder posits a German subculture by the side of the French one *within modern culture.* Moreover, in doing so he lays the basis for what will be later the "ethnic theory" of nationalities as against the "elective theory" in which the nation rests essentially on consensus, on Renan's "everyday plebiscite." We have just seen that the ethnic theory rests at bottom on the same equalitarian — i.e., individualistic — basis as the elective theory does. The two theories are therefore not completely independent of each other as it is often assumed nowadays.

They both apply, albeit on different levels, the same modern principle of equalitarian individualism.

It is fair to say that in Herder's cultural disquisitions the human individual is completely merged in the community or people taken as one. It is only on the most global level that we are able to descry the presence of the individualist principle. Here I must beg the reader's permission to introduce the hierarchical consideration: Herder asserts each concrete culture as a collective entity in which individuals are merged, and thus presents a holistic protest against the individualism of the Enlightenment, but this protest actually takes place at a subordinate level. At the superior level, the global level of consideration where the different cultures are assembled, they have equal rights, and this fact in turn shows, as against the ethnocentricism of naïve holism, adherence to modern individualism (transferred from the elementary to the collective level). I am aware that the reader might prefer to look at the combination in a different way, yet I am convinced that my formulation of it is right, or better that it is the most pregnant one from the point of view of the comparison of cultures and subcultures and their interaction. It is confirmed from other Herderian traits into which I cannot go here (only think of the later *Humanität*). The arrangement must be such as I describe it for Herder's thought to fall *within* modern culture and not outside it, for its subsequent impact to have been such as we know it. Moreover, if we admit that ethnocentricism is strong everywhere and if by anticipation we assume that German culture will show throughout a powerful tendency to holism, we may ask ourselves how well the Herderian equality between cultures will stand the test of subsequent generations of German thinkers. It is a fact that Herder's successors have more often hierarchized the cultures or nations, with their own at the top of the value scale, than they have valued them equally.

We may single out one hierarchical trait in Herder's first philosophy of history. In each historical period one particular culture or people comes to the fore and expresses for a time humanity at large, while the other contemporary cultures stand in the background as more or less subordinate. Thus in antiquity, there is a succession in which The Oriental, the Egyptian *cum* Phoenician, the Greek, and then the Roman have universal value as embodying each an age of ancient humanity, from infancy to old age. This identification of a given culture with humanity as a whole for a particular epoch is common among German thinkers after Herder, and we shall find it again, applied to modern times, in Fichte.

While leaving Herder, I should insist that I have signaled out one aspect only in his writings, an aspect that is fundamental for Herder's posterity both within and outside Germany. In German thought, Herder along with Schelling, originates one of the two currents or lineages of thought, the more distinctly romantic one, and his thought also spills out into or influences the other, more universalistic current. Outside Germany he had deeply influenced the acculturation and nationalisms of peoples exposed later on in their turn to the full impact of modern values, especially the Slavic speaking peoples of central and eastern Europe. The fact is well known and should cause no surprise given the formula we have isolated, which looks like a former blueprint for (positive) acculturation to modern conditions independently of time and place.

Fichte's philosophy is based on the primacy of the "I," initially of the individual, but ultimately also of the nation, that is, of the "folk" organized in a "state." Fichte in his turn has powerfully contributed to what was to become the German idea of the nation. Yet Fichte and Herder are poles apart. Fichte is a stranger to the Herderian and romantic, not to say monadic notion of the rich diversity of culture or peoples as embodying, each in its unique manner, humanity as a whole. Moreover, he has explicitly set out to be the philosopher of the French Revolution. He belongs, not to the particularistic but to the universalistic current of German thought. Actually, the individual "I" and the universal "I" are merged, become one and the same. In that sense, Fichte has often been considered in Germany as a forerunner of pan-Germanism, of the theory that sees in the state the incarnation of the collective will to power of a people and in the people the incarnation of the collective will. Here the reference is to his *Addresses* to the German nation, delivered in Berlin after Prussia's crushing defeat at Jena. Judging from the divergent interpretations that have been given them, these *Addresses* look problematic still today, and so does the social and political philosophy of Fichte in general.

The German historian Meinecke, writing before World War I, regrets that, while essentially exalting the German nation, Fichte still remains fettered by his universalism. The philosopher Martial Guéroult, the most thorough exegete of Fichte's philosophy in France, maintains in 1939 that Fichte has been all along a faithful adept of the French Revolution, and that his German characteristics are quite secondary, not to speak of the misrepresentations that have disfigured him.[6] Actually these two interpreters are agreed on one point: there is a universalist trend in Fichte. Let us even admit with Guéroult that this universalism is the essential, I would say the encompassing, component in Fichte's social thought, and in his *Addresses* in particular. Yet, we cannot acount for them through it alone, or with the mere addition of patriotism. Only remember that no German nation was in existence at the time. Some other elements, at least one, must be discovered that combine with Fichte's philosophical individualism to produce the *Addresses* as they are. It would not be difficult to find traces of holism in Fichte's thought, most notably in *The Closed Commercial State*, which poses a planned, essentially socialistic society, but there is one more decisive feature. I submit that the missing element is hierarchy, for a hierarchical form of thought is present, plain although unnoticed, all through Fichte's works.

One of his first books, written in 1793 in defense of the revolution, the *Contributions to the Rectification of the Judgement of the Public*, contains precisely a striking example of it. The book has a single figure.[7] It is intended to illustrate the subordination of the state to the individual and shows four concentric circles of which the largest includes — encompasses — the second largest, and so on: the "domain of consciousness," individualism in its moral form, "embraces" the domain of natural law, the latter in turn embraces that of contracts in general, and this last in the end embraces that of civil contract, or the state. Here is, repeated thrice, the very encompassing disposition through which I defined hierarchy in the above. Here is hierarchy in its pure form, and this occurs in a vindication of the Revolution against the attacks of Burke and Rehberg! This little event should put us thinking. In the first place, who in contemporary France would have hit upon such a view? Also, there is a subtle link between Fichte's staunch equalitarianism in political matters and the fact that he can practice the encompassing form of thought, far removed as it is from social subordination, without giving it its name.

Far more weighty than any occasional occurrence (and there are others) is the presence of the hierarchical opposition at the very heart of Fichte's system of philosophy, at the foundation of his *Wissenschaftslehre*, in that dialectic of the self and the non-self, the "I" and the "Non-I" that establishes the conditions of all knowledge. The disposition is the same as in the biblical case of Adam and Eve, the difference being that the I, being self-sufficient, posits the non-I within itself. There are similarly two levels: on the former level the I is undifferentiated, it is the absolute I or self; on the latter level we see facing each other the I and the non-I. We may thus say that, while not explicitly expressed, not "thematized," the hierarchical form of thought is fundamental in Fichte. It is a very remarkable trait indeed in a philosopher of the French Revolution, a trait obviously linked with the general German background, that is the more common recognition of subordination in society, as in Kant's dictum that man is an animal that needs a master. The rigorous philosopher has unwittingly salvaged hierarchy from its common tangle with power, and such a groping achievement could not but remain unperceived.

But once we have recognized in him this deep hierarchical perception, it takes no wonder that for Fichte one particular people, opposed to other peoples as the self to the non-self, embodies humanity, the human self as a whole. This goes far beyond occasional borrowings from the romantics.[8] It explains how Fichte could in 1807–8 join the predominant current of German thought. We thus come to an interpretation that does not split Fichte into two but takes him whole as someone who has, in cultural terms, *translated* the French Revolution into German, combining its message with a holistic sense of collective identity and with a strong hierarchy on the level of values.

All in all, Herder, Fichte, and the German thinkers in general have come to combine in a complex fashion traditional holism and modern individualism. To throw a little more light on the German conception of the nation in the nineteenth and the beginning of the twentieth century we may go back to a comparative definition of the nation itself.

A comparative view should stress the ideology. From that viewpoint, the nation — that of western Europe in the nineteenth century — is the modern socio-political group, that is the socio-political group that accompanies the ideology of the Individual.[9] As such it is two things in one: on the one hand a collection of individuals, on the other hand an individual on the collective level, facing other individuals, other nations. We may surmise that to combine both aspects is no easy thing, and the comparison of two subcultures, the French and the German, confirms the supposition.

Considering the predominating ideology in each of the two countries, I would characterize them as follows. On the French side, I am a man by nature, and I am French by the accident of birth. As in the philosophy of the Enlightenment at large, the nation as such has no ontological status: on this level, there is nothing, but a great void, between the individual and the species, and the nation is nothing but the widest empirical approximation of mankind that is accessible to me in experience. This is not just an arbitrary hypothesis, witness the main lines of force of French political life (in this century) or again the evolution of French opinion around the time of the two world wars. That is to say, in the global ideology the recognition of the nation as a collective individual, in particular that of other nations as different from the French, is very weak. The same is true of the recognition of antagonisms between nations: all along the nineteenth century French liberals, like the French revolutionaries before them, seem to have thought that once European peoples built themselves into nations all problems would disappear and peace would be assured. For that liberalism, the nation is a framework for the emancipation of the individual and this emancipation itself is the alpha and the omega of all political problems.

On the German side now, we shall take the ideology at the level of the great writers, but I see no reason to think that there is a discrepancy between their view and that of the common man. Here, I am essentially a German, and I am a man through my being a German. That is, man is immediately given as a social being. Subordination is very generally acknowledged as necessary in society, consubstantial to it. The need for emancipating the individual is less strongly felt than the need for communion and an ordering frame. Thus, in Germany, the first aspect we have distinguished in the nation, the nation as a collection of individuals, is weak.

The second, the nation as a collective individual, is very strong. While the French were content to think of nations as mere juxtaposed fragments of mankind, the Germans have been concerned *to order* the nations within mankind in terms of their value or of their might.

We may observe that the old ethnocentrism or sociocentrism which leads to exalting the *we* and despising the *others* survived in the modern era, but in a different way here and there. The Germans posited themselves and tried to impose themselves as superior *qua* Germans, while the French consciously postulated only the superiority of universal culture, but actually identified themselves with it so naively that they could look at themselves as the teachers of mankind.[10] Finally, French universalism on the one hand, pan-Germanism on the other, have a similar function or place in the whole ideological make-up, notwithstanding the different value we may attach to those nations. Both express an antinomy inherent in the modern concept of "nation," both translate the difficulty we experience when we try to apply modern ideology to the description of actual social life (intra- as well as inter-social life). The two different solutions the two nations have, so to speak, found to a common underlying problem have far-reaching consequences. Recent history shows that French ideology succeeds — at a very high cost — in remaining pure, unsullied by any compromise with actuality, and, as a consequence, poor in content. German ideology is richer. As a result of acculturation it has amalgamated traditional and modern elements. The amalgam, of which some aspects have been isolated here, is no genuine synthesis, it does not solve incompatibilities but only covers them up. That is why it has shown to be liable to a monstrous manipulation. Of course, all this belongs to the past, as postwar federal Germany has deliberately returned to modern values. Nevertheless, what once has been will not be lost and will continue to be effective in the future, although in formations and combinations that cannot be foreseen.

Notes

1. *Homo hierarchicus*, 1967; *Homo aequalis*, I, Genèse et épanouissement de l'idéologie économique, 1977 (in English: *From Mandeville to Marx*); in preparation: *Homo aequalis, II*, Individu et communauté dans la pensée allemande, 1770–1830.
2. Cf. "Toennies, Durkheim, and Weber," *Social Science Information*, 15–6, 1976, pp. 839–53 (etc.) and Werner J. Cahnman, *Ferdinand Toennies — A New Evaluation* (Leiden: E. J. Brill, 1973).
3. Cf. *Homo hier.*, 1979 coll. "Tel," pp. 396–403, and "La communauté anthropologique et l'idéologie," *L'Homme*, 1978 xviii–3/4, esp. 103–09.
4. Ernst Troeltsch, "The Ideas of Natural Right and Humanity," in Otto Gierke, *Natural Law and the Theory of Society*, translated with an introduction by Ernst Barker (Cambridge University Press, 1934), Beacon Press, 1957, pp. 201–22. German original: *Naturrecht und Humanität in der Weltpolitik*, Vor-

trag, Berlin, Verlag für Politik und Wirtschaft, 1923 (also in *Weltwirtschaftliches Archiv*, Band 18, Heft 3).

5. *Sämtliche Werke*, Suphan (ed.), pp. 477–586. I have used the French bilingual edition: *Une autre philosophie de l'histoire*, Paris, Aubier, 1964. On the complexity of the historical movement according to Herder, cf. the introduction by Max Rouché, *ibid.* pp. 48–73.

6. Martial Guéroult, *Etudes sur Fichte*, Paris, c. 1974, pp. 142–246, originally in *Revue Philosophique*, 64e année, vol. 128 (1939) (pp. 226–320); Friedrich Meinecke, *Weltbürgertum und Nationalität*, Ausgabe, München, 1915, pp. 96–125.

7. "Beiträge zur Berichtigung der Urtheile . . .," *Sämtliche Werke*, 1845, pp. 39–288. The figure is on page 133.

8. On the detail, see Xavier Léon, *Fichte et son temps*, 2 books in 3 vol., Paris, ed. 1954–59, II–1, pp. 433–63; II–2, pp. 34–93.

9. Cf. my "Nationalisme et Communalisme," *Homo hier.*, App. D. (in English in *Religion, Politics and History in India*, ch. 5). A brief statement of what follows was given in *Proceedings of the Royal Anthropological Institute for 1970*, London, 1971, pp. 33–35.

10. So did the publisher Bernard Grasset in a letter to the author which he made to follow the translation of a book by Friedrich Sieburg, *Gott in Frankreich* (*Dieu est-il français?*, Paris, Grasset, 1930, pp. 330, 335, 340, 342, 346.

3.

Structural Problems of Medieval Social History of Europe: Ideal types and the Specific Meaning of the Words in Latin Sources

Karl Bosl

In contradistinction to conventional historiography, it is the purpose of the present essay to stress the role and significance of the lower classes in the development of medieval society. Following Cahnman's and Boskoff's felicitous suggestion of a reunion and rapprochement between sociology and history,[1] a deliberate attempt will be made to combine the insights of a historiography that is not wholly ideographic with those of a sociology that is not completely nomothetic. The interpenetration of social science and history has long been frustrated by the application of ideal types and concepts employed in the analysis of modern societies and situations as if there were no differences in the human conditions of the past and the present. Words like "the state" were readily used to characterize the public order of medieval Europe, although medieval man spoke only of "rule" (*Herrschaft*) as equivalent of the ancient Roman Empire. As Jean Bodin has pointed out, *superioritas territorialis*, based on *advocatia*, not sovereignty, was the ancient principle, legally affirmed by the Peace Treaty of Westphalia (1648).[2]

O. Hintze and O. Brunner made a promising start in bringing sociological insight and methodology to medieval and modern history after K. Lamprecht had failed to persuade or even interest German historians with his *Economic History*. I therefore insisted after 1945 that German historiography's greatest need was not a renaissance of Ranke, still the ideal of many contemporary historians, but the acceptance of Max Weber. The collapse of the Third Reich had inevitably brought to an end the analysis of history — especially German history — exclusively in terms of *étatisme* and national state; it was time to look for new factors such as society, communal history, cooperation, liberty or representative institutions. However, before German historians had fully accepted Max Weber and the social sciences, a change in mental attitudes and a return to conservative views interrupted this process, affected many minds and brought about a setback in the influence of sociology in the fields of politics and human evolution, particularly in the empirical disciplines, and not in Germany alone.

Although sociology and social or societal history are often accused of being liberal sciences, there is no doubt that no science should be characterized in this manner since the fundamental aim of any science is to find the truth and describe reality. Of course, any history has some conservative implication insofar as it follows the traces of the past in order to reconstruct past society and mankind. But there can also be no doubt that social science and history have the effect of changing firm and orthodox views of men and the human past because history, according to Max Weber, is the social act of the individual in a changing society and civilization. "Change" as a basic factor of history besides "continuity" was invented after World War II. In any case I dislike using the concept of conservative and of liberal (non-conservative) history but prefer real, human, rational, emotional, continuous history in the long-range sense or, according to F. Braudel, changing, evolutionary and revolutionary history. We must distinguish between the historians' conservative and liberal ideologies as became clear during the recent German historical discussions on Fascism and Hitler and on society and the structure of government (conference at the German Historical Institute in London).

Today the structural concept of this question is represented by W. and H. Mommsen, M. Broszat, Tim Mason, and the individualistic concept by H. Hildebrand, K.D. Bracher, A. Hillgruber, E. Jaeckel. Out of the discussions of structural theories of fascism and of the "historical autonomy" of National Socialism as a "phenomenon sui generis" emerge Ranke's thesis and question whether a historical epoch is to be understood in itself or only from higher categories and aspects. The structuralists defend the view, based on their research, that Hitlerism was the "revolution of the petit bourgeois" and corresponded to the authoritarian mentality of the German lower middle class. But Hitler succeeded also, by representing himself as the idol of the man in the street, in convincing the majority of the indifferent and hostile working class and in integrating them despite the fact that he did not raise their standard of living. Only a hermeneutically sensitive attitude, not historical positivism, will solve the historical problems of National Socialism and the German people.[3] It is a curious phenomenon that near the end of the twentieth century historians have not yet reached a proper consensus on the methods of understanding and analyzing history, and that many rely only on the individualistic view of Ranke whose reputation is, however, not in question. It is interesting to note that 200 years of revolutions, mass and labor movements, nationalism and nation-states, of popular parties, public opinion and worldwide propaganda by mass media, of technological and industrial development and global civilization have not been able to convince historians that besides great men and little men the collective forces of society are no less dominant and decisive in history.

The reason for this is the limitation to modern and contemporary history, of the complex research needed for structural analysis and comparison, excluding medieval and early history although they need it as much as contemporary history which is the special target of combined social and economic research.[4] The German notion of "social" covers only modern economic society, not the entire concept of society and societal.[5] There can be no doubt that the Middle Ages are not only, as Ranke says, the field of action for popes, bishops, and monks, as well as emperors, kings, dukes and noblemen, but also the scene of a developing European society and civilization, a structural system of changing patterns and collective forces which becomes evident through comparison and complexity of viewpoints.

I focus in this essay on the rise of medieval society from the end of the tenth to the beginning of the fourteenth century because I believe that besides modern and contemporary society no other one is of such reality and interest for a socio-historical approach as this period, not only due to its model character but also because of its European-wide relevance to the nineteenth and twentieth centures.[6] My attempt to produce a structural analysis of medieval society and civilization was primarily concerned with the problem of usage of ideal types and concepts and the specific meaning of the relevant words in Latin and from national sources of the Middle Ages. In order to avoid unnecessary generalizations and useless positivism and artificiality, to demonstrate continuity and change, and to provide a convincing general and detailed picture of what we call European society and culture, concepts and patterns had to be found which could be used as continuous signposts in a changing world and history and could be understood as similar (anthropologically) elements of human action and life above all societal changes. These concepts and patterns, although taken from modern sociology, social science and contemporary history, had to correspond to words and concepts in medieval sources at least as far as the facts they expressed. No modern concept should be introduced that has no medieval equivalent in spite of specific differences.

In our days of profound social changes and predominant human, social and democratic demands and trends, states and governments are as extant and effective as ever but they have lost their reputations and are deteriorating. Instead, freedom and liberty are not only civil and moral values for all but are also decisive factors and aspirations of modern human, social and political development, and of primary concern to the historian. Liberty is equivalent to emancipation and liberation, both of which are basic elements of our society and civilization. Other fundamentals of modern and contemporary culture and progress are labor, labor movements, efficiency, profit, union and cooperation. A third crucial feature of our life is the poverty of whole tribes, nations and continents, and the proletarian way of life of many, many individuals. I hope to show that those factors of modern and contemporary history and evolution were also decisive in the rise of European society and civilization during the so called High Middle Ages. I believe this to be true because we find the same concepts and words with a similar meaning in the historical development especially of the eleventh and twelfth centuries which coincide with the emergence of the Middle Ages.

So far, not very many historians are aware that besides such well-known elements and patterns as feudalism, rationality or rule, three other real factors were predominant, concerning economy, society, public order and law, as well as the ideas and experiences of the upper and lower classes: poverty, labor and freedom (emancipation) — *paupertas, servicium, opus servile, libertas*. Nothing else, perhaps, makes it more clear and obvious how men, awakening from ancient and uniform rigidity, made rapid progress economically, socially, rationally and mentally in a period which I call the *Aufbruch* (the awakening or rising up) of Europe. Poverty, labor and liberty were also the background of the literary and humanist movements of the eleventh to thirteenth centuries, as much in the written and spoken word as in actual life experience. If they were isolated, they did not manifest their dynamic combination and explosive power. I am aware of the decisive importance of rulership and elite groups because a major part of my research was concerned with them,[7] but an exclusive interest in them obscures another dynamic element of the historical process. The medieval period of *Aufbruch* towards a societal (not social) evolution was no less important and secular than that of the nineteenth and twentieth centuries which were shaped by the same elements of poverty, labor and emancipation. That this is true becomes evident if we analyze the preceding ancient period in which power, rulership, wealth (the power to dispose of land and compulsory service), order (*ordo*), uniformity, symbolism, the totality of thought and action, were outstanding and prevailing in society and civilization.[8] During the period of *Aufbruch*, labor, poverty and emancipation had become conscious and variously noted motivations and forces of the historical process and had acquired opposing aims and positions which prevailed in the long run through evolution and revolution.

Labor[9] was held in contempt in ancient society; it was an evil in human life. In educated and literary tradition, the Virgilian term *labor improbus* was often quoted and repeated. It was a misfortune and calamity that had to be born humbly and obediently; it was the duty of the serf, of the lower classes which were collectively known as the *familiae* — the *Gesinde*, the servants [10] owned and ruled by king, nobility and church. The basic structure of medieval society comprised more than 90% of the whole population.

The *Aufbruch* movements of the period started at this structural point and were accelerated by the high vertical and horizontal mobility common since the eleventh century. From the dissolution of this basic structure arose the new classes of medieval society, situated between the nobility on the one side and serfdom and slavery on the other.[11] From these stem the *ministeriales* who replaced the old aristocratic elites of dynastic families which disappeared through physical exhaustion. They administered government and politics since the time of the Swabian emperor Frederic Barbarossa.[12] From the same *familia* arose also the middle classes in the urban centers of Europe, as well as the masses of free peasants who, as "pioneers" in the borderlands of Europe between settled and empty territories tilled new soil as homeland, an economic and political area for a new and increasing population. All of Europe, all the people were on the move at this time; economy, rulership, church, religion changed as fundamentally as never before or afterwards. It was generally an evolutionary dynamic.

The rise of the bourgeoisie and urbanism coincided with the liberation of labor and property in the towns and rural areas.[13] In the nineteenth century too, we may observe, the liberation of labor was the precondition of the democratic social process. During the so called High Middle Ages[14] the liberation of servile compulsory labor meant and caused emancipation of the working man from the compulsory service of *familia* and the free disposition of the power and profit of his labor. This initiated important changes and progress in the economy and society. The model of the large city of Regensburg in Southern Germany during the High Middle Ages proves that this was only the first step in the evolution of civic liberty, for the inhabitants of the towns did not achieve personal freedom through abolition of matrimonial compulsion and limitation of moving property to the *familia* of the lord until the end of the twelfth century. From then on they could marry outside the *familia* of the lord of the town and sell land and goods to anybody. That was the second step of liberation of the *familia* of their lord, or the lord of the town or manor. The servile ancestors of the townsmen, merchants, artisans, craftsmen and peasants bought themselves off *opus servile* (servile labor), a compulsory service for their lord, by a certain sum of money. The lord then transferred them to the holy patron of a church who thus became their fictitious lord to whose church or monastery they had to pay an annual tax. The graduation of this *census annualis* expressed the new gradation of society and social status according to which the taxpayer was a *ministerialis*, *civis* (citizen) or *servus operarius* (laborer). The *ministeriales* of this classification represented the oldest urban elite, a so called patrician circle of activities — the first "newcomers" before the arrival of the long-distance merchants and bankers. Merchants, artisans and laborers settled in the suburbs (*suburbia, portus*) of the old Roman cities of France, Italy and Germany, and after a longer or shorter interval were admitted into the expanded city walls. They were then integrated with the inhabitants of the old town nucleus to form a new urban community.

After liberation from service, work in cities and towns developed into autonomous occupations of trade and artisanship based on personal risk and venture. The workers, producers and traders accumulated money and expanded their businesses. As early as the thirteenth century an early form of capitalism developed though not in Weber's meaning of the term. Men worked for profit, calculated the chances and risks of their business and began to plan. None of that happened during the ancient period, but this is Weber's "rational trend" which became constitutive for European society and civilization. The beginning of this trend coincides with the rise (*Aufbruch*) of the eleventh century. This liberation and emancipation of labor-power resulted in constant expansion of production, increasing commercial activities by merchant and artisan communities throughout Europe, in expansion of interests, of the geographical and mental horizon of Europeans, in growing social prestige of the middle classes and in a new social morality. There were ample motivations for individual and collective initiatives; new geographical and material opportunities for expansive activities opened up; new ways of doing old things were sought in foreign countries. Europeans who are proud of their own urbanism should not forget that it is only due to lack of research and of cooperation between the different disciplines of medievalists that we do not know enough about the first continuous and civilized post-Roman urbanism in Islamic Asia Minor and Spain prior to that of Europe. We should also remember that between the ninth and eleventh centuries it was Islam and not Christianity which was the real global civilization, and that Arabic was the language of scholarship, science and literature prior to Latin.

The church and the clerics who held the intellectual monopoly in Europe until the twelfth century, always had a special feeling for changes in society; they were now convinced that new men needed a new *cura animarum* (pastoral care) if the church was not to risk the loss of control over the *fideles*, the faithful. The best proof of this is the creation of new reformed orders from the eleventh to the thirteenth centuries such as the monks of Hirsau, the Cistercians or the Mendicants, all of whom made labor and service a new religious and ethnical ideal. My own studies[15] have shown that the regular Canons, especially the Augustinian Canons as instruments of a second post-Gregorian papal and curial reform in the twelfth century, created a new curacy all over Europe to serve, in closest cooperation with reforming bishops, the itinerant people and restless masses of the new urban and rural society. A fundamental change took place from the self-sanctification of the older monasticism to the principle of *caritas* in the sense of active love and help for all according to St. Augustin.

That the old nobility submitted to the new ideal of work was a telling testimony to this effective change. Another consequence of the change in the church's attitude was the desire of the old ruling class whose economy and power had been based on its control of land and servile labor to benefit from the increasing wealth of the middle class because the former possessed no coined money. Hence it granted privileges to towns and burghers and honored labor at least as a spiritual, religious idea. The old monastic orders introduced the institution of lay-brothers which recruited even men of the highest nobility. The differences and contrasts between the ancient ideal concepts, the values of the nobility[16] and the new world of labor were not dissolved or abolished but resulted in an idealistic and religious compromise. The Cistercians highly appreciated the new idea of labor and organized new economic measures. They collected money and became known as the bankers of the twelfth century. A concentrated, more rational and specialized organization of labor and the economy gained momentum. By their *cura animarum* the Augustinian Canons not only raised the spirit of the rising classes in cities and along the main European roads, but also educated and instructed the maturing intellectuals in university centers such as Paris and Bologna. They produced such great creative thinkers as Hugh of St. Victor (Paris) and such "modern" critics like Gerhoh of Reichersberg.[17] For more than half a century the Augustinian Canons exercised the same centralized pastoral function for the Roman church as did the Mendicants of the thirteenth century and the Jesuits of the sixteenth.

Paupertas (poverty) was the ideology of the rising and emancipated urban and rural middle classes and the slogan of their critical objections to church, rulership and high society.[18] Two important events of the eleventh century formed the background of the tendencies and developments during the twelfth century. As a result of the so called Investiture Contest, better referred to as the first Roman church reform, king and noblemen lost the sacred legitimacy of their rulership and were subordinated to the law and judgment of church and public. That meant secularizing and demythologizing and disecclesiasticalization of rulership. The secular ruler was compelled to find an autonomous divine legitimation outside the church, a model of which was provided by Anonymus of York. As a result of this secularization, individualism, humanism, and secular sanctity were rising and expanding through theocracy, feudal monarchy and the principle of feudal contract.[19] Another crucial point was the demand in the growing communes of Italy by the rising civic and laic classes, not primarily by the church, that priests should remain unmarried and should be forbidden to buy their clerical and spiritual offices, and that priests of the latter kind should have no right to give the eucharist legitimately. The Pataria in Northern Italy made such demands but that did not prevent the reforming popes from having dealings wih them. Berengar of Tour formulated the theological background. Hence I believe that the reform popes, especially

Gregory VII, did not insist on celibacy or forbid simony on their own initiative or under the influence of the reform movement of Cluny, but accepted the demands of the restless classes and citizens of the northern Italian towns and agreed with their spirituality in this respect.

The spiritual and mental awakening of the rising classes had two consequences. It became increasingly necessary to organize a new centralized pastorate because the restless masses and their leaders intensified their criticism of the rich and mighty reigning church and compelled the clerics to discuss their demands. The call for abolition of simony hit the reigning churches of bishops who were losing their city-lordships in Italy, and in Germany were compelled to choose between organizing a new pastorate, as they did during the first half of the twelfth century, and becoming estates of the empire and territorial princes according to the empire's feudal law and neglecting *cura animarum*, as they did since the end of the century. There were many bishops in Europe during the first half of the twelfth century, e.g., in Salzburg, Regensburg, Passau, Halberstadt, or Paris, who used the Augustinian canons for this necessary task and tried to apply the ideal of *caritas* to guiding the faithful. They also wanted to link labor as an individual way of self-sanctification and individual poverty to the collective wealth and power of their churches and monasteries. At the end of the century, however, this idea was no longer accepted by the highly restless, excited and unsatisfied masses. Hence other persons and organizations had to establish a "modern" pastorate. It was the Mendicants who felt an urge to abandon the outdated burden of the church's collective wealth, who preached pure and total poverty, and who were ready to practice it in order to bring back the masses who had already started to follow the heretics. The Mendicants and above all St. Francis convinced pious people of being true and total *pauperes Christi* (Christ's poor) because these men and women saw themselves as such.

This new "social religion" corresponded to the religion of the masses (*religion populaire*)[20] and conformed to the social changes of a highly unstable society and to the desire for social status by the new urban and rural classes. Already in the eleventh century during the early stage of the *Aufbruch*, the church and secular rulers in France and Germany reacted by proclaiming the ecclesiastic Peace of God and the German *Landfrieden* (public peace). They thus protected the peaceful work of burghers and peasants and gained their loyalty and military supplies. King and aristocracy founded cities and towns, especially the Swabian emperor Frederic I who had taken note of the efficiency and power of labor, production and money in the growing communes of Northern Italy.

It must be understood that in this period of high feudalism and aristocratic rule the ideological contempt of work and workers did not disappear for a long time. The peasants did not obtain personal freedom, yet by the end of the eighteenth century they were the "poor people" which corresponds to the medieval Latin term *paupertas*. We can trace the development of the lower classes in Europe by means of the literary terms "the poor man," "the common man," "the little man." But the medieval sense of poverty was not the same as that of our modern era. The medieval sense, according to many cases found in the sources, becomes apparent by contrasting the words *potens* and *pauper*. The poor is not the man who lacks a minimum of livelihood, is not the outsider in a welfare society; he is the powerless, nonviolent and protected man. In times of feud and legitimate use of power, the poor, the worker, needed extensive protection because work can only be successful if performed in peace.

Why did the rising classes criticize the wealthy powers — the church and the secular rulers — since the eleventh century? In medieval thinking any "revolutionary" act can only mean reform and restoration of a previous situation. Imitation (of the old and tried values) is one way of progress, renewal, renaissance and reformation the others, for everything is embodied in a religious, eternal order (*ordo*). Retrospective thinking should not imply a violent social change. The reformers, too, were medieval in their thinking.

The critical objections were first expressed in the progressive cities of Italy, at Milan and in the Pataria movement; however, popes and emperors formed coalitions with them. In the middle of the twelfth century the Augustinian canon Arnold of Brescia, a student of Abelard, the famous Parisian teacher, turned the critical challenge into a revolution in Rome itself. It may seem strange to us that it was the urban laics, merchants and artisans, who demanded celibacy and drove out married clerics. The emancipative power of the new ideal of poverty became extremely effective in the movement of itinerant preachers in France, Italy and western and southern Germany who called themselves *pauperes Christi*. They wanted to restore the poverty of the original church, of the evangelists, of the apostles. Their ideals were the naked Christ on the naked wood of the cross and nakedly they followed the naked Christ. They also denied any secular power to the church. The main obstacle to understanding between the movement of poverty and the church was the leading position of the laics, the laic preachers and especially the women.[21] The movement of itinerant preachers caused the first emancipation of women in Europe. The Roman church brought this first church of the poor under its control but the second wave, since the middle of the twelfth century, was divided into the heretical groups of Cathari and Waldensians who left the church and were persecuted, and the orthodox poverty movement of the Mendicants who were clericalized and turned into an ecclasiastic order by Pope Innocent III, in the same way in which Innocent II had used the Augustinian canons. The Mendicants became militant priests, preachers and pastors of the urban and rural masses. Their activities postponed the reformation for 300 years.[22]

The poverty movement from the eleventh to the thirteenth century was a religious, a spiritual and a social phenomenon. It was born out of dissatisfaction with the social system of feudalism, with the feudal way of life of the ruling bishops and with the ancient mixture of worldly and transcendent elements. It was the expression of a desire for freedom and a preference for spirituality. Its consequence was a religious laicism inside and outside the church which corresponded to the first laic literature and the first secularization of rulership and society in the twelfth century. Other consequences were a new concept of Christianity and the individual Christian life, a new critique of life and of the doctrine of the church, a new morality of labor and far-reaching changes of society. At the end of the twelfth century the papacy and the new social classes which considered themselves nonviolent were at loggerheads. *Ecclesia spiritualis* of the poor of Christ stood up to the power of the church of priests. Heretical masses and clericalized Mendicants in the end represented the poor church of the spirit. Through liberation of labor the restless urban and rural classes were set free from the bonds of *familia*. Poverty became the ideology of the social critique of emancipated men and groups. Emancipation was the result of the great instability of this feudal society. The best proof of that was the emancipation of women and the acceptance of *ministeriales* by court society. But the outstanding evidence of this liberating, restless society was the *libertas ecclesiae* (liberty of church), the chief item of papal and ecclesiastic reform in the second half of the eleventh century. The reforming popes wanted to liberate themselves and their church from the bonds of a rulership that had been sanctified with the help of the high clerics of the Carolingian age and that had made the bishop of Rome an imperial bishop of the German king in the first half of the eleventh century. Thereby the popes tried to transform themselves into the universal power of Christianity face to face with the laic, decentralized and secularized emperor. By this act of emancipation the papacy succeeded for the first time in completing the universality of the Roman church throughout Europe and simultaneously in gaining spiritual and political hegemony over the continent.

Mutatis mutandis labor, poverty, liberation/emancipation were the most effective, decisive and predominant elements and factors of the social and historical process of modern and contemporary history as well as of the medieval period of *Aufbruch*. This observation may seem paradoxical and sensational and opposed to the ideas of historians and social scientists. However, not only the existence of the same notions in medieval sources with a comparable sense but also the possible and justified application of modern views and concepts make clear that the structural analysis combined with the history of ideas prove that Europe is a social and cultural unit. The impact of lower-class movements can be observed throughout the continent.

Notes

1. W. J. Cahnman and A. Boskoff, *Sociology and History* (New York: Free Press, 1964), pp. 1–7, 14–16, 560–80.
2. H. Mitteis, *Der Staat des hohen Mittelalters. Grundlinien einer vergleichenden Verfassungsgeschichte des Lehenszeitalters* (Weimar, 4th ed. 1953); *idem, Lehnrecht und Staatsgewalt* (Weimar, 1933); T. Mayer, *Fürsten und Staat* (Weimar, 1950); W. Schlesinger, "Burg und Stadt" in *Festschrift für T. Mayer — Aus Verfassungs — und Landesgeschichte I* (Konstanz, 1954), pp. 97–150; Karl Bosl, "Staat, Gesellschaft, Wirtschaft im deutschen Mittelalter" in Gebhardt, Grundmann, *Handbuch der deutschen Geschichte* (Stuttgart, 1970) I, pp. 640–833; *idem, Die Grundlagen der modernen Gesellschaft im Mittelalter. Eine deutsche Gesellschaftsgeschichte des Mittelalters*, 2 vols. (Stuttgart, 1972).
3. K. H. Bohrer, "Hitler oder die Deutschen. Englisch-deutsche Historikerkonferenz über das Dritte Reich. 'Revisionisten' contra 'Internationalisten'" in *AHF* (Arbeitsgemeinschaft ausser universitärer historischer Forschungseinrichtungen) in der Bundesrepublik Deutschland Nr. 3 (18.6.1979).
4. J. Kocka, "Theorieprobleme der Sozial- und Wirtschaftsgeschichte, Begriffe, Tendenzen und Funktionen in West und Ost" in H. U. Wehler, ed., *Geschichte und Soziologie* (Cologne, 1972), pp. 305–30; K. Borchardt, "Zur Theorie der sozialökonomischen Entwicklung der gegenwärtigen Gesellschaft," in T. W. Adorno, ed., *Spätkapitalismus oder Industriegesellschaft* (Stuttgart, 1969), pp. 29–47.
5. Karl Bosl, "Geschichte und Soziologie. Bemerkungen zum gleichnamigen Sammelband von H. U. Wehler (Hgb.)(Köln, 1972)" in *ZBLG* 39 (1976), pp. 893–909; *idem,* "Der 'soziologische Aspekt' in der Geschichte. Wertfreie Geschichtswissenschaft und Idealtypus" in *Historische Zeitschrift* 201 (1965), pp. 613–30; *idem,* "Der Mensch und seine Werke. Eine anthropologisch-humanistische Deutung der Geschichte" in *Wege und Forschungen der Agrargeschichte. Festschrift G. Franz: Zeitschrift für Agrargeschichte und Agrarsoziologie* 3 (1967), pp. 9–17; *idem,* "Der Mensch in seinem Lande. Stand, Aufgaben und Probleme der südostdeutschen Landesgeschichte" in *Rheinisches Vierteljahrblatt* 34 (1970); *idem,* "Reflexionen über die Aktualität der Geschichtswissenschaft. W. Schlesinger zum 65. Geburtstag" in *ZBLG* 36 (1973), pp. 79–98; *idem,* "Der Verlust der Geschichte" in *ZBLG* 37 (1974), pp. 685–98; cf. Eric Hobsbawm, "From Social History to the History of Society" in *Daedalus* (1971), pp. 20–45.
6. Karl Bosl, *Frühformen der Gesellschaft im mittelalterlichen Europa. Ausgewählte Beiträge zu einer Strukturanalyse der mittelalterlichen Welt* (Munich, 1964); *idem, Die Grundlagen der modernen Gesellschaft im Mittelalter* (Stuttgart, 1972).
7. Karl Bosl, *Die Reichsministerialität der Salier und Staufer. Ein Beitrag zur Geschichte des hochmittelalterlichen Volkes, Reiches und Staates*, 2 vols. (Nachdruck, 1968–69); *idem,* "Die Reichsministerialität als Element der mittelalterlichen deutschen Staatsverfassung im Zeitalter der Salier und Staufer" in T. Mayer, ed., *Adel und Bauern* (2nd ed.; 1967), pp. 228–76.
8. Karl Bosl, "Zu einer Soziologie der mittelalterlichen Fälschung" in *Historische Zeitschrift* 197 (1963), pp. 555–67; *idem,* "Der 'Adelsheilige.' Idealtypus und Wirklichkeit. Gesellschaft und Kultur im merowingerzeitlichen Bayern des 7 und achten Jahrhunderts" in *Speculum historiale* (1965), pp.

167–87; also in F. Prinz, *Mönchtum und Gesellschaft im frühen Mittelalter* (Darmstadt, 1976), pp. 354–86; *ibid*, "Eremus. Begriffsgeschichtliche Bermerkungen zum historischen Problem der Entfremdung und Vereinsamung des Menschen" in *Polychordia. Festschrift für F. Dölger* (Leyden, 1967), pp. 73–90; *ibid*, "Heiligkeit und Frömmigkeit. Bemerkungen zu den Zusammenhängen zwischen Religion, Kult, Herrschaft, Gesellschaft" in *Bayerisches Jahrbuch für Volkskunde* 1969–70), pp. 9–15.

9. L. H. Parias, *Historie générale du travail*, 2 vols. in series. P. Wolff and F. Mauro, *L'âge de l'artisanat* (Paris, 1960); Karl Bosl, "Die Sozialstruktur der mittelalterlichen Residenz- und Fernhandelsstadt Regensburg," in *Abhandlungen der Bayerischen Akademie der Wissenschaften* NF 63 (1966); *idem*, "Macht und Arbeit als bestimmende Kräfte in der mittelalterlichen Gesellschaft," in L. Petry, *Geschichtliche Landeskunde* (1968), pp. 46 ff; *idem*, Die Unfreiheit im Übergang von der archaischen Epoche zur Aufbruchsperiode der mittelalterlichen Gesellschaft," in *Sitzungsberichte der Akademie Wissenschaften* (Munich, 1973).

10. Karl Bosl, "Die Familie als Grundstruktur der mittelalterlichen Gesellschaft" in *ZBLG* 38 (1975), pp. 403–24.

11. Karl Bosl, "On Social Mobility in Medieval Society: Service, Freedom and Freedom of Movement as Means of Social Ascent," in S.L. Thrupp, *Early Medieval Society* (1967), pp. 87–102.

12. Karl Bosl, *Modelli di società medievale* (Bologna: Il Mulino, 1979), pp. 61–82; *idem*, "Die 'adelige Unfreiheit.' Zur Erneuerung der politischen Führungsschichten im Mittelalter," in *Bohemia Jahrbuch* 16 (1975), pp. 11–23.

13. C. Violante, *La Società Milanese nell'età precomunale* (2nd ed., Bari, 1972).

14. Karl Bosl, "Das Hochmittelalter in der deutschen und Europäischen Geschichte," in *Historische Zeitschrift* 194 (1962), pp. 529–67.

15. Karl Bosl, "Regularkanoniker (Augustinerchorherren) und Seelsorge in Kirche und Gesellschaft des europäischen 12. Jahrhunderts," in *Abhandlungen der Bayerischen Akademie der Wissenschaften* NF 86 (1979); A. Lazzarino del Grosso, *Armut und Reichtum im Denken Gerhohs von Reichersberg* (Munich, 1973); *idem*, *Società e potere nella Germania del XII secolo. Gerhoh di Reichersberg* (Florence, 1974).

16. Karl Bosl, "Leitbilder und Wertvorstellungen des Adels von der Merowingerzeit bis zur Höhe der feudalen Gesellschaft" in H. Scholler, ed, *The Epic in Medieval Society. Aesthetic and moral Values* (Stuttgart, 1977), pp. 18–36; *idem*, *Frühformen* (see note 6), pp. 106–34.

17. P. Classen, "Aus der Werkstatt Gerhohs von Reichersberg," in *DA* 23 (1967), pp. 31–92; R. Goy, *Die Überlieferungen der Werke Hugos von St. Viktor. Ein Beitrag zur Kommunikationsgeschichte des Mittelalters* (Stuttgart, 1976).

18. M. Mollat, *Les pauvres au moyen âge. Etude sociale* (Paris, 1978); *idem*, *Etudes sur l'histoire de la pauvreté* 2 vols. (Paris, 1974); O. Capitani, *La concezzione della povertà nel medioevo* (Bologna, 1974); E. Werner, *Pauperes Christi. Studien zu sozialreligiösen Bewegungen im Zeitalter des Reformpapstums* (Leipzig, 1956); A. Lazzarino del Grosso, *Armut und Reichtum im Denken Gerhohs von Reichersberg* (Munich, 1973); Bosl, *Frühformen* (see note 6), pp. 106–34; *idem*, "Das Problem der Armut in der hochmittelalterlichen Gesellschaft," in *Sitzungsberichte der Akademie der Wissenschaft in Wien* Phil. Hist. K1.294 H 5 (Vienna, 1974).

19. W. Ullmann, *History of Political Ideas in the Middle Ages* (London, 1968); *idem*, *The Individual and Society in the Middle Ages* (Baltimore, 1966);

idem, The Carolingian Renaissance and the Idea of Kingship (London, 1969); Karl Bosl, "Die 'Säkularisation' von Herrschaftsauffassung und Staatsideologie in der Stauferzeit. Der Zusammenbruch des geistlichen Monopols — Theokratie und Feudalprinzip" in *Festgabe für O. Höfler zum 75. Geburtstag* (Vienna, 1976), pp. 83–105.

20. R. Manselli, *La religion populaire au moyen âge. Problèmes de méthode et d'histoire* (Paris, 1975); E. Werner "Häresie und Gesellschaft im 11. Jahrhundert" in *Sitzungsberichte der Akademie der Wissenschaften in Leipzig* Phil. Hist. Kl. 117,5 (Leipzig, 1975); B. Töpfer, *Volk und Kirche zur Zeit der beginnenden Gottesfriedensbewegung in Frankreich* (Berlin, 1957).

21. Karl Bosl, "Armut, Arbeit, Emanzipation. Zu den Hintergründen der geistigen und literarischen Bewegung vom 11.–13. Jahrhundert," in *Festschrift für H. Helbig* (Cologne, 1976), pp. 128–47; *idem*, "Ideen, Gesellschaftswandel, Religion und Kunst im hohen Mittelalter," in *Sitzungsbericht der Bayerischen Akademie der Wissenschaften* (Munich, 1976).

22. H. Grundmann, *Religiöse Bewegungen im Mittelalter* (2nd ed. 1961), pp. 487–538; R. Manselli, "La religione popolare nel Medio Evo," in *Nuova Rivista Storica* 58 (1974), pp. 1–15; C. Violante, *I Laici nella società christiana dei secoli XI e XII* (Milan, 1968); A. Borst, *Die Katharer* (1953); M. Lambert, *Medieval Heresy: Popular Movements from Bogumil to Hus* (London, 1977); E. Werner, "Stadtluft macht frei, Frühscholastik und bürgerliche Emanzipation," in *Sitzungsbericht der Akademie Leipzig* Phil. Hist. Kl. 118,5 (1976); *idem*, "Haeresie und Gesellschaft im 11. Jahrhundert" in *ibid*. Phil. Hist. Kl. 117,5 (1975); M. Erbströsser and E. Werner, *Ideologische Probleme des mittelalterlichen Plebejertums. Die freigeistige Haeresie und ihre Wurzeln* (Berlin, 1960).

4.

The Operation of the Performance Principle as a
Task in the Shaping of Society*

K. M. Bolte

Translator's note: Leistung and *Leistungsprinzip,* the key terms of this paper (and with them such derivatives as *Leistungsbereitschaft, Leistungsgesellschaft, Leistungsbemessungsmasstäbe,* etc.), have no unambiguous single-term equivalents in English. None of several English terms that come to mind, such as "performance," "effort," "achievement" reflect the true meaning of the German *Leistung,* primarily because the German term implies both a process and its result, while the mentioned English terms refer only to the result, but not to the process that brings it about. The author himself points at an important difference: when used in physics and technology, *Leistung* has a clearly defined meaning to which corresponds a clearly defined measuring scale; while, when referring to the "work" or the "performance" or "effort" or "achievements" of a politician, an artist, a scientist, the term becomes vague and ill-defined and generally not susceptible to measurement. Yet the very problem of properly defining and measuring *Leistung,* so that the *Leistungsprinzip* can serve as a distributing principle for material goods and social chances in a given society is the main theme of this paper.

Between either selecting at any given moment the one English term that seems to express best what the author wishes to convey at that point, or using one single English term consistently throughout, the translator, after much agonizing, opted for the latter. The occasional awkwardness that follows from this appeared preferable to continuously switching back and forth between at least three or four English terms where the author uses only a single one in German and then perhaps feeling ever so often compelled to explain why at a given point one particular English term was chosen rather than another. When in consultation with several colleagues "performance" seemed to be suggested most often as the one single term to use, the translator at long last decided to settle for it — hoping thereby to do the least possible amount of injustice to the work of the author. P.N.

Introduction

We know that in every society life itself and the living together of human beings generate a number of "needs" that must be satisfied if life and living together are to be preserved. Certain needs exist obviously in all societies: goods and services must be produced; they must be distributed; there must be some common understanding about what is to be done with the aged, the sick, the weak and generally those who cannot provide for themselves; people who enter into the communal life as newcomers, e.g., children, must be familiarized with those modes of thinking and behavior needed for living within their society, etc.[1]

Depending upon through whom and how these needs are being satisfied, certain "systems of order" can be recognized in various societies, e.g., a certain system of production, a system of distribution, a system of social security, a system of education, etc. Behind the actually observable regulations may stand certain conceptions of the system, i.e., some model-like notion about how this or that should be regulated. The more "society" as such, i.e., human communal life in all its manifestations and problems, became, in the course of time, a subject of scientific reflection, the more clearly did such conceptions come to the fore which in turn led to considerable discussion about their respective advantages and disadvantages.

Besides basic notions of models of economic, educational and other systems there exist — and in fact influence these basic notions — other ideas about the principles according to which certain specific aspects of the communal life are to be patterned.

Well known principles of this kind, relevant for the universal ordering of society as a whole are, for example, the principle of democracy, the principle of pluralism and the principle of performance (*Leistungsprinzip*). The principle of performance, that will be the subject of the following discussion, is a principle of formation that refers primarily to the "Problematic of distribution," i.e., to the manner in which positions, incomes, chances, etc., are being allocated. It comprises the idea that individual performance should be the criterion for the allocation of material and social chances, usually with the hope that this mode of distribution will mobilize the readiness to perform.

In every advanced industrial society regulations can be observed that correspond to this performance principle. The performance principle as such, however, is by no means a product of industrial society; it can be demonstrated already in preindustrial societies. In addition the performance principle is neither the only distribution principle nor the only factor for the mobilization of performance in industrial society; it rather occurs in characteristic combinations with other principles of distribution and with other factors to mobilize performance. In addition, the operation of the performance principle in advanced industrial societies is by no means beyond dispute. Whereas some would like to see its dominance farther extended, there are others who consider it desirable to go beyond it and to replace orientation according to performance with orientation according to pleasure (e.g., H. Marcuse). A comparison between individual industrial societies leads to the realization that the performance principle has a quite different meaning in the several societies (e.g., in the United States, Japan, the Federal Republic of Germany), both as a principle of distribution and as a factor for the mobilization of performance.

From what has been said above it can be seen that the performance principle, in the form in which it is operative today in a given industrial society, is by no means a necessary consequence of the fact that this is an industrial society (in a certain stage of its development); it is rather a product of history and of actual impulses towards giving a certain shape to society. That in turn makes it clear that it is not only meaningful but actually necessary to rethink again and again the question after the consequences that follow from the specific manner in which the performance principle operates in each case.

It is the purpose of the following discussion to pursue this question in reference to the operation of the performance principle in the Federal Republic of Germany toward the end of the 1970s. In regard to the impact of the performance principle, too, the well known statement holds: "Only he who knows the past, can understand the present; and he who understands the present can shape the future." That makes it desirable first to bring back to memory a few historical developments and to have these preceded by a few conceptual clarifications.

Some Notes Concerning the Concept of "Performance" and the Historical Development of the Performance Principle

When talking about performance we shall first have to spell out what we mean by it; the concept is not unambiguous. Several sciences have formulated for their respective purposes their own concepts of performance. The best known is the performance concept in physics and technical sciences. Performance is work per unit of time, whereby work is defined as the product of force times distance. Practical as this definition may be for physics and technical sciences, it does not suffice to encompass suitably what we have in mind when we are talking about the performance of a politician, an artist, a scientist, etc. For the purposes of the social sciences it would seem useful to talk about performance when and where human action is understood either as contribution towards some goal or as an effort in that direction. Thus not every action and not any one specific action is performance; rather, human action is understood as performance when seen under one particular aspect: as contribution towards goals or as expenditure of effort in that direction.[2]

Performance in this sense has existed in all human societies. Performance in this sense appears to be one of the basic prerequisites for both individual and social existence. Even when and where some people were able to let others work for them, nevertheless, performance in this sense would have to be produced.

Mechanisms for the mobilization of performance can be demonstrated far back into history and special performances were in many cases especially rewarded. But even though performances have been produced at all times and certain performances were singled out for recognition, it was by no means in all societies considered as right and desirable to perform as much as possible and to distribute material and social chances in accordance with individual performance. This mode of thinking and behavior developed only under very specific historical conditions.[3]

If we go back in European history, for example, we note that in medieval society in Western Europe, to generate maximal individual performances was by no means considered an essential goal of life; on the other hand, there were in many areas numerous regulations that tried to obligate everybody to produce certain performances within the frame of certain groups to which one belonged (family, guild, community, etc.). As compensation he had — at least in principle — a standard of living assured to him commensurate with his status in the community. In those days the allocation of material and social chances did not take place primarily in accordance with individual performance but according to descent. Ordinarily, one entered by birth into certain groups and with that into certain positions, rights and styles of life, whose origins and gradations can be traced back to many and variegated developments in European history and not least to the prevailing distribution of power.

In spite of the dominance of the principle of descent as a mechanism for distribution we can discern, even in medieval times in Europe, in certain cases rules for distribution that followed the notion that he who does more should also receive more. Certain merits in war and special performances for the defense of the city, for example, were acknowledged with special "rewards," honors, and privileges. Such occasionally occurring allocations in accordance with individual performance were, however, not the dominating principle for distribution; the latter operated rather in accordance with the kind of group to which the individual belonged.

Since the sixteenth century new developments took place in Europe which led to a new attitude toward the performance of individuals and which generated significant impulses for performance. Three important developments may be briefly mentioned:

- In connection with the religious conflicts after 1500 AD, the idea took hold that man was called to participate in the creation of the Kingdom of God on earth. The work of the individual appeared as the medium through which his participation in this took place; with that his work appeared increasingly as an activity pleasing in the eyes of the Lord. Work was understood as divine service; sloth and plain loafing came close to sin and vice. These notions developed and spread mainly in the areas where Protestantism was influential, especially Calvinism, and with the latter they were diffused widely in England and the United States.[4]
- Together with Absolutism as a form of rule arising out of the disturbances towards the end of the Middle Ages, there grew up the officialdom of the civil service and with it the special form of an ethos of duty. Full and unconditional personal effort in discharging the requirements of the "office" entrusted to man by his overlord became a central occupational paradigm.
- In connection with the ideas of economic liberalism, especially in the eighteenth and nineteenth centuries, the notion took hold that every man should have the right to develop freely his own capacity for work, to offer the products of his labor in the market in free competition and to dispose freely of the proceeds of these products.

In connection with these liberal economic conceptions, the demand developed that the allocation of material and social chances be generally linked to the performance of the individual.[5]

The liberal economic bourgeoisie of the eighteenth and nineteenth centuries proclaimed this principle of distribution — the so called principle of performance — as a challenge toward the systematic reduction of what used to be social predetermination and arbitrary allocation through governmental authority. They believed that with this they had found an optimal principle for the shaping of social relations that not only guaranteed a just distribution through allocating to every man what was due him but that would, in addition, mobilize performance and with it bring progress and promote the general welfare.

In these briefly sketched processes that led to pressures toward individual performance; i.e., the proclamation of the performance principle as the dominating principle of distribution and the gradual spreading of these thoughts allied with the processes of liberalization and democratization of the preceding century, lay important roots for the rise of the "western" industrial societies — but also for many of our present problems.

As time went on, certain experiences, but also certain disappointments, came about in regard to both the realization and the effects of the principle. Already by the middle of the past century it was recognized that, as a consequence of changed economic conditions, the performance principle cannot, at least in some places, function as originally conceived. It had been conceived for use in a situation in which independent producers compete with one another in open consumer markets. For these it has, under the conditions of free competition, the effect of an impersonal distributing mechanism that rewards individual ability in relation to the production and marketing of goods and services. But under the conditions of production of large scale industry it is neither suitable for regulating the distribution of the proceed between capital and labor, nor can it within the places of work accomplish a scheme of paying the employees that does justice to their performance, as long as no special scales have been devised for the measuring of performance since the laws of the market have no validity in this context.

Likewise it was realized during the last century that for the sphere of the self-employed and individual enterprises too, the performance principle in its original conception functions less and less. The more the markets are being transformed into arenas of power plays, the more the conditions of perfectly free competition are disappearing.

A third important insight concerning the performance principle began to take shape during the past century. It was realized that if the performance principle were to operate fully with all its implications, its consequences would bring it into considerable conflict with other social values. The old, the sick, and those who, because there was no employment for them, were unable to perform at all, would under the conditions of a fully consequent performance principle end up in living conditions that appear to us today intolerable. Thus step by step an ever more differentiated social legislation, with regulations for distribution oriented along social considerations, developed as presumably the most important corrective and, in part, even competitive mechanism for the performance principle.

Finally, since the beginning of the present century, it was more and more realized that the performance principle, in order to be fully operative, presupposes not only the equality of equal rights but also a high degree of equality of chances.

The Impact of the Performance Principle in the
Federal Republic of Germany

When the Federal Republic came into existence, the performance principle was proclaimed from its very beginning. In connection with the regulations for access to public office and to civil service positions it is even mentioned in Article 33 of the Basic Law as follows; "Every German shall have equal access to any public office or civil service position according to his ability, qualification and actual performance." These were and are up to this day the "classical" arguments that are being adduced in support of the firm anchoring of the performance principle as a principle for the shaping of society. It is meant on the one hand to contribute towards a distribution of material and social chances that is felt to be just and on the other hand as a means for the mobilization of the willingness to perform.

The proclamation of the performance principle together with the "classical" arguments in its support lets us occasionally forget that it is actually no longer the "classical" performance principle that is operating in the Federal Republic today, but that it has already been modified, consciously limited, supported by a great number of diverse measures and that it has in many respects been watered down. We shall be coming back to this point.

The realization that the performance principle is unable to regulate the distribution between capital and labor has, in the Federal Republic, led, among other things, to the consequence that through the autonomy of the collective bargaining process a strategy for negotiations and conflict between employers and employees that is aimed at the problem of distribution has been linked with the performance principle. Thus the performance principle operates for many employess only as a kind of straightjacket that is placed on them before the mechanisms of negotiation can even begin to operate.

The realization that a valuation of the performance of employees might perhaps — although within limits — come about through market mechanisms and that for the performance principle to be operative at all it would be necessary to develop other methods for measuring performance than mere market valuations, brought into focus the problem of evaluating work and measuring performance. Since the 1920s in Germany the most variegated schemata and principles of measuring performance internally within individual enterprises have been initiated, practiced and discussed regarding the many problems connected with them. The discussions on this point are still going on.

The realization that the operation of the performance principle is endangered through the markets being transformed into arenas of power plays was brought back into focus again in connection with the process of concentration within the Federal Republic. The various waves of legislation against restrictions of free competition throughout the economy can be seen as a reaction to this.

From the very beginning of the Federal Republic the operation of the performance principle as a mechanism of distribution was, within the framework of the growing social legislation, pushed back in various places, in that distributing functions were assigned to various criteria that had been selected on the basis of social considerations (e.g., age, conditions of need, etc.). On the other hand, many measures were instituted with the intent of improving the operation of the performance principle through increasing the degree of equality of chances. Measures designed to reduce the influence of family situation and infrastructure upon education and vocational training, scholarships and fellowships, availability of educational equipment (books, etc.) free of charge, numerous experiments in the sphere of education, etc. can be named as attempts toward improving the equality of chances in the Federal Republic.

Thus the operation of the performance principle takes place in the Federal Republic from the outset within a framework of numerous legislative and other measures that are directly designed for that purpose and that in many respects limit, govern and regulate it. They can be related back to certain definite historical experiences.

For an understanding of the operation of the performance principle in the Federal Republic it must be taken into consideration that although important, it is by no means the only distribution principle in operation. It rather operates in combination, and, in part, even in competition, with other principles of this kind. In an earlier context we have already mentioned the principle of negotiations within the framework of the autonomy of collective bargaining, and the principle of social criteria. Besides these there are more than ten other legally ordained principles of distribution, beginning with the principle of inheritance, through the principles of age and seniority, to the principle of chance in parimutuel betting and lottery. Beyond these, finally, there exist mechanisms of distribution that are already at the outer edge or perhaps even already beyond the limits of legality and legitimacy (connections, favoritism, etc.).

In connection with the operation of the performance principle, ever new problems come into focus over the course of time in the Federal Republic, and these, in part, are under serious criticism. A few examples may indicate what is actually at issue.

The attempt to establish the performance principle as an integral part of higher level secondary education became a special trouble spot.** In the early 1950s this type of education was proclaimed as a kind of screening device for performance in our society and at the same time as a mechanism for reducing unjustified social inequalities. Without regard to social preconditions, all pupils were to be screened according to their ability and their will to perform. The school as a device for allocating social positions in a just manner based on performance appeared to embody the ideal of a democratic society and was an institution that fully corresponded to the underlying principle of performance.

Meanwhile a good deal of sobering up has taken place in this respect. It became quite clear that progress in school depends by no means only upon individual performance; it is also shaped, to a large extent, by other factors, e.g., through certain forms of behavior on the part of the teachers, through the content of subject matter, and the like. Attempts to overcome these problems through new types of schools and new teaching methods have, in connection with the educational autonomy of the individual states within the Federal Republic, led to a system of schools so highly differentiated that a new kind of social inequality has arisen between those who can see through those structures and are able to utilize them and those who are totally unable to comprehend them.

Of much more serious consequence, however, is the fact that, in combination with the distribution of rights and privileges within the school itself, performance stress and performance competition have begun to characterize the everyday life in the school itself. Choice of subject fields to study determined solely by the need for highest grades, reception of what is being taught under a persistent pressure to succeed, and transferring performance stress from the school to family life to such an extent that some newlywed women have mentioned anticipated problems with the schools as a reason for possibly not wanting children, are all contrary to the central pedagogic educational goals and guiding ideas of family policy in our society.

A second problem that is much discussed is the possibility that the operation of the performance principle may lead to completely nonsensical behavior patterns and genuine malperformances unless ways and means are found to balance the scales by which performance is measured exactly with those that set the goals of performance. For example: it is assumed that the activity of the physician shall primarily be aimed at making ill people well and at keeping healthy people healthy. But if the performance of the physician is measured not in terms of his success in healing (or the extent by which he keeps people healthy, because this also depends upon factors other than just the physician's own performance and these are, perhaps, not measureable at all) but it is measured by the number of home visits or by the number of radiations, etc.,[6] then, obviously, a physician behaves fully rationally who visits every patient, sees him in the office, gives him radiation, etc., as often as the patient is willing and able to tolerate this, until the capacity of the physician is fully utilized. Various "countervailing powers" can be thought of to counteract these and similar maldevelopments. Two of these are of special importance.

The first would be to establish a high degree of agreement between the goals of performance and the scales by which performance is measured. The second would be to develop a work ethic specifically directed at the activity itself; one that consistently directs the behavior (here: of the physicians) toward the "demanded" goal of the performance. In the case of the physician, this means that he would do with and for a patient no more and no less than exactly what, according to his best knowledge and conscience, would contribute to curing the patient or keeping him well. We shall be coming back to these problems.

A third problem is that during the last few years the political character of the performance principle has been more consciously recognized. The defenders of the performance principle act occasionally as though it were a kind of impersonal mechanism, whose impact is not influenced by group interests. Thus a few years ago, a well known German industrial economist wrote: "Furthermore it (the performance principle) as a measuring device is completely impersonal, not determined by some functionary or other but by the anonymous market and in that way to a much higher degree 'just.' " Those who fully see through the actual operation of the performance principle can see quite soon that if this statement has any validity at all, then it can have it only over a very small range. The great majority of all those who are performing are, within our society, subject to manners of operation of the performance principle that are to a high degree politically determined. Behind the mixture of the performance principle with other principles of distribution, behind the decision as to which kind of behavior is considered in this or that place as any performance at all, behind the choice of scales for the measuring of performance and the rewards or wages that are set for specific performances, etc., stand decisions that are determined by group interests that are political in nature.

These decisions are not something that contradicts the performance principle, rather they are its basis, without which it could not function at all. Considering these relations, the fear has repeatedly been voiced that the political character of the performance principle in our society is not clearly enough recognized, not sufficiently discussed, and that this principle thereby becomes an instrument of power, difficult to control, in the hands of those in our society who determine goals and scales of measurement for performance.

A fourth problem also arises. It has been proven many times during recent years that within our society there are developing ever more conditions of work within which the performance principle is either not operative at all or only to a limited extent. This refers first of all to cooperative relations in which it becomes ever more difficult to ascribe the results of work to individual workers. Then there is the growing number of those types of work — such as the control functions within the expanding sphere of automation — where it may at best be possible to establish whether somebody does or does not perform at all, but hardly whether he does it well or less well. Finally, some people seem to discern that with the tendency toward a society of services, those occupations such as administration, supervision, and teaching, in which performance is far less exactly measurable, will be growing proportionately faster than many positions within the production sector. With these, it is argued, it will become increasingly necessary to replace more or less exact measurement of performance with discretionary judgment. Experience gained from attempts at judging performance in civil service shows that this would lead one to expect a plethora of new difficulties in measuring performance.

The problem areas mentioned above are but a small fraction of the complexities that have been recognized in connection with the operation of the performance principle. Not only in the Federal Republic, but in other industrial countries, too, have unsocial consequences of the performance principle been discussed, such as the stress, neuroses, conflicts and nonsolidaric behavior that it produces, together with other negative aspects.[7]

The critics of the performance principle are, however, opposed by critics of the present form of operation of the performance principle who complain that the performance principle is too burdened with social measures; that for more performance not sufficiently more reward or compensation is either given or left (after taxes); and that measures of the welfare state, insufficient motivation, and certain forms of social-philosophical critique of society with utopian accent lead to a spreading lack of willingness and/or to outright refusal to perform. They are afraid that in this manner modes of thinking and behavior are being undercut on which rests the standard of living of advanced industrial societies, and that this will be the beginning of a decline of what has been achieved.

Considering this plethora of problems in connection with the performance principle — that obviously is going to grow even bigger in the future — some people have already earnestly suggested, some have even demanded that the performance principle as such be abolished altogether as a principle for the shaping of society. It is comparatively easy to demonstrate that for two reasons the abolition of the performance principle in the Federal Republic is at least at the present time hardly possible and that it would presumably be rather foolish to even try.

If we wanted to abolish the performance principle as a principle of distribution, we would have to go back for the regulation of distribution to principles, or to combinations of principles, that are already in operation besides the performance principle or that have already at some time and some place been in operation or that have been suggested as possible principles of distribution. We could then distribute either according to age, sex, descent, needs, etc., or give to everybody the same, or make allocations in accordance with some political purposes. First of all, evaluation and other problems that would arise from going back to these criteria would be considerable. Secondly, a distribution exclusively according to other criteria would appear from the point of view of our present value orientations as much less just than a regulation or distribution that includes the performance principle. Thirdly — and this seems to be the most essential — the abolition of the performance principle would lead to the disappearance of important spheres of freedom and guarantees of security. With all the annoyance with the principle of performance, one overlooks too easily that it offers to the individual considerable chances either to obtain certain things for himself in agreement with certain rules, or simply not to do so. In the struggle against all sorts of favoritism that are certainly in operation today, the orientation of distribution according to the performance principle offers to those willing to perform still the best chances and protection.

Those who consider the abolition of the performance principle must not only take its distribution function into consideration: another central function consists, as we know, in the mobilization of a willingness to perform. Of course, this willingness could also originate from other sources. If for the moment we disregard existential anxiety and external compulsion as factors of mobilization of performance, then both historical and contemporary comparisons between societies show that among important motivating forces of performance have been, among others: the will to convert into reality certain ideas; the thought to serve God with a certain kind of action; the personal satisfaction that goes with the fulfillment of certain values and deeds; feelings of obligation towards certain people or certain groups to whom one considers oneself as belonging (King, nation, fatherland, family, etc.); the wish to develop one's own personality; "ability acquired with one's education" and the like.[8] All of these factors of motivation for performance are certainly even today operative in the Federal Republic — some to a greater extent, others only minimally. But it seems quite remarkable that, whenever in our society factors for the mobilization of performance are being discussed, it is always the performance principle that is being emphasized as the primary mobilizing factor. It is anticipated and hoped for that people will perform because they will get something for it. This priority is due, not least, to the fact that another factor of considerable importance in other societies is hardly emphasized in ours.

A comparison between societies makes it easy to see that in various historical societies, very clearly in the eastern European, but also in most western European industrial societies, the obligation of the individual within the frame of society is an important factor for mobilization of performance besides the performance principle as such. I.e., in the course of his socialization every individual is equipped with the awareness that society is a cooperating union that can in the end exist only if every participant is willing to render performances in it and for it.

In the Federal Republic one is very reluctant to pronounce these in themselves natural things openly and to translate them into an appeal for performance. The explanation is presumably that the Federal Republic developed in explicit contrast both to the time of National Socialism and to the Socialist forms of society in their East-European form, i.e., in contrast to social relations in which the obligation of the individual towards society took on extreme forms.

The primacy of the performance principle as a mobilizing factor for performance is by no means rendered questionable through the fact that the performance principle does not encompass all spheres of society. We have already pointed out earlier, that with certain forms of work (e.g., with control administration, teaching, etc.), it is less thoroughly operative than with others. Certain spheres of action it does not encompass at all. The educational performance of parents, the performance of aid by neighbors, many performances that are carried out in an honorary capacity, all of these are outside of the operation of the performance principle. Which leads first to the question whether these important types of performance are perhaps not sufficiently appreciated and rewarded in our society and secondly to the question what it really is, that keeps the motivation for performance alive within these particular spheres of action. Nevertheless the fact remains that with us the performance principle is of the highest importance as a factor for the mobilization of performance. Thus the abolition of this principle would, for this reason alone, generate considerable problems.

Sociopolitical Approaches

A review of the preceding discussion in its full context makes it quite clear that, based upon an analysis of the operation of the performance principle and considering the experience with this principle but also considering our present-day ideas concerning values, one can neither insist on the total implementation of the performance principle nor its complete abolition. It does, however, appear as meaningful to contemplate where, given the situation and the problems that exist in connection with the performance principle, one might perhaps think of new approaches to influence its operation. In what follows, ten aspects shall be pointed out that this writer considers in this context as essential regarding the situation in the Federal Republic. In other words, the following statements are intended not as scientific-analytic, but as sociopolitical considerations.

As a presupposition for everything that follows it appears necessary to see to it that the importance of performance and the performance principle within our society be clearly recognized by as many people as possible and that both are accorded their proper place in the scheme of things. That means first of all to make everybody aware that performance is a basic requirement of both human and social existence; that the performance principle can be an important motor for the mobilization of the willingness to perform; and that performance and the performance principle constitute by no means a contradiction to our humane and social guiding principles.

The following quote may illustrate the point: "The concept of performance does not conflict either with the idea of the personal self-development of man or with the social idea of a humane order of society. Concerning man's right to personal self-development it can, I believe, be shown that the highest form of human self-fulfillment can be observed exactly where man is challenged, where he is egged on to performances, where, to quote Goethe's Faust, he is 'with effort striving.' As for society, the material basis of its existence rests exclusively upon the capacity of its economy to perform. The humanity of a thus organized society consists, I believe, in providing for every human being, even those who are economically less able to perform, the basis for a dignified human existence. On the other hand, our experience shows that nobody must deceive himself about the fact that the ability of the so called welfare state to perform is in the first place a function of the capacity of its economy to perform. But the capacity of our economy to perform would certainly deteriorate without the motor of the performance principle."[9]

An important problem concerning the shaping of society is related to the question of what the combination of the performance principle with other principles of distribution should be like and whether we could or should be satisfied with the present combination.

Two distribution principles have above all others again and again been under discussion in competition with the performance principle. First there is the inheritance principle which consistent defenders of the equality of chances would like to see restrained vis-à-vis the principle of performance, as far as the inheritance of the means of production is concerned. The other is the social principle. Here the problem is seen in the distance between work income and social income in several places becoming narrowed to such a degree or even disappearing completely, that with it the willingness to perform is altogether lost.

There is no patent solution for the combination of the performance principle and other distribution principles. Behind every one of these principles stand ideas of goals and configurations of interests that are competing with one another. But in changing the relative weight of any one principle (e.g., with the expansion of the social principle), it would always have to be kept in mind whether and to what extent this affects at the same time other principles of distribution. If the expansion of other principles of distribution takes place at the expense of the performance principle, it must be carefully considered whether this might not in the end close the source from which all the other principles are obtaining everything they are distributing.

Together with the question just discussed, to what extent the performance principle should in general be combined with other principles of distribution, it must be considered within which spheres of society and to what extent, it should be operating. An overview of the total present situation and discussion does seem to indicate, on the one hand, quite a number of points in favor of making it operative as far as possible, at any rate within the occupational sector. That would mean that it should even within the sphere of the civil service be allowed to operate much more than has hitherto been the case. In spite of several efforts in this direction during the past few years, there also have been clear tendencies in the opposite direction. On the other hand, it seems urgently necessary to contemplate whether the operation of the performance principle should not be considerably reduced in the area of the schools. Of course, the school must educate towards willingness and capability to perform. But the pressure towards performance and towards competition in performance should obviously not become operative so early in a manner that destroys the joy of performance or steers the ability to perform in false directions or has the other problematical consequences indicated above. In order to provide the potential of performance necessary for our society, it seems that, as far as the schools are concerned, the raising of personalities capable of performance and co-operation should have a higher priority than the raising of competitors who are conscious of competition and conflict.

A further task lies in seeing to it that in those areas where one has decided to institute the performance principle, it functions as optimally as possible, without getting watered down. Many details could be added at this point. As examples, two aspects may be pointed out:

First, it seems important that one repeatedly re-examine the question whether the goals of performance are clearly formulated and whether the scales for rewards are adequate for these goals. The example of the physician discussed above may be remembered.

Next to the agreement between performance goals and performance measuring scales, it seems of decisive importance for the ability of the performance principle to function, that for greater performance visibility more must be given or more received. It is, of course, not possible to state here absolute numbers. But where, among those who work, the feeling is spreading that it does not pay to work more because one does not receive sufficiently more, or because not sufficiently more is left after taxes, thresholds are being reached that touch upon the ability of the performance principle to function as a mobilizing factor for the willingness to perform. It is quite possible for advocates of the performance principle to consider as desirable a certain levelling of the differences in earnings between certain occupational groups. But those who oppose clear differentiation of rewards according to performance within certain spheres of work belong certainly among the gravediggers of the performance principle itself.

In an earlier part of this discussion it was pointed out that the performance principle is essentially political in nature. This means that it operates within a framework of numerous legislative regulations and of variegated confrontations of interests. It means that its very ability to function is based directly upon political-decision processes that precede it. Thus those who are for the performance principle and who are interested in its preservation and in the development of its ability to function must clearly realize that they must also take care of its political basis. Measuring and valuation of performance are not merely technical and apolitical processes but are, on the contrary, either consciously or unconsciously saturated with the considerations of interest groups. It seems unavoidable and only natural that in all spheres of our society those affected by the performance principle would wish to take part in the formulation of the fundamental measuring scales through which it operates. The highest possible degree of consensus of all concerned about these fundamental scales would presumably even be the safest guarantee for its meaningful operation. One should never lose sight of this: the performance principle is not in and of itself a just principle. It becomes just in its mode of operation only when the criteria for measuring and valuation are so selected and formed that they correspond to our notions of justice.

If it should be true that in our society those forms of work are increasing, for which the accounting of individual performance becomes ever more difficult (team work); if — with the tendency towards a service society — activities are increasing, for which performance is no longer accurately measurable; if, therefore, tendencies become visible that make the performance principle ever less operative as a factor for the mobilization of performance, then it would become important to develop other mobilizing factors besides the performance principle. That would also become important if the performance principle were to be further restricted in favor of other distributing principles (e.g. the social welfare principle). In this context two possibilities appear:

First, much greater efforts than have been up to now, would have to be undertaken to limit places of work and to form their outward conditions in such a manner that pleasure and genuine interest in work and the work's content becomes possible. Efforts towards the "humanization of work," especially within the general frame of "delegation of responsibility" go in that direction. But much more remains to be done.

Secondly, within the Federal Republic, too, we could more clearly emphasize that we are a kind of social cooperative organization whose existence depends upon the readiness of its members to produce performances within it and for it. That has nothing to do with the revitalization of any community — or collective ideology — and it does not contradict our guiding principle that man is not born for the benefit of social institutions but that these should, in the last analysis, exist for the development of the individual. It is solely a reminder of a fact and would counteract tendencies that let those appear as clever who are avoiding their social obligations and are trying to exist as types of "border moralists" at the expense of others.

Worthy of more intensive consideration in connection with the problem of performance is the question of whether in the future certain performances should be specifically rewarded that are not being rewarded today.

For example, discussion has been going on for some time as to whether parents or mothers should receive a special pay for their educational work. In regard to various kinds of honorary and voluntary activities, too, it would seem worthy of contemplation whether they might not be more recognizably appreciated than has been the case up to now.

In some spheres of performance, the performance principle does not operate at all (e.g., the educational performance of the parents). In this case motivation for performance cannot come through the operation of the performance principle. Also, the performance principle itself can function only if it is brought into clear relation with goals. In light of these observations, it seems necessary to revitalize within our society, and again to a higher degree, the discussion of values and goals. Within individual occupational spheres, revitalizing the discussion of so called occupational and work ethics is called for. These are not philosophical games; these are matters of considerable importance for the security of behavior in human society.

Human life is — aside from providing the basic necessities of food, sleep, drink, etc. — not by nature directed toward definite goals. A desirable quality of life, guidelines for our efforts, must be formulated and justified. People must then be motivated to live and to perform toward attainment of these goals. Only when this does take place, can performances be secured that are necessary for life itself and only then can we achieve the operation of the performance principle so that it does not contradict any humane and social goals, but functions in agreement with the guiding principles of our lives. It must become clear that the challenge is not only to perform because of the rewards, but also because of the goals.

When we talk about performance, readiness to perform, mobilization for performance, etc., it must be kept in mind that the point is not only the performance of the individual but also what shall be called "social performance." Individual performance takes place within an institutional frame. In order to arouse individual willingness to perform and to have individual performances accomplished, and then to have this utilized according to social goals, it is necessary to create functioning systems of education, continuing education, places of employment for all, limiting legal conditions, etc. The production of individual performance and its evaluation and utilization thus presuppose a variety of "social performances" and vice versa.

Not only school, occupation, and society today make demands for performance upon the individual, but the individual has, in turn, in our society which constitutes a web of social institutions, a claim that in and with these institutions the necessary basic conditions be provided for the development and utilization of his own individual capacity to perform. The individual has a claim to performances on the part of society.

He has a claim to education and further training. Because only those who have the opportunity to continuously learn will be able to perform continuously within a continuously developing society. He has a claim to a place of work because only where a place of work is assured to everybody does it seem meaningful and defensible to educate people in schools for a whole decade primarily in preparation for their later ability to do some work. He has a claim to security when he finds himself in social need and to other things as well, because only in this way can it be justified that ever larger parts of the rewards for his performance are not being placed at his personal disposal but are assigned to social institutions to be utilized by them. The production of individual and social performances are two inseparably interwoven aspects of the problem of performance, and their meaningful intertwining is an absolute necessity in every modern industrial society.

A society that depends on performances for its own existence and that goes to considerable length to educate members of the society who are both willing and able to perform, should have an interest in such performances not being wasted but being utilized in accordance with its individual and social guidelines. A lackadaisical method of "letting things run their course," however, and a senseless wasting of performances are no exceptions in our society.[10]

It is, therefore, an important task to counteract such tendencies. It is obviously senseless if, on the one hand, performances are being forced and then, on the other hand, used up in a wasteful manner. All those who are interested in performance and all those of whom performances are demanded, should pay special attention to this problem.

So much for the enumeration of several aspects whose discussion and formation in regard to the present-day operation of the performance principle appears to be essential.

The performance principle has not yet come to an end. Its operation is going to continue to present us with problems but also with opportunities. Let it be said once more: today it does not constitute a realistic set of alternatives to think of either an absolutely consistent operating performance principle or of its total abolition. The only realistic chance for the future lies in shaping the operation of the performance principle in such a manner that it is in agreement with our currently proclaimed ideas concerning the goals of our society. If today some people recommend that the performance principle be abolished (whatever they mean in practice), simply because in some places there are annoyances connected with it, then this must seem, as a kind of therapy, equally senseless as if a physician were to suggest "off with the head" as a cure for headaches. We find ourselves in a historical period in which, in the wake of worldwide industrialization processes, competition between individual countries is increasing. In this situation of competition we shall be able to make our contribution to the solution of worldwide problems only if we ourselves have a secure relation to performance. A society that today thinks that it can afford not to perform would soon not be able to afford anything at all.

Our attitude toward performance today is different from that in former times. We do not look upon work as a form of divine punishment. But, by the same token, we do not look upon performance as our sole purpose in life either. Today we have instead a rather instrumental understanding of performance. We see performance as a necessary means for obtaining our real life goals. To learn, to perform, to live, appears to us a meaningful sequence. Without learning, no performance; without performance, no life.

Life is more than performance — much more — but performance is a necessary prerequisite for it. The solution of problems that come about in connection with performance is thus an essential contribution towards the sharing of our own future.

Notes

* The present article, originally entitled *Das Wirken des Leistungsprinzips als gesellschaftliche Gestaltungsaufgabe,* follows to a large extent a lecture given by the author at the "Eisenhuettentag" in Duesseldorf on November 10, 1978. Translation by Professor Paul Neurath.

1. This problematic has been treated many times in sociological literature as the question after the functional prerequisites of human communal life, e.g., in the writings of T. Parsons.

2. For the development of a concept of performance that would be applicable to the social sciences, see e.g. K. M. Bolte, *Leistung und Leistungsprinzip* (Opladen 1977), p. 20 and literature that is cited there.

3. See, e.g., W. Fischer, "Gewinn und Lustorientierung in sozialhistorischer Perspektive," in G. Hartfield (Hg.), *Das Leistungsprinzip* (Opladen, 1977), p. 54.

4. See, e.g., M. Weber, "Die Protestantische Ethik und der Geist des Kapitalismus," in *Gesammelte Aufsätze zur Religionssoziologie* Vol. I, 4th Edition (Tuebingen, 1974).

5. This is contained, e.g., in the writings of John Locke (1632–1704), Adam Smith (1723–1790), David Ricardo (1772–1823), and Saint-Simon (1760–1825).

** *Footnote by Translator P.N.:* The term used at this place by the author is *allgemeinbildende Schulen,* which refers to several types of schools that are in their totality still far less all-inclusive than American highschools, but at the same time far less elitist and upper class than the old-style *Gymnasium.*

6. The tendency in this direction was given in the Federal Republic where, when it comes to accounting, the parties are not physician and patient but physicians and the institutions of health insurance.

7. See the German literature on the subject, e.g., K. M. Bolte, *loc. cit.*; H. P. Dreitzel, "Soziologische Reflexionen über das Elend des Leistungsprinzips," in A. Gehlen and others, *Sinn und Unsinn des Leistungsprinzips* (München, 1974); G. Hartfield (ed.), *loc. cit.*; H. Lenk, *Sozialphilosophie des Leistungshandelns* (Stuttgart, 1976); C. Offe, *Leistungsprinzip und Industriegesellschaft* (Frankfurt, 1970).

8. E.g., H. Heckhausen, "Einflüsse der Erziehung auf die Motivationsgenese," in Th. Herrmann (ed.), *Psychologie der Erziehungsstile* (Goettingen, 1966), p. 140.

9. K. Sontheimer, "Zwischen Leistungsglück und Leistungsdruck," in *IBM-Nachrichten 240* (Stuttgart, 1976), p. 88.

10. H. Markus, *Die faule Gesellschaft*, 6th edition (Duesseldorf, 1974).

5.
Locke's Liberal Theory of Parenthood

Edmund Leites

I.

Parents today are sometimes uneasy about their right to exercise authority over their children; they are not sure they have any real right to command their children's obedience. Mothers and fathers who are unsure of their right to govern may nonetheless require submission from their children, at least in some matters. They may come to this out of a despairing conviction that things will just not work out at home if they do not exercise some rule. But the underlying insecurity about the legitimacy of parental authority can remain.

Mothers and fathers may regard the use of parental authority as bad because they think it encourages "authoritarian" attitudes in their children. If parents bring up their child to be submissive to their wills, is it not likely that he will become an adult who is willing to be ruled in a similar way by political figures? He will submit to a similar authoritarian rule in the wider world, outside the family, and expect others to do likewise. And as he grows older, he will find or seek to find a powerful, commanding, and awesome father in the nation's capital to take the psychological role once held by his own father. Writings of Wilhelm Reich, A. S. Neill, and members of the Frankfurt School (Max Horkheimer, Theodor Adorno, Herbert Marcuse, and others) can sustain these suspicions about the political implications of parental authority.

There are opposing views, however, about the parental right to command children. These views ought to be examined with care, especially if they are supported by considerable philosophical and psychological insight. For this reason, John Locke's views on the legitimacy of parental authority and its political meanings are well worth our attention. He sees a certain use of parental authority as very much contributing to the creation of adults who will govern themselves by their own reason; they will not be children with respect to political authority. This view makes sense; there

61

are problems with his notions of child-rearing, but as I shall argue, they lie elsewhere.

Although Locke remained a bachelor without children throughout his life, he had much experience in raising and educating children. From 1660 to 1666, as part of his duties as lecturer in Greek at Christ Church, Oxford, Locke had students under his care and tuition. His tutorial duties, writes James Axtell, "consisted primarily of ministering to the intellectual and domestic needs of up to ten pupils ranging in age from thirteen to eighteen." He was truly *in loco parentis*; his account book indicates that he spent money on one pupil's behalf for "door keys, paper, laundry, bedmaker, butler, caution money, nurses, doctors and medicine for illnesses, and tutor's fees" (Locke, 1968: 38).

Locke's interest and studies in medicine led to his meeting Anthony Ashley Cooper, Lord Ashley (later the first Earl of Shaftesbury), in 1666. Ashley took a liking to Locke and in that same year invited him to London to be his medical advisor and general aide. At Exeter House, the London home of Lord Ashley, Locke took on both pediatric and pedagogical duties. He was given full educational and medical charge of Ashley's fifteen-year old son and sole heir, who was of sickly constitution. Later, after the son's marriage (in a match arranged by Locke himself), he supervised the education and general upbringing of the seven children, male and female, of this marriage. The eldest son, and heir (who became the third Earl of Shaftesbury and a philosophical luminary of late seventeenth-century England), was put under Locke's particular charge. Shaftesbury writes that Locke had "the absolute direction of my education." Locke did more than raise and educate Shaftesbury; he even assisted at his birth, in his capacity as household physician (Locke, 1968: 45).

In 1675, after the first Earl of Shaftesbury had lost his government offices, Locke left Exeter house and voyaged in France. But this was not the end of his career as an educator and guardian of youth. After a year and a half in France, at the behest of Shaftesbury and his friend Sir John Banks, he undertook the care of Bank's son, Caleb, "to let him see the manners" of the French. From 1677 to 1679, Caleb was in his charge in Paris and other parts of France; only snow in the Alps prevented their visiting Rome. After 1679, Locke never again had children or young men under his personal supervision; but by this time, as Axtell puts it, he "had passed through a whole spectrum of gentlemanly educational experience — Oxford don, pediatrician, private tutor, and travelling governor on the grand tour" (Locke, 1968: 47).

II.

Locke was never a parent; but as is evident from the foregoing, he had much experience acting in the place of parents. His interest and experience in political matters is well known. In the following pages, I shall explore his views on the duties parents have toward their children, the authority they rightly have over them, and the meaning of the use of their authority for political life.

In the second of his *Two Treatises of Government*, Locke writes that "all *Parents*" are, "by the Law of Nature," "*under an obligation to preserve, nourish, and educate their Children*," who are "the Workmanship" of God. He defines parental responsibility in matters of education in these broad terms: parents must give "such vigour and rectitude" to their children's minds as will make them "most useful to themselves and others" as adults. More specifically, they must prepare their children for the freedom to which they have a right as adults. For while children are not born in freedom, they are "born to it." Young children's want of judgment makes them stand in need of restraint and discipline; parents therefore have a right to govern them. But a child ends his nonage when he "comes to the use of *his Reason*." This permits him to know "the Law of Reason" which ought to govern all his acts. He then has a right to rule his own will by the light of his own understanding of this common "Law of Nature" (*Treatises* II, §§55–57, 64, 173, 174.)[1]

If the child and his father live "under the positive Law of an Establish'd Government," he now has the capacity to know these laws as well, and to rule his will in accordance with them; so he now has a liberty, equal to his father's, "to dispose of his Actions and Possessions according to his own Will, within the Permission of that Law." Moreover, he now has a relation to the law of the established government which he did not have as a child: he now has the ability to ascertain whether the government and its laws conform to the higher law of reason which defines and limits the purposes and powers of civil government: for government has a rightful claim to his obedience only if it does so. As an adult, he should evaluate his government for himself in the light of this higher law; in this, as in all other matters, he should govern his "*Will*" by his *own* "Understanding" (*Treatises*, II, §§59, 149–51, 55).

What must parents to do bring up children who will be self-reliant in this way? We should not expect a full theory of childhood education from Locke in his *Two Treatises*, since it is a work on government, but what we do get is curious: he tells us that since a child is born into the world, "in an Estate, wherein he has not *Understanding* of his own to direct his *Will*; he is not to have any Will of his own to follow: He that understands for him, must will for him too; he must proscribe to his Will, and regulate his Actions" (*Treatises*, II, §5). At first sight, it is hard to see how his method of education makes it likely that children will become adults who will be self-reliant in judgment and masters of their own will. Children are to have no will of their own, and are to subject their will in all things to the understanding of their parents; how does this prepare them for the freedom and responsibilities of adulthood?

Yet Locke does think that this regime, *as part of a larger scheme of childhood education*, will lead children to become adults who will govern their conduct by judgments they made for themselves. For a full statement and explanation of his belief, we must turn to some *Thoughts concerning Education*. There, he says that a resolution of the natural struggle between parent and child which establishes the full authority of the parents, can help greatly to resolve the natural struggle between reason and willfulness that also occurs, within the child, as he moves toward adulthood.[2]

The struggle between parents and child begins early, for a child loves "*Dominion*" even more than he loves "Liberty . . . And this the first Original of the most vicious Habits, that are ordinary and natural. This love of *Power* and Dominion shows itself very early . . . Children as soon almost as they are born . . . cry, grow peevish, sullen, and out of humour, for nothing but to have their *Wills*. They would have their Desires submitted to by others." This love of dominion leads a child to contend with his parents "for Mastery," the parents must win, for if they do not, they will not only end up his slave, but make him a slave to his own willfulness. "When their Children are grown up," parents who did not take their children in hand when young, "complain that the Brats are untoward and perverse;" they should not be surprised: since their children had their way over parents and tutors when young, why should they not continue to be willful when older? (*Thoughts*, §§103–104, 38, 78, 35). But if parental mastery is achieved in the name and spirit of reason, it allows the child to grow into an adult who will turn to his own reason for guidance in matters of conduct and belief. The rigorous rule of a young child is therefore justified because it enables him to rule himself as an adult.

The same willfulness, the same demand to have whatever one desires, which is expressed in children's desire to have their own way over their parents, is at work within their souls; there, its opponent is their own good judgment, weakly developed, and at first having little power over their conduct. How shall they develop the habit of giving the reins to reason, rather than to their willful desires?

Locke does not believe that a power sufficient to command conduct will accrue to children's reason without help from adults. Modern parents sometimes suppose that children are most likely to grow up to be adults who will regulate themselves if they are left to regulate themselves as children, without parental interference. The earlier adults call upon children to govern themselves by the use of their own reason, the better. Parental interference is thus seen as a check upon the growth of a child's self-governing habits. Locke observes that rationality attracts children at an early age, for the growth of their rational capacities is a sign to them of their maturity, their growth toward adulthood. "If I mis-observe not," he writes, "they love to be treated as Rational Creatures sooner than is imagined" (*Thoughts*, §81). To treat them in this way is to begin to give them some of the dignity of adults. But their attraction to their own rationality is a weak force compared to the power of other desires, including, above all, their desire to have their own way, no matter what. Hence their own reason is at first, and must remain for some time, a weak opponent. Parents cannot expect their child's own rationality to command the field against his desires. On their own, children *cannot* tame themselves in the name of reason.

Parents must therefore tame their children's will for them, in the name and spirit of a reasonableness which is too weak in the children themselves. To tame this willfulness in one's children is to create within them a firm and unswerving habit of submission to reason, even if it is, at the outset, the reason of the parents. But "he that is not used to submit his Will to the Reason of others, *when* he is *Young*, will scarce hearken to submit to his own Reason when he is of an Age to make use of it" (*Thoughts*, §36).

Parents should not gain this submission by a general use of corporal punishment, but by creating, as soon as possible, a sense of awe in their children which will lead them to willingly conduct themselves as their parents wish. "Every one will judge it reasonable, that their Children, *when little*, should look upon their Parents as their Lords, their Absolute Governors, and, as such stand in Awe of them." This ought to give parents their "first power" over their children's minds (*Thoughts*, §§51, 77, 41, 42). A child's experience of the affection which his parents naturally have for him, and his experience of their conscientious concern for his good, which they ought to have, will make it easier for him to submit to their will. He will love them. But awe consists of more than love: there must also be a certain distance between parents and their child, and he must deeply fear offending them (*Thoughts*, §99). With awe of his parents as a basis, his submission to parental judgment can be gradually transformed into a willing submission to his own reason.

Readers may object that Locke's method of training is authoritarian; that children who are not permitted to judge for themselves are not likely to become adults who will habitually govern their conduct by their own reason. But Locke says that children (and adults) have a natural desire to act as they see fit; if a parental regime is not too harsh, chidren's spirits will not be broken; they will retain this desire; they will be submissive to their parents, but wish for the freedom of adults. Yet this desire cannot be left untouched, for if it is, submissive children may become adults who simply do what they like, however unreasonable their actions may be. If they are to become adults who rely on their reason to govern their conduct, parents must offer the proper example. Chidren want to be adults; their idea of adulthood is formed largely by the behavior of those who govern them: if parents not only govern their children but also *themselves* in the name and spirit of reason, they will give their children a strong desire to govern themselves by reasonable means. They need not fear that their example will go to waste; even at an early age, children can often perceive when adults are acting in the spirit of reason.[3]

Locke grants that a child's attraction to the use of reason is not solely based on an emulation of parental example. In some way (Locke does not make clear how) children come to the idea that the use of reason is an essential element of maturity, whether or not their parents make much use of it; parents who fail to be rational thus may rightly fear their children's disrespect. "Frequent, and especially, passionate *Chiding*," Locke writes, is of "ill consequence. It lessens the Authority of the Parents and the Respect of the Child; For . . . they distinguish early betwixt Passion and Reason: And as they cannot but have a Reverence for what comes from the latter, so they quickly grow into a contempt of the former; . . . natural Inclination will easily learn to slight such Scare-crows, which make noise, but are not animated by Reason" (*Thoughts*, §77).

But the natural respect which a child has for rationality, as an element of maturity, competes with another idea of adult life: grown-ups are free to do whatever they want, reasonable or not. Parents must regulate their conduct in the name and spirit of reason, if they wish the former idea to mean more to their child than the latter. Counseling fathers on the upbringing of a son, Locke writes,

> If anything scape you, which you would have pass for a Fault in him, he will be sure to shelter himself under your Example, and shelter himself so as that it will not be easier to come at him, to correct it in him the right Way. If you punish him for what he sees you practice your self, . . . he will be apt to interpret it, the Peevishness, and Arbitrary Imperiousness of a Father, who, without any Ground for it, would deny his Son the Liberty and Pleasures he takes himself. Or if you assume to your self the liberty you have taken, as a Privilege belonging to riper Years, to which a Child must not aspire, you do but add new force to your Example, . . . For you must always remember, that Children affect to be Men earlier than is thought: And they love Breeches, not for their Cut, or Ease, but because having them is a Mark or Step towards Manhood (*Thoughts*, §71).

If children are habitually willful, their emulation of rationality in adults, strong as it is, will not be able to match the power of their habit of self-indulgence. But if their willfulness has been tamed by their parent's rule, their desire to govern themselves as their parents do can meet with success, for their own reason can manage their already-tamed desires. Hence, as they grow older, they can gradually become self-reliant adults. Locke says that once a child easily submits for the reasonable rule of his parents, they should prepare him for his freedom by encouraging him to rely on his own judgment in matters within the reach of his understanding: as children "grow up to the Use of Reason," the rigor of parental government should be "gently relaxed" (*Thoughts*, §41). It should be relaxed

> as fast as their Age, Discretion, and Good-Behaviour . . . allow it; even to that degree, that a Father would do well, as his Son grows up, and is capable of it, to talk *familiarly with* him; nay, *ask his advice*, and *Consult* with him, about those things wherein he has any knowledge, or understanding. By this, the Father will put . . . serious Considerations into his Son's Thoughts, . . . The sooner *you treat him as a Man*, the sooner he will begin to be one . . . (*Thoughts*, §95).

Once children are in proper awe of their parents, their faults should be dealt with by calm words and reasons adapted to their understanding. Locke does not suppose that girls and boys "in Hanging-Sleeves" should have "the Reason and Conduct of Councellors;" yet apart from a true obstinacy, which may require physical punishment, "there will never want such Motives, as may be sufficient to convince them" of "the Vertue they should be excited to" or "Fault they should be kept from." If no other reasons seem suited to their minds, "there will always be intelligible, and of force to deter them from any Fault, fit to be taken notice of in them (*viz.*). That it will be a Discredit and a Disgrace to them, and displease you" (*Thoughts*, §§39, 81).

When obstinacy is the source of a child's misbehavior, however, physical punishment may be used if words do not work, but only if there is some hope that the child will become truly more willing to obey his parents. If whippings do not have this effect, Locke asks, "to what purpose should they be used?" (*Thoughts*, §§78, 87).

Even if we grant that Locke's method of education may create adults who look to their own reason for guidance, they may still find Locke's method of child-rearing rather harsh. Hence it should be noted that he thinks the use of parental authority is a delicate matter. Mastery of impulse is essential to virtue, but energy and spirit must also be strong in anyone who is to do much for himself or others. Too harsh a parental regime, even if done in the name of reason, will break the mind or spirit of the child. He will be a "*low spirited moap'd Creature*" who, when grown, will be of as little use to himself as he is to his friends. "The true Secret of Education," Locke writes, is to know "how to keep a Child's Spirit, easy, active and free; and yet, at the same time, to restrain him from many things he has a Mind to, and to draw to things that are uneasy to him" (*Thoughts*, §§51, 46; also see §65).

Curiosity and a spirit of playful inquiry are not encouraged by the heavy hand of parental authority; but Locke thinks these motives should play a large part in the intellectual growth of a child. Therefore, when it comes to the learning of reading, writing, and other elements of a proper curriculum, he contends that parental commands should ordinarily not be used to force a young child to study. The right way to teach children reading, writing, foreign languages, etc., "is to give them a Liking and Inclination to what you propose to them to be learn'd; and that will engage their Industry and Application" (*Thoughts*, §72).

III.

Locke says that by his methods, children will gain "an ingenuous Education" (*Thoughts*, §45). This means, on the one hand, an education designed to bring up a child to be "noble in . . . character . . ., generous . . . high-minded"; on the other hand, it may also mean an "education befitting a free-born person" or "one of honourable station" (*Oxford English Dictionary*. Today we might say that Locke's object is a *liberal* education: see the *OED* and see Garforth, in Locke, 1964:60). These two distinct senses of "ingenuous" raise problems, however. For is Locke's method of education suited to those who lie in such servile positions that a reliance on their own judgment of what is permitted by law, civil or moral, such that it will only make their lives miserable, if they survive at all? Shall day laborers, wholly dependent upon the economic good will of others, speak and act their mind as gentlemen do? Shall servants who live in the family, and are considered to be under the parental authority of the master of the house, have this self-reliance? Shall women, even gentlewomen, govern themselves as gentlemen do? Is this method really suited, or meant for, *all* children?

We can raise these same questions in the light of the unequal distribution of political rights in late seventeenth-century England. Locke is no democrat; he does not advocate the extension of suffrage to poor adult males or to women. Can we suppose that he nonetheless thinks that all should be educated so that they will act in the light of their own judgment of what law requires? Why would Locke believe this education is suited to all if he thinks that most must rest content to be ruled by others, in politics, marriage, and work?

Such questions might lead us to conclude that his system of moral education was meant only for the sons of gentlemen. As adults, they could make good use of a self-reliant attitude in moral and legal matters. Politics would be open to them; they would be nobody's servant or humble wife, and their economic well-being would free them from having to act in a servile manner in order to make a living. This conclusion would be reinforced by Locke's own statements concerning the purpose of this book.

He introduced the *Thoughts* by saying that it is aimed at "*our* English

Gentry," for he is concerned "*that young Gentlemen should be* put into (*that which everyone ought to be solicitous about*) *the best way of being formed and instructed.*" If those of the rank of gentlemen "*are by their Education once set right, they will quickly bring all the rest into Order.*" He concludes his book by saying that he desired only to present "some general Views, in reference to the main End, and aims in Education, and those designed for a Gentleman's Son" (*Thoughts*, The Epistle Dedicatory, §216).

I would nonetheless argue that Locke believes his method of moral education is fit for all. Locke's statements concerning the purpose of his book are made with reference to the *whole book*; but it does not mean he believes that only gentlemen would benefit from the methods described; some are particularly suited to gentlemen (or their betters), but the fundamental elements of moral training have wider application.

Young gentlemen require "Breeding"; they need to be taught the carriage and manners which will prepare them to act and feel in a manner suitable to their station in life. They should not be given the manners suitable to a "Prince" or "Nobleman"; nor should they be given the breeding suitable to someone of lower station. Gentlemen are in the middle of the social hierarchy; they must know how to conduct themselves with appropriate dignity in the presence of their equals, their inferiors, and their superiors (*Thoughts* §§216, 141–143; also see §94).

Gentlemen must also be given an education fit for the leisure they will have as adults; thus their tutors should introduce them to science, mathematics, philosophy, and other subjects which they may pursue more deeply, if they wish, as adults. Their leisure will also permit them to take a responsible part in public life; to do so is their proper calling (*Thoughts*, §94). Hence a gentleman's child must learn sufficient history, law, and political theory, and have sufficient experience in political life (when he is of a suitable age to gain it) to play an intelligent part in the public world (see "Some Thoughts Concerning Reading and Study for a Gentleman," in Locke, 1968: 387–404). In his private affairs, he may be faced with substantial matters of business, investment, finance, and the like; therefore he must be prepared, "step by step," for these things as well. It is of more import for a son to learn how to "manage his affairs wisely" than it is for him to learn to speak Greek and Latin (*Thoughts*, §94).[4]

All of these things should be taught those who will be gentlemen; but the chief object of education, the creation of a virtuous character, which must include moral self-reliance, is not reserved for gentlemen, noblemen, or princes. *This* is an object that should guide the education of anyone, high or low, male or female. Reflecting on the education of a son, Locke writes, "I place Vertue as the first and most necessary of those endowments that belong to a *Man* or a Gentleman, ... Without that I think, He will be happy neither in this, nor in the other World" (*Thoughts*, §135, my italics).

Women deserve no less. He writes that "the principal aim of his . . . Discourse is, how a young Gentleman should be brought up from his Infancy, which, in all things will not so perfectly suit the Education of Daughters; though where the Difference of Sex requires different Treatment 'twill be no hard Matter to distinguish" (*Thoughts*, §6). It does not affect Locke's methods of moral education. *Some Thoughts Concerning Education* is based on a set of letters he wrote to Edward Clarke concerning the education of his son, Edward, Jr. At one point in the correspondence, Mrs. Clarke requested Locke to counsel her on the education of their daughter, Elizabeth. In his response, Locke wrote, "since . . . I acknowledge no difference in your mind relating . . . to truth, virtue and obedience. I think well to have no thing altered in it from what is [writ for the son]" (Locke, 1968: 344). We should also note that in illustration of his thesis that parents must not brook obstinacy on the part of their children, Locke praises the *mother* "who was forced to whip her little *Daughter* at first coming home from Nurse, eight times successively the same morning, before she could master her Stubbornness and obtain a compliance in a very easie and indifferent matter" (*Thoughts*, §78, my italics).

IV.

Does Locke's theory of parental responsibility have a political implication? It does: parents must gain an absolute submission from their child so that when he is grown, he shall see none of his superiors as fathers or mothers, to whom he owes the obedience he owed his parents when he was young. Locke will not have the relation between parents and children be a model for relations found outside the family (*Treatises*, II, §§77–86; also see §2).[5]

In so doing, he goes against a common seventeenth-century English practice: any relation of superiority and subordination was thought to be like that of parent and child. The religious teaching of the Church of England,

> . . . existing without an interruption at least from the reign of Edward VI, consisted of a social and political interpretation of the duty to obey parents and enjoined by the Decalogue; the simple requirement to "Honour thy father and mother" was expanded to include loyalty and obedience to the king of all magistrates, as well as to masters, teachers, and ministers. This reading of the Fifth Commandment appeared in . . . the catechism, which . . . all members of the Church of England had to learn (Schochet, 1975: 6).

Children in New England were by no means exempt: "Puritan children, studying the famous catechism prepared by John Cotton, learned to answer the question '*Who are here* in the fifth commandment *meant by Father and Mother?*' with the words, 'All our Superiors, whether in Family, School, Church, and Common-wealth' " (Cotton, 1656: 4; quoted in Morgan, 1966: 19).

Of course, those who used the Fifth Commandment in this way were not required to suppose that the duties and rights of magistrate, or clergyman, or landlord, were *in all respects* like that of a father or mother to their children; each office could be understood to have its distinct duties and privileges. (See Schochet, 1975: 78–81). What all superiors had in common was that they were set over their inferiors by God's will and law, as parents were set over Children by His law; all of them deserved"Revereance and Obediance, Service and Maintenance, Love and Honour" (Brailsford, 1689: 40; quoted in Schochet, 1975: 80–81), just as parents did.

The family was thus seen as the natural and appropriate place to prepare children to take part in larger social realities; for the relation of parents to child within the family was like those which the child would encounter throughout his life; it was but the first. One Puritan teacher wrote that

> a family is a little Church, and a little Common-wealth . . . whereby tryall may be made of such as are fit for any place of authority, or of subjection in Church or Common-wealth. Or rather it is as a school wherein the first principles and grounds of government and subjugation are learned: whereby men are fitted to greater matters in Church or Commonwealth (William Gouge, *Of Domesticall Duties*, first published in 1622; quoted by Haller, 1941–42: 246).

This use of the relation between parents and children had support from the Stuart kings, for they believed it would reinforce their own claim to the loyalty of their subjects. The Stuart kings were not alone in the view that a willingness to submit to parental power was the best preparation for obedience to a strong monarch: in 1639, a French royal declaration stated that "the natural respect of children toward their parents is the bond of the legitimate obedience of subjects to their sovereigns" (Quoted in Stone, 1975: 55). Paternal power was particularly favored by the "new Renaissance State" in France and England. The Stuart and Bourbon kings sought to centralize power in their own hands and direct all political loyalty to the throne; thus they were firm opponents of loyalties to cousins and distant kin, especially among the aristocracy. Such networks of allegiance were "a direct threat to the States' own claim to prior loyalty." But a stress on the subordination of children to their *own* father within the smaller nuclear family was no such threat; indeed, it was seen as a basis for a firm and unswerving obedience to the sole and absolute rule of the monarch. "The seventeenth-century State was as supportive of the patriarchal family as it was hostile" to the family oriented to kin (Stone, 1975: 24, 55).

Locke rejects the view that the family is a microcosm of the larger social world. The attitude that young children should have toward their parents is not the attitude they should have as adults to political, or any other, superiors. The powers of kings, or of any magistrates of the civil order, are not forms of "Parental Power"; hence Locke rejects Filmer's claim that kings have a right to command the obedience of their subjects because they are the proper heirs to the paternal power which Adam had over his children. "The right which . . . Parents have by Nature, and which is conferred to them by the 5*th* Commandment, cannot be . . . political Dominion," Locke says; for it "contains nothing of the Magistrates Power in it" (*Treatises*, II, §§52, 63; also see §66). In my concluding remarks, I shall outline some of Locke's reasons for saying this; especially those which bear upon his notions of child-rearing.

The law of reason and nature gives parents the right to command their young children and sets limits upon the use of this authority. But parents cannot expect that their young children will give them the obedience which the law of reason requires *out of an ultimate* loyalty to the law itself; children must begin their moral growth with a firm and ultimate allegiance to their own parents. It must go no farther than that. If parents embody the spirit of rationality in their own acts and speech, in time the law of reason can become detached in a child's mind as a separate object of deep devotion. This loyalty to an abstraction cannot take place at first, however. At first, parents should not seek to distinguish the authority of reason from the authority of their own persons. Their children should experience them as one.

But this is just what should not take place in civil society. The powers of a magistrate should never be seen as in his very person, for law, either natural, or civil, is the sole source of the legitimate powers of any element of civil government. Subjects should see civil authority in this way. The "Allegiance" which they should give to the executor of the laws established by their legislature should be "nothing but an Obedience according to Law"; they should be careful to distinguish the executor's person from the laws themselves; their loyalty to the latter should alone lead them to obey him. If he violates the law, "he has no right to obedience, nor can claim it otherwise than as the publick person vested with the Power of the Law, and so is to be considered as the Image, Phantom, or Representative of the Commonwealth . . . declared in its Laws; and thus he has no Will, no Power, but that of the Law" (*Treatises*, II, §151).

The executor of the laws has power by virtue of the laws of the commonwealth; these laws themselves must be made by legislators who act on its behalf. But the members of the commonwealth should no more give their ultimate allegiance to their legislators, than they should to the executor of the laws; for legislators can lose their legitimacy as well. They do so when they go against the rational purpose of a legislature, which is to protect the rights and liberties of all subjects. Therefore, the people must make a sharp distinction between the persons of the legislators and the rational purposes which may justify their rule:

> The Legislature being only a Fiduciary Power to act for certain ends, there remains still *in the People a Supream Power* to remove or *alter the Legislature,* when they find the *Legislature* act contrary to the trust reposed in them . . . Thus the *Community* perpetually *retains a Supream Power* of saving themselves from the attempts and designs of any Body, even if their Legislators, whenever they should be so foolish, and so wicked, as to lay and carry on designs against the Liberties and Properties of the Subject (*Treatises*, II, §149).

A parent may rightfully govern the will of his young children without their consent, for the law of nature or reason gives this power to parents "for the Benefit of their Children during their Minority, to supply their want of Ability, and understanding how to manage" themselves. But "*Voluntary Agreement*" alone "*gives . . . Political Power to Governours*" (*Treatises*, II, §173). In the ordinary course of affairs, this consent to their rule is implicitly given by our very use of the freedom which they sustain; for example, by our ownership of land which they protect, or even by our use of the roads of the commonwealth (*Treatises*, II, §§119–122). But this consent may properly be withdrawn when they no longer rule in accord with the law, civil or natural, which sustains their authority. Children must give their ultimate allegiance to the persons of their parents, for they cannot govern themselves by their knowledge of the laws they are under; but adults must give their ultimate allegiance to no other person; they must not find other "mothers" and "fathers." Their knowledge of law alone should command their obedience to civil authorities.

By rejecting a familial model for the political order, Locke gives up a most convenient way to integrate the family and the larger social world. The awe which parents can command from their children can easily be transferred in later life to other social superiors. Readers of the *Two Treatises* may well wonder how Locke proposes to bridge this gap between family and polity. In this essay, I have sought to show how he thinks childhood awe can lead to the rule of law. His views make sense: the defects in his notion of childraising lie elsewhere.

V.

Parental love does not have much of a role, perhaps none, in Locke's theory of how children should grow. By "parental love," I mean something more than good will, something which, by the way, parents ought to have for their children. For good will, as I use the term, does not require much of an involvement in the emotional life of those for whom we care; we need not feel joy at their pleasures, nor sorrow at their pains. This is because we do not have to identify very strongly with those for whom we have good will; we may be pleased at their triumphs and saddened at their defeats, but neither the one nor the other need strike us very deep. But parental love, in my use of the term, does involve such an identification. For parents who have such a love, there is more than a bit of themselves in their children. They feel the triumphs, the joys, the defeats, and the sorrows of their children in an intense and deep way, as if they were their own.

Perhaps Locke thinks that such a love is one of the reasons why parents would take the trouble to concern themselves with the moral and intellectual education of their children. On the whole, Locke remains suspicious of it. In *Two Treatises of Government*, he prefers to emphasize the obligation of parents to educate their children; in *Some Thoughts Concerning Education*, he does not appeal to parental love, but tells us, at a number of points, that the discipline which parents must impose upon their children is *for the convenience of the parents themselves*, who would otherwise suffer for the rest of their lives under the tyranny of their own offspring. His suspicion of parents identifying themselves with their children is revealed, above all, in his attacks upon mothers and fathers who spoil their children: "Parents, being wisely ordain'd by Nature to love their Children, are very apt, if Reason not watch that natural affection very warily, are apt, I say, to let it run into *Fondness*. They love their little ones, and 'tis their Duty: But they often with them, cherish their Faults too" (*Thoughts*, §34, my italics).

What are the moral faults which parents cherish when love of their children runs into "fondness?" Ultimately, they all run into one fault, the fault of unrestrained self-assertion. Children

> . . . must not be crossed, forsooth; they must be permitted to have their Wills in all things. . . . The Fondling must be taught to strike, and call Names; must have what he Cries for, and do what he pleases. Thus Parents, by humoring and cockering them when *little*, corrupt the Principles of Nature in their Children . . . (*Thoughts*, §§34–35).

The identification of parents with their children — their "fondness" for them — means that they accept, and delight in, the assertiveness of their children. Inasmuch as he is self-assertive, the child has a sense that his own feelings are important to him, just because they are his; therefore they should be expressed in his actions and words. Moreover, he is willing to ask others, press others, even require others, to satisfy his desires, just because they are *his*; he is willing to let others suffer his anger and disappointment, when he is crossed, for no other reason than that he has been foiled.

A parent may well take pleasure in the self-assertiveness of his own child, if he has the sense that it is not a separate being who is assertive, but he himself. His love of the assertiveness of his own child may be all the more pleasurable if he feels, on the one hand, that his own freedom to assert himself in the world of adults is extremely limited, and, on the other hand, that he really can satisfy the desires of his own child. For then his child can be assertive to a degree far greater than that permitted him, yet suffer no penalty.

For Locke, all such parental feelings are the stuff of disaster. Fond parents breed willful adults — not to mention willful children — who will never respect others, nor care for themselves, as reason requires.[6] He tells us that we, as parents, should turn away from such fondness and let our children know that we take no delight in their self-assertion: "The first thing they should learn to know should be, that they were not to have any thing, because it pleased them, but because it was thought fit for them." Their attempts to get others to give them what they want by crying should be firmly punished; thus they should never be "suffered to have what they once cried for" (*Thoughts*, §38).

Given all this, it is no wonder that Locke tells us that the true secret of education is to maintain "a Child's Spirit, easy, active and free," while instilling a habit of submission to parental authority and rational standards. For by "Spirit," Locke means that self-assertiveness which if lacking makes even our devotion to reason of little use. As Locke says, we will be of little use to ourselves as we are to our friends. "If the *Mind* be curbed, and *humbled* too much in Children; if their *Spirits* be abased and *broken* too much, but too strict an Hand over them, they lose all their Vigor and Industry, and are in a worse state" than those children who have not a mastery over their inclinations. "For extravagant young Fellows, that have Liveliness and Spirit, come sometimes to be set right, and so make Able and Great Men; But *dejected Minds*, timorous and tame, and *low Spirits*, are hardly even to be raised, and very seldom attain to any thing" (*Thoughts*, §46).

Locke supposes this "Spirit" to be so innate in Children that, it will survive, and even flourish, although they are taught with some force "that they were not to have any thing, because it pleased them, but [only] because it was thought fit for them." Would not a parental regime based on this principle be more likely to create either a rebellious child or a "*Low spirited moap'd Creature*"? Perhaps not, for one likely outcome is a child who somewhat unconsciously transforms what he desires into a goal which his conscience requires him to seek. What was originally his desire becomes an object of his duty. Inasmuch as it become this, he is free to give all his energies to its attainment. Self-assertion thus becomes conscientious devotion to one's calling, among other things.

This psychology was clearly present in seventeenth-century Puritanism, and perhaps in other English milieus as well. It made it easier for parents as well as their children, for it provided a way for parents to identify with the wills of their children even while they actively sought to tame them. All men and women in Puritan society were to have a calling. It was the responsibility of parents to see that their children were brought up in one which was "profitable both to themselves, and the Commonwealth," to use the terms found in the Massachusetts Laws of 1648 (Farrand, 1929: 11; quoted in Morgan, 1966: 66). It is not difficult to imagine how parents could express their love for the assertive self of their child by delighting in his successfully making his way in his studies or apprenticeship, although their delights would have to be expressed in moral terms. Puritan preachers were perhaps aware that parents' anxious concern that their child succeed in his calling would be but a thin disguise for a rather more wordly and less "rational" interest in his success. Cotton Mather tells parents that "if your *main concern* be, to get the *Riches* of *this World* for your Children, and leave a *Belly full* of this *World* unto them, it looks very suspiciously, as if you were yourselves People of *this World*, whose *Portion* is only in *this Life*" (Mather, 1721: 9; quoted in Morgan, 1966: 87).

The transformation of desire into duty runs many risks, not the least of which is a certain willingness to overlook much that is morally questionable in order to continue to seek one's own way in the name of reason and duty. To those from other cultures and civilizations, where a transformation of desire and self-assertion into duty is perhaps less readily achieved, this psychology may seem like sheer hypocrisy. "Dabei kommen die wunderbaren Ergebnisse heraus, die in der nichtangelsächsischen Welt stets so viel Erstaunen hervorrufen," writes Levin Schücking (1964: 24).

Our Lockean upbringing makes it likely that we will make much that is morally dubious our duty, but it also makes it likely that we will tailor our desire somewhat so that it can become the voice of reason. A person brought up on Lockean principles will only feel comfortable, after all, if he thinks he is acting out of reason. No doubt, this encourages a great deal of moral deception, but it also gives his conscience a card to play which it would not have in civilizations and cultures where people feel more at home with their desires, reasonable or not. Conscience will surely have a say in just how far desire can speak in its voice.

But we pay an emotional price for this, even when we come to experience our desire to forward ourselves and have our way as the call of duty. For our desire undergoes a certain transformation when it becomes "the voice of conscience," even if conscience makes the objects of our desire its own. Desire must accommodate itself to the tone that we believe is appropriate to the workings and judgements of conscience itself. In Locke's view, the appropriate tone is one which is fundamentally "cool"; our moral reason cannot allow itself to fly off into the emotional fantasies of the enthusiasts.

A certain sobriety must be maintained. Such a view of the mood appropriate to conscience has its merits, but it causes some real problems when we seek to assert ourselves largely through the medium of duty. We can, to a certain degree, express anger and other aggressive emotions in a sober tone, although the satisfaction in doing so is sometimes quite limited. The cool tone, however, does not permit us to give very adequate expression to our sexual desires. The ecstatic and enthusiastic may have little rightful place in conscience, but our erotic life is poverty-stricken without them. To the sober conscience, however, the ecstatic and passionate sides of sexual desire seem to promise a dangerous breakdown of moderation and self-control.

Locke's theory of parenthood is particularly suited to encourage a political and economic order which relies upon individual self-restraint and a willingness to act within the forms of law, and at the same time, expects a considerable degree of self-seeking and self-assertion in the name of civic, legal, and moral duty. It should therefore come as no surprise to realize that Lockean principles of childraising were popular in eighteenth-century England, which, speaking very generally, had such an order. In sexuality, too, we find what we might have expected: "good" people come to have an intense discomfort with their own sexuality. This attitude is well expressed in Richarson's *Pamela*: his eminently virtuous heroine, at the height of her adolescent sexuality, approaches the consummation of her marriage with terror. How different from Juliet's longing for Romeo:

> *Come, civil night,*
> *Thou sober-suited matron, all in black,*
> *and learn me how to lose a winning match,*
> *play'd for a pair of stainless maidenhoods.*
> *Hood my unmann'd blood, bating in my cheeks,*
> *With thy black mantle; till strange love, grown bold,*
> *Think true love acted simple modesty.*
> (Romeo and Juliet, *3.2.10–16)*

Notes

This is a revised and expanded version of a paper first published (under the same title) in O'Neill and Ruddick, 1979; 306–18. The comments of Martin Wangh (of the New York Psychoanalytic Institute) on this earlier version were of great help, as were my discussions on Locke with Paul Desjardins (of Haverford College). I have also benefited from F. W. Garforth's intelligently edited and abridged version of Locke's *Thoughts Concerning Education* (Locke, 1964).
1. Locke's *Two Treatises* was first published in 1689, with a publication date of 1690 on the title page. I quote throughout from Peter Laslett's edition of the *Treatises* (1963), which is based on the third printing (1698), as corrected by

Locke. "I" indicates the *Second Treatise.* I refer to the sections of this *Treatise,* rather than to pages of Laslett's edition, for the convenience of readers who use other editions.

2. *Some Thoughts concerning Education* is based on a set of letters which Locke wrote to Edward Clarke in 1684 and 1685, in answer to Clarke's request for counsel on the education of his son, Edward Jr. It was first published in 1693. I quote throughout from James Axtell's edition of the *Thoughts* (1968), which is based on the fifth edition, published in 1705. This was the last edition to undergo revisions by Locke, who died in 1704. I refer to sections of the *Thoughts* for the convenience of readers who do not have ready access to Axtell's edition.

3. We must distinguish two senses of rationality to understand what Locke means when he says that even young children can perceive the rationality of many adult actions. An act is rational *in spirit* if it is guided by considerations genuinely thought to be reasonable by the agent; but an act is *substantively* rational if it is truly appropriate, when judged from a rational point of view. Locke believes that very young children can often tell when their parents' conduct toward them is rational in spirit, even if they cannot judge its substantive rationality. Addressing parents, Locke explains that when he says that children "must be *treated as Rational Creatures,*" he means that "you should make them sensible by the Mildness of your Carriage, and the Composure even in your Correction of them, that what you do is reasonable in you, and useful and necessary for them: And that is not out of *Caprichio,* Passion or Fancy, that you command or forbid them any Thing. This they are capable of understanding" (*Thoughts,* §81).

4. "*Wisdom* . . . in the popular acceptation," writes Locke, "is a Man's managing his Business abley, with forsight in this World" (*Thoughts,* §140).

5. For that matter, Locke will not use the relation between parents and children as a model for other relations *within* the family, such as husband and wife. More generally, he rejects *any* use of the family as a model for relatons in the larger society.

6. This coddling is as unfortunate on the physical level as it is on the moral: Locke warns mothers that "most Children's Constitutions are either spoiled, or at least harmed, by *Cockering and Tenderness*" (*Thoughts,* §4).

References

Brailsford, Humphrey, *The Poor Man's Help* (London, 1689).

Cotton, John, *Spiritual Milk for Boston Babes* (Cambridge, Mass., 1656).

Farrand, Max, ed., *The Laws and Liberties of Massachusetts: Reprinted from the Copy of the 1648 Edition in the Henry E. Huntington Library* (Cambridge, Mass., 1929).

Haller, William and Malleville, "The Puritan Art of Love" *Huntington Library Quarterly,* V (1941–42), 235–272.

Locke, John, *Two Treatises of Government,* ed. by Peter Laslett (Revised ed. New American Library, New York, 1963).

Locke, John, *Some Thoughts Concerning Education,* abridged and ed. by F. W. Garforth (Barron's Educational Series, Woodbury, N.Y., 1964).

Locke, John, *The Educational Writings of John Locke,* ed. by James L. Axtell (Cambridge University Press, 1968).

Mather, Cotton, *A Course of Sermons in Early Piety* (Boston, 1721).

Morgan, Edmund S., *The Puritan Family* (Revised ed. Harpter & Row, New York, 1966).

O'Neill, Onora and Ruddick, William, eds., *Having Children: Philosophical and Legal Reflections on Parenthood* (Oxford University Press, New York, 1979).

Schochet, Gordon J., *Patriarchalism in Political Thought* (Basil Blackwell, Oxford, 1975).

Schücking, Levin, *Die Puritanische Familie in literarsoziologischer Sicht* (Francke Verlag, Bern, 1964).

Stone, Lawrence, "The Rise of the Nuclear Family in Early Modern England: The Patriarchal Stage," in *The Family as History*, ed. by Charles G. Rosenberg (University of Pennsylvania Press, 1975), 13–57.

6.

Vico's View of Jewish Exceptionalism

Joseph B. Maier

In the first book of the *New Science,* Vico makes it clear that, after the Fall of Man, the Jews alone through revelation retained direct contact with God. They were human from the beginning, and even physically of "normal human stature," to which the descendants of the giants, the founders of gentile humanity, stemming from Ham, Japheth, and Shem (who had renounced the true religion of Noah, their common ancestor) only gradually returned.[1] The Jews did not undergo the long and arduous process of domestication. Unlike all other nations, they did not have to pass from a brutish condition through "the age of the gods" and "the age of the heroes" in order to attain rational humanity, "the age of men, in which all men recognized themselves as equal in human nature."[2] Unlike all gentile religions, the religion of the Jews was founded on the "natural prohibition" of divination, "as something naturally denied to man," for the God of the Jews is Spirit, "not sensed in the way of vulgar wisdom" in accordance with the principle of *Nihil est in intellectu quin prius fuerit in sensu.*[3] Jewish history is exceptional. Since the Fall, and especially after the great flood, the rest of the human race has been on its own, guided only by the imminent law of God's providence embodied in human nature and its instincts.

Apart from this belief in the separate origin of the chosen people, one need not be either a pious Catholic or an orthodox Jew to feel reluctant about dismissing Vico's view of Jewish exceptionalism as wholly abstruse. Jewish history, both before and after the people's exile from its ancestral land, before and since the renewal of Israel's statehood, has been so unique as to defy facile analogy and frustrate comparative research. Its utter singularity would rather incline one to assume with Vico that, in addition to "the ordinary help from providence which was all that the Gentiles had," the Jews were accorded "extraordinary help from the true God."[4] We cannot undertake to penetrate the veil that surrounds the mystery of the Jewish career. It is, however, the thesis of this article that Vico's assertion of

81

Jewish exceptionalism is not as categorical as it may seem and neither is Jewish consciousness of the miracle of Israel's persistence from antiquity to modern times. To substantiate it I shall, first, sketch what appears to be Vico's central position; second, suggest that the important point of his work is not the conventional distinction between biblical and profane history but the scholarly sobriety with which he compares the true religion of the Jews and the false religions of the heathens, thus reducing the difference between poetic imagination and revealed truth; third, indicate the extent of his familiarity with Jewish culture; and, finally, proceed to elucidate, however briefly, the meaning of "Israel's eternality" in the work of three important Jewish writers — Nachman Krochmal (1785–1840), Moses Hess (1812–75), and Franz Rosenzweig (1886–1929). The exploration of the relationship between Vico and these authors is intended as an investigation into a possible affinity of ideas rather than an attempt to demonstrate a biographical or factual dependence of the three on Vico.

It is true, as we said above, that Vico notes many decisive differences between the Hebrews and the gentiles.[5] But at the same time, he draws many parallels between Hebrew and gentile history and institutions.[6] Eventually, however, the distinction loses importance and Vico abandons the Bible as a historical source in spite of his many attempts to prove its truth from profane sources. As his concern is with history, with the city of fallen man, not the City of God, he does not interpret it in terms of revealed religion. There is a vast difference between Vico's civil theology and St. Augustine's theology of history, where gentile history depends upon the destiny of the exceptional Jews. By confining revelation to the history of the Jews, Vico breaks the Scriptural framework that still confined even Hobbes and Spinoza.[7] He sees no progression to fulfillment in the earthly history of the fallen gentile world, only repetition, from *corso*, to fall, and *ricorso*, though on different levels and with modifications, as the most natural and rational form of historical development. Even after the fall, man remains attached to God through instinct. There are three instincts, especially, that all nations possess — the belief in providence, the recognition of parenthood, and the instinct to bury their dead. Religion, marriage, and burial are universal institutions. Civilization is based on these instincts, on them is built the whole structure of the arts and sciences.[8] Vico's emphasis throughout is on the rise and decline of ancient Rome as the pattern of universal history and "the marvelous correspondence between the first and the returned barbarian times" in the history of the Middle Ages.[9]

What links the true religion of the Hebrews with the false religions of the gentiles, Vico believes, is the all-embracing providence of historic developments. Providence established a continuity between the primitive belief in Jupiter and the true belief in the true God. How did providence forge this link between the fabled god of the sky and the spiritual God of Israel?

Through the "vulgar wisdom" of the great poets who created the first divine fable, "the greatest they ever created: that of Jove, king and father of men and gods, in the act of hurling the lightning bolt."[10] It was an image so powerful and instructive that its creators themselves believed in it, "worshipped it in frightful religions," and attributed to it whatever they saw, imagined or even made or did themselves — their institutions, their customs, their morals and manners, their whole world. This, says Vico, is the civil history of Virgil's expression, "*Iovis omnia plena*" The ignorant, rough, wild, and savage men of yore apprehended the first great benefit Jove conferred on mankind in not destroying it with his bolts "by a hidden sense the nations have of the omnipotence of God."[11] Apprehended by such human sense as they had and, in despair of nature's succors, they desired something superior to nature to save them. It was divine providence itself that "permitted them to be deceived into fearing the false divinity of Jove because he could strike them with lightning. Thus, through the thick of clouds of those first tempests, intermittently lit by those flashes, they made out this great truth: that divine providence watches over the welfare of all mankind."[12] The false is not the opposite of the true, but contained within it as a necessary stage in the attainment of the whole truth. For this is Vico's important discovery — the hidden truth of mythology.

As to the extent of Vico's familiarity with Jewish sources, there are, of course, his references in the *New Science* to Philo and Josephus. Indeed, his conception of Jewish singularity varies little from those of the Jewish authors. Among his contemporaries, there was Giuseppe Attias of Leghorn, a correspondent of Vico who mentions him in his *Vita*.[13] Attias was a man of broad culture and thoroughly at home with the Hebrew language, a student of the Bible, mathematics, and philosophy, and very much in touch with the intellectuals and scholars of the University of Pisa. Although Vico mistakenly considers him to be Giuseppe ben Abraham Attias of Cordova, well known for his edition of the Old Testament, there can be no question about Vico's acquaintance with Jews and Judaism. A more than casual and superficial acquaintance, we should think. While there appears to be no reference to the work of the sixteenth century Jewish writer Azaria de Rossi in any Vichian writing, we may consider it very likely that Vico knew about Rossi through his friend Alessio Simmaco Mazzocchi, a distinguished biblical scholar and antiquarian.[14] Mazzocchi has been credited with having preceded Robert Lowth in formulating the theory of parallelism as the metrical basis of biblical poetry,[15] but the same theory is also attributed to Rossi. Could it be that the Jewish scholar was unknown to Mazzocchi? It seems reasonable to assume that such was not the case and that Vico, too, was acquainted with the work of Rossi.[16]

Vico's view of the uniqueness of the Jews and of Jewish history notwithstanding, his "philologic" approach — the logic of myth, language, religion, poetry — would suggest no categorical break between Jewish and gentile history. On the contrary, his suggestion of the equivalence of the terms *logos* and *davar* as meaning "word" as well as "deed" would seem to indicate the comparability of the substantial traditions of the Greeks and the Hebrews, even as Martin Buber's conception of "saga" as the "predominant method of preserving the memory of what happens" (as in the story of Moses and Sinai) would suggest an extension of the Vichian view.[17] Historians assure us that Greek and Hebrew texts and archeological evidence show that at least from the tenth century B.C. onward — not to speak of the Mycenean age — Greeks went into Palestine as sailors and merchants, and that King David appears to have employed Cretan mercenaries.[18] Yet, they say, there is no sign before Alexander the Great that the Greeks knew the Jews by name or had any information about their political and religious peculiarities, reminding us that Herodotus went to Tyre, not to Jerusalem. The Jews before Alexander, on the other hand, to judge from the Bible, knew a little more about the Greeks, though not much. They had a name for them — *Yavan*, i.e, Ionia — and there is a promise to Yavan in the last chapter of Isaia (late sixth century?) as one of the nations to whom God will declare his glory.

Confirmation of the suggestiveness of Vico's "philologic" approach, however, seems to come from another quarter strongly affirming the common background of Greek and Hebrew civilizations.[19] Archeological discoveries at sites like Ugarit, says Cyrus H. Gordon, prevent us from regarding Greece as the hermetically sealed Olympian miracle, or Israel as the vacuum-packed miracle from Sinai, and he adduces an impressive amount of evidence in support of his thesis that Greek and Hebrew civilizations are parallel structures built upon the same East Mediterranean foundation. Since 1929, he maintains, Ugarit has yielded an especially important corpus of literary tablets bridging the gap between the oldest Greek and Hebrew compositions. Ugaritic literature often parallels subsequent Greek and Hebrew texts simultaneously, showing that Israel and Hellas drew on a common East Mediterranean heritage of the second millenium B.C., more particulary, its last half, the heroic age. The text of Homer about the Mycenean age with its memories of the Trojan War, and the Hebrew text dealing with the conquest through David's reign, cover ground with much in common geographically, chronologically, and ethnically. The customs of both Greeks and Hebrews in the heroic age were often alien to their respective descendants in the classical periods. We should remember that the gulf separating classical Israel (of the great Prophets) from classical Greece (of the scientists and philosophers) must not be read back into the heroic age when both peoples formed part of the same international complex. The Greco-Hebrew parallels, Gordon says, need not conceal the evident and profound Greco-Hebrew differences. No two nations forming part of a large cultural sphere are identical. Everyone knows that Homer is different from the Bible. What is not sufficiently known is the fact that the two share a common East Mediterranean heritage.

In Jewish consciousness, too, scripture is a warrant of the people's sacred *and* profane history. On the one hand, the Jewish people is chosen — "a kingdom of priests, and a holy nation" (Exodus 19, 6); on the other, it is "like all the nations" (I.Samuel 8,5). The covenant comes from beyond time and enters into time to create this people. It has a beginning in time and place, as this is true for every people, for every time and place. The *Midrash* tells us: "Before God gave Israel the Torah, He approached every tribe and nation to offer them, that hereafter they might have no excuse to say, 'Had the Holy One, blessed be He, desired to give us the Torah, we should have accepted it.' " But all the nations of the world rejected the Torah, saying: "We cannot give up the law of our fathers, we do not want Thy Torah, give it to Thy people Israel." Upon this He came to Israel and asked them, "Will ye accept the Torah?" They answered: "All that the Lord has spoken will we do and be obedient."

Nachman Krochmal systematically articulated that consciousness. As Maimonides had offered a *Guide to the Perplexed* in the realm of philosophy of the Middle Ages, so Krochmal fashioned a *Guide to the Perplexed of This Time* to illumine the essence of Judaism in the vast field of his people's history.[20] It may well be that his intellectual world was characterized by the idealism of Schelling and Hegel. That, after all, was a matter common to a variety of philosophical movements of the nineteenth century. Krochmal's concept of spirit, all-embracing and even "absolute spirit," would seem to lend a certain plausibility to this view.[21] Undeniable and much more striking, however, is Vico's influence on Krochmal's approach to history and the philosophy of history.[22] There is, first, Krochmal's principle of movement, which governs human evolution. Like Vico, who held that men make their history both deliberately and unintentionally in response to the challenges of the physical environment, he looks upon "growth" as a law of nature, a law like "all the other laws of Providence." Providence turns men's instinct to the creation of institutions. They evolve "naturally," with imminent necessity. As in Vico's "first men, the stupid, insensate, horrible great beasts,"[23] who, wandering in the forests of the earth, unerringly hit upon universal principles of conduct to govern their lives, so there is in the awe felt by Krochmal's lowest savages inhabiting the wilderness "a spiritual core which abides through the infinite number of external and material changes to which it gives rise."[24] It is the same evolutionary doctrine which leads both men to maintain that "this was the order of human institutions: first, the forests, after that the huts, then the villages, next the cities, and finally the academies,"[25] even as both share the conviction that, in the main, it is religion that creates and preserves the social bond, that drives men on their disciplining journey from savagery toward "humanity" and makes them men.[26]

Both Vico and Krochmal view the history of mankind as "an ideal eternal history traversed in time by the history of every nation in its rise, development, maturity, decline, and fall."[27] Nature itself, and most assuredly human nature, is defined by them in terms of their principle of development, a process of growth at once spiritual and physical, social, political, intellectual, and artistic, from "crude beginnings" to higher and higher forms.[28] Krochmal shows that the particular history of the Jews traverses the same universal path, in varying ways and time frames, to be sure, but in the same unalterable order, with each stage arising and coming to fruition out of the actualized potentialities of the preceding phase. Rise, maturity, and decline, the three cycles of Jewish history, are seen to manifest themselves in three subcycles. Thus, the successive stages of the first cycle stand out as the periods of Abraham to the exodus from Egypt, the conquest of Canaan to the death of King Solomon, and the division of the kingdom to the destruction of the first temple. There are, likewise, distinct substages to the maturity phase that extends from the Babylonian exile to the death of Bar Kochba and Rabbi Akiba, and the phase of decline and fall that reaches from the termination of the *Mishnah* to about 1700.

What Krochmal thought of the further course of Jewish history, whether he considered Moses Mendelssohn and the age of Enlightenment as the first phase of a new cycle, is hard to say. He ventured no predictions and offered no blueprint of the future. But that there would be a future for the Jewish people, a *ricorso* after the *corso*, there was not the slightest doubt in his mind. His philosophy of religion is the best testimony to that. Krochmal's "absolute spirit," the God of Jewish monotheism, is, as Vico would say, the "only true God." He is separate from, not the resultant of, the particular spirits. The latter are cultural emergents, they evolve in the course of men's innate drive to realize themselves. Men make their own history, but not wholly, not unaided. The finger of God provides the divine spark, or, as Vico says, "without human discernment or counsel, and often against the designs of men, Providence has ordered this great city of the human race."[29] To Krochmal the "absolute spirit" is both the guardian angel of Judaism and the warrant of its timeless identity and oneness. As "God accompanies Israel in all his migrations," exceptional eternity may be claimed for the Jewish people. Indeed, its history, although otherwise subject to the ordinary natural processes, is not merely a stage in the objectivization of the "absolute spirit" but its eternally recurrent self-realization.[30]

Moses Hess is surely more Hegelian than Vichian in his initial interpretation of Jewish existence and destiny. This "utopian socialist" and *Kom-*

munisten-Rabbi, as Karl Marx was scornfully to dubb him, suggested that in the beginning men lived in an undifferentiated unity of spirit and matter, a state of primitive communism, before the evil invention of property. That unity was broken by Christianity with its greater emphasis on spirit. The historical dialectic, harmonizing Schelling and Saint-Simon, would now bring about a more perfect reconciliation of spirit and matter. It would issue into a "social humanity," where private property is abolished and men are guided by love and social justice. Thus would the Hebrew prophets be vindicated, although the Jews would disappear as a people. They had been necessary, to be sure, to give birth to Christianity and, most assuredly, there had been much that was great in the ancient Jewish state — a unity of religious, social, and political life, a whole world ruled by one law. Then men strayed from God. Now "the ancient law will rise again, transfigured. . . ." Having conquered the world spiritually, having fulfilled their mission of being a light unto the nations, the present task of the Jews was to disperse and assimilate. They had played their historical part by making possible, first, Christianity and then socialism. Now they had better leave the scene. "The people chosen by their God," he said, "must disappear forever, that out of its death might spring a new, more precious life."[31]

It is to Hess's eternal credit, Isaiah Berlin has said, that in the end he permitted himself no such triumph of doctrinal fashion over "the direct evidence of experience."[32] Thus in *Rome and Jerusalem*, his most important work, in rather Vichian terms he comes straight to the point of his concern — the Jews, their present, and their possible future: "The thought of my nationality, which is inseparably connected with the ancestral heritage and the memories of the Holy land, the Eternal City, the birth place of the belief in the divine unity of life, as well as the hope in the future brotherhood of men."[33] Nations, like families and physical types, are real. They are a natural historical growth. The Jewish people which for "two thousand years has defied the storms of time . . . has conserved its nationality in the form of religion and united both inseparably with the memories of its ancestral land."[34] To demonstrate that his position is in consonance with the viewpoint of modern *Jüdische Wissenschaft*, Hess quotes the famous Jewish historian Heinrich Graetz (1817–91): "The history of the Post-Talmudic Period still possesses a national character; it is by no means merely a creed or church history. As the history of a people, our history is far from being a mere chronicle of literary events or church history. . . . The literature and religious development, just as the tragic martyrdom, are only incidents in the life history of the people, not its substance."[35]

In this "genetic view," as Hess calls it,[36] nature, life, history, and Judaism form a basic unity, sustained by the creator. That God is the ground and origin of all being, he reasons, has been the fundamental expression of the Jewish genius from the time of Moses and the prophets down to Spinoza and modern days. Its manifestations are not a supernatural phenomenon, but "form a part of the great eternal Law which governs all three spheres, the cosmic, organic, and social."[37] Rise, growth, and maturity characterize the development of these spheres. The social sphere, however, is the Jewish people's special field of operation. This people conceived "being" as "becoming" and "sees reality as an everlasting succession of birth and rebirth."[38] Judaism is rooted in the love of the family, and nationalism is the flower of its spirit. It is not a "passive religion" but an "active life factor" that coalesced with the national consciousness into "one organic whole." Even the belief in immortality is the product of that remarkable family sense which links the Jew with the distant past of the patriarchs and the remote future of the Messiah's reign. It is his conception of the family that gave rise to "the vivid belief in the continuity of the spirit in human history."[39] The Jewish people created "the noblest religion of the ancient world" and continued to develop it, even as that religion, with its soul-stirring Hebrew prayers, has preserved the people and to this day constitutes "the tie which binds into one people all the Jews scattered around the globe."[40] While social life had its beginning in the family of the individual, it will come to maturity with the family of nations. From the beginning of their history and throughout the storms of their exile, the Jews "have clung fast to their mission, namely to bring about not only the sanctification of individual life, but also the social life of man."[41] Social justice, the harmonizing of the opposing forces of modern life — this is a "mission," says Hess, they can fulfill only in their ancestral home, as "a nation which is politically organized; such a nation alone is able to realize it practically by embodying it in its institutions."[42]

Thus in his view of both the particularism and the universalism of Jewish history, Hess may well be said to be Vichian. Like Vico, he was convinced that natural affections and solidarity, the desire for individual freedom and social justice within historically continuous groups like families, religious bodies, and nations were not anything ephemeral and transient, but the permanent and ever evolving stuff of history. Moreover, Hess was not only Vichian in his outlook, he was right. His predictions of the fate of European Jewry proved to be uncannily accurate. And it is also clear that "the State of Israel, whatever attitude may be adopted towards it, could not have come into being if the Jews had in fact been not such as he, but as his opponents supposed them to be, whether they were orthodox rabbis, or liberal assimilationists, or doctrinaire communists."[43] In any case, it cannot be denied that the socialist morality Hess "so pureheartedly preached, as well as the type of nationalism . . . he idealized, have, on the whole, proved more enduring and productive of human happiness than the more 'realistic' solutions of his more Machiavellian rivals, both on the right and on the left."[44]

Vico's assertion of Jewish exceptionalism appears to be mild, indeed, compared with Franz Rosenzweig's radical and penetrating interpretation of Jewish history and destiny.[45] Jewish life, says Rosenzweig, is not governed by ordinary temporal realities. The "eternal people" creates its own circular time, Sabbath after Sabbath throughout the year, in the succession of generations. In contrast to the history of other peoples, the earliest legends about the Hebrew tribe say nothing of its attachment to its native soil. Only the father of mankind, Adam, sprang from *adamah* — from the earth itself. Israel's father Abraham came from the outside, and his story, as it is told in scripture, begins with the Lord's command to leave the land of his birth and go to a land that the Lord will show him.

There was, Rosenzweig continues, a relatively short period of political independence in ancient Israel, when the Jews, too, were rooted in, and ruled, the land. But for the most part, Jewish history has since moved in an entirely different direction, and elements latent in the original deposit have since become manifest. The significant turning point in the history of Jewish antiquity came, politically, with the destruction of the temple in the year 70 C.E., and, culturally, with the appearance at about the same time of Rabban Johanan ben Zakkai. Thenceforth, the road taken by the Jewish people was marked, on the one hand, by the abandonment of the temple as the sole elected place of divine service, the abandonment of the priesthood as the sole performers of divine service and keepers of the law, if not the abandonment of the claim to separate political existence altogether. On the other hand, it was marked by the substitution of the *bet hamidrash* and the *bet haknesset* (the house of learning and of assembly) for the temple, of the people's rabbi for the priestly nobleman, of Torah learning and the practice of *hesed* for the sacrifice. Indeed, it was only after its loss of land and political independence that the Jewish people regained its vitality and stepped into "the bright light of history." In the most profound sense possible, says Rosenzweig, "this people has a land of its own only in that it has a land it yearns for — a holy land. And so even if it has a home, this people, in recurrent contrast to all other peoples on earth, is not allowed full possession of that home."[46]

Vico and Rosenzweig are at one in their belief that for the peoples of the world, language and customs and law are the carriers of life, expressing profound institutional processes and structures. There is, indeed, a striking similarity in their "philologic" (as distinct from plain logic) approaches.

But once again Rosenzweig is much more sanguine than Vico in the claim that the Jews are special. For the "eternal people," he argues, land and language, custom and law have long left their time-bound moorings and have been raised to "the rung of holiness."[47] Down to the most subtle detail, the languages of the peoples follow the changes in their destinies. Language is alive because it too can die. Precisely because it is not eternal, precisely because it is a reflection of the destiny of a people among other peoples, does it deserve to be called a people's most vital possession. And that is precisely why the "eternal people" has lost its own language and, all over the world, speaks a language dictated by external circumstances. Its own language has ceased to be the language of daily life. Yet it is anything but a dead language. It is, as the people themselves call it, a holy language, employed not in everyday contexts, but in prayer, in the ultimate, loftiest region of life. In addition to their own land and their own language, the increase in custom and the renewal of law provide the peoples of the world with the strongest guarantee of their life. Their myth waxes and wanes, parts of the past are constantly forgotten and others remembered as myth. The myth of the "eternal people," however, becomes eternal and does not change. Its law is supreme, a law that can be forsaken but never changed. This people has long ago been robbed of all the things in which the peoples of the world are rooted. "But we are still living," says Rosenzweig, "and live in eternity. Our life is no longer meshed with anything outside ourselves. We have struck root in ourselves."[48]

As we near the end of our reflections on the Jewish exception, we view our problem as arising from the persistent tension between the claims of a categorical ideal and the demands of ongoing history. Taking our departure from Vico's belief of Jewish singularity, we have sketched three attempts to resolve the tension between the perennial essence of Judaism and Israel's existence in the temporal life of the secular world. Nachman Krochmal viewed the historical experience of the Jewish people from the standpoint of the absolute value of Judaism. He tried to show that, although God as source and origin is distinct from all that derives from him, the most complete, inclusive embodiment of the "absolute spirit" in the religion of Israel was the ground for this people's persistence into infinity.

Franz Rosenzweig's undertaking is wholly different. Thoroughly existentialist in outlook and motivation, he seeks to define the sphere of the Jewish people's "real existence" here and now. He does so by showing that this people bought its eternity at the cost of its temporal life. For it, and for it alone, the moment has petrified. With its customs and laws, it lives in what Rosenzweig calls a "changeless present." Between Krochmal's and Rosenzweig's views of Jewish exceptionalism are those of Moses Hess. While less profound and systematic, and regardless of their greater or lesser affinity to Vico's conception of history, they are more in consonance with the experience of these Jews who "resolved to enter history to preserve the people and sustain their faith."[49] It is an unfinished experience and a history that is still being made, but an experience and a history in which "the constant unity of life endured: *the people*, which lives in its religion and through its religion (and everyone uproots himself when this religion is weakened within himself, and everyone separates himself when he gives up this religion); and *the religion*, which speaks to all men and is to exist as universal truth for all men and which, nevertheless, exists on earth only through this one people and must therefore be lost from earth when this people dies."[50]

Notes

1. *The New Science of Giambattista Vico* (hereinafter NS), translated by Thomas G. Bergin and Max H. Fisch (Ithaca: Cornell University Press, 1968), par. 369–373.
2. NS, par. 31.
3. NS, par. 363.
4. NS, par. 313.
5. NS 126, 165, 167, 301, 313, 329, 350, 369, 401, 940.
6. NS 165, 423, 433, 527, 530, 533, 557, 715.
7. Cf. John Herman Randall, Jr., *The Career of Philosophy* (New York: Columbia University Press, 1970), 957.
8. Ibid., 958.
9. NS, par. 1046.
10. NS, par. 379.
11. NS, par. 383.
12. NS, par. 385.
13. *The Autobiography of Giambattista Vico*, translated by Max H. Fisch and Thomas G. Bergin (Ithaca: Cornell University Press, 1975), pp. 173–174. A good entry on Giuseppe Attias is to be found in the *Dizionario biografico degli Italiani*, 4, pp. 525–526.
14. I am indebted for this suggestion to the Vico scholar Professor Gustavo Costa of the University of California in a personal communication of March 1, 1979.
15. Cf. *Enciclopedia Cattolica*, VIII, col. 535.
16. The most recent and most astute comment on Rossi's historical scholarship is by Yosef Hayim Yerushalmi, "Clio and the Jews: Reflections on Jewish Historiography in the Sixteenth Century," in Salo W. Baron and Isaac E. Barzilay (eds.), *American Academy for Jewish Research*, Jubilee Volume, Proceedings Vols. XLVI–XLVII, 1979–1980, esp. pp. 632–638.
17. Cf. Werner J. Cahnman, "Vico and Historical Sociology," *Social Research*, Vol. 43 (Winter 1976), No. 4, pp. 831–832 and NS, par. 401. Also Joseph Maier, "Vico and Critical Theory," *Social Research, ibid.*, pp. 849–850.
18. Arnaldo D. Momigliano, "Jews and Greeks," *Midstream*, Vol. XXIV (Aug./Sept. 1978), p. 48.
19. Cyrus H. Gordon, *The Common Background of Greek and Hebrew Civilizations* (New York: W. W. Norton, 1965), *passim*; also "Homer and the Bible," *Hebrew Union College Annual*, Vol. XXVI (1955), pp. 43–108.
20. Krochmal's work was published posthumously by Leopold Zunz, the famous founder of the *Wissenschaft des Judentums* and historian of Hebrew literature. He gave it the title, *Guide to the Perplexed of This Time (Moreh Nebuken ha-Zeman)*, to indicate its continuity with traditional Jewish thought, especially the philosophy of Maimonides. Krochmal himself wanted to call his work *Sharey Emunah Tserufah (Gates of Pure Faith)*. Cf. Nathan Rotenstreich, *Jewish Philosophy in Modern Times* (New York: Holt, Rinehart & Winston, 1968), p. 265.

21. Cf. J. Guttmann, *Philosophies of Judaism* (New York: Holt, Rinehart & Winston, 1964), p. 365 ff.
22. Cf. Simon Rawidowicz, "War Nachman Krochmal Hegelianer?," *Hebrew Union College Annual*, V (1928), pp. 535–582.
23. NS, par. 374.
24. *Nachman Krochmals Werke* (hereinafter NKW), edited by Simon Rawidowicz (Berlin: Ajanoth, 1924), pp. 25, 54.
25. NS, par. 239.
26. NKW, p. 34 ff.
27. NS, par. 349.
28. NKW, p. 54.
29. NS par. 342.
30. Cf. Salo W. Baron, *A Social and Religious History of the Jews* (New York: Columbia University Press, 1937), II, 221, 443 ff.
31. Quoted in Isaiah Berlin, "The Life and Opinions of Moses Hess," in Philip Rieff (ed.), *On Intellectuals* (New York: Doubleday, 1970), p. 142.
32. Ibid., p. 153.
33. Moses Hess, *Rome and Jerusalem*, translated by Meyer Waxman (New York: Bloch Publishing Co., 1945), p. 40.
34. Ibid., p. 35.
35. Ibid., p. 37.
36. Ibid., p. 187.
37. Ibid.
38. Ibid., p. 222.
39. Ibid., p. 58.
40. Ibid., p. 85.
41. Ibid., p. 209.
42. Ibid., p. 103.
43. Isaiah Berlin, "The Life and Opinions," *op. cit.*, p. 179.
44. Ibid., p. 181.
45. Franz Rosenzweig, *The Star of Redemption*, translated by William W. Hallo (New York: Holt, Rinehart & Winston, 1971).
46. Ibid., p. 300.
47. Rosenzweig, *The Star of Redemption, op. cit.*, p. 305.
48. Ibid.
49. Nathan Rotenstreich, *Jewish Philosophy, op. cit.*, p. 254.
50. Leo Baeck, *This People Israel*, translated by Albert H. Friedlander (New York: Holt, Rinehart & Winston, 1964), p. xviii.

7.

The Sociobiological Theory of Jewish Intellectual Achievement: A Sociological Critique*

Lewis S. Feuer

I.

The noted mathematician Norbert Wiener, writing his autobiography, meditated upon the significance of the Jewish family for the Jewish contribution to scholarship and science. He set down briefly what we might call the sociobiological theory of the Jewish intellectual endowment. Wiener wrote:

> At all times, the young learned man, and especially the rabbi, whether or not he had an ounce of practical judgment and was able to make a good career for himself in life, was always a match for the daughter of the rich merchant. Biologically this led to a situation in sharp contrast to that of the Christians of earlier times. The Western Christian learned man was absorbed in the church, and whether he had children or not, he was certainly not supposed to have them, and actually tended to be less fertile than the community around him. On the other hand, the Jewish scholar was very often in a position to have a large family. Thus the biological habits of the Christians tended to breed out of the race whatever hereditary qualities make for learning whereas the biological habits of the Jew tended to breed these qualities in. To what extent this genetic difference supplemented the cultural trend for learning among the Jews is difficult to say. But there is no reason to believe that the genetic factor was negligible. I have talked this matter over with my friend, Professor J. B. S. Haldane, and he certainly is of the same opinion. Indeed, it is quite possible that in giving this opinion I am merely presenting an idea which I have borrowed from Professor Haldane.[1]

Other writers have independently proposed the same theory as that stated by Norbert Wiener and J. B. S. Haldane. Thus, Mr. Nathaniel Weyl in his book *The Creative Elite in America* has argued vigorously "that Jewish intellectual eminence can be regarded as the end-result of seventeen centuries of selective breeding for scholars."[2]

The Wiener-Haldane hypothesis is certainly consistent with mathematical genetics. Haldane was not only a most distinguished mathematical geneticist (the editor of the *Journal of Genetics*) but he was also the leading English Marxist scientist (an editor of the London *Daily Worker*). Curiously, the notion of selective breeding for intelligence was also quite compatible with historical materialism. For one could argue that according to the sociobiological hypothesis, the genetic traits of a population were themselves the outcome, in large measure, of cultural circumstances, which in turn, in the present case, were founded on the place of Jews in the European economy. There was, however, no evidence adduced that as a matter of sociological fact European history had seen a large-scale experiment in cultural selective breeding for intelligence on the part of the Jewish population. The facts, though scattered, sparse, and fragmentary, scarcely sustain some of the major propositions of the Wiener-Haldane hypothesis. While they corroborate part of the hypothesis, they suggest the operation of cultural factors quite other than those of selective breeding.

II.

Selective breeding, to be effective, usuallly depends on three conditions: (1) the mating of certain selected members of the population is encouraged while others are discouraged; (2) the favored members of the population reproduce themselves in greater numbers than the unfavored; and (3) the favored members survive more than proportionately under the exigencies of existence. To what extent did the family practices of the Jewish population during its long history conform to these conditions?

From Talmudical times onward, the Jewish ethic and social practice placed a tremendous pressure upon everyone to get married. Marriage was a social imperative upon every individual. In Lithuania, for instance, at the beginning of the twentieth century, as the sociologist Arthur Ruppin observed, "the old Jewish tradition prevails that every Jew and every Jewess should marry." "In Carpatho-Russia hardly any Jewish girl remains single."[3] "In Galicia for instance, there is only an infinitesimal number of Jewish bachelors, while an old maid would be looked upon as a monstrosity."[4] The *shtetl* (the small Jewish community) did not provide a place for an "alteh moyd" (old maid): "To be a spinster is a dreadful fate which fortunately occurs far more in the anxious forebodings of girl and parents than in fact."[5]

The pressure on young men to marry was equally unremitting. The Talmudical rabbis had warned against any waste of human semen.[6] And Ben Sira before them had warned against celibacy: "Where no hedge is, the vineyard will be derelict, and where no wife is, a man is waif and stray." The Talmud reiterated: "If you are twenty and still celibate, you will be thinking of sin all your days." The precepts indeed expressed what was the practice of the Jews.[7] "The fraternity of bachelors was not popular with Jews, the Talmud speaking of the wifeless man as deficient in humanity, whilst Ben Sira stigmatises him as a vagabond, wandering up and down," wrote the learned scholar Solomon Schechter.[8] Bachelors were consequently rare in Jewish communities.[9] Early marriage was the norm insisted upon by the rabbis. The *Mishnah*, the core Talmudical text, regarded the age of eighteen years as the normal one for marriage, but Moses Maimonides, the celebrated medieval philosopher and sage, effectively reduced the norm to seventeen years by interpreting the age of eighteen to mean a man's eighteenth year.[10] In Jerusalem, it was said, no man was allowed to reside who, when over twenty and under sixty, was without a wife.[11]

The transmitters of Jewish values, the teachers, were especially under the social mandate to be married; in turn, they inculcated a similar mandate in their pupils. Medieval Christendom entrusted its teaching of children to celibate priests and monks; the latter conveyed values and attitudes to their pupils which were in keeping with St. Paul's denigration of the married status. Not so with the Jewish teachers. "An unmarried man was forbidden to teach, since he would have frequent contact with the mothers who brought their children to school."[12] In Moravia, the rabbis were actually forbidden to confer the first academic rank of *Haber* on a bachelor; the degree-receiver was required to have been married for at least two years. For the higher title of *Morenu*, the candidate was required to have been married for at least five years. If he had been a part-time, post-yeshivah student because he had been engaged in trade or business, he was required to have been married for at least fifteen years.[13]

Since there was a system of virtually universal education for boys, the high valuation of marriage was reinforced as a basic tenet in the entire Jewish community. Flavius Josephus, in his polemic with Apion on the relative merits of the Hebraic as compared to the Roman-Hellenic civilization, boasted: "Above all we pride ourselves on the education of our children, and regard as the most essential task in life the observance of our laws and of the pious practices, based thereupon, which we have inherited." "It orders that they shall be taught to read, and shall learn both the laws and the deeds of their forefathers. . . ."[14] This tradition was preserved right into modern times. "Even small communities consisting of ten householders were expected to appoint a teacher and to support poor pupils if they could afford to do so."[15] Besides private schools, the communities supported public schools, taxing their members for this purpose, and using the threat of excommunication to collect these revenues. A community without a school, it was said, deserved to be excommunicated as a whole.[16]

Thus, almost every Jewish man and woman was guided toward marriage. No mechanism of social selection operated to exclude any particular class, section or stratum from the married status. Were scholars, however, the preferred choices as husbands for the ablest and healthiest women? Did they have a relatively higher number of children? Were learning and intelligence thus the preferred traits in a sexual selection which made for a selective breeding?

III.

The self-taught Jewish philosopher Solomon Maimon, who at the end of the eighteenth century made the transition from the Talmud to Kant's philosophy, observed in his *Autobiography*: "The study of the Talmud is the chief object of higher education among our people. . . . A wealthy merchant, leaseholder or professional man with a marriageable daughter does everything in his power to acquire a good Talmudist as son-in-law. In other respects the scholar may be deformed, diseased, and ignorant: he will still have the advantage over rivals."[17] Such indeed is the customary account of the privileged status of the scholar as a marital prospect throughout Jewish history. The novelist Isaac Bashevis Singer recalls that in Poland at the beginning of the twentieth century women accepted it as their "lot to bear children, cook, run the household, and earn a living — while the man studied Torah. Rather than complain, our grandmothers praised God for providing them with husbands who were scholars."[18] Many Jewish parents indeed took pride in securing a young yeshivah student as their daughter's husband, and supported him in his studies for years afterward.[19] The more talented the student was, it is said, the greater the effort to have him marry young, even at fourteen or fifteen. Fathers interrogated prospective sons-in-law on their Talmudical erudition, though they realized that the wives of these "perennial students" would have to support them.[20]

Far more parents were evidently loath to marry their daughters to the perennial Talmudists. Jewish fathers took a lot more into account in judging prospective sons-in-law than their book-learning. Thus, as Salo Baron writes, in the seventeenth and eighteenth centuries, educational leaders complained frequently "that the communal plutocracy no longer cared to give its children training in rabbinic law or, via marriage, to attract young talent from among the students of the yeshivot . . ."[21] The change in attitude in the eighteenth century toward the young scholars was drastic, as the latter declined in general high esteem. "Rabbi Jonathan Eybeschütz, one of the most prominent yeshiva heads of his day, deplored the fact that only the poor married off their daughters to scholars, . . ."[22] In Germany especially wealthy men were reluctant to have their daughters marry the Talmudical students. "Moses Samson Bacharach accused them of even going so far as to mock these students for devoting their whole time to the study of the Torah."[23] In the later Middle Ages, fathers saw their daughters deserted by wandering Jewish student sons-in-law who, more than emulating the goliards, left their wives behind as they went seeking the Lilith of learning in one center after another.[24] Curiously, the classical authorities, the Talmud and Ben Sira, had warned against marriage in which the wife supported the husband as unworthy and degrading. Ben Sira wrote: "There is anger and impudence and great reproach if a woman maintains her husband."[25] The Talmud had called on every Jew to learn a trade, and not to live by his learning. But European Jewry did not always follow classical wisdom.

Moreover, it must be borne in mind that the ordinary teacher in a Jewish community suffered an extremely low status. As far back as the Palestinian academies, the scholars learned in the oral law had looked down on the ordinary school teacher, whose learning was encompassed in a reading knowledge of the Bible. The latter was regarded as only a little higher than the ignoramuses, the "am ha-aretz." The rift between the upper and lower intellectuals grew deeper with time. "Centuries later the gap between the Bible-centered teachers and the scholars who championed the Oral Law widened considerably."[26] The Jewish teacher became an object of ridicule, and the *heder*, his schoolroom, the cynosure of pupil and parent cynicism. The rector-rabbi who presided over a yeshivah retained something akin to the status of a university president in the United States before 1960, but the social distance between him and the ordinary teacher (the *melamed*) was immense. The latter, usually poverty-stricken, was often regarded as trying desperately to make as much money from his charges as possible. To eke out his living, he frequently combined his teaching with some trade or business. A pamphlet published in Lublin in 1635 ascribed the low state of the Jewish schoolroom to the low fees for instruction, the difficulty in collecting them, and the tendency of many parents to change teachers every half-year; the teacher was said to promote pupils simply because he feared to lose them.[27] In rural districts, especially, the *melamed*'s status was low. Parents, moreover, "were more concerned with training their children for some occupation than providing them with religious instruction. They therefore employed any 'ignoramus' to teach their children, and in some cases, even men-servants were expected to devote some of their time to teaching the children of their employers."[28] Teachers who furthermore migrated from their native localities bore the opprobrium for having abandoned their wives.[29] Learning was indeed widespread. As Solomon Maimon wrote: "the majority of the Polish Jews consist of scholars, that is, men devoted to an inactive and contemplative life; for every Polish Jew is destined from his birth to be a rabbi, and only the greatest incapacity can exclude him from that rank."[30] When the massacres of 1648 took place, a contemporary chronicler wrote that out of fifty adult male Jews in an average community, twenty had the title *Morenu*. "This is doubtless an exaggeration," writes Salo Baron, "but there is no question that a considerable number of Jews, whether or not possessing the title *Morenu*, were very learned."[31] But the actual rabbis and the governing officials of communities, synagogues and *yeshivot*, were an extremely small percentage of the people. Maimon wrote with some bitterness that the Jewish people were ruled by "a perpetual aristocracy under the appearance of a theocracy. The learned men, who formed the nobility, have for many centuries been able to maintain their position as the legislative body with so much authority among the common people that they can do with them whatever they please."[32] There was thus a high intellectual establishment, small in numbers, surrounded by a mass of literate citizenry. How small the establishment was can be seen from an official report in 1842 in Russia that found in the whole country 604 synagogues, 2,340 prayer-houses, 3,944 schools, but only 954 rabbis.[33] The latter were the professional, salaried rabbis, not the larger number of those who, by virtue of their learning and respected character, would usually in their later years be accorded the honorary title. The total Jewish population was then approximately two million out of a European Russian population of over fifty million.[34]

Under such circumstances, one can understand how a Jewish father would weigh carefully the prospects of the young scholar who was seeking his daughter's hand. What chance did the scholar have of rising into the genuine administrative rabbinate? Or would he evolve into a despised teacher of children in a dark and dank pretense of a schoolroom? Or would both father and daughter have to toil to maintain the academic ne'er-do-well as a perpetual bookworm? One can understand why the disaffection with the scholars became widespread, and that it was the poor, evidently seeking a spiritual upward mobility where the material kind was not to be had, who continued to seek young scholars as their daughters' husbands. Only occasionally did wealthy fathers select impoverished scholars as their sons-in-law.[35] That a selective mating of wealthy and healthy daughters with the most intelligent young men was taking place can hardly be shown.

Rich families, moreover, were a highly transient phenomenon in the annals of Jewish communities. A wealthy family never retained its wealth long enough to become a genetic center for the breeding of intelligence. "It is difficult to trace any wealthy dynasties, of the type which exist today; the children of Aaron of Lincoln or Benedict of New York enjoyed at the best a modest competence."[36] Among the great gentile banking families, such as the Fugger and the Medici, there was indeed a certain stability of fortune from generation to generation. But among the Jews of wealth in the Middle Ages, "it seldom happened that this wealth passed from father to son. Generally, it was strictly personal; and the confiscatory measures which followed the death of a wealthy Jew (the whole of whose fortune legally passed to the crown) prevented his son from enjoying it."[37] Moreover, the number of rich Jews was a small fraction of the Jewish population. The lists of contributors to the Jewish taxes in Angevin England, for instance, "show that there were many more poor Jews than rich," and they all lost most of their wealth when they were expelled from England in 1290.[38] When conditions of greater stability evolved in the eighteenth century, they were coeval however with a growing rejection of pure scholars as sons-in-law by wealthy families.

In any case, the eminent Jewish scholars, contrary to the Wiener-Haldane hypothesis, did not generally have large families. As the distinguished historian Cecil Roth wrote: "Few of the eminent Jewish scholars of the Middle Ages, Rashi, Rambam, and so on, are known to have had large families which would have been considered of more than average number even today."[39] Indeed, "the families of some outstanding personalities were very small: for example the great financier of the twelfth century, Aaron of Lincoln . . . had only two sons. . . ." The Jewish families on the average were small in size; when the Jews of Munich were massacred, the records showed that the modal family had two children.[40] In early modern times, the Jewish family became much larger, but then the trend reversed, and in Prussia, for instance, by the end of the nineteenth century, families with only two children were dominant.[41]

Legal documents have always been a valuable source on the structure and relations of families. The case histories which Irving Agus has assembled in the second volume of his *Urban Civilization in Pre-Crusade Europe* provide information as to the size of Jewish families in that medieval period. Of the 33 families involved in the described legal proceedings, the largest group was childless; 11 families had no children. Seven families had one child each; three families had two children; seven families had three children each; only five families had four children each. In the last three groups, ambiguities in the data involve variations of one in the statement of the family sizes. The impressive fact is that the average family in these proceedings, generally involving merchants, had only 1.6 children. Usually these cases, arising from such circumstances as the father's death, pertained to completed families, not those low in offspring because the family itself was still young. The high frequency of childless marriages in this middle-class group suggests still another difficulty in the way of a theory of selective breeding.

IV.

It seems doubtful that the intellectual class among Jews enjoyed a higher rate of survival than their more ordinary fellow Jews. The likelihood is that in the massacres, pogroms, and legal measures directed against Jews, it was the intellectual class which sustained a disproportionate loss of numbers. The evidence here is indirect, but it was the case, for instance, that after the summer of 1096 when the chief communities of German Jews were destroyed by lynching bands of crusaders, scholarship was utterly interrupted. Rabbi Gershom, in the first quarter of the twelfth century, acquired a great reputation mainly because "the students of the students of the great teachers of Mayence did not survive the holocaust of the First Crusade."[42] "A good many Jews" were hanged in England in 1278–79 for alleged coin-clipping — three in Bedford, five at Canterbury, four at Norwich. They were all houseowners; evidently poor, property-less Jews were exempt from this risk.[43] Polish Jewry subsequently became the most populous center for Jewish culture. Their numbers were estimated as having increased from 50,000 in 1501 to 500,000 in 1648.[44] But in the spring of 1648 their massacres began under the direction of the Cossack commander, Bogdan Khmelnitzki, and his "semi-barbarous" followers from southern Russia. The catastrophe brought the Jews losses that exceeded those they had borne during the Crusades and the Black Death. Chroniclers reported that anywhere between 100,000 and 500,000 Jews were killed during the next decade. The Jewish communities on the left bank of the Dnieper virtually disappeared, while on the right bank, "only about one-tenth of the Jewish population survived." Seven hundred Jewish communities in Poland suffered massacre and pillage. Can we venture any plausible inference as to how the Jewish intellectual class fared relative to their fellows in these catastrophes?

In the similar calamities of our own time, the survivors, it has been observed, have tended not to be intellectuals or scholars, but rather simple people, mistrustful of all authorities; unencumbered by possessions, they were ready to leave and hide with little more than the miserable garments on their backs. When the Nazi army on its first day in Odessa executed a mass slaughter, "thousands of persons, most of them Jews including many intellectuals, were murdered in the first 24 hours."[45] Intellectuals, "rationalizers," as Raul Hilberg has said, were more apt, for instance, to invent plausible, relatively benevolent explanations as to why the Germans would want the Jews to assemble at a certain place at a certain time.[46] The survivors acted instinctively at short notice and ran away. They had the will to live and the readiness to live on near nothing. They could dissemble, and in a peasant's hut, pass themselves off as domestics. The faces of the scholar-intellectuals, lit by the lamp of learning, were far more recognizable. Probably the scholars of the Polish Jewish community in 1648 perished similarly in disproportionate numbers. The community as a whole soon revived, numbering in 1788 in Poland and Lithuania 617,032 out of a total population of 8,790,000.[47]

A traumatic period of massacre was generally followed by a lowering of the permissible age of marriage. Thus, in the fourteenth century, after the

Crusades had reduced the number of Jews, the prohibition against child marriage was relaxed.[48] Similarly, after 1648, the permissible age of marriage declined three to four years below the Talmudic and Maimonidean norm of eighteen and seventeen. The institution of the marriage broker likewise first emerged during the Crusading era, and was strengthened after 1648, because Jewish society was so disintegrated by the impact of massacres and expulsions that go-betweens were required to mediate between the families in isolated villages and hamlets.[49] Until modern times, the matchmakers were almost always rabbis and scholars; the fees were lucrative, varying between two and three percent of the dowries.[50] The marriage brokers are said to have operated on the principle of mating like with like, and therefore of not mating tall with short, young with old, or learned with ignorant.[51] The pattern of mating defective or sickly persons might have led through reinforcement to their genetic extinction, while the healthy would have grown relatively more numerous. On the other hand, the matchmakers became famous for their loquacious over-depiction of the eligible clients, and a whole department of Jewish jokes evolved on this theme. The marriage broker became preeminently a functionary among those who for one reason or another seemed to be failing to get married through the normal social channels. Apart from maximizing the number of married persons, it is doubtful that their intervention contributed to a higher degree of selective breeding than the available autonomous choices of the families and their young would have secured.

When the great waves of migration of Jews to America began after the pogrom of 1881, the rabbis and scholars tended to remain behind in disproportionate numbers. America was regarded as irreligious, as a place where Jews would fall away from their belief and ritual. Many immigrants departed for America as if by stealth, in a sort of shame at leaving the fold. Young lads, making the decision to migrate, shed Talmudic erudition for the lore of the Singer sewing machine: "Whoever recollects the beginnings of the Jewish emigration from Russia knows that almost every Jew who contemplated emigrating learned to operate a Singer sewing machine. What else could they do? To learn a 'trade' was the only way, and the easiest and quickest thing to learn was the ways of the Singer machine."[52] Thus recalled one who had emigrated. The traditionalist rabbis and scholars who remained behind were during the next decades decimated by wars, Polish, Ukrainian, and Russian pogroms, the Nazi holocaust, and Bolshevik intolerance. Survivors in the traditional Jewish communities were more likely the materially resourceful and adaptable rather than those adept in the scholarly discipline.

V.

Perhaps the most potent factor, however, for the selective loss of highly endowed Jewish intelligence over the centuries was the conversion of Jews to the Christian and Moslem religions. The impact of conversion on the ranks of Jewish intellectuals has rarely been discussed but there can be no doubt that this phenomenon, especially in the latter Middle Ages, affected the intellectual Jews far more than it did their ordinary co-religionists.[53]

The number of Jews in the world (as indicated by the evidence) declined from the time of the Roman Empire in the third century A.D. to that of the papacy in the thirteenth by approximately 66 to 85 percent.[54] According to a reasonable estimate by Dora Askowith, there were at the time of Nero 4.5 million Jews within the Roman Empire, which then had a total population of 54 million.[55] Salo Baron, on the other hand, reckoned the Jewish population in Claudius' time at almost 7 million.[56] By the middle of the seventeenth century, however, the Jewish population was diminished tremendously both in absolute and relative terms; the Jews are estimated approximately to have numbered not more than 900,000 out of a total European population reckoned at 100 million. They had evidently declined from between nearly seven to ten percent of the European population to less than one percent.[57] What were the causes of this decline of the Jewish population? Probably the Jews shared in the general decline of the birth rate which commenced in Europe during the latter days of the Roman Empire. Physical destruction, too, had its part in the depopulation of Jews. But there was also, writes Cecil Roth, "the gradual seepage of individuals, not many at a time, but in the long run very numerous." There were such instances, as for example in Portugal at the end of the fifteenth century, when a mass conversion of a community as a whole took place; the threat of massacre was a catalytic agent for this type of social process. More significant, however, than massacre and mass conversion, writes Cecil Roth, was the continuous, "constant pressure of environment, of social advantage, of conviction, of petty annoyances, of Ghetto pressure, of conversionist sermons and the rest of an elaborate system organized mainly with a view to breaking down the resistance of the Jew."[58]

One sociological generalization emerges from the facts concerning Jewish conversions throughout the centuries: to the extent that the surrounding society was one which offered liberal intellectual, political, economic, and social opportunities, to that extent the rate of Jewish conversion to Christianity was high. The Jews of Italy, for instance, were not massacred, nor did they emigrate; nevertheless, their actual number tended to remain stationary, or to diminish; whereas in 1638 they constituted about two in a thousand of Italian population, in 1938 they had declined to one in a thousand. What had occurred was a steady assimilation of Jews into the Christian population: "There was a perpetual procession from the Synagogue to the Church. Between 1634 and 1700 no less than 1,195 Jews were baptized in Rome alone."[59] The Jews in Britain found a liberal society with a high civilization; therefore, the founders of the Anglo-Jewish community were soon asssimilated into English society. Often they intermarried with aristocratic English families, such as those of the Duke of Norfolk and the Marquess of Salisbury; then too there were families whose calling was for service in the British Army — the Pereira, Aguilar, and Barrow.[60] "[T]here can be little doubt that the majority of them [the descendants of the founders of the Anglo-Jewish community] are outside," writes Cecil Roth.[61]

Montagu Frank Modder has described the assimilation of the British Jewish elite into the English Christendom: "When Sampson Gideon, the head of the Jewish community in the latter part of the 18th century, determined to bring up his children as Christians, he set an example which was followed by many of the chief Jewish families during the remainder of the 18th century and the early years of the 19th. The wealthy classes found that as Jews they could not satisfy their social and political aspirations. They saw, too, that conversion to Christianity would remove the obstructions which made their position intolerable. So a number of prominent families, the Bernals, the Lopezes, the Riccardos, the D'Israelis, the Aguilars, the Besavis, and the Samudas, for instance, severed their connection with the Synagogue, and allowed their children to grow up without any religion, or in the Established Church. In the main, these secessions arose not from religious convictions, but from social and personal causes."[62]

Apart from the effects of sheer physical force, in threat or actuality, two types of motives swayed the individuals who converted to Christianity. The highly ambitious and able often felt the wish to enter, remain, or rise in the governing elite.[63] Then, too, the rebellious in temperament often found the religion of their fathers stale, parochial, stifling, uninspiring. Both these kinds of persons tended to be extremely intelligent, although the second variety often exhibited neurotic traits in their revolt against their fathers. By contrast, the ordinary plebeian, impoverished Jew had no such compelling call to convert to Christianity. Ignorant of the gentile culture, he was scarcely a candidate for political or social advancement; no reading or immersion in gentile works had awakened in him a discontent with his father's religion. If some rebellious impulse moved him, it was more likely to express itself in allegiance to a Jewish sectarian movement, as Hasidism was, or fealty to another rabbi. The consequence was that conversion probably operated to drain a disproportionately large percentage of Jewish genetic intelligence into the Christian (or Moslem) ranks.

The converts from Judaism thus often achieved a high degree of eminence. Many Jewish doctors were converted to either Islam or Christianity; sometimes they then composed literary works devoted to attacking Judaism, and defending their new faiths.[64] Among the Spanish Jews, two eminent medieval scientists were converted to Christianity; Moses ha-Sephardi was baptized at the age of forty-four as Petrus Alfonsi, then, appointed as physician to Henry I, king of England, he introduced Arabic mathematical-astronomical science to that country;[65] Joseph Vecinho, physician to the king of Portugal, was consulted in 1484 on the practicability of Christopher Columbus' proposal. Vecinho was the translator of Zacuto's nautical tables, and had made improvements in the astrolabe; he accepted conversion in 1487.[66]

Many of the converts not only became priests, but achieved renown as the most zealous proselytizers and champions in disputation with the Jews. Some rose or had descendants who rose to high station in the hierarchy of the church.[67] The apostates led the ideological onslaught against the Jewish culture and religion in every center, moved often by zeal against their forebears.[68] In Rome, Pope Gregory XIII, prompted by a converted Jew, Joseph Tzarfati, instituted in 1584 a requirement that Jews were to attend weekly conversionist sermons.[69] The practice persisted in an attenuated form until 1847, when it was finally terminated. The conversionary discourses were usually given by apostates, who were not only zealous, but skillful in argument. How different were they in their intellectual character and desire for assimilation from the Jewish section of the Soviet Communist party, which directed the Marxizing, antireligious campaign in 1921–22? "The campaign was conducted almost exclusively by Jews against other Jews. . . . In fact, the *Evsektsiia* jealously guarded its monopoly over the persecution of the Jewish religion," writes a historian of the Jews in the Soviet Communist party.[70]

VI.

Thus, diverse types of apostasy have recurred in the history of the Jews. If there were those who, in Yitzhak Baer's words, "had entered their new faith as penitents, become monks, and appeared chiefly as persecutors of and missionaries to their former co-religionists," a larger class was moved rather by "political considerations"; conversion provided "an 'admission ticket' to a world that was wholly secular and to a career in the civil and political bureaucracy."[71] Philosophical influences in every historical period have tended to reduce the tenacity of the specifically Jewish religious culture. The powerful influence of the Averroist philosophy, which was felt by Moslem, Jewish, and Christian thinkers alike, thus tended to devaluate the significance of any particular religious forms and organizations. The Averroist philosopher placed all religions on an equal footing; hence the Averroist enlightenment mitigated the trauma of religious conversion; for the religious myths and symbols, in its view, were matter for the masses, not for the rational philosophers. The Averroist influence was not unlike that of Renaissance humanism in Italy, Kantianism in the early nineteenth century in Germany, and Marxism in Eastern Europe in the twentieth century.

Jewish teachers who explicated the Hebrew language to Pico della Mirandola and his fellow humanists became converts to Christianity; thus, Flavius Mithridates, a translator of Hebrew works, was such a Renaissance convert.[72] Not essentially different in kind were the philosophical conversions to Christianity that took place in Germany beginning in the early nineteenth century. Karl Marx's father, Heinrich Marx, when his livelihood as a lawyer was threatened by an anti-Jewish decree, found his path to conversion facilitated by his Kantian leanings.[73] The philosopher Solomon Maimon, in the Kantian era, proposed to convert from Judaism to Christianity, because, in his words, "in practical use the latter has an advantage over the former; and since morality which consists not in opinions but in actions, is the aim of all religion in general, clearly the latter comes nearer than the former to this aim."[74] During the Romantic period, the children and grandchildren of Moses Mendelssohn, the famed intellectual leader of German Jewry, were converted to Christianity; the daughters embraced Roman Catholicism, whereas the sons were drawn to Protestantism. When Abraham Mendelssohn, Moses' eldest son, hesitated about having his children baptized, his brother-in-law Bartholdy wrote to him: "You say you owe it to your father's memory (not to abandon Judaism). Do you think that you are committing a wrong in giving your children a religion which you and they consider the better? In fact, you would be paying a tribute to your father's efforts in behalf of true enlightenment, and he would have acted for your children as you have acted for them. . . ."[75] Thus the world of liberal European culture, with its opportunities for advancement, beckoned to the ablest and most ambitious of the Jews. Theodor Herzl, the founder of organized political Zionism, had as a youth been restive with "the dull compulsion of the Ghetto." After a party he attended, he wrote to his parents: "Thirty or forty ugly little Jews and Jewesses. Not a very refreshing sight." As late as 1893, he indulged in a grandiose fantasy of a mass conversion to Catholicism. He would negotiate with the pope: "Help us against anti-Semitism, and I in return will lead a great movement amongst the Jews for voluntary and honorable conversion to Christianity." Then, "in the broad light of day, at noon on a Sunday, a solemn and festive procession accompanied by the pealing of bells shall proceed to the St. Stephen Cathedral in Vienna. There shall be no furtiveness and no shamefacedness, as hitherto; it shall be done proudly and with a gesture of dignity."[76] The realities of the Dreyfus case abrogated such fantasies on Herzl's part; they illustrate, however, precisely the cultural and social forces that moved many of the ablest Jews to conversion to Christianity. Among the Polish Jews as well, it was the "well-to-do Jewish neo-phyte" who sought to enter the Roman Catholic Church, not the handicraftsman or proletarian.[77] And in Russia, in the nineteenth century, notes Salo Baron, "quite a few Jews, whether in the armed forces among the more easily assimilated intelligentsia, or in the group of straight careerists, joined the dominant faith."[78] The number of Russian Jews thus converted is estimated to have been 84,536.

Apart from the philosophical intellectuals and the politically ambitious, there were a certain number of Jews to whom a good business was worth a mass. "Arrant scoundrels," Cecil Roth calls them, yet the picaresque insouciance of these characters, stands in refreshing contrast to the zeal alike of the monks, penitents, and disputationists, and the careerism of the bureaucrats. Moses Israel of Salonica, for instance, made a kind of "racket" of baptism; he enjoyed the experience several times, and earned the temporal reward of a license to manufacture arquebus powder.[79] There were forced converts who managed to quit Portugal not because they wished to renew their Judaic religion but because they were attracted by commercial opportunities outside the Iberian peninsula. Whether they remained Christians because of religious indifference, or whether they felt that when in Rome, one must do as the Romans do, or whether they were mindful that a commercial traveller might as a Christian be better received in some lands, the seepage of talented Jewish men to the Gentiles was significant.[80] A man of brilliant abilities in finance might decline to renounce his life's calling in order to adhere to what he regarded as the meaningless dogmas of a religion. Thus, for instance, Don Samuel Abravanel, an "expert at figures and familiar with the royal revenues in the reigns of Henry II and John I," converted to Christianity around 1391, and was appointed chief accountant to the king of Castile.[81]

As we have seen, where the host culture is perceived by an alien minority as equal or superior, and nonrepressive of its own, the rate of voluntary conversion is high, especially among persons of intellectual abilities. Where the host culture has been perceived as inferior to one's own, the rate of conversion has been low. Thus, "in Czarist Russia up to 1917 . . . to a certain degree the Jewish cultural level was superior to that of the surrounding population."[82] The consequence was a low rate of conversion. Vienna, from 1901 to 1905, had a conversion rate of 39 Jews per 10,000 yearly; Russia, on the other hand, from 1891 to 1897 had an annual average of only 2. Germany from 1896 to 1900, and in 1904 had an annual average of 8.[83] The figures mirror the situations in which Viennese, German, and Russian Jews found themselves with respect to their host cultures. Earlier in the nineteenth century, however, many of the most talented Jews in Germany had adopted Christianity as a way of obtaining their passports to universal culture: Heinrich Heine, Ludwig Börne, joined later by Leopold Kronecker and Georg Cantor; the ranks of the converted or their sons had genius not inferior to that of their greatest contemporary loyalists.

A marginal type of apostate has been rather ignored in our histories that have stressed economic, social, and philosophical considerations. In the Middle Ages, Jewish men and women evidently on occasion wished to marry Christians and therefore converted to Christianity. The converse process, of Christians converting to Judaism, was virtually out of the question. "Converted Jews were more numerous in the twelfth century than has sometimes been allowed," writes H. G. Richardson in *The English Jewry under Angevin Kings*.[84] Among the women who were converted, there were such as Constance who married the tailor Gerin.[85] The reverse process was so dangerous that when a deacon at Oxford fell in love in 1222 with a Jewish girl, he was degraded, and executed by the king's bailiffs.[86] If one can judge from the later romances of young Jews from the eighteenth to the twentieth centuries, love choices of Gentiles by Jews were far more frequent occurrences among the intellectuals and well-to-do than among the poor. Probably erotic motives therefore augmented a continuing disproportionate seepage of Jewish genetic intelligence into the Christian ranks through the centuries.

In modern times, conscious apostasy, in response to conversionist propaganda, has been a negligible phenomenon among the Jews. The largest organization with this aim in the United States, the American Board of Missions to the Jews, founded in 1894, claimed that by 1966 they had converted 2,500 Jews.[87] Far more important than conversionary efforts were the purely social and impersonal forces making for the assimilation of the Jews into American society. For many persons the Jewish religion became a vestigial set of symbols; one then chose that religious community most congenial with one's social preferences.

VII.

It is often asserted that a large percentage of the eminent Jewish men of science are the descendants of rabbis; such a finding would naturally tend to confirm the hypothesis that a selective breeding for intelligence in rabbinical families made for their subsequent relatively higher contribution to science. Curiously, an empirical test of this hypothesis largely contradicts it.

Let us, for instance, examine the class of the most recognized eminent Jewish scientists, the winners of Nobel Prizes. Forty-nine such names are listed in the *Encyclopaedia Judaica*. This work, the most recent and authoritative, might well be expected in its biographical articles to emphasize any rabbinical parentage or ancestry in the scientist's background. Only one scientist out of forty-nine is described as having had such a rabbinical background. Those for whom no rabbinical antecedents were indicated were the following: Adolf von Baeyer (mother Jewish), Robert Barany, Felix Bloch, Konrad Bloch, Niels Bohr (mother Jewish), Max Born, Sir Ernest Boris Chain, Melvin Calvin, Paul Ehrlich,, Albert Einstein, Joseph Erlanger, Richard P. Feynman, Fritz Haber, Gustav Hertz (Jewish father), Herbert Spencer Gasser, George Charles de Hevesy, Murray Gell-Mann, Donald A. Glaser, Robert Hofstadter, François Jacob, Sir Bernard Katz, Arthur Kornberg, Sir Hans Krebs, Lev Landau, Karl Landsteiner, Gabriel Lippmann, Otto Loewi, Salvador Luria, André Lwoff, Elie Metchnikoff (mother Jewish), Otto Meyerhof, A. A. Michelson, Henri Moissan (mother Jewish), Hermann J. Muller, Marshall W. Nirenberg, Max Perutz, I. I. Rabi, Tadeus Reichstein, Emilio Segré, Julian S. Schwinger, Igor Tamm, Selman A. Waksman, George Wald, Otto Wallach, Otto Warburg and Richard Wilstaetter. No facts were provided concerning one laureate, Julius Axelrod. The only Nobel laureate who was identified as the scion of a rabbinical family was the geneticist Joshua Lederberg.

Thus, only slightly more than two percent of the Nobel laureates, only one out of a class of forty-nine, are identifiable as of rabbinical antecedents.[88] Acknowledging the possible loss of transmission of information from generation to generation, there is still no basis for the claim that a large percentage of Jewish scientists are the descendants of rabbis.

By contrast, the eminent rabbis were generally the sons of rabbis, or descended from rabbinical families. *Men of the Spirit*, a volume by Rabbi Leo Jung, is devoted to the biographies of twenty-eight famed rabbis of modern times.[89] Let us review the relevant entries: Akiba Joseph Schlesinger, "of a family renowned for its rabbis"; Levi Itzhak, "descended from a long line of rabbis" through "twenty-six consecutive generations"; Samuel Mohilever, whose family had bred rabbis for twenty-two generations; Israel of Sklov, his father a rabbi, his grandfather a Gaon; Edward Biberfeld, a scion of rabbis on both sides; Naphtali Berlin, of "a family rich in Rabbinic traditions"; Jonathan Eibeschuetz, on both sides; Michael Kahn, whose mother's rabbinical family continued back to the sixteenth century; Nathan Birnbaum and Shmuel Margulies, both of rabbinical descent. Those whose father was a rabbi: A. I. Karelitz, Y. E. H. Herzog, Y. Z. Soloweitchik, H. Ehrentreu, I. Salanter, Z. W. Gold, B. Z. Safran, M. S. Glasner, Yosef Hayyim, and Hayyim Medini. M. Friedland's mother was the daughter of a rabbi; M. Bar-Ilan's grandfather was a well-known rabbi. No mention of rabbinical descent was made concerning M. Gaster, S. Mendlowitz, H. Zeitlin, J. Duenner, J. Aszod, or M. Schick. With twenty-two of the twenty-eight eminent rabbis descended from or the sons of rabbis, it seems clear that a strong dynastic principle prevailed in the rabbinate. Joseph Duenner's father was a poor tavernkeeper, Moshe

Schick's father a merchant, and Judah Aszod's father a tailor. Such cases, however, were exceptional.

Possibly selective breeding heightened the acumen of rabbinical intelligence; it may also have extinguished qualities of venturesomeness and originality. The rabbinical abilities, in any case, scarcely played any part in the scientific movement among the Jews. The Jewish scientists emerged rather from the mercantile and artisan classes. Less encumbered by traditionalism, their children moved quickly into the frontiers of scientific research, into the exploration of the unknown. Rabbinical law indeed posed intellectual obstacles to some branches of science. The injunction upon "Torah-true priests (Kohanim)" not to defile themselves by contact with any dead body led some to avoid a medical career, involving, as it did, the dissection of bodies.[90] Jews are said to have "apparently played no part in the renaissance of modern biology."[91] Perhaps a residual influence of Jewish traditional culture may have assisted in this cultural selective retardation.

In Germany and Austria, before the advent of Nazi rule, the Jews had achieved a foremost scientific place. Very few, however, of the scientific community had sprung from rabbinical roots. The names of 245 scientists were set forth in a volume by Sidney Osborne entitled *Germany and Her Jews*.[92] Unfortunately, in only 66 cases were facts concerning religious influences indicated. Of those 66, only five were described as having had a father who was either a rabbi or a Jewish scholar, while seven had some relative other than one's father, characterized by such associations. Only eight were described as having had received a Jewish education. Probably the vast majority of the less documented 179 scientists had no rabbinical linkages whatsoever, for such facts have generally been prized by the writers on the contributions of Jews and were scarcely repressed in their encyclopedias and biographical dictionaries. The eighteen percent of the 66 cases who had some rabbinical or scholarly relative would probably be little more than five percent if more ample data were available.

VIII.

We have thus seen how the universality of marriage among Jews of all classes; the seepage of a large percentage of the ablest stratum through conversion and assimilation into the gentile population; the ambivalent attitudes of Jewish communities toward their rabbis, students, and teachers; and the frequent nondescent of Jewish scientists from rabbinical families all tend to indicate that social selective breeding was of small moment to the later scientific achievement. The Jews probably only held their own, with a certain constancy, as far as the genetic endowment of intelligence was concerned. Yet it may well have been true that at the outset of the Middle Ages the small nucleus of surviving Jewish people was the most intellectually gifted in Europe. It is not generally realized how small were the numbers of European Jewry in the Middle Ages. Irving Agus estimates cautiously that "in the year 800 . . . the Jews of Northern Italy, Germany and France, must have numbered no more than eight to ten thousand souls." Thus, "the ancestors of Ashkenazic Jewry, in the year 800 C.E., numbered but about ten thousand."[93] The most reliable document on the population of the Jews among later medieval sources is the remarkable *Book of Travels* of Benjamin of Tudela. Probably for about 14 years, from 1159 to 1173, Benjamin journeyed through towns of Spain, southern France, Italy, Greece, the Aegean archipelago, and on to Middle Eastern and North African centers. He faithfully recorded the numbers of the Jewish communities, their occupation, and their state of scholarship. One gets a sense of how sparse the Jewish numbers were: Marseilles with 300 Jews, Genoa with only 3, Pisa with 20, and Rome notably with only 200. In Europe, only Constantinople and Thebes had sizeable Jewish settlements, each with 2,000 persons.[94] The recorded number of Jews in all the places he visited in Europe, including those of the Aegean archipelago, added up to 14,574. Benjamin seems, however, to have counted only the adult Jewish men in the communities; hence his figures should be multiplied by about 3.5 to include women and the average number of children. Thus the total number of Jews in the communities he visited was about 51,009. Excluded from Benjamin's travels and enumeration were 14 German towns where Jewish communities existed, but these as Agus indicates, could not have totalled more than twenty thousand Jews. In England there seem to have been no Jews prior to the Norman Conquest in 1066; then a small migration of French Jews began. By the 1270s, the total population of the English Jewish communities was not more than 3,000.[95]

Thus, European Jewry at the outset of the Middle Ages may have consisted, indeed, of only about 10,000 persons. St. Jerome had remarked on the decline of the Jewish population toward the close of the fourth century when he wrote that "in comparison to their previous multitude, there hardly remained a tenth part of them."[96] The spread of Christianity, conversions, and persecutions all operated to diminish their number. Yet the handful who chose to survive as Jews at the beginning of the Middle Ages was probably among the most highly endowed intellectually in Europe. They were a group of "exceptionalists," intellectually, economically, and politically.[97] Intellectually, they had remained relatively immune to the waves of irrationalism that grew pronounced in the later Roman era. They remained in aloof detachment as the Christian theologians of diverse orthodoxies and heterodoxies argued over the trinity and virgin birth. Their monotheism, despite their own superstitions, tended by contrast to be reinforced as a simple rationalistic doctrine. Joinville, in the crusading thirteenth century, described a typical response to argument with the Jews.

The Jew, asked by a knight whether he believed in the virgin birth, "replied that of all this he believed nothing." Whereupon the knight smote him. "And so ended the disputation." The knight warned against any further disputations, "for there were a great many good Christians there who, before the disputation came to an end, would have gone away misbelievers. . . ."[98] Those who intellectually could not yield to the complexities of Christian theology, who found it contravened their principle of simplicity in philosophizing, were among Europe's most scientific in spirit. As Europe receded into the decentralized separatism of feudal societies, the surviving Jews were those who chose to remain outside the feudal economic and political structure.[99] They became merchants and artisans even as trade everywhere was diminishing, and the lines of commerce between countries and continents were being largely severed. The Jews continued to undertake voyages to distant places, selling their wares in the towns.[100] Every small Jewish community was an outpost, a wayfaring station, where the commercial traveller felt at home — a surviving international of commerce. A background in Talmudic learning was economically helpful to the merchant, for it guaranteed a warm reception from fellow Jews on one's travels; thereby Talmudic learning was "a strong factor in providing security of life and property to these travellers."[101] The Jews, pioneers of capitalism, stood altogether outside the system of lords, vassals, and serfs. No Christian oath of fealty bound them; inevitably they were partisans of the towns and the slowly emerging national kings. In medieval England and Normandy, for instance, the Jews were exempt from local customs and tolls, and "could sue and be sued only in the king's court" or the courts of the keepers of the king's castles; "As against all other men, except the king, he was protected."[102] As artisans they were linked to the division of labor and the exchange market. At Thebes, Benjamin of Tudela found that the Jews were "the most eminent manufacturers of silk and purple in all Greece"; at Saloniki, they lived "by the exercise of handicrafts"; at Brindisi, all of them were dyers; and at Constantinople, many were "manufacturers of silk cloth."[103] In medieval Sicily, where records are available, "the bulk of the Jews of the lower classes were stevedores, dock-laborers, metal workers and so on"[104] — surviving cells of workingmen in the feudalizing society. The average villager in medieval Europe was so isolated that, as G. G. Coulton estimates, he probably never saw more than a hundred people in his life.[105] In this structure of social isolates, the wandering Jew brought news, ideas, and portents of things to come. Those who chose to be Jews during the period in the early Middle Ages, when Europe declined intellectually, economically, and religiously, were probably persons who were, on the average, intellectually far ahead of their surrounding culture. It was not until several centuries later that the advancement of gentile culture made conversion in the absence of force a more likely alternative for rationalist intellectuals.

IX.

Once the Middle Ages were under way, there is no real evidence that there existed practices of selective breeding that would have raised the average genetic endowment of Jewish intelligence. Nevertheless, though Jewish intelligence probably remained roughly constant, the genetic level of intelligence among Christian Europeans may well have tended on the average to decline during the course of centuries. Christian social institutions and practices did make for a selective, dysgenic breeding against intelligence.

A decline of intelligence had perhaps begun during an earlier era toward the close of the Hellenic period. The intelligence of the ancient Greeks, conjectured Francis Galton, was probably much superior to that of modern Europeans, while according to the founder of British genetics, William Bateson, the decline of Greek civilization might have arisen from the mixtures that were introduced into that remarkable genetic stock. Bateson wondered if the reforms of Cleisthenes (507 B.C.), which sanctioned foreign marriages and admitted aliens and freedmen to citizenship, were "the effective beginning of a series of genetic changes which in a few generations so greatly altered the character of the people."[106] Apart from the problematic consequences of genetic mixtures in Hellenic society, there can be little doubt that the homosexuality which became widespread among the Greek intellectual class tended to reduce their relative fertility. Hans Kelsen, the distinguished Austrian scholar, noted: "The characteristic of homosexuality must remain an exceptional one, it can and may not be the general rule if society is not to be destroyed (by becoming extinct)."[107] Where it specifically affects the intellectual class, homosexuality then would entail a probable differential loss in the intellectual endowment of that given society. Aristotle had been aware that there was a relation between homosexuality and population decline, for he wrote in his *Politics* that homosexuality was fostered in Crete in order to reduce overpopulation.[108] And in Plato's *Laws*, one can read the warning that homosexuality "destroys the seeds of human increase, or sows them in stony places, in which they will take no root."[109] The intellectuals rarely had children, if one can judge from the accounts in Diogenes Laertius' *Lives of the Philosophers*. Among the Jews, on the other hand, homosexuality, as Cecil Roth wrote, was "hardly to be traced" at any place or time in their many-centuried history.[110] Meanwhile, the Roman Empire in its last centuries had to face the combined impact of homosexuality, celibacy, and the will to childlessness. The Christians not only favored celibacy but were averse to large families; especially among the Roman middle classes did childless families become the fashion, so much so that a scarcity arose of persons from the propertied classes eligible for appointment to town councils.[111]

Throughout the first part of the Middle Ages, "the great era of population decline coincided with increase in the strength of the Roman Catholic Church," as J. C. Russell has noted.[112] Although this trend was reversed in the latter part of the Middle Ages, the heritage of a depopulation-culture persisted; "so that many of its forms of expression partake of ideas derived from the preceding age."[113] The number of celibates in the laity was probably not high; a volume of the hearth taxes in a Belgian county in the early sixteenth century shows that the celibates numbered only 2 percent of the household population.[114] But the impact of the monasteries throughout Europe was toward reducing a large part of its superior genetic intelligence. One-third of the population of Spain is said to have been at one time in monastic orders,[115] and allowing for exaggeration, with an undoubted adverse consequence for the average intelligence of Spaniards. In England, as J. C. Russell observed: "Quantitatively, the effect of celibacy was probably not great. The English poll tax of 1377 showed about 30,000 clergy in an aggregate of 1,400,000 or about 2.3 percent. Qualitatively, the story may be quite different. A study of the medieval German nobility tends to show that the entrance of so many noble families into the Church hastened their extinction. . . ." Monasticism appealed to the most energetic and ambitious as well as to the more contemplative of educated persons then.[116] And precisely the latter class of intellectuals did not transmit its proportionate genetic heritage to Christian Europe.[117]

The triumph of celibacy as an ideal in the era from 200 to 900 A. D. is a fascinating episode in the oscillations of human history. Christianity spread most rapidly in urban areas where depopulation and depression were having their greatest effects. A sense of exhaustion came upon the intellectuals.[118] A longing grew for supernatural intervention. The sentiment for celibacy increased so strongly that the Christian emperors abolished the penalties against it, despite the fact that larger families were needed. The laity elected celibate monks as their bishops rather than secular married clergy.[119] "Great numbers of Christians entered monasteries voluntarily," renouncing those ties of family which the Romans had once prized.[120] By the fifth century, the Christian church was supreme in the religious domain, "rooting out religious dissent except among the Jews."[121]

As late as the beginning of the twentieth century, Spanish liberals, seeking to bring their country into the mainstream of European history, sensed that clerical celibacy was a principal enemy. "If we could only get rid of our monks as easily as our colonies!," a Spaniard is represented as declaring in one of the comic papers of Madrid during the world war, an aspiration voiced by many Spaniards of all classes.[122] As Charles Darwin wrote, the decline of the Spanish nation was probably the consequence of its institution of celibacy. In Darwin's words: "Almost all the men of a gentle nature, those given to meditation or culture of the mind, had no refuge except in the bosom of a church which demanded celibacy; and this could hardly fail to have had a deteriorating influence on each successive generation." Added to this, "some of the best men," the doubters, the questioners, "were eliminated during three centuries at the rate of a thousand a year." The "evil" wrought was "incalculable."[123] In 1646, Fray Luis de Miranda complained how the plethora of monks and their celibacy was draining Spain of its best seed: "The towns are almost all depopulated and deserted. . . . Our Spanish monarchy is being consumed away hour by hour and moment by moment. . . . [The religious orders are carrying off] the bravest men, the healthiest, the most upstanding, those with the best faces, the most talented and skillful. There is not among them a cripple, nor hardly a dwarf, nor one that is ugly, or dull, or ignorant. . . . In the world [remain] only the dregs and dross of men."[124]

Castile's population had commenced in the sixteenth century to decline sharply. In the fifteenth century, it had numbered between 7,900,000 to 9,500,000 persons, but by 1590 it had fallen to 6,250,000.[125] The religious vocation meanwhile continued to absorb a considerable number: "The Cortes of 1626 stated that there were then 9,088 monasteries, not counting the convents. Thus the fields were unpeopled and the factories empty."[126] In the last years of the eighteenth century, when industry and the entry of foreign immigrants had been much encouraged, the population of Spain which reached 10,541,221 still included, acccording to the historian Altamira, 168,248 ecclesiastics.[127] Thus, a class of more than 1.5 percent of the male population, including doubtless a disproportionate number of highly intelligent, was being subtracted from the Spanish heritage.

In Britain, during the latter part of the Middle Ages, monasticism grew at a rate that far exceeded that of the population. "A wave of enthusiasm for monasticism followed the Conquest and set up a system which included probably twenty times as many members by 1300 as in 1066. During the same period the population increased about 3.5 times. Probably the peak of the numbers was reached about 1275-1300 although the population of England continued to increase until the Black Death. . . . The decline was in about the same proportion as the loss in general population between 1346 and 1377." Subsequently, the monastic population tended to be stable until the dissolution of their institution, while the population increased about fifty percent.[128] In 1377, the combined numbers of the religious and secular clergy were about 35,000, or 1.6 percent of the total population of 2,200,000.[129]

Long after the Protestant Reformation had withdrawn the universities from the Roman Catholic fold, the ethic of celibacy continued to exert its influence on English scientists. As J. B. S. Haldane remarked: "Fellows of Colleges at Oxford and Cambridge lost their jobs on marriage up till the late nineteenth century, and the tradition of celibacy still persists. One result of this has been a lesser fertility of the educated.[130] In 1882, there were evidently not more than sixty families, and hardly ten young women in all Cambridge. Then the University of Cambridge removed the ban on marriage for their fellows. At once, a "stampede" for marriage ensued.[131] Several centuries of genetic disendowment, however, had been wrought against British scientific capacity.

Is there any way of estimating, even roughly, the decline of intelligence that may have taken place in the Christian community as a result of clerical celibacy? J. B. S. Haldane wrote in 1938 that "if the existing differences in fertility of social classes continue, [we may] expect a slow decline perhaps of 1 or 2 percent per generation in the mean intelligence quotient of the country. That is, on the whole, deplorable."[132] Haldane was particularly mindful of the lower fertility of the professional classes — the "doctors, clergymen, teachers, and so on," because apart from that stratum "the well-to-do do not have children appreciably more intelligent, as judged by these tests, than the remainder of the population."[133] Of course, European countries have varied considerably as far as their relative numbers of clergy are concerned; moreover, one must bear in mind the degree of the clergy's commitment to celibacy as well as the date of the country's reception of the Christian religion. If we assume that the average western and central European country adhered to a celibacy-practicing Christianity on an average of ten centuries, and if each century is taken as having consisted of four generations, and lastly, if we assume that the differential fertility of their celibate clergy was at least that of the Western professional class (a very modest assumption), then the negative impact on the mean intelligence quotient must have been very large indeed. To be sure, once the most intelligent had been eliminated, the dispersion of its remaining groups with respect to intelligence would have been lessened. The differences in the intelligence, in other words, between priest and parishioner would have become smaller. The law of diminishing intelligence under a negative differential fertility would have had a milder effect as the population lost its most talented. The damage inflicted would have grown proportionately less. Meanwhile, however, European intelligence would have sustained a traumatic injury especially in the region of the highest ability.

This whole domain of the rise and fall of civilizations and their genetic states continues to be enveloped in obscurity. If some geneticists have deplored the consequences of certain racial intermixtures which took place in antiquity, the eminent R. A. Fisher, on the other hand, has declared: "The fact of the decline of past civilizations is the most patent in history, and since brilliant periods have frequently been inaugurated, in the great centres of civilization, by the invasion of alien rulers, it is recognized that the immediate cause of decay must be the degeneration or depletion of the ruling classes."[134] To what extent alien infusions have been like external sources of energy counteracting an entropic trend is unclear. The historian Tenney Frank felt that the Roman decline was coeval with racial mixture.[135] What, might one ask, was the effect on Arab civilization in North Africa of admixtures with such peoples as the Berbers and the Sudanese Negroes? If sheer conquest has a revitalizing potential, one might perversely argue that the pogroms and rapine committed against the Jews had an intermittent eugenic effect through the agency of ethnic or racial mixture. The areas of ignorance here are immense: which racial mixtures are deleterious, which favorable, and in what respects and in what degrees, remains virtually *terra incognita*. Many, moreover, would prefer that these problems remain unexplored.[136]

X.

Mark Twain once wrote that the Jew's "contributions to the world's list of great names in literature, science, art, music, finance, medicine, and abstruse learning are . . . way out of proportion to the weakness of his numbers." He felt that "nine-tenths of the hostility to the Jews comes from the average Christian's inability to compete successfully with the average Jew in business. . . ."[137] Justice Oliver Wendell Holmes, Jr. in 1926 told his friend the British jurist Sir Frederick Pollock, that it was "queer" to see the widespread prejudice against the Jews. To which Pollock replied that the others were "jealous."[138] Hitherto, explanations for this high attainment have been either racial or environmental. It has been felt that the choice was between these two hypotheses; the racial hypothesis proposed that the Jews as a race were primordially biologically endowed with a higher intelligence; the environmental hypothesis held rather that the higher achievements were due to such social influences as the tradition for scholarship, the closeness of the Jewish family, the persecution of the Jews which led them to prefer the learned professions, and the pessures on the Jewish child to work harder in order to survive and prosper in a hostile world.

The modified sociobiological theory, on the other hand, is neither racial nor environmental. No hypothesis is proposed that the Jews as a race *ab initio* were endowed with a genetic basis for intelligence superior to that of other races. In their origins the races may have been equal or unequal in intelligence; no assumption is made concerning the original state. The modified sociobiological theory rather affirms: whatever the primordial genetic endowments of races, certain values and practices in sexual relations will maintain the constancy of that endowment, whereas other practices, especially a differential adherence of the intellectual class to celibacy and homosexuality will tend to diminish that endowment.[139] The biological basis of intellectual achievement is thus not a constant among the various races and peoples; the social practices with regard to sexuality can elevate the average genetic endowment for intelligence of a given race, or lower it.

The sociobiological theory of intellectual achievement does not, however, reduce to a case of sociological determinism. Standing, for instance, outside the deterministic model was the decision of ten thousand or so Jews, a small minority of them, to resist at the outset of the Middle Ages the sociological processes of assimilation and conversion. Their decision, exceptional as it was, arose from no requirement of the late Roman or early medieval mode of production, nor was it rational in terms of helping one's chances to survive. Such "exceptional" decisions can, however, be crucial in the evolution of a culture and a people.

Notes

* I am grateful to my friend Professor William Peterson for his advice on the final version of this essay. The responsibility for its shortcomings, however, is wholly mine.
1. Norbert Wiener, *Ex-Prodigy: My Childhood and Youth* (New York, 1953), pp. 11–12. Also cf. J. B. S. Haldane, *Heredity and Politics* (New York, 1938), p. 162.
2. Nathaniel Weyl, *The Creative Elite in America* (Washington, 1966), p. 92. Also cf. Lewis S. Feuer, *The Scientific Intellectual: The Psychological and Sociological Origins of Modern Science* (New York, 1963), p. 308. Raphael Patai, *The Jewish Mind* (New York, 1977), pp. 306, 334.
3. Arthur Ruppin, *The Jews in the Modern World* (London, 1934), p. 79.
4. Arthur Ruppin, *The Jews of To-day*, tr. Margery Bentwich (London, 1913), p. 73.
5. Mark Zborowski and Elizabeth Herzog, *Life Is with People; The Jewish Little-Town of Eastern Europe* (New York, 1953), p. 129.
6. Salo W. Baron, *A Social and Religious History of the Jews,* Vol. II (New York, 1952), p. 210.
7. Cf., the proverbs on "celibacy" in Reuven Alcalay, ed., *Words of the Wise* (Jerusalem, 1970), p. 62.
8. Solomon Schechter, *Studies in Judaism; Second Series* (Philadelphia, 1908), p. 95.
9. Salo Wittmayer Baron, *The Jewish Community: Its History and Structure to the American Revolution*, Vol. II (Philadelphia, 1942), p. 308.
10. Israel Abrahams, *Jewish Life in the Middle Ages*, New Ed. (London, 1932), p. 183.
11. Ibid., p. 106.
12. Max Arzt, "The Teacher in Talmud and Midrash," in Jewish Theological Seminary of America, *Mordecai M. Kaplan Jubilee Volume*, ed. Moshe Davis (New York, 1953), p. 45.
13. Isidore Fishman, *The History of Jewish Education in Central Europe from the End of the Sixteenth to the End of the Eighteenth Century* (London, 1944), pp. 30–31.
14. *Josephus*, tr. H. St. J. Thackeray (London, 1926), Vol. I, pp. 187, 375.
15. Isidore Fishman, *The History of Jewish Education in Central Europe*, p. 17.

16. Ibid., p. 38.
17. Solomon Maimon, *An Autobiography*, tr. J. Clark Murray, ed. Moses Hadas (New York, 1967), p. 16.
18. Isaac Bashevis Singer, *In My Father's Court* (New York, 1966), p. 44.
19. Isidore Fishman, *The History of Jewish Education in Central Europe*, p. 125.
20. Zborowski and Herzog, *Life Is with People*, pp. 131, 136, 276, 272.
21. Salo W. Baron, *The Jewish Community*, Vol. II, p. 362.
22. Chaim Wolf Reines, "Public Support of Rabbis and Scholars" in *Yivo Annual of Jewish Social Science*, Vol. VII (New York, 1966), p. 44.
23. Isidore Fishman, *The History of Jewish Education in Central Europe, p. 125.*
24. *Salo W. Baron, The Jewish Community, Vol. II. p. 187.*
25. Cf. Schechter, *Studies in Judaism*, Second Series, pp. 95–96.
26. Max Arzt, "The Teacher in Talmud and Midrash," p. 43.
27. Cf. Elijah Bortniker, "Education," *Encyclopaedia Judaica*, Vol. 6 (Jerusalem, 1971), p. 414.
28. Isidore Fishman, *The History of Jewish Education in Central Europe*, p. 56.
29. Ibid., pp. 62–63.
30. Solomon Maimon, *An Autobiography*, p. 52.
31. Salo Wittmayer Baron, *Steeled by Adversity: Essays and Addresses on American Jewish Life* (Philadelphia, 1971), p. 155.
32. Solomon Maimon, *An Autobiography*, p. 108.
33. Salo W. Baron, *The Russian Jew under Tsars and Soviets*, New York, 1964, p. 139.
34. In 1820, the Jews numbered 1,600,000 out of a European Russian population of 46,000,000. This rose in 1851 to 2,400,000 Jews in a population of 61,000,000 in European Russia.
35. Salo W. Baron, *The Jewish Community*, Vol. II, p. 81
36. Cecil Roth, *The Jewish Contribution to Civilization* (London, 1938), p. 229. The estate of Aaron of Lincoln, "the wealthiest Jew of his time," was evidently mostly confiscated by the king at his death in 1186, so that his two sons actually were not his heirs. Cf. H. G. Richardson, *The English Jewry under Angevin Kings* (London, 1960), p. 115.
37. Cecil Roth, *The Jewish Contribution to Civilization.*
38. *H. G. Richardson, The English Jewry*, pp. 5, 229.
39. Cecil Roth, "The Ordinary Jew in the Middle Ages," in *Studies and Essays in Honor of Abraham A. Newman* (Philadelphia, 1962), p. 22.
40. Ibid., pp. 23–24.
41. Raphael Straus, *Regensburg and Augsburg*, tr. Felix N. Gerson (Philadelphia, 1939), p. 228. Arthur Ruppin, *The Jews in the Modern World*, London, 1934, pp. 71–72.
42. Irving A. Agus, *Urban Civilization in Pre-Crusade Europe*, Vol. 1 (Leiden, 1968), p. 40.
43. H. G. Richardson, *The English Jewry under Angevin Kings*, pp. 219–220.
44. S. M. Dubnov, *History of the Jews in Russia and Poland*, tr. J. Friedlaender (Philadelphia, 1916–1920), Vol. I, p. 66.
45. Dora Litani, "The Destruction of the Jews of Odessa in the Light of Rumanian Documents," in *Yad Vashem Studies on the European Jewish Catastrophe and Resistance*, ed. Nathan Eck and Aryeh Leon Kubovy (Jerusalem, 1967), p. 137.

46. Discussion with Raul Hilberg, author of *The Destruction of the European Jews*, Burlington, Vermont, June 14, 1972. The first lists of survivors, narrated Simon Wiesenthal, the organizing spirit in the search for Nazi war criminals, were "nomads, vagabonds, beggars." Cf. Gerh Korman, ed., *Hunter and Hunted: Human History of the Holocaust* (New York, 1973), p. 290. Also cf. Helen Epstein, *Children of the Holocaust: Conversations with Sons and Daughters of Survivors* (New York, 1979), pp. 161, 166. Also cf. Yehuda Bauer, *Flight and Rescue: Brichah* (New York, 1970), pp. 3–4.
47. Dubnov, *History of the Jews in Russia and Poland*, pp. 263–264.
48. Abrahams, *Jewish Life in the Middle Ages*, p. 169.
49. Ibid., p. 171.
50. Editorial Staff, "Shadkhan," *Encyclopaedia Judaica*, Vol. 14, pp. 1254–1255.
51. Zborowski and Herzog, *Life Is with People*, p. 273. Felix Aron Theilhaber, *Die Schädigung der Rasse durch soziales und wirtschaftliches Aufsteigen, bewiesen an den Berliner Juden* (Berlin, 1914).
52. Jacob Milch, "New Movements amongst the Jewish Proletariat: VII." *The International Socialist Review*, Vol. VII, No. 10 (April 1907), p. 605.
53. Moses Hadas has suggested a distinction between the terms "apostate" and "convert." "The term apostate has a more unfavorable connotation than that of convert; whereas the convert may have acted from conviction or self-protection, the apostate is felt to have changed his religion for selfish purposes." The usages are, however, vaguely differentiated, and the terms are often used interchangeably. "Apostasy" has a more voluntary connotation than "convert"; thus, although the literature often discusses "forced conversions," there is no such usage as "forced apostasy." Also, "apostasy" is more often used to refer to an individual's decisions, in deviation from his group, whereas "conversion" refers more often to a collective phenomenon. The opprobrium attached to "apostate" reflects the close in-group feeling attached to the "deviationist," or "renegade," or excommunicate. Cf. Moses Hadas, "Apostates," *The Universal Jewish Encyclopedia*, Vol. I (New York, 1939), p. 427.
54. Cecil Roth, "Are the Jews Unassimilable?" *Jewish Social Studies*, Vol. III (1941), p. 5.
55. Dora Askowith, *The Toleration of the Jews under Julius Caesar and Augustus* (New York, 1915), p. 52.
56. Cecil Roth, "Are the Jews Unassimilable?," p. 5.
57. Ibid., p. 7.
58. Ibid., p. 7.
59. Ibid., p. 9.
60. Ibid., p. 10.
61. Ibid. Also cf. Cecil Roth, *A History of the Jews in England*, Third Ed. (Oxford, 1964), pp. 209, 225.
62. Montagu Frank Modder, *The Jews in the Literature of England to the End of the 19th Century* (1939, reprinted, Cleveland, 1960), p. 82. The novel *Reuben Sacks*, published by the unhappy Anny Levy in 1888, depicted vividly the emotional strains of the educated youth among upper class Jews in England.
63. The role of Jews in the medieval bureaucracy is discussed in Heinrich Graetz, *History of the Jews*, ed. Bella Lowy (London, 1892), Vol. III, pp. 299–301, 527–538.
64. Salo Wittmayer Baron, *A Social and Religious History of the Jews*, Vol.

VIII, Sec. Ed. (New York, 1952–1973), pp. 246, 249. Among the list of Jewish medical writers in Arabic during the Middle Ages, the names of converts to Islam recur frequently. Cf. Harry Friedenwald, *The Jews and Medicine: Essays* (Baltimore 1944), Vol. I, p. 172, ff.
65. Cf. Barry Spain, "Mathematics," *Encyclopaedia Judaica*, Vol. II, p. 1122. Baron, *A Social and Religious History of the Jews*, Vol. VIII, p. 173.
66. Cecil Roth, *Gleanings: Essays in Jewish History, Letters and Art* (New York, 1967), p. 174.
67. Ibid., p. 35. Cecil Roth, *A History of the Marranos*, Sec. Ed. (Philadelphia, 1959), pp. 14, 48. Also, Haim Hillel Ben-Sasson, "Apostasy," *Encyclopaedia Judaica*, Vol. 3, pp. 202–211.
68. Cf. Cecil Roth, *The Jewish Book of Days*, Rev. Ed. (New York, 1966), pp. 45, 195, 143, 215–216.
69. David Philipson, *Old European Jewries* (Philadelphia, 1894), pp. 143–145. Louis Wirth, *The Ghetto* (Chicago, 1928), pp. 59–60. Cecil Roth. *A History of the Jews in Italy* (Philadelphia, 1946), pp. 316, 409.
70. Zvi Y. Gitelman, *Jewish Nationality and Soviet Politics: The Jewish Sections of the CPSU, 1917–1930* (Princeton, 1972), pp. 298–299.
71. Yitzhak Baer, *A History of the Jews in Christian Spain*, Vol. II (Philadelphia, 1966), p. 93. Also cf. Heinrich Graetz, *History of the Jews from the Earliest Times to the Present Day*, Vol. III, tr. Bella Löwy (London, 1891), pp. 179, 299, 301, 527, 533, 538. "[A] large number of Bolshevik leaders and active party members were of Jewish parentage; but they had been completely assimilated . . ." Solomon M. Schwarz, *The Jews in the Soviet Union* (Syracuse, 1951), p. 93. The Jewish socialist parties, on the other hand, opposed the Bolshevik Revolution. Consequently, the Commissariat for Jewish National Affairs had difficulty in finding persons who could write in Yiddish for their Communist Jewish newspaper. Ibid., pp. 94–95.
72. Cf. Haim Hillel Ben-Sasson, "Apostasy," *Encyclopaedia Judaica*, Vol. 3, p. 206.
73. Lewis S. Feuer, "The Conversion of Karl Marx's Father." *The Jewish Journal of Sociology*, Vol. XIV (1972), pp. 154–157.
74. Solomon Maimon, *An Autobiography*, p. 89.
75. Gustav Karpeles, *Jewish Literature and Other Essays* (Philadelphia, 1895), p. 308.
76. Alex Bein, *Theodore Herzl: A Biography*, tr. Maurice Samuel (Cleveland, 1962), pp. 49, 94, 35. *The Complete Diaries of Theodore Herzl*, tr. Harry Zohn (New York, 1960), Vol. I, p. 7.
77. Beatrice C. Baskerville, *The Polish Jew: His Social and Economic Values* (New York, 1906), p. 331.
78. Baron, *The Russian Jew under Tsars and Soviets*, p. 81.
79. Cecil Roth, "Forced Baptisms in Italy," *Gleanings*, p. 243.
80. A. S. Halkin, "A *Contra Cristianos* by a Marrano," *Mordecai M. Kaplan Jubilee Volume* (New York, 1953), p. 399.
81. Baer, *A History of the Jews in Christian Spain*, Vol. I, p. 378.
82. H. H. Ben-Sasson, "Apostasy," *Encyclopaedia Judaica*, Vol. 3, p. 207.
83. Ruppin, *The Jews of To-day*, p. 185.
84. H. G. Richardson, *The English Jewry under Angevin Kings* (London, 1960), p. 28.
85. Ibid., pp. 29–30.
86. Ibid., p. 35.

87. Robert E. Blumstock, "Mission to Jews: Reduction of Inter-Group Tension," *Practical Anthropology*, Vol. 14 (1967), p. 39. Robert Blumstock, "Fundamentalism, Prejudice, and Missions to the Jews," *The Canadian Review of Sociology and Anthropology*, Vol. 5 (1968), p. 31.
88. Some error may arise from the fact that some scientists of Jewish ancestry have been extremely recalcitrant to any effort to link them to the Jewish community. Perhaps some data were suppressed, although journalists and biographers, eager for information, would make this difficult. "There was the celebrated case of Karl Landsteiner, a Viennese Jew, the famous discoverer of various blood groups, who sued the editors of a Jewish encyclopedia for libel because they dared to mention that he was of Jewish extraction." Cornelius Lanczos, *Judaism and Science* (Leeds, 1970), p. 2.
89. Leo Jung, ed., *Men of the Spirit* (New York, 1964).
90. Ibid., p. vi.
91. Mordecai L. Gabriel, "Biology," *Encyclopaedia Judaica*, Vol. 4, p. 1030.
92. Sidney Osborne, *Germany and Her Jews* (London, 1939). My assistant, Deena Mandel, has helped me with the research on the names in this volume.
93. Irving Agus, *Urban Civilization in Pre-Crusade Europe*, Vol. I, pp. 12–13.
94. *The Itinerary of Rabbi Benjamin of Tudela*, tr. A. Asher (reprinted, New York, 1927), Vol. I., pp. 36, 37, 38, 47, 55. The appellation "rabbi" was evidently honorific. Also, cf. Cecil Roth, "Benjamin of Tudela," *Encyclopaedia Judaica*, Vol. 4, p. 538.
95. H. G. Richardson, *The English Jewry under Angevin Kings*, p. 216.
96. S. W. Baron, *A Social and Religious History of the Jews*, Vol. II, p. 210. Also, Cecil Roth, *The History of the Jews of Italy*, p. 34.
97. In the Soviet Communist party, the number of Jews was likewise disproportionately large among the "deviationists," both left and right, who were embattled with Stalin and the dominant group. Cf. Z. Y. Gitelman, *Jewish Nationality and Soviet Politics*, p. 449 ff.
98. Villehardouin and De Joinville, *Memoirs of the Crusades*, tr. Sir Frank Marzials (London, 1908), p. 148. St. Jerome much earlier had complained of the Jews' polemical powers in the disputations between church and synagogue. Cf. S. Krauss, "The Jews in the Works of the Church Fathers," *The Jewish Quarterly Review*, Vol. VI (1894), p. 239.
99. "In the midst of a social organization where the populace was attached to the land, and where everyone was dependent upon a liege lord, they (the merchants) presented the strange picture of circulating everywhere without being claimed by anyone." Henri Pirenne, *Medieval Cities*, tr. Frank D. Halsey (Princeton, 1925), p. 131.
100. L. Rabinowitz, *Jewish Merchant Adventurers: A Study of the Radanites* (London, 1948), pp. 9–10, 15–22.
101. Agus, *Urban Civilization in Pre-Crusade Europe*, Vol. I, pp. 56–57.
102. H. G. Richardson, *The English Jewry under Angevin Kings*, p. 110.
103. *The Itinerary of Rabbi Benjamin of Tudela*, pp. 47, 49, 55, 45.
104. Cecil Roth, *Gleanings*, p. 26.
105. G. G. Coulton, *The Medieval Village*, p. 393.
106. *William Bateson, Naturalist, His Essays and Addresses*, ed. Beatrice Bateson (Cambridge, 1928), p. 311. "The average ability of the Athenian race is, on the lowest possible estimate, very nearly two grades higher than our own. . . . It has been a severe misfortune to humanity, that the high Athenian breed decayed and disappeared. . . ." Francis Galton, *Hereditary Genius: An*

Inquiry into Its Laws and Consequences (London, 1869, Sec. Ed., 1892), pp. 330–331.

107. Hans Kelsen, "Platonic Love," *The American Imago*, Vol. III (1942), p. 9. Flavius Josephus writes of "the contempt for marriage" which had prevailed among the Lacedaemonians, and "the unnatural vice so rampant" among the people of Elis and Thebes. Cf. *Josephus*, Vol. I, p. 403.

108. Aristotle, *Politics*, tr. William Ellis (London, 1912), p. 58.

109. Cf. Kelsen, "Platonic Love," p. 39.

110. Cecil Roth, *The Jews in the Renaissance*, Philadelphia, 1959, p. 45.

111. Arthur E. R. Boak, *Manpower Shortage and the Fall of the Roman Empire in the West* (Ann Arbor, 1955), pp. 80, 84, 129. Tenney Frank, "Race Mixture in the Roman Empire," *The American Historical Review*, Vol. XXVI (1916), pp. 704–705.

112. Josiah Cox Russell, "Late Mediaeval Population Patterns," *Speculum*, Vol. XX (1945), p. 171.

113. Ibid.

114. J. C. Russell, "Recent Advances in Medieval Demography," *Speculum*, Vol. XI (1965), p. 97.

115. Cf. Trout Rader, *The Economics of Feudalism* (New York, 1971), p. 58.

116. Josiah Cox Russell, "Medieval Population," *Social Forces*, Vol. 15 (1937), p. 506. In England, it should be observed, the number of the religious was halved by the plague, evidently being affected more than the population generally. Cf. J. C. Russell, "Late Medieval Population Patterns," p. 170. The four great orders of mendicant friars, Dominican, Franciscan, Carmelite, and Austin were, however, exempted from the poll tax andrecords of 1377. Their numbers have been estimated respectively as 1,889; 2,219; 945; and 765. Cf. Josiah Cox Russell, "The Clerical Population of Medieval England," *Traditio*, Vol. II (1944), p. 209.

117. The sociological factors, apart from the theological, which impelled the church toward a discipline of celibacy were discussed at length by Henry Charles Lea, *History of Sacerdotal Celibacy in the Christian Church* (New York, 1907), Vol. I, pp. 60–63, 408–409.

118. E. M. Sanford, "Contrasting Views of the Roman Empire," *American Journal of Philology*, Vol. LVIII (1937), pp. 454–456.

119. J. C. Russell, "The Ecclesiastical Age: A Demographic Interpretation of the Period 200–900 A.D.," *The Review of Religion*, Vol. V (1941), pp. 142–143. H. R. Betterman, "The Beginning of the Struggle Between the Regular and the Secular Clergy," *Medieval and Historiographical Essays in Honor of J. W. Thompson*, ed. Cate and Anderson (Chicago, 1938), p. 25.

120. J. D. Russell, "The Ecclesiastical Age," p. 145.

121. Ibid.

122. "A century and a half ago there was one priest to every thirty inhabitants in Spain," wrote Havelock Ellis, with some exaggeration. Havelock Ellis, *The Soul of Spain*, New Ed. (London, 1937), pp. 395–396.

123. Charles Darwin, *The Descent of Man and Selection in Relation to Sex*, Sec. Ed., (New York, 1874), p. 160.

124. Américo Castro, *The Structure of Spanish History* (Princeton, 1954), pp. 645–646.

125. Harold Livermore, *A History of Spain*, Sec. Ed. (London, 1966), p. 278. Another estimate for Spain as a whole which confirms this trend is given in Massimo Livi Bacci, "Fertility and Nuptiality Changes in Spain from the 18th to the Early 20th Century," *Population Studies*, Vol. XXII (1968), p. 83.

126. Altamira, op. cit., p. 137.
127. Ibid., p. 164. According to another source, the Spanish clergy at this time numbered 182,564 out of a population (including Minorca) of about ten and a half million. Antonio Domínguez Ortíz, *La Sociedad Española en el Siglo XVIII* (Madrid, 1955), pp. 58, 123.
128. Russell, "The Clerical Population of Medieval England," p. 212.
129. Ibid., p. 179.
130. Cf. J.B.S. Haldane, "Alfred Kinsey," *Kinsey: A Biography*, ed. Cornelia V. Christenson (Bloomington, 1971), p. 230. Charles Edward Mallet wrote that "prolonged celibacy" has tended to make the College fellows "dreary and vinose." Cf. *A History of the University of Oxford* (London, 1927), Vol. III, p. 348. "A don of thirty," wrote Leslie Stephen, "was ten years older than a rising young barrister of forty." Sheldon Rothblatt, *The Revolution of the Dons: Cambridge and Society in Victorian England* (London, 1968), p. 191.
131. George Gordon Coulton, *Fourscore Years, an Autobiography* (Cambridge, 1943). p. 94. Joseph John Thomson, *Recollections and Reflections* (Toronto, 1936), pp. 74, 90, 274. Sheldon Rothblatt, *The Revolution of the Dons*, p. 242.
132. J. B. S. Haldane, *Heredity and Politics* (New York, 1938), p. 126.
133. Ibid.
134. Ronald Aylmer Fisher, *The Genetical Theory of Natural Selection* (Oxford, 1930), p. 237. J. B. S. Haldane, *Heredity and Politics*, p. 21.
135. Tenney Frank, "Race Mixture in the Roman Empire," *American Historical Review*, Vol. XXI (1916), p. 705 ff.
136. H. J. Eysenck, *The Inequality of Man* (London, 1973), pp. 14, 24. R. J. Herrnstein, *I.Q. in the Meritocracy* (Boston, 1973), p. 45.
137. Mark Twain, "Concerning the Jews," *Literary Essays*, Vol. 24, New York, pp. 275, 286.
138. Mark De Wolfe Howe, ed., *Holmes-Pollock Letters: The Correspondence of Mr. Justice Holmes and Sir Frederick Pollock 1874–1932* (Cambridge, Mass., 1941), Vol. 2, pp. 191–192.
139. The later distinguished Nobel laureate in genetics, and at that time a Marxist and admirer of the Soviet Union, H. J. Muller, once wrote that "it is easy to show that in the course of a paltry century or two . . . it would be possible for the majority of the population to become of the innate quality of such men as Lenin, Newton, Leonardo, Pasteur, Beethoven, Omar Khayyam, Pushkin, Sun Yat Sen, Marx." The list indeed was a curious conglomerate. Muller, however, feared that the Nazis would avail themselves of genetic knowledge to breed instead for "a maximum number of Billy Sundays, Valentinos, Jack Dempseys, Babe Ruths, even Al Capones." H. J. Muller, *Out of the Night: A Biologist's View of the Future* (New York, 1935), pp. 113–114.

8.
Some Sociohistorical Perspectives on Race Relations

Lester Singer

The study of "race relations" and, therefore, the understanding of social existence in American society are beclouded by, *inter alia*, certain persisting questions which are ignored or whose answers are mistakenly taken for granted. Some of the questions revolve around the nature of race relations and certain assumptions concerning their persistence. Assertions such as, e.g., "race relations, i.e., racial antagonism, are inevitable" or "that's the way it has always been," reflect a fairly common misreading of the past — or else are a poor substitute for the study of history. Such statements, and others like them, help to perpetuate ignorance, to generate confusion, and, ultimately, to delay the resolution of issues critical to all of us.

The foregoing should not be taken as an indication that my view of human relationships, and especially of intergroup relations, is rosy-hued and saccharine. Rather, my intent is to grasp the realities as clearly as possible so as to provide a basis for understanding race relations — which I conceive to be one variety of intergroup relations.

Race Relations as a Variety of Intergroup Relations

> *Either you're with us or you're against us —*
> *you're not with us, you're one of them.*
> (Anonymous)

All people are aware of many sorts of social differences. All of us have uttered or heard one or another form of the quotation above which distinguishes "us" from "them." At this stage of our knowledge it appears that the quotation attributed to Anonymous should be attributed to Everyman. It appears to be an expression of a fundamental dimension of many social phenomena but especially of intergroup relations — even in the absence of intergroup conflict.[1]

It may well be that the ubiquity of this sort of binary thinking[2] leads us into error in our interpretation of social existence. One consequence is to regard any social difference or ethnic conflict we encounter as having always existed. With such a view, the ideas that "blacks and whites are natural antagonists" and, of necessity, "racial friction will always be part of the human condition" are compelling.

At any rate, fundamental to intergroup relations in general is the characteristic distinction people draw between "us" and "them," between "we" and "they." To be a member of a group means, among other things, distinguishing between "us" (the "in-group") and "them" (the "out-group").[3] Goodhearted folk may find this distressing. Some people seem to think that this fact of social existence bears out the "compelling" ideas just noted, i.e., that there have always been racial distinctions and antagonisms and, hence, race relations and, further, that this will always be the case.

The first several times I encountered the view that "it has always been this way," i.e., antagonistic race relations have always been a feature of human existence, I brushed the notion aside uncritically with the comforting rationalization that such an assertion could only be the expression of a prejudiced or ignorant mind. I did not feel alone in this posture. Most writers either ignore the question of origins or simply assert that race relations as we know them are a "modern" phenomenon or a phenomenon of nineteenth century origin.[4] At some point, for reasons which I cannot recall, I remember asking myself — with a chilled feeling in my viscera — "What if it's true?," "Has it really always been this way?" A chilled feeling indeed, for if the present were merely an exacerbated version of the past all hopes for the elimination of the racial problems of American society, or any other society, were groundless.

Starting with the question "has it always been this way?," an examination of the anthropological and historical evidence provided a clear "no!" I was then faced with two obvious questions: "when, and under what circumstances did race relations begin?" and "what was it like before this?"

Before turning to the question of origins a definition of *race relations* is in order. A naive, uncomplicated view of race relations would suggest that race relations are relations between races, between people(s) who are physically distinguishable, i.e., biologically distinguishable, "born that way."

Distinguishability alone, however, is insufficient to explain race relations — which we find to be fraught with tension, animosity, conflict, and the like. Furthermore, a moment's reflection makes it obvious that among white Americans[5] there are redheads, blondes, brunettes, hazel-eyed, brown-eyed, blue-eyed, tall, fat, thin, short, etc., individuals. These easily distinguishable differences apparently do not make a difference, i.e., they do not make for race relations.

The key to the significance of distinguishability for race relations lies in the socially shared notions — combinations of beliefs, values, and judgments, in short the stereotypes — which cause some differences to be deemed significant in social relations and which render others relatively unimportant.[6] Once this key is grasped it is unnecessary to belabor the principle: if people believe something to be true, they will act as if it were true.[7]

A usable definition of race relations must include, then, the notion that in a situation of race relations the distinguishability of the peoples involved is important when it is interpreted as a sign of something else which is value-laden in the society, e.g., inferior or superior intellect, ingenuity, dishonesty, amiability, dependability, childishness, etc. Furthermore, in such situations these qualities are believed to be innate — just like the physical traits with which they are linked in the belief system. It becomes understandable, then, that in such circumstances proponents of a racist view frequently talk in terms of keeping the "blood" or the "race" pure, i.e., they espouse an anti-miscegenationist policy.

There is little need to extend the list of characteristics that is symbolized in the appearance of various peoples. It is important to stress, however, that people (who are distinguishable in a way that is significant for race relations) when viewing one another and responding to the significant signs, do not simply catalog or add up the signs. Rather their tendency is to respond to a *gestalt*, a total configuration, dominated by one or two "important" cues. Their response is a complex but unified experience of recognition, revulsion or warmth, fear and animosity, or friendliness and security. (After all, we recognize "us" in just the same way as we recognize "them.")

In this way individual behavior in a situation of race relations is dominated by the socially shared understanding of the significance of some particular kind of distinguishability — or, if you will, dominated by the significance imputed to the distinguishable signs and guided by the appropriate behavioral expectations (norms).

When we move from the individual level to the group level — when the relations between groups are dominated or, to be more accurate, rationalized by the significance imputed to certain "distinguishable" signs — we have a situation of race relations. In such circumstances the consequences of individual responses can be seen to have cumulated in all those phenomena we call collectively *discrimination*. Discrimination, in this sense, is but one aspect of inequality in the distribution of power among the peoples or groups in a society or social system. Such a state of affairs is typically evident in such indicators as differences in: average life span, types of jobs, rates of unemployment and underemployment, rates of infant mortality and maternal mortality, residential locations, income, etc.

We have come quite a distance from the statement that race relations are relations between people(s) who are physically distinguishable. Instead of an emphasis on biology, a more appropriate definition is one which stresses sociocultural aspects. A usable definition of race relations emphasizes relations not race because, in the final analysis, rather than race causing relations it is the relational context that makes for "race."

A useful working definition of race relations would be something like the following: race relations refers to those relations between (or among) peoples wherein the interaction and institutional arrangements are rationalized by shared beliefs and judgments concerning the essential, i.e., innate, characteristics of the depressed group (i.e., "race") and the oppressing group (i.e., "race"). It is important to understand that the more powerful group, the members of which fill the controlling positions in the major organizations of the social system, defines the "innate" characteristics of the less powerful, the depressed, group as well as the traits of its own group.[8]

In such a situation the presence of some readily recognizable characteristic helps in drawing the line between the superior (i.e., more powerful) and the inferior (i.e., the suppressed) group. If physical differences characterize two unequal (in power) groups and if these are viewed as significant signs of imputed biological differences, we have a situation of race relations! If, in a situation of superordinate/subordinate relations, no such physical characteristic differences exist, they may be created! An example of this was the designation of Jewish Germans as an inferior "race" by the German government during the Hitler regime and the legal requirement that Jewish Germans (otherwise largely indistinguishable on a physical basis from other Germans) wear a six-pointed yellow star on their outer garments in order to render them distinguishable.

The notion of the overriding importance of biological characteristics — rather than relational structures — in the development of race relations does not die easily. Only an examination of the evidence will be convincing.

Has It Always Been This Way?

The problem of race relations is not new. . . . Whenever . . . two people of significantly different characteristics have come in contact with each other, or have sought to occupy the same area, a problem of race relations has inevitably developed.[9] *[I.e., It has always been this way!]*

Is it reasonable or realistic for men of good will to go on assuming that blacks and whites, at least on the crucial continents of Africa and North America, are ever going to live amicably side by side in genuinely multiracial societies?

My answer is emphatically "No."[10] *[I.e., It will always be this way!]*

Our species has existed for quite some time — on the order of fifty thousand years. The earliest writing, however, dates back only c. 5,000 years. Thus, the first difficulty I faced was with the term "always." How far back would "the record" take me? What kinds of data did it contain? What of prehistoric peoples? What about preliterates? In the absence of written material was there any pictorial evidence?

Among the archeological findings is a portrayal of humans by preliterates. Though not very ancient it is an expression of a preliterate view. It is a rock-painting (petroglyph) of what appears to be "cattle-rustling."[11] The figures driving off the cattle are being pursued by figures carrying bows and arrows. The pursuers are much taller and more slender than the smaller, stockier raiders. In short, the painting shows clearly that the preliterate painter was capable of distinguishing physical types which, incidentally, correspond to contemporary Bushmen (of the Kalahari Desert) and Bantu-speaking pastoralists (in East Africa).

The painting is mute, however, with regard to the significance of the differences depicted. We cannot tell, from an examination of the painting, what the indicated distinctions meant to the painter and to the people for whom the painting was made.

To contemporary American minds the depiction of differences suggests invidious distinctions — on a racial basis. It may very well have been the case that the differences depicted did suggest invidious distinctions of the sort "we are good and they are bad." The most reasonable chain of inference from our knowledge of preliterate peoples suggests, however, that the invidious distinctions had a cultural, i.e., an ethnocentric, basis and not a racial basis.

What knowledge and what inference could support such a statement? To start with, we have no direct information of the thought processes of prehistoric (preliterate) peoples. It seems reasonable (at least in this realm of inquiry, i.e., ideology, mythology), to extrapolate from what we know of the thinking of contemporary preliterates.

Typical of contemporary preliterates — and, by inference, of prehistoric preliterates — is the use of a single term for themselves and the concept "people." For example, the word (the name) which the Navaho call themselves means "the people." It is not difficult to imagine the implications, at least in earlier times, for non-Navaho, i.e., "non-people." The same kind of usage was the case with the ancient Egyptians who referred to themselves as "Rot" or "the men," and with the Zuni, with the Kung, and many of the Bantu-speaking peoples of east and south Africa, as well as with many other preliterate peoples.

In short, preliterates distinguish sharply and invidiously between themselves and other peoples — between "us" and "them." The *content* of the distinction for preliterates is to separate "us" (among whom each person has a status-set and a relationship to every other one of "us") from "them" with whom no clear relationships exist. It should be added that in order to simplify social existence among preliterates, as well as among civilized peoples, every "one of us" is marked in a number of more or less noticeable ways: language, clothing, hair style, tattoo, application of color to the face and body, to name a few kinds of distinguishing signs. (Note that typically such "status symbols" also help us to distinguish the relative status of "one of us" when we meet someone whom we do not know on a face-to-face basis.)

As I have indicated, all people draw a "line." The important point with preliterates is that their invidious distinctions are *not* based on the conception that "they" are *biologically* different. The distinction is not based on the belief that "they" are "born that way," and, therefore, cannot change. The proof of this lies in the fact that among preliterates the line — that divides "us" from "them," which is based on a simplistic ethnocentrism — can be crossed.

The permeability of the barriers among preliterates is demonstrated by the existence of adoption. In other words in the case of preliterates one of "them" can become one of "us" by going through the appropriate ceremony replete, of course, with rituals, oaths, etc. The outcome of the adoption ceremony is that the former stranger achieves thereby a status, which is to say a position, in the relational network which makes up the "we" or "us" in question. The notion of adoption is so widespread among contemporary preliterates that it seems safe to conclude that the barriers between prehistoric preliterate peoples were not based upon biological, i.e., racial, ideas.

Since the phenomenon whose origin we seek, race relations, is said to be a product of Western society, an appropriate next step is to examine the ancient period of Western civilization. For the earliest periods the written record is vague with regard to the area of our concern. We do have some pictorial evidence, in the form of tomb paintings of the XIX dynasty dating back about 3,000 years (1314–1194 B.C.). In these instances, the Egyptian painters in depicting "us" and "them" not only differentiated figures by dress but also used different pigments for complexions: faces were painted red for "us" (i.e., the Egyptians), white for the people to the north, black for the people to the south, and yellow for the people to the east.

At this point the reader may be saying, "Well! This sounds familiar." Its "familiarity" is misleading, however. What we have here is simply a grander version of the earlier (preliterate) ethnocentric distinction between "us" and "them." For the Egyptians of the time, the people to the north and south were deemed culturally inferior (a view comparable to the later Greek view of barbarians), and the people to the east — particularly the inhabitants of the Mesopotamian Valley — were enemies. Furthermore, the distinctions the Egyptians made did not prevent "others" from being assimilated into Egyptian society, i.e., there was no racial barrier. This was also the case with the Greeks and the Romans and is well documented by recent scholarship. In the summation of his study, Snowden points out that the Greco-Roman view of human beings (based on considerable contact with black and brown Africans as well as black and brown Indians) "developed no special theory as to inferior dark or brown peoples and attached no stigma to color. . . . It is intrinsic merit, says Menander, that counts."[12] In short, race relations had not yet appeared or, more properly put, race relations had not yet been invented. Here also the "line" or barrier was permeable and could be crossed by acculturation.

The advent of civilization did make some difference. The content of group identity among the great civilizations was cultural, i.e., ethnocentric. In the fertile crescent and the areas west of it all of the civilized societies were marked — not surprisingly — by unifying creeds "and the myths which grew up to support traditional beliefs assumed under these circumstances a rational and an ideological character."[13]

Robert Redfield illuminates clearly the differences between preliterates and the ancients in this respect. First of all for preliterates:

> . . . each set of prejudices as to other peoples is *local* for the people who hold it. Each world of thought is small and ends with that band or tribe. In the next band or tribe one finds some other set of attitudes toward ethnic groups known to that little people. Primitive life is a patchwork of cultures-and-societies; and ethnic prejudices are part of the patches. No one great set of prejudices as to the goodness or badness of people who follow this god or have this custom, or show this skin color, breaks loose from the local cultures and establishes its influence over many of the patches, becoming a widerunning, prevailing, tincture of the human scene.

> The other generalization is even more negative. Ethnic prejudice is — to use a word in an unusual sense — *unprincipled*. It is not grounded in a choice of principles for including some and excluding others; for exalting my people and degrading others. A principle is such a reason for an attitude as compels action in accordance with it in unanticipated cases, even against conflicting considerations. The relations between two primitive ethnic groups are not so governed . . . . one cannot correctly speak of race relations in these societies for there is no emphasis on "purity of blood," or any particular innate characteristics.[14]

In contrast to the localism and "unprincipled" character of preliterate ethnic relations, there developed among the ancient civilizations another principle as an addition to but overriding their ethnocentrism, namely universal religion. To draw on Redfield again:

> The religions of civilization, the "world religions" get to have a certain separateness from local life and come to be taught and extended to many kinds of

people. A great religion is a principle for ordering the relations of men. It emphasizes one difference, that between believer and unbeliever, and it tends to deny or reject other kinds of differences among them.[15]

By the time the Greeks, the Hellenes, came to challenge the Persians for the domination of the world they knew (the Mediterranean and the Fertile Crescent), they had shifted from the earlier, local, unprincipled exclusiveness of preliterates to this grander type of ethnocentrism. A clear expression of this was Aristotle's scorning condescension[16] toward the fair-skinned barbarians (the word comes from the Greek term for jabberers), and toward the Asian peoples because of their obvious cultural inferiority — obvious, that is, to Greeks. Hellenized Asians were *not* scorned precisely because they were *hellenized*. The position was clearly based on cultural and religious distinctions and was not a plea to "keep Greek blood pure."

It fell to Aristotle's pupil to begin the process from which there emerged yet another principle for ordering relations among people. Alexander the Great left a mark upon history in the form of the concept which we have come to know as "citizenship." For it was with Alexander's empire that the distinction began to be made between a person of the empire — whether Greek, Syrian, Persian, etc. — and the rest, the outsiders, the noncitizens.[17]

The idea of citizenship came to full bloom in the Roman Empire with the clear distinction between citizens and others, i.e., barbarians. And so, with Alexander's social invention, by the end of the ancient period there were three types of principles for ordering intergroup relations: cultural, religious, and political — separable in thought, frequently intermixed in practice.

The medieval period — from the fall of Rome and the rise of Islam to the fall of Byzantium to the Turks in the fifteenth century — witnessed in western Europe simply more of the same. The greatest stress, however, was on the religious principle. (Indeed, one view of the Middle Ages is that the whole period was a centuries-long religious war between Christians and Moslems.)

It should be clear that with religion, as with the other two "great principles" of division, the barrier between "us" and 'them" can be penetrated. The process of passing over the line in the case of religion is called conversion, and is, in principle and in practice, possible with all the great religions, with only some variations in difficulty. (The parallel political transformation is called in English, interestingly enough, naturalization.)

Before leaving late medieval Europe, let us look at the internal "them," the Jews of Europe. One can discern some similarities between the treatment of Jews in Europe during the high Middle Ages and the treatment of the German Jews under the fascist regime of Adolph Hitler. I refer to the insistence, in various localities and at different times, upon distinctive dress for Jews, occupational restrictions, etc. However, the similarities — distressing as they were to the people involved — are, from a sociological point of view, superficial; for the Jews in medieval Europe, the outsiders, were constantly urged to become insiders, i.e., to convert to Christianity. One may make deprecating comments about some of the methods employed by, let us say, the Inquisition — but no one can deny that the despised outsiders could, by conversion, enter the community of believers. In Nazi Germany, on the other hand, all of the social devices were used not merely to exclude Jewish Germans from participation, as Germans, in the life of Germany. The social devices were expressions of a racial notion — namely, that Jews were biologically impure, immoral, etc. Note that this kind of principle or barrier does not permit shifts in identification from "them" to "us." The impermeability (in theory) of this kind of barrier, based on notions of innateness, distinguishes *race* relatins from other types of intergroup relations.[18]

Before continuing with the historical sweep it is also important to clarify an issue which has both a psychological and a sociological aspect: the import of prejudice as a personal attribute and the nature of the relationship between prejudice and social existence. On the basis of what is known about human behavior, social phenomena, history, etc., it is safe to say that ever since there have been people, most persons have been prejudiced against some other person(s). However, in the absence of a supporting social matrix, even though such prejudice may have had a racist core, the prejudice remained solely a personal, i.e., a psychological, phenomenon and was not a guiding societal principle. Ruth Benedict offers some historic examples: "Cicero writing to Atticus (first century B.C.) 'Do not obtain your slaves from Britain because they are so stupid and so utterly incapable of being taught that they are not fit to form part of the household of Athens.'"[19] She also quotes Said of Toledo (a Moorish scholar writing in the eleventh century A.D.): "Races north of the Pyrenees are of cold temperament and never reach maturity; they are of great stature and of a white colour. But they lack all sharpness of wit and penetration of intellect."[20]

Now, because citizenship, i.e., being a Roman or not, was the guiding principle for ordering intergroup relations in Cicero's time, and religion was the guiding principle in the time of Said of Toledo, the statements just cited have a peculiar sociological significance. Their significance consists only in illustrating the absence of race relations despite the presence of "race prejudice" in some individuals. The sociological point, simply put, is: individual prejudice is apparently *not* the source of race relations.

What does it take to generate the racial principle? The material already examined can be distilled to yield some general answers. First of all, being a member of a society, say Society X, means not only that I am not a member of Society Y but also, almost necessarily, it means that for me Society X is better than Society Y.[21] (I could have written *Tribe* K, or *Nation* E, or adherents to *Religion* U.) Further we have seen that intergroup relations seems to have started with unprincipled, local ethnocentrism, and it was only slowly, over centuries and millenia, that new general principles governing intergroup relations were "invented," i.e., socially shared, in different social contexts.

The simplest way to make the issue clear is to point out that many ideas appear "before their time" (note the "racism" of Cicero and Said of Toledo) simply because human beings are marvelously creative. In order for any particular new idea to become a *social invention*, i.e., a socially shared belief or value, it must "fit" the setting. Let me elaborate this sociological point.

In any given social setting, the new idea must make sense in the judgment of the "culture bearers," i.e., those who dominate the setting. To make sense requires, in turn, that it be perceived by them as serving their interests. Once this occurs, this dominant elite or ruling group then endeavors to make the rest of "us" think it serves to our advantage. This is not always a simple matter. (One can imagine the diehards back home on the Attic penninsula grumbling when Alexander had his generals marry Persian noblewomen.) In brief, the ruling group in a given setting, wittingly or unwittingly, uses ideas regarding intergroup relations — or any other ideas for that matter — for its own advantage, as perceived within the bounds of the *Weltanschauung* of their time. As we shall shortly see, this last qualification is very important in the development of race relations, i.e., in the invention of the racial principle to order social relations. In passing, we should note that, since race relations have not appeared up to now in our historical search, Bryce, Cox, Frazier, and others are sound in their position that race relations are a modern phenomenon and, further, the assertion that "it has always been this way" is simply *not true*![22]

How Did It Get To Be This Way?

Racial determinism was the form taken by the advancing wave of the science of culture, as it broke upon the shores of industrial capitalism. It was in this guise that anthropology first achieved a positive role alongside of physics, chemistry, and the life sciences, in the support and spread of capitalist society.[23]

Let us go back to western Europe for it was there that "race" as a grand principle for ordering social relations was invented. We are left with answering such questions as "Why the Europeans?" "Which Europeans?" "Under what circumstances, i.e., in what relational settings?" In the attempt to answer these questions we shall see the importance of the social setting, i.e., the importance of *relations*, in race relations and the relative unimportance of "race," i.e., biology. Further, as the contact of the western Europeans with the Africans is sketched, it should be kept in mind that Africans south of the Sahara had been in contact with Arabic-speaking "whites" long before the first Portuguese set foot on Africa — without the development of race rleations. And this with a long history of an overland slave trade in Africa.

After the Iberian peninsula had been conquered by the Moslems at the beginning of the eighth century A.D., the Portuguese (i.e., the people who eventually became the Portuguese) were dominated by Moslems — Moors for the most part — for the next several centuries. (It was during this period that Moslems — and Jews — brought medicine, mathematics, music, and philosophy to the Christian world; in Spain and Portugal the dark-skinned Moors were the main transmitters.)

By the early fifteenth century the Portuguese broke free of Moorish domination and even carried the battle across the Straits of Gibraltar into the Moorish stronghold of Ceuta. The leader of the Portuguese forces was Prince Henry, known to most of us as Henry the Navigator. He earned the epithet because he developed the plan of exploration that ended with Portuguese ships finding their way to India and the wealth of the Orient.

The fifteenth century witnessed Portuguese expeditions creeping down the west coast of Africa (the state of western navigation and popular belief required sailing within sight of land). The records these Portuguese captains brought back indicate that when these expeditions touched land sometimes they were well received and sometimes greeted with hostility.

The Portuguese, of course, looked down on the Africans — not, however, for racial reasons. A "pep-talk" by the captain of a caravel before attacking an unsuspecting west coast community reveals the Portuguese attitude:

> . . . although they are more in number than we by a third yet they are but Moors and we are Christians one of whom ought to suffice for two of them. For God is He in whose power lieth victory, and he knoweth our good wills in His holy service.[24]

Rather than a racial principle, here was the religious principle in action. The Portuguese not only believed in the cultural capacity of the Africans, they made every effort to convert captured Africans to Christianity. According to Portuguese writers of the time, the captives were easily assimilated into the population. Many were eventually freed and married into Portuguese families. In the eyes of the Portuguese of that time, conversion to Christianity made the Africans the same as any other Christians. (By the way, while religion was an important motivating force — and a rationalizing device — in the activities of the Portuguese,[25] it should be remembered that the Portuguese Crown also sought unimpeded access to the fabled wealth of the Orient. The Portuguese explorations and Vasco de Gama's successful voyage to India were really "end-runs" around the Venetians, Pisans, Genoans, and Moslems who blocked the direct route to the east.)

Finally, mention must be made of the beginning of the overseas, as opposed to the overland, trade in African slaves. This trade is coincidental with the Portuguese explorations. It began with Moorish captives and continued with pagan Africans captured from the various tribal societies the Portuguese conquered, or purchased from the various kingdoms they dealt with.

African slaves were in great demand in Portugal, especially in the southern section of the country where the fight against the Moors had depleted the population. Consequently, by the middle of the sixteenth century, in the southern part of Portugal (indeed as far north as Lisbon), "black" Africans outnumbered "white" Europeans. Furthermore, in the absence of a racial barrier, there was "free" intermarriage. It is quite clear that race relations had not yet developed.

The next Europeans to emerge in the Age of Explorations were the Spaniards. Portuguese successes were a spur, and the return of Columbus was followed by many expeditions to what was finally recognized as the New World. The incipient competition between the Spaniards and the Portuguese was eliminated through the intervention of the pope with the famous bull (3 May 1493) drawing a line on the map of the world, from pole to pole, 100 leagues west of this line to Spain and all those east of the line to Portugal. The Portuguese crown was unhappy and a rapid renegotiation, which resulted in moving the line farther west (to 370 leagues west of the Cape Verde Islands) was formalized in the Treaty of Tordesillas on 7 June 1494. Unknown to all parties involved was the fact that the new line passed through the eastern tip of South America. Aside from lessening friction between Spain and Portugal, the treaty had two other important consequences: Brazil became a Portuguese colony and the Portuguese had a monopoly of the overseas African slave trade during the early part of that traffic.

It was not long before the Spanish conquistadores encountered the mineral wealth — gold and silver — of the Aztecs and the Incas. With this discovery there commenced an extractive process which staggers the imagination. Cortez's comment to one of the Aztecs to the effect that the Spaniards had a sickness of the heart which could only be cured by gold was more than a bitter metaphor. In a world that still "counted in pennies," where there was very little in the way of capital, liquid or otherwise, the mint in Mexico City produced (from 1570 to 1821) two billion Spanish dollars, another two billion were exported in bars, and Peru accounted for another billion or so.

It is almost unnecessary to add that the mineral wealth was not extracted by Spaniards. The work was done by Indians, for the most part, and their labor was garnered either in the form of tribute (*encomienda*) or by labor levies (*repartimientes*).

The Spanish presence in the New World was not simply an economic and political presence; it was also a religious and, of course, a biological presence. With regard to these latter impacts, among other things there was incessant activity directed at the conversion of the Indians to Christianity. While on the one hand the Indians were being decimated as a result of the heavy demands of the *encomendieros* for labor (especially in the mines under the most unhealthy circumstances), on the other hand the crown and the church attempted to soften the demands, to abolish the virtual enslavement of the Indians, and to end the *encomiendas*. Further, in a biological sense: (1) the Indians were also being decimated by the new biota, in the form of diseases, introduced by the Spaniards, and (2) miscegenation — in the forms of intermarriage, concubinage, and casual liaison — was going on as usual, i.e., as usual in instances where the newcomers were predominantly males.

Clearly, in the case of New Spain, i.e., the Spanish colonies in the New World, the objectives and interests of the colonists, especially of the *encomendieros* (i.e., those to whom *encomiendas* had been granted by the crown) and the objectives and interests of the crown and church were in conflict. The issue was brought sharply to a head when (due largely to the efforts of the Bishop of Chiappas, Bartolomé de Las Casas, on behalf of the Indians) Charles V signed the "New Orders" (at Barcelona, 20 November 1552). The "New Orders" ended all *encomiendas* at the death of their holders (thus abolishing the right to levy labor tributes) with no new ones to be awarded.

The prospect of being deprived of "their Indians" — their source of labor — aroused the *encomendieros*. There were representations to the crown and threats of resistance in the New World. In fact, in Peru the Spanish colonists killed the viceroy who brought the news. (The *encomiendas* were not effectively abolished until the eighteenth century, although Indian slavery did gradually disappear.)

The case of the Spaniards in Mexico in the sixteenth century is interesting because they were on the edge of the very development we seek. "In the opinion of many of the Spanish settlers, the Indians were an inferior species; they were *gente sin razon*, creatures more animal than human, destined by God for slavery or serfdom."[26] Here was the kind of rationalization which was needed as justification for an inescapably exploitative situation — and which would have clothed it in racial garb.

Counterposed to this view was the view of the crown (desiring wealth and land) and of the church — itself dominated by the crown. Both of these forces expressed themselves within the frame of reference of Roman Catholicism, namely, the equality of souls under the fatherhood of God. It is my contention — along with that of others[27] — that in this conflict it was the institutionalized religious views of Spanish society supported by the dominant power of the crown, which prevented the Spaniards from "inventing" race relations. They came close, but did not achieve it. Additional factors had to be present before race relations could be invented, before the racial principle could become part of a cultural frame of reference.

From the early part of the sixteenth century, starting about 1510, African slaves were landed in the Spanish colonies. (Las Casas' suggestion, which he subsequently regretted, that African slaves be imported to save the natives, the Indians, very likely helped speed the development of the traffic.) With Spain the major colonial power in the New World at that time, the Spanish colonies had the greatest need for imported, i.e., slave, labor. In addition to the vast territory held by Spaniards, the need for imported labor was great because the Spaniards had decimated or eliminated many of the Indian societies they had encountered, particularly in the Caribbean. Still, in a relational context where they held the reins of power, the Spaniards in contact with Indians and Africans did not develop "race" relations, i.e., they did not invent the racial principle as a means of organizing intergroup relations.

In its early days, the overseas slave trade was in the hands of the Portuguese. Subsequently, French, Dutch, and English slavers competed with the Portuguese and, in the eighteenth century, the English gained primacy in the Atlantic slave trade with the grant of the *asiento* — the Spanish contract to supply slaves to the Spanish colonies. (This slave trade was an important source of capital. It meant not merely, for example, the making of Liverpool as a great port, it was an important part of the process of capital accumulation which laid the basis for the Industrial Revolution in England.[28])

In the sequence of Europeans emerging from both the cocoon of feudalism and the European land mass, there are a number of societies which were active during the Age of Exploration. The most important for our purpose — the development of the racial principle — are the Dutch and the English. The Dutch require mention only because of two points: (1) their role in the African slave trade (already noted above) and, more importantly, (2) the imprint they left on the southern end of Africa in the form of a religiously justified and politically enforced race relations system in the Union of South Africa. This latter instance has been, until recently, so isolated as to have little if any bearing on the development we are tracing. It is of interest, however, as a sort of corroborative parallelism to the "western" development.

With the appearance of the northern Europeans upon the colonial scene several new elements were added to the historical process. Emerging from Europe in the late sixteenth century and flourishing in the seventeenth and eighteenth centuries, the Dutch and the English were somewhat less mired in medieval, i.e., feudal, conceptions of politics and economics than their predecessors at their times of exit (fifteenth and early sixteenth centuries). Further, the Portuguese and Spanish colonies were crown colonies, dominated from the home countries, thus local control over legislation regarding slaves was diluted. The Dutch and the English, on the other hand, tended (and this more and more as time went on) to operate with limited liability companies (a recent invention) in which royalty invested along with merchants and enterprising nobility. One immediate consequence was that in the British colonies (and in Dutch South Africa) the regulations regarding slaves were of local origin and tended more to express clearly the interests of the slaveholders and to depress and restrain the slaves.[29]

Whether one stands with Karl Marx or Max Weber on the influence of Protestantism upon the development of capitalism, and especially the capitalist "spirit," it is impossible to deny the effect of Protestantism and especially of Calvinism upon the world-view of the Dutch and the English. These were folk who tended less to think of all souls as the same in the eyes of the creator (especially in view of a belief in predestination) and to think more in terms of worldly advancement as a sign of grace and, consequently, a low estate in life as sure of damnation. The development of Protestantism was a large step in the direction of "freeing" western European minds from what Cox has called "the influence of the Roman Catholic Church with its mystical inhibitions to the *free exploitation of economic resources.*"[30]

We should take notice of at least two consequences of the new ideological force. The first is the tremendous individuating effect of Protestantism, especially of "ascetic Protestantism" (Weber's term) upon its believers. (See, e.g., Bunyan's allegory, *Pilgrim's Progress*, in which the protagonist, Pilgrim, i.e., the pious Christian, leaves home on the journey to find his own salvation, pressing his fingers to his ears to shut out the pleas of his wife and children as well as the advice of friends and neighbors.) The second is the effect upon the attitudes of the growing entrepreneurial class toward the laboring classes. This can best be summed up in what Edgar Furniss has called "the doctrine of the utility of poverty."[31] The general idea was that workers should be paid subsistence wages (otherwise they would not continue to work), idle workers should be compelled to work, and as for education: "To make the society happy and people easy under the meanest circumstances, it is requisite that great numbers of them should be ignorant as well as poor."[32] If the laboring classes had to be educated, they should receive vocational training, for any other education "would teach them to despise their lot in life, instead of making them good servants in agriculture, and other laborious employments to which their rank in society has destined them; instead of teaching them subordination it would render them factious and refractory. . . ."[33]

Keeping in mind that this was the tone of the English view toward labor, not just in the eighteenth century but in the seventeenth as well, let us turn to the British colonies of North America where the initial labor force consisted largely of indentured servants. The English did not establish slavery immediately. The importation of Africans did not begin until the end of the second decade of the seventeenth century. These African "servants," however, were initially treated much like the indentured English, Scots, Irish, and Welsh.

It was not until the last quarter of the seventeenth century that the colonial regulations began to make clear the form of the slave labor system. The Virginia Acts, for example, distinguished *"all servants not being Christians brought in by sea who were declared for life"* (emphasis added) from the Christian servants, i.e., the indentured servants who served for a term of years.[34] The Africans, to quote Handlin, "never profited from these enactments. (The provision limiting the effectiveness of the act to Christians is not surprising in view of contemporary English attitudes; thus another act of the same year excluded Quakers altogether.)"[35] It is important to note that the distinctions in the early colonial legislation were drawn on the basis of religion and not on the basis of biology.

By the end of the seventeenth century the English took over a major portion of the Atlantic slave trade and the middle and lower seaboard colonies were inundated with slaves. This coincided with a shift in the colonial economy from providing naval stores to the cultivation of rice, indigo, and cotton. Large scale operation became advantageous, i.e., profitable. The large number of slaves, in turn, hastened the sharper definition and further depression of the legal status of the African slaves — finally to that of a chattel. Here is a clear instance of local, dominant elites (in the various English colonies) insuring their interests by utilizing the institutional means which they controlled. (In short, the slave holders passed laws protecting their own property interests; the slaves, of course, had no representation in the proceedings.)[36]

The eighteenth century saw little change. Slavery was an established labor system in the European colonies of the New World and Africa, but nowhere was this justified on the basis of biological differences. The slaves were deemed and perceived as inferior for the simple reason that they were inferior in law (by definition), in social fact (they were under coercion), and in religion (they were heathens or the descendants of heathens). There still was no "racial principle" operative.

By the third quarter of the eighteenth century, however, an intellectual development surfaced which was to produce, *inter alia*, the racial principle and thus was to provide the ideological justification for colonial oppression and exploitation after slavery was abolished. I am referring to the development of the scientific attitude in biology.

In his study of the formation of the modern scientific view, Hall[37] placed the "biological revolution" in the nineteenth century. But the biological revolution is merely a stage in that massive transformation of Western thought which started with Copernicus. The names we link with this upheaval and new perspective — Kepler, Brahe, Gallileo, Newton, Boyle, Hooke — are those of astronomers, physicists, and chemists who burst into the forefront in the sixteenth and seventeenth centuries. The biologists (Leeuwenhoek, Malpighi, Harvey, and Redi) had been working meantime, but it was not until the eighteenth century that the grand systematic overview of the biological world commenced to be built. First Ray, working at the end of the seventeenth and the beginning of the eighteenth centuries, and then Linnaeus in the latter half of the eighteenth century, opened the last act of the process which Copernicus unwittingly began — the displacement of mankind, "God's noblest work," from the center of the universe to a minor planet of a third-rate sun at the edge of one of many galaxies in a boundless universe. Finally, mankind became a subject for scientific investigation on a par with gravity. The Linnean taxonomy formed the basis for Darwin's hypothesis, in the mid-nineteenth century, that we and the apes and monkeys had a common ancestry. The ideological point is that not before the end of the eighteenth century did scholars, in a systematic way, apply the new scientific view to man as a species.[38]

Linnaeus, in his monumental classification of the animal kingdom, listed four varieties in the section on mankind (the species homo sapiens in which were included all living people): Homo Europaeus, Homo Asiaticus, Homo Afer, and Homo Americanus. In his *Systema naturae per regna tria naturae* (Vol. 1, 1789), Linnaeus uses skin color, temperament, hair color, and body structure as the criteria for distinguishing the four types. Linnaeus was, of course, not the first to make such a schema. (One of the most noted of his predecessors was George Louis Leclerc, Comte de Buffon, who appears to have been the first to successfully introduce the term race into the language of the natural sciences, 1749. He also considered mankind a single species which he divided into six races based on skin color — the differences in which he attributed to climate.)

Johann Friedrich Blumenbach — the "father of anthropology" — in his doctoral dissertation on human varieties (1795) also assumed a single human species and attributed the visible differences among the varieties predominantly to environmental influences. His scheme consisted of: Caucasian variety, Mongolian variety, Ethiopean variety, American variety, and Malay variety. Blumenbach's distinctions were based on physical attributes only, with no reference to intellectual, temperamental, or behavioral characteristics.

Not only did biologists become interested in this new line of inquiry, but so did many of the intellects of Europe. The lines were quickly drawn between "monogenists" (who posited a single origin of the species homo sapiens) and the "polygenists" (who posited different origins for each of the "races"). Names such as Voltaire and Kant, as well as Cuvier, Lamarck, and Hunter could be found on both sides of the dispute. Also, the proponents of various schemes of racial classification — ranging from two races (with four sub-races) all the way through twenty-five races (with 39 sub-races) to one schema consisting of two hundred races! — loudly proclaimed their positions throughout the period. This overly brief account could be extended considerably, but the point is made. The point is that as biology was coming to maturity as a science, there was a great deal of concern with the varieties of mankind, with what they called at the time the "races of man," and this concern became part of the mental climate of western Europe (part of the mental furniture of western Europeans and Americans).

It was only a matter of time before some of the students of the subject started to make invidious distinctions. Blumenbach had expressed only an aesthetic preference in his writing, alluding to the "Caucasian variety" as "in general that kind of appearance which according to our opinion of symmetry, we consider most handsome and becoming." But others, such as Lord Kames (the Scottish jurist, 1774) and Dr. Charles White (an English physician, 1799) spoke differently. Sir William Lawrence in a series of lectures at the Royal College of Surgeons, echoing Dr. White, talked of the "lower" races as midway between apes and men, i.e., Europeans. In the United States, the argument over origins — polygenism *versus* monogenism — carried on by such people as Dr. Samuel George Morton (regarded by Benjamin Silliman of Yale as the outstanding American authority on geology), Louis Agassiz, and John Bachman not only spread awareness of the race idea but also the notion that some races are superior to others.

Gobineau, the nineteenth century forerunner of Sorokin and Toynbee, did a sweeping examination of history[39] in an endeavor to uncover the answer to the mystery of the rise and fall of civilizations. After eliminating a number of possible causal factors, e.g., climate, topography, religion, etc., he fixed upon *the answer of the time*: race! He concluded that the "Caucasian race" (and in particular the "Aryan branch") was responsible for the major civilizations. These fell, he concluded, due to the degeneration that followed upon their expansion and absorption of inferior peoples.

By this time (mid-nineteenth century), the place of the race concept in Western thought, especially the notion of superior and inferior races, was assured, both for the scientists and intellectuals as well as in popular thought.[40] This was not surprising, for this scientificaly supported, seemingly logical view of our species provided a rationalization, a justification, for the exploitative practices that the leading Western societies had been engaged in, as well as those which they were carrying on or planning. In Cox's words, "This clearly was in answer to an urgent necessity for such an authoritative explanation; the whole world, so to speak, was calling for it."[41] Cox's reference to "the whole world" means, of course, the whole world of the exploiters, the colonialists, the imperialists, not the exploited and the oppressed.[42]

Notes

1. See, e.g., Henri Tajfel, "Experiments in Intergroup Discrimination," *Scientific American*, Nov. 1770, pp. 96–102. See also, M. Sherif, "Experiments in Group Conflict," *Scientific American*, Nov. 1956.
2. Edmund R. Leach, "Genesis as Myth," in John Middleton, ed., *Myth and Cosmos* (Garden City, New York, Natural History Press, 1967), p. 3.
3. *Cf.* H. Tajfel, "Experiments," especially pp. 98–99.
4. *Cf.* J. Bryce, *Race Sentiment as a Factor in History* (1915), cited in Wm. C. Boyd, *Genetics and the Races of Man* (Little Brown, 1955), p. 186; O. C. Cox, *Class, Caste, and Race* (Doubleday, 1948); E. F. Frazier, *Race and Culture Contacts in the Modern World* (Knopf, 1957). Of the three, only Cox talks of racism as caused. He attributes the development of racism to the development of capitalism (pp. 321 ff).
5. In this instance the term "white" is being used as a relatively undefined catchall to mean simply all Americans *not* of *known* African, Asian, or Native American (Amerindian) ancestry.
6. The issue of the relationship between societal racism and individual beliefs and prejudices is dealt with below.
7. The classic sociological dictum is: "When men define a situation as real, it is real in its consequences." *Cf.* W. I. Thomas and F. Znaniecki, *The Polish Peasant in Europe and America* (University of Chicago Press, 1918), "Methodological Note," pp. 1–86. The oldest bit of folk wisdom embodying the same idea is, to my knowledge, an ancient Chinese proverb: "If two people believe it, dirt becomes transformed into gold."
8. *Cf.* John Rex, "The Concept of Race in Sociological Theory," in S. Zubaida, ed., *Race and Racialism* (Tavistock Publications, 1970): "We shall speak of a race-relations structure or problem in so far as the inequalities and differentiation inherent in a social structure are related to physical and cultural criteria of an ascriptive kind and are rationalized in terms of deterministic belief systems, of which the most usual in recent years has made reference to biological science," p. 39. For Rex's explanation of "a deterministic belief system" see note 18, below. His deterministic/undeterministic dichotomy corresponds to my distinction between permeable/impermeable barriers between groups discussed in this paper.
9. Dr. G. T. Gillespie, D.D., president emeritus of Belhaven College, Jackson, Mississippi, in an address made before the Synod of Mississippi Presbyterian Church in the United States, 4 Nov. 1954, published by the Citizen's Council, Greenwood, Mississippi.
10. Peregrine Worsthorne, "Black and White Reality — A British Observer's View," *U.S. News & World Report*, 1 July 1963, p. 62.

11. See, E. O. Christensen, *Primitive Art* (Bonanza Books, 1955), pp. 330, 331 — after G. W. Stow and D. F. Bleek, *Rock Paintings in South Africa from parts of the Eastern Province and Orange Free State* (London, Methuen).
12. F. M. Snowden, Jr., *Blacks in Antiquity, Ethiopians in the Greco-Roman Experience* (Harvard University Press, 1970), pp. 216, 217. *The New York Times*, 15 Feb. 1971, reported on an acquisition by the Brooklyn Museum: "a marble head of a black man of the Hellenistic period . . . [was recently] acquired by the Brooklyn Museum. . . . The face 'with an indescribable expression of dominance, haughtiness and innate nobility' must have belonged to an important person 'worthy of having likeness in stone made by an artist of outstanding ability.' " The person quoted is Bernard Bothmer, curator of ancient art.
13. R. E. Park, "Race Ideologies," *Race and Culture* (Free Press, 1950), pp. 304–305.
14. Robert Redfield, "Ethnic Relations, Primitive and Civilized," in J. Masuoka and P. Valien, eds., *Race Relations: Problems and Theory; Essays in Honor of Robert E. Park* (University of North Carolina Press, 1961), p. 32 (emphasis added).
15. Ibid., p. 33.
16. Aristotle, *Politics*.
17. *Cf.* S. Davis, *Race Relations in Ancient Egypt*, 2nd Ed. (Humanities Press). (Davis explains in his introduction that "the term 'race' is used in this book as applicable to a group with common cultural features, not in a biological sense . . ." This is the pre-modern usage which makes the term equivalent to *folk, tribe, nation*, or, technically, *ethnic group*.)
18. John Rex, "The concepts" (p. 49), makes a similar kind of distinction: "There are, however, two quite distinct kinds of belief system that, for lack of a better word, we may call deterministic and undeterministic. When the former are applied to the justification of a social structure the social structure comes to be seen as inevitable and unalterable, and transition from one kind of role to another, may be held to be impossible.
    The clearest example of such a deterministic theory is the one to which the term racist is often confined. What happens in this case is that the fact that a particular group suffers discrimination is attributed to an incapacity to perform a role or a special capacity to behave in particular ways that is determined by genetic inheritance. This is the most completely deterministic theory in that it is argued that *nothing any individual can do can alter the situation and the pattern of rights in the society*" (emphasis added).
19. Ruth Benedict, *Race: Science and Politics* (Modern Age Books, 1940), p. 10.
20. Ibid.
21. *Almost* necessarily. That the distinction need not be an invidious one is evident from the anthropological literature which offers a few exceptions. One occurs in the highlands of western Guatemala. There, "the Indians of one local community do not prejudge the Indians of many other local communities as either bad people or good people; they think of them as having different ways, and that is their affair. Much travel and much commerce brings Indians of many communities together superficially; an Indian trader meets a people of another dialect, costume, and custom in almost every town to which he comes; and ethnic variety is a commonplace." Robert Redfield, "Ethnic Relations, Primitive and Civilized," p. 31. Another example is the relationship between the Tewa and the Hopi.

22. Marvin Harris disagrees. *Cf.* Thomas Y. Crowell, ed., *The Rise of Anthropological Theory*, 1968, p. 81, where he writes: "Certain Marxists (Cox, 1948) insist that racism itself is confined to the capitalistic epoch, but such a view can find no support in ethnographic facts. Folk racism, a popular system of prejudice and discrimination directed against one endogamous descent group by another, is probably as old as humanity." His unfortunate choice of the term "folk racism" for what I have called ethnocentrism apparently causes him to overlook certain sociological facts, namely, the *permeability* of the barriers in most situations of intergroup relations and the "impermeable" barrier which develops in situations of race relations. (*Cf.* John Rex's distinction between *deterministic* and *undeterministic* belief systems, note 18, above.) See also the statement by Harris immediately below.
23. M. Harris, Ibid., pp. 80, 81.
24. Azurara, Gomes Eannes de, *The Chronicle of the Discovery and Conquest of Guinea*, tr. by C. R. Beazley and E. Prestage (London, 1896–1899, reprinted by Burt Franklin, publisher, New York, no date), p. 138. (Also in Cox, *Class, Caste, and Race*, p. 327n.)
25. Azurara, *The Chronicle*, p. 83, in reporting on the division of the slaves brought back by one expedition, writes as follows: "The infant (Prince Henry, L.S.) was there, mounted upon a powerful steed, and accompanied by his retinue, making a distribution of his favours, as a man who sought to gain but small treasure from his share; for of the forty-six souls that fell to him as his fifth, he made a very speedy partition of these (to others); for his chief riches lay in (the accomplishment of) his purpose; for he reflected with great pleasure upon the salvation of those souls that before were lost."
26. H. B. Parkes, *A History of Mexico* (rev. and enl., Houghton Mifflin, 1950), p. 89.
27. *Cf.*, e.g., Cox, *Class, Caste, and Race*; D. Pierson, *Negroes in Brazil* (Southern Illinois University Press, 1967, 1942); F. Tannenbaum, *Slave and Citizen, the Negro in the Americas* (Knopf, 1947); John Rex, "The Concept of Race," p. 51.
28. See, e.g., F. Tannenbaum, *Slave and Citizen.*
29. Cf. O. Handlin, *Race and Nationality in American Life* (Little, Brown, 1957, c. 1948); F. Tannenbaum, *Slave and Citizen.*
30. O. C. Cox, *Class, Caste, and Race*, p. 330. Emphasis added.
31. E. S. Furniss, *The Position of Labor in a System of Nationalism* (Boston, 1920), pp. 119–120; (cited in Cox, *Class, Caste, and Race*).
32. *Cf.* Mandeville (1723) in E. F. Heckscher, *Mercantilism*, M. Shapiro, tr. (George Allen & Unwin, 1935) (cited in Cox, *Class, Caste, and Race*). "Mandeville, as usual, put the matter the most provocatively. . . . From what has been said it is manifest that in a free Nation where Slaves are not allow'd of, the surest Wealth consists in a Multitude of laborious Poor. . . . As was always the case with Mandeville, he stated what most people of his time were thinking. . . ." Heckscher, *Mercantilism*, Vol. II, p. 164.
33. Giddy, 1767–1839, president of the Royal Society, in Hammond, J. L. & B, *The Town Laborer*, 1760–1832 (London, 1917) (cited in Cox, *Class, Caste, and Race*). The Hammonds, further on this same point, write: "Windham who, after the death of Fox, was the best scholar in the House of Commons . . . declared himself a sceptic as to the value of the 'diffusion of knowledge'. . . . He also quoted Dr. Johnson as saying it was not right to teach reading beyond a certain extent in society. 'The danger was, that if the teachers of good

and the propagators of bad principles were to be candidates for the control of mankind, the latter would be likely to be too successful' " (p. 56).

34. O. Handlin, *Race and Nationality*, p. 16.

35. Ibid., pp. 15, 16.

36. Ibid., pp. 16, 17. Handlin writes: "But slavery for life (referring to the Virginia act of 1670, L.S.) was still tenuous as long as the slave could extricate himself by baptism. . . . So that they could be 'freed from this doubt' a series of laws between 1667 and 1671 laid down the rule that conversion alone did not lead to a release from servitude. Thereafter, manumission, which other servants could demand by right at the end of their terms, in the case of Negroes lay entirely within the discretion of the master." It should be added that colonial legislation made manumission progressively more difficult. (*Cf.* Tannenbaum, *Slave and Citizen*.)

37. A. R. Hall, *The Scientific Revolution, 1500–1800: The Formation of the Modern Scientific Attitude*, rev. ed. (Beacon Press, 1962).

38. *Cf.*, Annemarie de Waal Malefijt, "Homo Monstrosus," *Scientific American*, Vol. 219, #4, Oct. 1968. Malefijt makes the point that for millenia the savants of the west believed that remote regions were populated by monstrous creatures and that it was not until the nineteenth century that general agreement concerning the unity of living men, i.e., homo sapiens, developed.

39. Gobineau, Joseph Arthur, Comte de (1816–1882). Published in English as: *The Inequality of Human Races*, tr. Adrian Collins (H. Fertig, 1967).

40. *Cf.*, e.g., Thomas Henry Huxley, the famous biologist, who said in a public lecture: "It may be quite true that some negroes (sic) are better than some white men; but no rational man, cognizant of the facts, believes that the average negro is the equal, still less the superior, of the average white man. And, if this be true, it is simply incredible that, when all his disabilities are removed, and our prognathous relative has a fair field and no favour, as well as no oppressor, he will be able to compete successfuly with his bigger-brained and smaller-jawed rival, in a contest which is to be carried on by thoughts and not by bites. The highest places in the hierarchy of civilization will assuredly not be within the reach of our dusky cousins. . . ." T. H. Huxley, "Emancipation — Black and White (1865)," in *Lectures and Lay Sermons* (E. P. Dutton, 1910), pp. 115–20, cited by H. G. Birsch, "Boldness and Judgment in Behavior Genetics," in M. Mead, T. Dobzhansky, E. Tobach, R. E. Light, eds., *Science and the Concept of Race* (Columbia University Press), pp. 50–s51.

41. Cox, *Class, Caste, and Race,* p. 335.

42. It should be remembered that it was during the nineteenth century that the world was transformed into a single economic community, governed largely by "market" principles, which affected the lives of almost every living person. This community was dominated by the growing capitalistically organized societies. The structural transformations within and among these dominant societies and the dominated societies were, of course, accompanied by changes in cultural frames of reference — the development of racism being only one of these changes. (*Cf.*, e.g., Karl Polanyi, *The Great Transformation*, Beacon Press, 1956, c. 1944.)

9.

A Race or Not a Race: The Question of Jewish Identity in the Year of the First Universal Races Congress

Harriet D. Lyons and Andrew P. Lyons

The congress, which provides the central focus for the issues and debates to be examined in this article, is an appropriate subject for inclusion in a volume dedicated to Werner J. Cahnman. Attended by Ferdinand Toennies, the congress has implications both for the historical understanding of the social sciences and the attempt of twentieth century Jews to understand and affirm their identity. Both of these concerns have figured prominently in the professional and humanistic endeavors of Professor Cahnman.

From July 26–29, 1911, there met in London, at the university, the First Universal Races Congress.[1] Initiated by Felix Adler, professor of social ethics at Columbia University and an early leader of the ethical culture movement, the conference seems to have been closely identified with liberal Jewish opinion on both sides of the Atlantic, and it certainly excited considerable interest among leading members of the Jewish community in Britain. On January 6, the *Jewish Chronicle* announced the forthcoming congress and published an interview with Lord Weardale, who was to be its president.[2] Among the anticipated delegates to the congress, according to the article accompanying the interview, were "the leading anthropologists and sociologists," and, indeed, among those reading papers were Franz Boas; Ferdinand Toennies; Sir Harry Johnston; Dr. Giuseppe Sergi, the Italian raciologist who had defended the superiority of *The Mediterranean Race*; and C. S. Myers, the Cambridge psychologist who had been on the Torres Straits expedition.[3] C. G. Seligmann, famous for his work in the Torres Straits and subsequently for *Pagan Tribes of the Nilodic Sudan* (coauthored with Brenda Seligmann), did not address the meeting, but was present at a planning session held in May at the London home of Mr. and Mrs. Stuart Samuels,[4] and was among those who voted for the following motion, proposed by C. S. Myers:

> That this meeting heartily approves the objects of the forthcoming Universal Races Congress, which is to promote friendly relations between the races of mankind, and resolves that the congress is worthy of the moral and material support of all right thinking men and women.[5]

At the congress itself, the question of "the Jewish race" was discussed at length by Israel Zangwill, whose address was printed in full in the *Jewish Chronicle* of August 4,[6] despite competition for space by a number of important community concerns, including the death of the chief rabbi just a fortnight before. The connection between the interests of "leading anthropologists and sociologists" and those of prominent members of the Jewish community is certainly a topic worthy of investigation, particularly if that investigation can tell us something beyond the conventional (if accurate) opinion that a number of leading Jewish anthropologists, including Franz Boas, who were instrumental in bringing about the decline of racial determinism as an explanatory concept within that discipline, were interested in questions of race at least partly because of their own struggle against anti-Semitism. The opinions expressed at the conference by Zangwill, and by a number of others, social scientists and laymen alike, before and after it, not only serve to illustrate the relationship between the notion of cultural relativism and the Jewish experience before the First World War, but also bring to light certain paradoxes in the anthropological study of Jews and Judaism, which in turn have some bearing on the logical problems experienced by anthropology in discussing racial matters generally. The paradoxes to which we refer become unavoidable whenever a desire to promote racial and ethnic self-esteem coexists with a predisposition to distrust those who would make racial classifications. That just such a situation existed in the early years of this century among Jews who gave thought to racial matters becomes evident upon examination of the reaction of British Jews to the First Universal Races Congress and certain other events occurring at the same time that drew attention to the question of Jewish racial identity.

Although Zangwill's was the only paper at the First Universal Races Congress to deal extensively with matters of direct and explicit concern to the Jewish community, the Congress had been initiated by Jewish interests[7] and the Jewish press indicates that positive results were expected from it. In the January 6 interview mentioned above, Lord Weardale was asked if the congress might be expected to pass resolutions favorable to the Jewish cause, or if it proposed only to debate general scientific issues concerning race. Weardale assured them that resolutions would be passed, and that it was likely that the congress would have no objection to resolving its support for amelioration of hardships suffered by Jews, provided no individual governments (25 of them had agreed to send delegates and officially receive copies of the proceedings) were singled out for unfavorable mention.[8]

It is certainly understandable that Jews in 1911 were interested in any prestigious support they might obtain for their cause; the pages of the *Chronicle* for the entire year are full of reports of pogroms in Russia and extreme persecution suffered by Jews in Rumania. On May 26, Sir Arthur Conan Doyle sent to the *Chronicle* a report of a meeting of the General Jewish Colonising Association, dedicated to the establishment of a settlement in "the Orient" (though not necessarily in Palestine) as a refuge for persecuted Russian Jews. Doyle summarized a dispute between Zionists and non-Zionists at the meeting and apologized for his own absence, remarking:

> An outsider like myself cannot possibly choose between various Jewish schemes. He can only feel that the general condition of this Jewish question is a scandal to Christendom.[9]

One did not have to travel to Russia to witness "the general condition of this Jewish question" at this period, however.

The last two decades of the nineteenth century had witnessed an increasing tide of international anti-Semitism. This was the period in which the demagogue Edouard Drumont wrote *La France Juive* (1886) and H. S. Chamberlain's writings appeared in Germany. In the 1890s French society was rocked to its foundations by the Dreyfus case. The persecution of the Jews by the Rumanian and Russian governments, combined with the miserable living conditions of the Jews of Eastern Europe, produced a mass emigration to Britain and the United States. In both countries, the new immigrants were regarded with fear and suspicion by many elements of society, particularly by workers, insofar as they accepted low wages, and by small businessmen, insofar as they were perceived as rivals who were unwilling to accept the conditions of trades from which all attempts had been made to exclude them.

Britain was largely a way station for immigrants from Poland, Russia, and Rumania en route to the United States. However, many immigrants did stay and populated the insanitary ghettos of the East End, Manchester, and the Leylands (Leeds). The conditions in the sweatshops appalled both *The Lancet* (1884) and Beatrice Potter (Webb). Before it became evident that a stream of migration was to ensue, the British Jewish community, which had gained political emancipation when Lionel de Rothschild took his seat in the Commons in 1858, had given the immigrants a cautious welcome. However, the Jewish "cousinhood" developed a somewhat jaundiced view of its less fortunate brethren. During the reign of Edward VII, powerful Jewish families, such as the Rothschilds, Sassoons, Waleys, and Cohens, enjoyed royal favor and a limited degree of acceptance in the highest circles.[10] Doubtless, they felt threatened by the swarming masses of the

East End and worried by a rising tide of popular anti-Semitism. An exception to this trend was Sir Samuel Montagu M.P., a resolute defender of the immigrants' interests.

In 1904, the anti-Jewish lobby persuaded the Tory government to introduce a restrictive new Aliens Bill into the Commons. The agitation in the Commons was led by Major William Eden Evans Gordon (conservative, Stepney Division, Tower Hamlets) and Sir Howard Vincent (conservative, Sheffield). Sir Charles Dilke and Charles Trevelyan, both liberals, led the opposition to the bill on the second reading, and it was defeated.[11] The young Winston Churchill also opposed the bill, and sought to remove some of its more offensive provisions. In 1905, a somewhat milder but still restrictive bill was passed. The new liberal government in 1906 enforced the act, but not to its full rigor.

Although the act, as interpreted by the liberal government, was primarily aimed at stopping immigration via overcrowded and insanitary immigrant ships, its psychological effect was indisputable. The door was no longer open. For all that, immigration continued, impelled further by the Kishinev massacre and the Russo-Japanese war. By 1911, some 120,000 East European Jews had settled in London.[12]

The period preceding the Universal Races Congress witnessed a number of disturbing incidents. On December 16, 1910, three policemen had been killed and two wounded in Houndsditch, a Jewish area in the East End, by assailants repeatedly described in the press as "alien," "foreign," and "nihilists."[13] There were, of course, Jewish anarchists in London,[14] although they were peaceful anarchists and, needless to say, did not receive universal support in the Jewish community. The Houndsditch assailants, who had met in a building used by an anarchist group, were jewelry thieves with no anarchist affiliations. The ensuing events included the famous Sidney Street Siege, in which Winston Churchill, the home secretary, was prominently involved. The thieves were allowed to perish when their shelter caught fire and burnt to the ground.

The press, including *The Times*, exploited to the full the somewhat dubious political penumbra of this event. A degree of covert as well as overt anti-Semitism was an important aspect of the newspaper coverage. One newspaper article took the trouble to mention that the house to which one of the criminals had fled had formerly been rented to a S. Cohen, who had stored second-hand clothing there.[15] An editorial which appeared in *The Times* on December 19 contained the statement: "A savage delight in taking life is the mark of the modern continental anarchist criminal. We have our own ruffians, but we do not breed that type here, and we do not want them."[16]

Indeed, the general furor surrounding the Houndsditch murders had led to the suggestion in Parliament of an Aliens Act even stiffer than the 1905

Act. There was hardly an issue of the *Jewish Chronicle* during 1911 that did not contain either some reference to the debate over a new Aliens Act or some report on injustices committed by the courts in the interpretation of the old one.

Anti-Semitism in Britain at this period was sometimes overt, sometimes subtle. Shortly before the Houndsditch murders, a discreet article had appeared in *The Times*, informing readers that a Russian immigrant, recently arrived in Toronto and suffering from cholera, had spent several days while en route visiting relatives in the East End. Doctors, according to the article, believed the organisms causing the disease had been transported in the immigrant's supply of Russian black bread.[17] On the other hand, direct, even violent attacks on Jews were not unknown. In August 1911, a railway strike in the region of Tredegar and Ebbw Vale erupted into a number of attacks on Jewish residents of the district, apparently as a result of resentments against Jewish landlords and certain Jewish businessmen who had attempted to collect outstanding debts. A series of violent incidents ensued, during which Jewish shops and homes were broken into, windows shattered, and Jewish citizens attacked in the streets. The story of the attack and its aftermath ran in the *Jewish Chronicle* throughout the autumn and into the winter.[18] A minor diversion from the Tredegar incidents was provided by the Bethnal Green dairy dispute in September: the Board of Guardians of Bethnal Green West awarded a contract for milk delivery to a gentile firm, although its bid had been ½d per gallon higher than that of a competing Jewish-owned firm. R. G. Style, chairman of the West Bethnal Green Conservative Association, said at a meeting at which the contract was discussed, "We don't want any Jew contractors."[19] A Mary James added that "the Jews wouldn't buy food from us" and was loudly cheered.[20] At the next meeting of the board, the decision was reversed, and Style remarked that the whole thing had been blown out of proportion by a press seeking to arouse hysteria over anti-Semitism.[21] In the end, the Great Eastern Dairy wrote to the board of Guardians of Bethnal Green, saying that their dignity and self-respect would not allow them to accept the contract.[22] Such was the rather problematic situation of the Jewish community in the country which hosted the First Universal Races Congress.

If British Jews were concerned with exposing and correcting the disabilities suffered by Jews in their own country and elsewhere, they were also, in 1911, concerned with the scientific questions which they expected would be raised at the conference. It is in the nature of that concern and the debate that accompanied it that we may find some lessons about the relationship between the struggle against anti-Semitism and Jewish attitudes about race.

The Jewish community of Britain hoped, in general terms, that the scientific study of race would shed some favorable light on the Jewish question. They were willing, even eager, to provide a forum for those who had anything to say on the question of Jewish racial inheritance and attainments which might ultimately improve their position; the trouble was that there was no consensus as to just what sort of statements would improve their position. On the one hand they wished to assert their pride in a unique and superior racial heritage; on the other they feared that an overemphasis on race could play into the hands of anti-Semites.[23] The two points of view are well summed-up in a debate that took place between C. S. Myers and Lucien Wolf at the May planning meeting for the congress.[24] The subject of the debate was whether there was, in fact, a Jewish race. Myers, speaking in favor of the motion of support for the congress, asserted that such a race did, indeed, exist, although he felt obliged to acknowledge the work of Boas concerning the plasticity of Jewish immigrants in the United States, as well as that of Maurice Fishberg, whose book, asserting among other things, that Jews in the Diaspora tended to resemble physically their host populations,[25] was published in Britain that year. As all these studies tended to support some environmental influence on racial type, he hoped the congress would investigate this topic more fully.[26] Meanwhile, Jews could learn from the Celtic movement; Celtic languages and mythology were being enthusiastically revived and preserved — "a Jew who had any spark or feeling for, or pride in, his race, could never fail to realize that he belonged to a race which was apart and which he should make every effort to keep intact."[27]

Wolf argued that stressing the notion of Jewish racial separateness played into the hands of anti-Semites, even if the notion should turn out to be true. Wolf supported Myers' motion of support for the congress, which he hoped would aid in the fight against anti-Semites.[28]

The next issue of the *Jewish Chronicle* printed a letter from Meyer Akiba Dutch, in which Dutch asserted that the whole tone of debate was alien to race pride and seemed particularly worried that the matter should be open to scientific debate, including animal experiments. Such experiments might even lead to the conclusion that intermarriage was acceptable, so long as Jewish superiority of faith was taken as proven.[29]

The editors of the *Jewish Chronicle* might have wished some years later that they had shared Dutch's fear of scientific experiment in the matter of Jewish racial identity. In February 1911, the journal gave a quite respectful interview to Karl Pearson, the biometrician, anthropologist, and prominent eugenicist, who was then engaged in a study of the alien Jewish population of London. When the results of this study were eventually published in 1925, Pearson and his collaborator Margaret Moul asserted that the inferiority of alien Jewish children in "unbiased" tests led to the conclusion that Polish and Russian Jewish immigration ought to be strictly controlled in the interests of Britain;[30] even if the inferiority were slight, only proven superiority would be grounds for unrestricted immigration. In 1911, however, Pearson insisted that his study was still in its early stages and it was far too soon to draw any firm conclusions regarding the existence of a Jewish racial type in Britain, or of the quality of such a type vis-à-vis the host population. Pearson[31] said that Jews ought to welcome his study of alien school children, as it was to be completely unbiased. He appealed to Yiddish-speaking women to volunteer as home visitors for his study.

Asked what he had found in regard to Jewish school children, Pearson stressed the preliminary status of his studies, but stated that some "curious facts" had already emerged. Eyesight of Jewish children was "below the normal level and corresponding more to the German standard than to that of the English children." At first he had thought it might be "due to the use of Hebrew type," but girls, who read less Hebrew than boys, had no better eyesight. "It is possibly a racial characteristic."[32] Asked about "maturity in relation to age," Pearson replied, "This has not been investigated, but from other experience, I should say the Jewish children are a little more Eastern, that is, mature earlier than the Germanic races."[33]

Asked about the general relationship between heredity and environment, Pearson responded, "I think that heredity plays by far the larger part, but it is one of the objects of the investigation to find out which plays the larger part. We are not beginning with any dogmas on the subject."[34]

Pearson continued by saying that the local government had reported on the debilitating effects of back-to-back houses, but that he was of the opinion that only the weak find themselves in a position of having to live in such places initially.[35]

Pearson further asserted that he attributed the long survival of the Jewish people to their emphasis on large families; in a large group some better types were bound to occur. The Jews, on the other hand, were now, in Pearson's opinion, threatened by the tendency of the poorer classes to have larger families than the better classes.[36] The dietary laws, Pearson remarked, had been useful: Moses was a long way ahead of his time.[37] The readership of the *Jewish Chronicle* had to draw what comfort it could from this "unbiased," "scientific" account of the situation; it did not really provide grounds to assert, *simultaneously*, racial separateness and racial superiority on the one hand, as well as the capacity of the Jews to assimilate satisfactorily with the British population on the other.[38]

The spiritual, intellectual, and moral capacity of the Jew continued to receive space in the *Chronicle* in the months immediately preceding the congress, although a great deal of space was taken up in the June issues by accounts of the coronation of King George V, in line with a general tendency to emphasize the patriotism of the Jewish population of England. (There are even two rather saccharine poems written by socially prominent

Jews in the June 22 issue, one of them utilizing Hebrew phrases.) An article by S. W. Melamed on "The Psychology of the Jewish Mind," which appeared in two parts in the May 26 and June 6 issues of the *Chronicle*, is worthy of note, insofar as it draws attention to certain philosophical and theological stereotypes about Jews and Judaism that formed part of the intellectual baggage of the European tradition. Melamed[39] points out that two contrasting characterizations of Jewish religious thought are to be found in the classic works of philosophy and theology. On the one hand, Judaism has been said to be social and political, not really religious at all. According to Melamed, Machiavelli, Voltaire, Kant, Houston Stuart Chamberlain, Renan, and Schopenhauer had all taken this view and used it to build a negative portrait of Judaism. It is, moreover, a view that those of us concerned with the sociology and social anthropology of Judaism, particularly historical Judaism, confront even in such tremendously valuable work as that of Weber and Robertson Smith. Melamed further says that the sociopolitical characterization of ancient Judaism had a longstanding rival for acceptance in the view that Jews possessed (and possess) a special spiritual genius — this is the view of Schiller, Huet, Guizot, and John Stuart Mill, according to Melamed. Melamed rejects the notion of a historically consistent Jewish personality, as well as the attribution of historical events in general to national character, pointing out some of the dangers of such attribution which later came to obsess the so-called "culture and personality" school of American anthropology. This group has, perhaps with only partial accuracy, been identified with Jewish interests within the anthropological profession, and certainly included, and continues to include, a number of prominent associates of Franz Boas, already mentioned as an important speaker at the First Universal Races Congress. Melamed put the central issue succinctly:

> How can personality, itself a product of history, dominate history? . . . Because modern historiography follows individualistic tendencies is by no means a ground for asserting that personality alone is the driving force in history. . . . Evolution is partly destructive of individuality, because it develops and transforms it.[40]

What continuity Melamed does acknowledge in the Jewish mind over the centuries, he attributes largely to abnormal patterns of living resulting from anti-Semitism.

The Jewish community in Britain, then, social scientist and layman alike, was concerned at the time of the congress with questions of whether there was a unique Jewish mind, whether it was housed in a unique Jewish body, and what influences the surrounding environment might have on the physical and mental characteristics of the Jew. Was assimilation possible, and, if so, was it desirable? In their different ways, at least three of the papers delivered by Jews at the congress attempted to deal with these questions, two indirectly and one directly. C. S. Myers' paper, "On the Permanence of Racial Mental Differences" (see note 27), allows for environmental influences over the very long haul and real racial types in the here and now, resulting from those same influences. Boas's paper, "Instability of Human Types," was essentially a repetition of his earlier and well-known work on the head forms of immigrants and descendants of immigrants in the United States, and stressed at least a limited plasticity in a new environment. Israel Zangwill delivered a fairly lengthy address, in which he dealt with all of the paradoxes discussed earlier, and concluded that some form of Zionism was the only escape from them. This address, judging from the space given it in the *Chronicle*, seems to have been the one which most caught the fancy of the lay Jewish public.

The Jews, said Zangwill, were faced with a more difficult dilemma than Hamlet's: "to be *and* not to be."[41] He says that the Jews' concern for survival in a hostile world has led them everywhere to develop chameleon-like qualities. One result of this has been a fossilization of Judaism. He points out that the last revolution celebrated in the Jewish ritual calendar took place two thousand years ago and that agricultural festivals continue to be celebrated at their original seasons, completely out of phase with the seasons in the lands where Jews now often find themselves. The Ladino language of the Sephardic Jews is more akin to the language of Cervantes than to modern Spanish. Jews, according to Zangwill, work so hard on the masks they must wear in order to survive as Jews at all that they neglect the development of Judaism. Many lands have produced Crypto-Jews like the Marranos, who practice their Judaism in secret; a less extreme illustration of the same phenomenon is the disproportionate success of Jews in the performing arts. The successes upon which Jews pride themselves in scholarship, finance, and even chess rest upon the Jews' cosmopolitan personality. Of particular interest to historians of anthropology is Zangwill's prediction that Jewish thinkers will be led to reject the notion of race itself, as their own success at assimilation belies the concept of fixed racial types.[42] Insofar as the views of Boas, expressed at the congress, represented an important stage in the decline of the notion of racial determinism in anthropology, Zangwill's prediction was accurate; indeed, there has been a tendency, when contemporary anthropologists assess the vast changes their discipline underwent in the early part of this century, to ignore the countercurrents within Jewish opinion concerning the question of race which form the subject of this account, stressing the roles of Boas and his associates in the rejection of racial determinism.

Discussing assimilation, Zangwill says that it has been necessary to Jewish survival, and that Jews have proven themselves adept at it; on the other hand, Jewish survival *as Jews* demands assertion of racial identity, which in turn demands a homeland where Jews can be free of the pressure to assimilate. Assimilation, says Zangwill, is particularly hard on the lower classes, who tend to get left behind, a particular pity in his opinion, as he believed that the strict observance of Jewish law had rendered the Jewish lower classes superior to their lower class neighbors, while the Jewish upper classes were, if anything, inferior to the non-Jewish European upper class.[43] Perceptive enough to see the logical conclusions to be drawn from Jewish adaptability, Zangwill's concern for the preservation of Jewish culture is strong enough to cause him to reject them. To put the matter simply, racial pride demands assertion of racial identity.

Denial of racial identity in response to pressure from the gentile community in the long run carried too high a price in terms of destruction of racial pride. If Jews could not agree on whether they constituted a race, there was also some disagreement as to whether they should identify with non-Jewish white Europeans in their suppression of the colored races. Some time before the congress, Joseph Hertz had written South Africa to complain that Smuts had promulgated laws in the Transvaal that made it possible to treat Jews "like Kaffirs," though this was not being done at the moment.[44] On August 25, at the height of the furor over the S. Wales riots, the *Chronicle* published an editorial saying that the First Universal Races Congress had not happened a moment too soon, that it was the duty of Jews, as longstanding victims of racial injustice, to stand at the forefront of the fight for racial tolerance. In particular, the writer condemned the lynching of a Negro prisoner, accused of killing a white policeman, from a hospital bed in Philadelphia, and the acquittal, in Rhodesia, of a Jewish father who had shot a black accused of insulting his daughters.[45] Over the next several weeks, a dispute ensued between a Hyman S. L. Polak, who supported the editorial stance wholeheartedly, and a D. Greenberg, who failed to commit himself concerning the editorial, but vociferously opposed Polak. Polak had pointed out that the Jewish mayor of Durban had inexcusably required British Indians in that city to celebrate the recent coronation separately from the rest of the British community there; this attitude reminded him of the treatment of Jews in Russia.[46] Greenberg replied that the persecution of Jews in Russia was carried out on religious grounds; there had been no attempt in South Africa to deprive the Indians of their religion! Rather, the need to keep them separate was an economic one: accustomed to living on next to nothing, they would present unfair competition to the European business community if allowed total freedom. Moreover, what did Polak think would be the result for Jewish-gentile relations in South Africa if the Jews dissented from prevailing racial policies?[47]

What have we to learn from all this? At the very least, this survey of one year in the annals of an influential and prestigious Jewish journal should teach us that there was no single "Jewish position" on race that was absorbed *in toto* by a social science dominated by liberal Jews, an opinion often heard in America, if not so often in Britain. Rather, the conflict over race in anthropology was mirrored by and linked with similar controversy within the Jewish community. At times the madness for scientific proofs of Jewish singularity could even descend to the ridiculous; witness the case of Redcliffe Salaman,[48] who published in the *Journal of Genetics* certain conclusions concerning intermarriage which he consented to expound in an interview for the *Jewish Chronicle*, published on October 20 under the title "Mendelism and the Jew." He admits that he is no anthropologist, but says that his experiments with Mendelian crossings on potatoes have led him to certain conclusions about Jewish intermarriage which might be of interest to anthropologists: that Jewishness, as evidenced by the Jewish face (an "easily recognizable" trait), is inherited as a simple Mendelian recessive, thus explaining Fishberg's finding that Jews tended to resemble their host population and allowing Salaman to argue, as Fishberg did not, that Jews must be particularly vigilant about intermarriage in order to preserve their racial purity.

The very extremes to which debate could go, as evidenced by the interview with Salaman, are themselves evidence of just how open was the question of racial identity in Jewish circles at the time we have been discussing. The question, moreover, was one which could not easily be resolved, for any position that might be taken could, and did, furnish support for adverse statements about Jews and Judaism. Assertions of racial identity could, and did, prove compatible with tragic doctrines of Jewish racial inferiority. On the other hand, denials that Jews constituted a distinct race fed into the hands of those would label the Jews a mongrel people, a *Mischmaschvolk*,[49] with equally tragic implications. When the luxury of defining a national identity is not one which oppressors are willing to grant to the oppressed, "objective" science has frequently become a dangerous and double-edged weapon.

Notes

(The *Jewish Chronicle*, London, has been abbreviated *J.C.*)

1. The proceedings of the congress were published in a volume entitled *Papers on Inter-Racial Problems*, communicated to the First Universal Races Congress, edited by G. Spiller (London, 1911).

2. *J.C.*, 6 January 1911, p. 16. Lord Weardale (1847–1923) was the son of the Fifth Earl of Stanhope, a prominent Tory politician and historian. Before his elevation to the peerage in 1906 he had three times been a liberal member of Parliament. Weardale was a philanthropist, a philo-Semite, and a pacifist who had opposed the Boer War. In 1906 he had become president of the Inter-Parliamentary Union. (See his obituary, *The Times*, March 2, 1923.)

3. G. Spiller, ed., *Papers on Inter-Racial Problems* (London, 1911).

4. This planning session was reported in the *Jewish Chronicle* on 12 May 1911, p. 19.
5. *J.C.*, 12 May 1911, p. 19.
6. *J.C.*, 4 August 1911, pp. 14, 17–19.
7. Jews did not form a majority of contributors to the congress, although many prominent Jewish scholars spoke. Indeed, it was the stated policy of the Congress that papers concerning a particular race were to be given by a member of the race in question, and accordingly several African and Asian delegates addressed the assembly, as did W.E.B. Du Bois.
8. *J.C.*, 6 January 1911, p. 19. In the light of this stated wish not to offend individual delegations, it may be apposate to make some remarks about some of the twenty-five national organizations which were organized to plan the congress. It is interesting to note that Russia, the leading center of anti-Semitism, appointed a general committee to the congress. Furthermore, the German general committee included not only some of the most liberal of German and Jewish academics but also Ludwig Schemann, head of the Gobineau Vereinigung, and Eugen Fischer, who was later to become one of the Nazis' leading scientists (On Fischer see Max Weinreich's *Hitler's Professors*, New York, YIVO, 1946). Students of American sociology might be interested to note that the American general committee included Jane Addams, founder of Hull House, one of the early settlement houses, James Breasted, Maurice Bloomfield, Franz Boas, John Dewey, George Dorsey, W.E.B. Du Bois, Charles Ellwood, H. P. Fairchild, Franklin Giddings, A.E. Janks, Albert Keller, A.L. Kroeber, George H. Mead, Charles Peabody, Ulrich B. Phillips, F.W. Putnam, Albion Small, William Graham Sumner, and W.I. Thomas. Most of these individuals were liberals, but we might note the presence of Ulrich B. Philips, the great historian of slavery who is regarded as an anthropologist for "the peculiar institution" (for a list of those involved with the congress see Spiller, 1911, pp. xvii–xlvi).
9. *J.C.*, 26 May 1911, p. 31.
10. See Cecil Roth, "The Court Jews of Edwardian England," pp. 282–295 in his *Essays and Portraits in Anglo-Jewish History* (Philadelphia: Jewish Publication Society of America, 1962).
11. See Paul Foot, *Immigration and Race in British Politics* (London: Penguin, 1965), pp. 87–96; also *The Times*, 26 April 1904.
12. For general details of this period, see Gartner's fine book, *The Jewish Immigrant in England 1870–1914* (Detroit: Wayne State University Press, 1960).
13. *The Times*, London, 17 December 1910, p. 10; 19 December, p. 10.
14. See Gartner, 1960, pp. 130–137.
15. *The Times*, London, 19 December 1910, p. 10.
16. *The Times*, London, 19 December 1910, p. 11.
17. *The Times*, London, 2 December 1910, p. 5.
18. It should, in fairness, be pointed out that the official Christian position in Britain was still tolerance. Indeed, on September 29, the *Jewish Chronicle* printed the following announcement: "Humiliation services have been held (in Tredegar) in several of the local churches and chapels, the themes of the sermons being the rioting and looting. The ministers have not flinched from speaking very plainly to their Congregations in regard to the recent outrages" (p. 21).
19. *J.C.*, 15 September 1911, p. 8.
20. Ibid.
21. *J.C.*, 22 September 1911, p. 12.

22. *J.C.*, 29 September 1911, p. 10.
23. For an extended discussion of this problem, see *The Question of Race in Anthropology From the Time of Johann Friedrich Blumenbach to That of Franz Boas*, Andrew P. Lyons, unpublished D. Phil. thesis, University of Oxford, 1974, pp. 399–407.
24. It is interesting to note that Wolf had been involved in a discussion of the question with his friend Joseph Jacobs at a meeting of the Anthropological Institute some twenty-five years earlier. Jacobs was later to become editor of *Folklore*, and an expert on fairy tales, particularly Celtic fairy tales. He also became president of the Jewish Historical Society and literary editor of the *Jewish Encyclopaedia*. Jacobs died in Yonkers in 1916. The young Jacobs was much influenced by the eugenicist Sir Francis Galton, then president of the Anthropological Institute. In his 1885 paper on the "Racial Characteristics of Modern Jews," Jacobs affirmed that Jews were anatomically distinct from other races, although they were not specially different in their liability to or immunity from certain diseases such as tuberculosis. He had applied Galton's "composite portraiture" technique in the study of the physical type of some Jewish boys. Eight composite photographs were obtained. There could be no doubt that they portrayed "the Jewish expression."

In a paper given later that year, Galton's loyal protégé proclaimed that the average Jew had 4 percent more ability than the average Englishman, and 2 percent more than the average Scotsman. Jacobs was not discussing Eastern European Jews, and he little realized he was playing a dangerous game. Raciology was yet to turn its full attention to Jews.

In the discussion of Jacobs' first paper, Lucien Wolf denied that Jews had a peculiar immunity to consumption. Wolf, who was later to become a prominent journalist and Jewish historian, collaborated with Jacobs in the *Bibliotheca Anglo-Judaica* (1887).
25. Maurice Fishberg, *The Jews: A Study of Race and Environment* (London, 1911).
26. *J.C.*, 12 May 1911, p. 19.
27. Ibid. Although it does not refer to Jews directly, Myers' own contribution to the congress does deal with the apparent paradox posed by the simultaneous assertion of environmental influence on physical characteristics and the reality of racial types: environment itself creates racial distinctions; however, over a long time, perhaps many thousands of years, the distinctions can be broken down by environment. There is thus the hope that primitives may advance to the level of civilized man; those he had met on the Torres Straits expedition were certainly already at the level of the European peasant classes. C.S. Myers, "On the Permanence of Racial Mental Differences" in *Papers on Inter-Racial Problems*, ed. G. Spiller (London, 1911), pp. 73–77.
28. *J.C.*, 12 May 1911, p. 19.
29. *J.C.*, 26 May 1911, p. 22.
30. Karl Pearson and Margaret Moul, "The Problem of Alien Immigration into Great Britain Illustrated by an Examination of Russian and Polish Jewish Children," originally published in *Annals of Eugenics*, Vol. 1, 1925, reprinted in Ashley Montague, ed., *Frontiers of Anthropology* (New York, 1974), pp. 412–420.
31. *J.C.*, 17 February 1911, p. 18.
32. Ibid.
33. Ibid.

34. Ibid.
35. Ibid.
36. Ibid.
37. Ibid.
38. On page 6 of the January 13 issue, the *Chronicle* has printed an article protesting against anti-alien hysteria immediately above another castigating a letter writer in the *Daily Telegraph* for reporting that the Jews are assimilating so well that they even have plum pudding at Christmas!
39. S.W. Melamed, "The Psychology of the Jewish Mind," *J.C.*, 26 May 1911, p. 26.
40. Ibid.
41. Israel Zangwill, "The Jewish Race," G. Spiller, ed., *Papers on Inter-Racial Problems* (London, 1911), p. 277.
42. Ibid., pp. 268–277.
43. Ibid., pp. 277–278.
44. *J.C.*, 6 May 1911, p. 10.
45. *J.C.*, 25 August 1911, p. 6.
46. *J.C.*, 1 September 1911, p. 21.
47. *J.C.*, 8 September 1911, p. 8; *J.C.*, 6 October 1911, p. 20.
48. *J.C.*, 20 October 1911.
49. The term *Mischmaschvolk* was actually used to describe the Jews by Heinrich Class of the *Alldeutscher Verband*, who was later to become an acquaintance of the young Hitler. (See Lyons, 1974, p. 405.)

10.
Urban Development: From Urban Types
to Urban Phases

Alvin Boskoff

Careful analysis of urban areas and their patterned activities effectively began about one hundred years ago, with Fustel de Coulanges (1955). But increasing urbanization and advances in scholarly resources and techniques have created a staggering and somewhat bewildering mass of relevant works. For convenience, these may be classified as: urban economic history (Bautier, 1971; Duby, 1974; Gras, 1922; Hodgett, 1972); urban demography (Hauser & Schnore, 1965; Herbert & Johnston, 1976); urban sociology (Boskoff, 1970; Mellor, 1977); urban archeology (Adams, 1966; Braidwood & Willey, 1962); the "new" urban (social) history (Abrams & Wrigley, 1978; Clark & Slack, 1976; Davis & Haller, 1973; Dyos, 1968); and most recently, urban anthropology (Eames and Goode, 1977; Fox, 1977; Gutkind, 1974; Friedl & Chrisman, 1975). Although varied objectives may be found in this academic avalanche, perhaps the underlying theme is a search for key aspects of urban dynamics, or more directly, an understanding of the causes and conditions of urban growth, development, and change.

In this multifaceted quest, perhaps two major strategies can be identified. One approach tries to derive a simplified causal factor or dimension from rich historical data for specific cities and for a limited time period — such as Fustel de Coulanges' analysis of the declining role of religion in Athens and Rome (Fustel de Coulanges, 1955); Pirenne's theory of the economic (commercial) base of urban revival following the Crusades (Pirenne, 1925); Childe's technological theory of the "urban revolution" in Mesopotamia and Egypt (Childe, 1951). A significant variant of this approach, however, offers a more complex explanation of urban development — for example, R. Adams' emphasis on technology, religion, and stratification in Mesopotamia and preconquest Mexican cities (Adams, 1966).

Despite the immense labor and detail in these studies, and their creative contributions to interpretation of urban experience, they share some common limitations. Methodologically, these "theories" or explanations are simply plausible assertions, bold and intuitive judgments, about the genesis of descriptive patterns (structure, growth, or long-term alteration). In the absence of adequate *comparisons*, or concern for relevant differences, these explanations rely on faith or logic, rather than demonstration. Indeed, given this basic deficiency, it is impossible to choose among conflicting theories of urban development (e.g., economic, technological, religious, political-organizational), or to determine the specific utility of any one theory for some range of cities or historical eras.

In short, these theories have been imposed on cavalierly selected portions of a conceptually chaotic urban "field." Consequently, what was needed was a strategy (or strategies) for *classifying* or ordering this diversity so that appropriate comparisons might be devised, both for descriptive and explanatory purposes. Urban typology, therefore, became a serious and variegated phenomenon of urban analysis, from the 1930s to the present. The accompanying table contains a fairly representative listing of such classifications, testifying perhaps to the ingenuity and perseverance of urban scholars. I would like to review the basic character of this second strategy and also to suggest its probable achievements and also its theoretical shortcomings.

Urban Typologies

Since urban typologies themselves can be classified in at least four categories, it is necessary to sample each category, although this must be somewhat brief.

Technological Typology

The prime example of this type is Sjoberg's distinction between preindustrial and industrial cities, based on the simple presence or absence of manufacturing methods (Sjoberg, 1960). Although he acknowledged the importance of social and political organization, Sjoberg assumed that internal differences in each type were not significant enough for subclassification. Instead, he concluded that preindustrial technology per se is associated with basic similarities in urban ecology, economic system, and stratification.

However, as Cahnman has indicated (Cahnman, 1966), this typology is excessively simple, ignoring considerable differences in historical periods, national settings, and cultural milieux — all of which severely restrict the use of the technological dimension in responsibly developing an urban typology (Daunton, 1978: 258). In addition, the industrial type itself, which is the focus of much social science investigation, encompasses a range of

TABLE 10.1
The Diversity of Urban Typologies

AUTHOR	SPECIFIC URBAN TYPES
A. Technological Base	
Sjoberg	Preindustrial city, industrial city
B. Demographic-Ecological Base	
Schnore	Patterns A-E, each representing a different concentration of educational levels in cities
Timms	Modern city, feudal city, colonial city, immigrant city, preindustrial city
Taylor	Infantile, juvenile, early mature, mature types
C. Economic-Functional Base	
Duncan	National metropolis, diversified manufacturing, specialized manufacturing, regional metropolis, regional capital, submetropolitan
V. Jones et al.	Manufacturing, industrial, diversified manufacturing, diversified retailing, retailing
Stanback and Knight	Nodal, nonnodal
Boskoff	Orthodox ecological city, cultural-symbolic ecological city
Lefebvre	Political city, commercial city, industrial city, "zone critique"
D. Organizational-Political Base	
Braudel	Open towns, closed towns, subject towns
Pirenne	Flemish type, Liege type
Weber	Ancient city, medieval city
Mumford	Eopolis, polis, metropolis, megalopolis, tyrannopolis
Redfield and Singer	Heterogenetic city, orthogenetic city
Hoselitz	Generative city, parasitic city
Gordon	Commercial city, industrial city, corporate city
Fox	Regal-ritual city, administrative city, mercantile city, colonial city, industrial city

empirical forms that escape identification in this "reductionist" typology. In short, Sjoberg's scheme ambitiously devours urban phenomena, but results in a superficial and theoretically naive dichotomy. Yet Sjoberg at one point (Sjoberg, 1960: 68–69) clearly recognized that development and expansion of cities (presumably toward differentiated types) were limited by social power and political stability, although he was not ready to apply this conclusion in developing his typology.

Demographic-Ecological Typology

Given the rich reservoir of demographic data for cities and related areal units, urban demographic typologies have become popular — particularly since the application of factor analytic techniques (Berry, 1972; Hadden & Borgatta, 1965). However, one of the more interesting examples is Timms' transformation of Shevky and Williams' "social area analysis" into a complex typology of cities (Timms, 1971). Briefly, social area analysis sought to locate internal differences by ranking census tracts in terms of three dimensions: social rank (i.e., occupation and income); family status (e.g., percent working women, fertility); and ethnicity (i.e., percent nonwhites). Timms added the dimension of migration pattern, but also postulated that the interrelation of these four dimensions offers the basis for a viable urban typology. Thus, the "modern city" reflects relative independence of these dimensions, while in the "feudal city" all are highly intercorrelated. In the "immigrant city" type, ethnicity is highly correlated with migration pattern and family status, whereas social rank is independent of the remaining dimensions.

This typology is imaginative, intriguing, and yet unused. However, it suggests several possibilities and perhaps some cautions. First, it provides a generally useful method of describing basic demographic differences (not simply size) between cities, for any historical period or national setting. Second, this method yields a more faithful picture of urban variety, unencumbered by adherence to any single variable (such as technology, density, or topography). Third, it focuses on patterns of *residential* variety within cities, as reflections of underlying economic and political processes. However, the connection between demographic and economic-political patterns is rather vague, while the question of similarities or differences in such connections for each urban type is neither posed nor provisionally answered. Finally, the relations among the various urban types remain problematical. How do cities of a given type acquire the characteristics of alternative forms? Is there an "evolutionary"scale implied by this typology, or do types of cities develop in distinctive ways?

Economic-Functional Typology

The most popular form of urban typology, understandably in the Western world, emphasizes urban economic patterns and influences (Stanback & Knight, 1970) Duncan and associates limit their analysis to U.S. cities, but the classification can be applied to other developed nations with little difficulty. Essentially, Duncan's typology employs two dimensions: dominant economic activity (e.g., manufacturing, transportation, finance), and area of economic influence. His typology deals not with each type per se, but with each type as a component in a complex national urban system. Viewing cities and their dependent areas as a diversified economic network, Duncan can therefore "locate" cities (arbitrarily limited to those of 300,000 population and over) in a given type in terms of their limited or extensive "contribution" to the national economy — from the national metropolis type to the specialized manufacturing type (Duncan, 1960).

Such a typology, which incidentally was unable to handle nine "special cases" (Washington, San Diego, San Antonio, Miami, Norfolk, Wilkes-Barre, Tampa-St. Petersburg, Knoxville, Phoenix), is of course historically limited and also is "insensitive" to noneconomic (cultural, religious, and political) components of urban regions. It is instead wedded to the premise that cities develop distinctive patterns primarily in response to locational factors, to population size, and to economic opportunities that derive from the preceding factors. Consequently, it is implied that — after a certain point — cities tend to remain "locked" within a given type because of the restraining effect of other urban types within the overall urban system.

Organizational-Political Typology

Significantly, urban typologies that focus on crucial differences in social structure and distribution of power-authority have generally been applied to premodern towns and cities (i.e., to antiquity and medieval communities) (Abrams & Wrigley, 1978; Braudel, 1973). Perhaps the prime example is Weber's distinction between "ancient" warrior-patrician cities and "medieval" burgher-oriented cities. Weber's famous discussion is rich in detail and somewhat rambling and tentative, studded with various subtypes and analysis of "deviant" or mixed cases. But he apparently contrasted an urban power base derived from a military elite and a closed status system with one in which major power was more widely shared by merchants and then artisans, to encourage "rational" economic pursuits, bolstered by locally devised legal systems (Weber, 1958). Yet Weber's analysis was primarily descriptive; he was not concerned with tracing the mechanisms of urban transformation (cf. Weber, 1923).

Hoselitz's discussion of generative and parasitic cities (which is somewhat related to Redfield and Singer's typology of heterogenetic and orthogenetic cities) explicitly applies to a wider historical range, and both to developed and underdeveloped urban settings in the contemporary world (Hoselitz, 1960). Briefly, the generative type is notable for encouraging economic development in its region and nation, while the parasitic type greatly inhibits such developments. Hoselitz thus classifies cities on their direct and indirect impact beyond their borders. In addition, he suggests that generative cities exercise their "power" by applying economic (achievement) values, whereas parasitic cities lack such effects because of predominant cultural-political (ascriptive) values. We must further assume (although Hoselitz does not examine this issue) that each set of dominant values is espoused by a unique configuration of strata and/or interest groups. Furthermore, Hoselitz recognizes that a given city may shift into an alternative form — either temporarily or long-term — but the dynamics of such changes is not considered.

Though urban typologies have explored several avenues of interest to students of cities, with variably useful forms of conceptual-empirical patterning, their collective contribution to a deepened understanding of urban dynamics has been limited. Perhaps the methodology of classification itself is the prime difficulty, with its focus on either gross distinctions or on a search for roughly simultaneous forms. On the other hand, it may well be that the methodology of typology has been inadequately applied — a position that has some merit, in my opinion. There are at least three pertinent criticisms that seem warranted for urban typology in general, or for specific examples.

1. Most urban typologies have been based on a single dimension of urban functioning (population, technology, economic structure). Each favored dimension appears to have been selected on faith or on grounds of sheer availability of information for that dimension. There is no compelling theoretical reason for selecting any dimension for an exercise in urban classification, nor is there any reasonable basis for adopting any of the competing urban typologies.

2. Closely related is the general neglect of a crucial question: what processes, factors, or conditions can be identified as promoting the unique features of *each* type within a given typological scheme? For example, the preindustrial–industrial typology descriptively contrasts the demographic, ecological, and institutional accompaniments of each type, but essentially ignores the issue of the emergence of "preindustrial cities," and assumes that industrialization unleashes all the "typical" characteristics of the "industrial city." The same deficiency can be found in demographic-ecological and economic-functional types, where qualitative correlations of features tend to overshadow concern for causal or quasi-causal processes.

Parenthetically, in the social sciences, which are distinctively concerned with understanding empirical similarities and differences in human behavior and social organization over time, types cannot be simply *classifications*. Social and/or cultural types that deal with social systems (families, complex organizations, communities, regions, national societies) necessarily entail multiple variables and thus potentially different combinations of those variables. Types must therefore be constructed to include some specification of (a) the genesis of each configuration, (b) the means by which each unique pattern is sustained (i.e., remains true to type), and (c) the points at which significant variation might be expected to occur.

3. Finally, then, urban typologies have generally avoided the problem of transformation. If cities can (and have) develop or change in organization and functioning — so that they can be legitimately "transferred" from one type to another — what processes "explain" such changes, for some cities but not others, in given time spans but not others? Of the typologies listed in Table 10.1, perhaps only three or four have included some discussion of this issue. But their proponents have been content with superficial or question-begging solutions — such as, the pressure of technological development, or economic rationality, or the inevitability of class conflict.

In short, the urban typological approach has been predominatly descriptive rather than theoretical in intent. Likewise, while it has utilized more or less rich historical materials, it has failed to locate and investigate the complexities of urban variation and change in any sustained fashion. But the shortcomings of urban typology entail a salutary search for more useful analyses, for fundamental rethinking about urban phenomena and their potential explanation. In my opinion, this has already begun in earnest, and we can recognize the germ of significant improvement in two respects: a reexamination of urban dimensions, and an embryonic development of the methodology and explanation of *urban phases*.

Urban Dimensions

There has been much contention about the distinctive features of urban communities and the viability of the concept of the "rural-urban continuum" (Dewey, 1960; Castells, 1977; Wirth, 1938). But urban forms are relatively new in human experience, and thus urbanness must possess some special characteristics. However, the old problem of *distinctiveness* (as well as the more immediate problem of urban development) is inseparable from the question of identifying crucial variables or dimensions by which one can estimate similarities and differences, and continuities and changes. In recent years, serious concern for such dimensions has focused on five prime candidates.

Briefly, urban areas (and related forms of complexity) have been analyzed in terms of population, space or land, technology, basic values, and social organization and its behavioral correlates (Lampard, 1969; Boskoff, 1970; Remy & Voyé, 1974). Usually, investigators and thinkers emphasize one or two of these dimensions. However, there has been no clear rationale for such a choice, or for the assumption that all dimensions are equally important. There is some agreement, based on a growing literature of urban "case studies" (Baugh, 1975; Dyos & Wolff, 1973; Everitt, 1973; Foster, 1974; Walker, 1971; Warner, 1968), that the social organizational aspect of urban communities is the focal theoretical dimension and that organizational alterations (or continuities) account for significant differences (and similarities) between urban areas.

This distinctively sociological approach to urban dimensions and urban structure — as contrasted with sociological "flirtation" with demographic, ecological, technological, or psychological foci — should not be viewed as a simple reflection of a traditional sociological bias (i.e., that the character of social organization largely accounts for patterns of social behavior and typical cultural productions). In fact, sociologists have frequently strayed from that presumed disciplinary nexus, perhaps in response to seductive themes from sister disciplines (psychology, psychiatry, economics, biology). More appropriately, it is now fairly evident that such important ingredients as population, space, technology, and values function as tools, resources, possibilities — which provide clues for social behavior and sequences of interaction. On the other hand, social organization, explicit or implicit, formal and informal, is crucial in implementing, applying, interpreting, correlating, and channeling the impact of those basic dimensions. But the organizational aspect is even more significant for the analysis and understanding of urban experience, because the urban arena is typically marked by insistent and complex pressures from those dimensions, pressures that in practice cannot be ignored, filed away, or simply reacted to tropistically. The dynamics of organization, in variably identifiable forms, thus must be the intellectual strategy for enhanced understanding of towns, cities, and urban regions.

Urban Phases

Significantly, this new strategy in its earliest form involved the notion of urban organizational *phases*, which were interpreted as orderly, reasonable transformations rather than strictly necessary, "evolutionary" stages. Perhaps the first full-blown analysis was that by the economic historian N.S.B. Gras, who distinguished a *town economy* phase from the *metropolitan economy* phase on the basis of western European and North American material (Gras, 1922). Following the traditional orientation of economics, Gras located organizational features in the consequences of specific economic behavior and roles (e.g., specialized traders and their formal associations, categories of craftsmen, regulation of weights and measures, price and wage standards). As a consequence, relations between towns and dependent areas (villages, rural areas) were regularized on a limited, local basis, through control of areal markets for specific goods of commodities. Organization is likewise indirect and market-oriented in the more complex metropolitan economy. But the number and range of dependent communities is considerably greater, principally with the addition of the core city's ability to control transportation, wholesale and other middleman activities, financing for commercial and industrial purposes, storage facilities, and the encouragement of new services and productive enterprises.

Some forty years later, Wilbur Thompson, an urban economist, developed a more detailed series of "urban growth stages," with somewhat less emphasis on the organizational component of these developmental phases. Thompson postulated four degrees of urban complexity: (1) moderate influence, due to specialized export of one or two commodities; (2) wider influence, related to an "export complex" of several valued goods to other communities; (3) an economic maturation phase, in which the city has become capable of generating and serving multiple markets within its own enlarged boundaries; and (4) the regional metropolis phase, which by multiple exports to a network of neighboring cities and towns and by servicing its own varied economic demands, creates an intricate but informal economic empire (Thompson, 1965).

Both of these schemes assume that efficiency and variety of economic services promote orderly and continuous growth, without help or hindrance from noneconomic sources — a typical nineteenth century approach to economic analysis. Under this notion, governments and politics are of minor significance, wars and revolutions are ignored, and urban populations are assumed to be ethnically and ethically homogeneous and static. However, urban history continually belies these assumptions, and sociology during the last half century repeatedly uncovers evidence of the weighty role of nonrationality, power, and social conflict in urban functioning in varied national settings. What, then, is a more faithful approach to phases in urban organizational forms?

In retrospect, the extended controversy over "community power structure" in cities can be interpreted as reflecting an implicit and groping search for variations and changes in the organization of urban power. Despite the apparent differences in orientation between political scientists and sociologists (symbolically led by Dahl and Hunter), between the so-called pluralist and elitist theorists, perhaps the crucial aspect of this long debate is the fact that they were studying cities with differing degrees of autonomy in developing local organizational structures (Clark, 1968; Gilbert, 1972). But these aspects were hidden by the ideological presuppositions of researchers (conservative and radical) and by related fixations on selected methodological and technical approaches to urban power (reputational, positional, and issue or decision-making). Indeed, the dominance of this ideological and methodological mixture effectively clouded the *theoretical* potential of the community power approach until quite recently.

Reanalysis and theoretical probing by such writers as Gilbert (1972), Clark (1968), and Walton (Clark, 1968) strongly suggest that cities develop and change through the empirical correlation of two sets of variables: dominant function (economic, cultural, administrative, etc.); and formal or informal mechanisms of coordination and control, of encouragement and restriction. As Gilbert (1972: 64), for example, has concluded from her analysis of 166 such studies, the more diversified the city's functions (particularly in the economic realm), the more pluralist the structure of power. However, this conclusion is based on investigations that were largely cross-sectional in nature. Consequently, the intriguing question arises: to what extent does functional change for specific cities accompany, precede, or follow "meaningful" change in power structure? Clearly, this reformulation of the "community power structure" problem requires adequate historical depth for specific cities and perhaps an ordering of our knowledge of urban power structures for different historical periods (e.g., comparisons of classical Greek cities, Roman cities of the republic and the empire, medieval towns in north and south Europe, early industrial towns, and "modern" metropolitan centers in Europe and North America).

Such an ambitious project also requires new or revised intellectual tools. Of greatest importance is a conception of urban phases (Boskoff, 1968; 1973) that adequately deals with variations in the social organization of change. Second, in identifying and classifying specific phases, we need greater concern for the key features of participants — both those in strategic positions and those comprising urban populations. Finally, the use of urban phases should be accompanied by a theory (or theories) that provides responsible explanations of either (a) change of phase or (b) maintenance of a given phase. Essentially, with such achievements, it will be possible to salvage some of the existing urban typologies, by enhancing their ability to account for specific kinds of urban change (or stagnation).

1. In my opinion, an orientation to urban phases must recognize alternative (and often implicit) emphases in the organizational or power structure of cities and urban regions. Empirically, these emphases appear to comprise basic attitudes toward dominant and competing urban functions, and toward the consequences of altering or maintaining key urban functions. Thus, urban organizational phases may be tentatively classified as being: conservative (maintaining a given function); expansive (exploiting or extending a given urban function); radical (seeking to replace one dominant function by another); and reactionary (concerned with resuming a previously dominant function).

2. The social organization of power clearly depends on the social sources of crucial decisions — strategic individuals, families, or social categories, whether locally based or derived from broader contexts (more influential urban regions, states or provinces, the national government). Historically, urban power centers have included: priestly castes, military leaders, kings, mercantile families and/or fraternities, industrial leaders, financial potentates, elected officials, key civil servants, powerful labor unions. In line with the previous suggestion, surely it is imperative to determine (a) the typical orientation to change of each such category, and (b) the process by which typical forms of urban power achieve their ascendancy.

3. In view of the characteristic heterogeneity of urban areas, we would expect some divergence of interests, skills, and concerns about the dominant thrust of urban organization. Urban history is marked by recurring internal conflicts, by competition for power, by orderly or bloody disputation on priorities, goals, functions, means, distribution of costs and benefits. We therefore need to identify significant changes in the *composition* of urban populations, in their ability to *articulate* their viewpoints and interests, and their commitment to the city and/or the larger urban region.

4. Admittedly, the most difficult portion of this enterprise is devising (or reconstructing) a viable theoretical scheme that can account for differentiation of phases, phase movement, and stability or phase maintenance. Currently, there seem to be two potential sources — of quite contrasting substance, and with very different objectives as to applicability.

Briefly, one theoretical source derives from Marx and is addressed to urban developments in Western Europe and North America from the seventeenth century to the present. As recently amplified by Gordon (1977; 1978), this approach rigidly locates power solely in the economic realm during the early, intermediate, and current stages of capitalist economic structuring. It assumes that urban power is essentially exploitative and marked by the dominance of a strategic and unified economic class (first merchants, then industrialists, and finally corporate administrators). However, in my opinion, the Marxian orientation to urban dynamics contains two serious defects. First, it has inadequate historical breadth, given the approximately 10,000 years of urban experience. Second, it implicitly assumes change or development only in *technology*, while positing a fundamentally continuous (and inevitable) pattern of social organization — an issue that is prematurely closed, rather than investigated by proponents of this theory.

The simplified dynamics of Marxian urban theory, as was also evident in earlier "historical" theories and the urban typological approach, is basically unsuited to the empirical variety and complexity of urban areas in different periods and settings. A more flexible approach may be discerned in a theoretical framework that allows the student to search for different, varying, and even competing sources and conditions of urban power, with some concern for accounting for changing dominance among alternative sources. This framework is the much-used and yet highly criticized "social system" or "structural functional" orientation, which was not originally conceived for urban areas. But with some interpretation and extension, it may provide a tentative theoretical base for the phase-orientation urban analysis seems to require.

Essentially, the theory underlying social systems analysis involves three crucial premises (Parsons, 1951): (1) social systems are complex entities that function by specialization of interactive components (sub-systems); (2) at any given time, specialization is accompanied by minimal degrees of coordination, which is provided by the operation of a strategic subsystem and its constituent groups or associations; (3) as social systems evolve and/ or confront changing pressures from the larger environment (physical and sociocultural), there is a tendency toward change in the sources and objectives of the coordinative subsystem. However, there is little evidence of a rigid, deterministic sequence of such changes, presumably because of unforeseen variations in external conditions and also because internal interactions seem to follow patterns of probability rather than unmodified causality.

In the Parsonian version of social systems theory (Parsons, 1951), the major subsystems are classified into four empirical categories: adaptive (technological-economic, scientific); goal-attainment (political-administrative); integrative (religious, philosophical); and pattern-maintenance (kinship, educational, recreational, artistic). Furthermore, Parsons assumes an "existential strain" toward development (or relative focus on subsystems) in the order just presented.

Urban Phases

How can these theoretical clues be employed or adapted to the problem of urban phases, given the vast panorama of urban experience? Provisionally, we may identify four "phases" of urban development, with the explicit caution that these are not inevitable, irreversible, or neatly divisible into equal time periods.

Technical-Professional Phase

The earliest and perhaps the most crucial phase of urban functioning is essentially *protective* in nature, concerned with the assurance of safety and emotional welfare for a relatively large, concentrated population. Military and religious skills of a high order are therefore relatively uncontested bases of power-authority over such activities as production, storage, and exchange. Urban power and social organization thus emphasize *adaptation* to the immediate geosociological environment and to a culturally associated supernatural environment. Normally, then, power is used conservatively, for containment and insulation.

Entrepreneurial Phase

The "take-off" phase in urban areas begins with processes that erode isolation and/or encourage the quest for growth, expansion, risk, achievement. Normally, opportunities for growth or development tend to emerge from external sources — trade with other regions or political units, economic or political needs of kingdoms and nations, significant technological innovations (in navigation, manufacturing, warfare), and newly enacted laws or regulations that offer potentialities for new or enhanced manipulation of skills and resources. Entrepreneurial organization distinctively replaces an adaptive-conservative emphasis with a bold stress on various forms of expansion (in size, production, range of influence, application and stretching of norms or rules). In practice, this means greater (but somewhat selective) coordination of urban resources (land, capital, labor, administration, and any unique advantages of location, information, or political influence currently associated with a given urban community).

The entrepreneurial phase may be stimulated by military cliques, businessmen in industry, commerce and finance, local political leaders, or any combination of these. Historically, the most significant source in the Western world has generally been a corps of economic notables (in trade, industry, or mining), whose quest for profit and wealth entailed increased demands for employment and also some expansion of "public services." But political figures likewise have assumed key entrepreneurial roles, in promoting crucial local alliances or facilitating decisive policies for urban development (e.g., Joseph Chamberlain in Birmingham, William Hartsfield in Atlanta). In general, as Marx and Engels observed in their famous Manifesto, the urban bourgeoisie — the striving, rising, determined middle classes — and the historically correlated "system" of capitalist forms and congenial interstices contributed the essential ingredients for this second phase, largely during the nineteenth and early twentieth centuries. Incidentally, most cities appear to function at this phase or stage, in various parts of the urbanized world (Wiebe, 1967).

The Bureaucratic Phase

Imperceptibly, the fruits of entrepreneurial exuberance also contain costs, in the form of practical difficulties. Entrepreneurial expansion ultimately requires complexity of administration (both private and public) and the accumulation of records, regulations, authoritative decisions, legal disputes. At this point in urban development, entrepreneurial values confront serious competition from enlarging categories of legitimated "watchdogs" of various urban activities in virtually every institutional realm. "Urban bureaucrats" — in specific cities and in regional and national foci — in effect inhibit or decelerate processes of further expansion (with the exception of their own numbers) and instead emphasize the sanctity of rules rather than achievements, of precedent rather than special or unique opportunities, of caution and control rather than coordination. In some respects, this phase resembles Parsons' "pattern-maintenance" function — particularly in its emphasis on received values and restriction of variation.

But while the pattern-maintenance phase is conceived as an interlude — a salutary pause — the bureaucratic phase seems to have a longevity that is notably sturdy and is apparently immune to normal attempts to alter the dominance of the guardians of documents.

Many large metropolitan areas began to enter this phase in the 1930s — as a result of the Great Depression, and the enlarged domain of governmental activity and surveillance following World War II. It became evident that cities in the limbo between entrepreneurial and bureaucratic dominance could not adequately deal with accumulated urban difficulties, such as continued poverty, interracial conflicts, increased levels of taxation, irregular spatial development, high and diversified crime rates, housing shortages and deteriorated housing stocks, corruption, deficiencies in local implementation of state and national urban policies. Perhaps these and other problems reflect a basic failure in urban social organization: a structured incapacity to achieve or sustain coordination of its variegated segments.

An Embryonic Phase: Planning

A few cities — Stockholm, Amsterdam, London — have experimentally opened a fourth and somewhat misty phase of urban development. Despite a voluminous urban planning literature since about 1940, we must separate hopes and ideals and theories from actual implementation experiences with "urban planning." Much of what has been called urban planning is either entrepreneurial or bureaucratic in fact, a situation that confuses and discomforts many who are concerned with realistic confrontation of urban problems and with serious attempts at developing unrealized urban potentialities.

From the evidence of planning ventures and the distinctive ethos of planning goals, the urban planning phase is a response to the unregulated expansiveness of the entrepreneurial phase and the intricately structured immobility of the bureaucratic phase. It therefore seeks guided, balanced development, with an effective ability to contain the special power of any interest group or organized activity. Urban planning thus requires delegation of power-authority to a fiduciary "integrating" cadre of planners, who by training and achievement are able to combine innovation with order, relevant facts with overarching values, present needs with anticipated futures, municipal with regional resources and needs.

Since urban planning is still sporadic and tentative in practice (dating arbitrarily from the 1940s), it is difficult to trace its necessary preconditions. "Necessity" is clearly not an adequate explanation; compelling arguments for urban planning were made before the turn of the century (Howard, 1955; Geddes, 1968), but were either derided or ignored. From scattered clues, however, it seems that at least two conditions are necessary (but perhaps not sufficient) for genuine movement into a planning phase. One such condition is a strong, widely held communal-socialist ideology, which defines community welfare as encompassing a wide spectrum of legitimate interests over a considerable time span. This is, of course, a rather difficult ideology to develop as a voluntary product (currently, found only in Scandinavia and Britain). A second condition is widespread recognition and understanding of urban crisis, the judgment that current norms and procedures are dangerously unequal to clearly defined problems and desired practical goals. In the past, deep economic depression has been the prime contributor; serious and continued energy shortages may become an alternative source of urban crisis.

It is important to remember that each urban phase was associated with characteristic organizational forms. The technical-professional phase was marked by disciplined military formations, professional organizations or guilds, or formalized religious systems. The entrepreneurial phase had the corporate form, local public government (civil courts, self-imposed taxation, elections), labor unions, political parties, private foundations. The bureaucratic phase contributed computer technology, filing and retrieval systems, examination systems, civil service, administrative law, mechanisms of promotion and succession. Explicitly or implicitly, all these innovations were means of attaining or sustaining strategic power, and thus of creating "order." Sociologically speaking, the planning phase appears to possess only one distinctive organizational innovation — metropolitan government — and this has been a rather weak organizational prop thus far (e.g., in Toronto, Miami, Minneapolis, London).

Conclusion

Urban phases — theoretically and practically — reflect preparatory and accompanying structural changes in urban areas and in their relation to larger systems. Indeed, it seems likely that urban development cannot be adequately understood without using a "phase orientation" and its necessary incorporation of problems and solutions to repeated or typical patterns of change (or its obverse). Urban typologies normally skirt theoretical issues of change because typologies are devised to classify or pigeonhole large numbers of cities either for very narrow or indefinable time periods. Such typologies need not be jettisoned. They can be reconceptualized in more specific ways (with more types, as empirically required); and where proper theoretical questions and data are used, typologies can be selectively converted into some valid set of urban phases — applicable to a limited number of cities for extended time periods, or as a means of searching for general directions among varied urban areas in different eras and cultural-political settings (Chalklin, 1974; Mohl & Betten, 1970; Strauss, 1966; Wade, 1959).

The above conception of urban phases can only be tentative and exploratory. Given the complexity of urban phenomena, this pattern of phases may well be too simple in some respects, too narrow in its relevance for non-Western urban areas. There is certainly room for much more empirical study of cities, and for reconsidering or rethinking available investigations by various disciplines and fields. But this additional work must be guided by a flexible "phase" framework, to be altered or replaced as experience develops, as "goodness of fit" is either approximated or negated in an evolving confrontation of past facts and present concepts or categories.

Of course, with a little effort, one can find whatever one desires in the world of manifold facts. However, if we view urban phases as sets of structural possibilities for change or development (Mannheim, 1940), we can search for evidence for or against these possibilities in subsequent periods for specific urban areas. It then becomes as necessary to account for maintenance of a phase as for replacement of one phase by another, because both strike the same chord: the relative ability of urban areas to adapt to or exploit their environments. From this general standpoint, likewise, we may be able to interpret significant urban *difficulties* as reflecting understandable inabilities to shift into a more "workable" phase. There is an expandible agenda before us; it is perhaps time to be conceptually bold and discard the Idols of the Tribe that have impeded our imperative intellectual grasp of urban dynamics.

References

Abrams, Philip and E.A. Wrigley, eds., *Towns in Societies: Essays in Economic History and Historical Sociology* (Cambridge: Cambridge University Press, 1978).

Adams, Robert M., *The Evolution of Urban Society* (Chicago: Aldine, 1966).

Baugh, Daniel A., ed., *Aristocratic Government and Society in Eighteenth Century England* (New York: New Viewpoints–Franklin Watts, 1975).

Bautier, Robert-Henri, *The Economic Development of Medieval Europe* (New York: Harcourt, Brace Jovanovich, 1971).

Berry, Brian J.L., ed., *City Classification Handbook* (New York: Wiley–Interscience, 1972).

Boskoff, Alvin, "Urban Power Structures and the Management of Innovation: A Typology and Related Theoretical Considerations." Paper given at meetings of the American Sociological Association, 1968.

Boskoff, Alvin, *The Sociology of Urban Regions*, 2nd ed. (New York: Appleton-Century-Crofts, 1970).

Boskoff, Alvin, "Urban Role–Complexes and Urban Development." Paper given at meetings of the American Sociological Association, 1973.

Braidwood, Robert J. and Gordon R. Willey, eds., *Courses Toward Urban Life* (Chicago: Aldine, 1962).

Braudel, Fernand, *Capitalism and Material Life 1400–1800* (New York: Harper and Row, 1973).

Cahnman, Werner J., "The Historical Sociology of Cities: A Critical Review," *Social Forces*, 45 (December, 1966), 155–161.

Castells, Manuel, *The Urban Question: A Marxist Approach* (Cambridge: MIT Press, 1977).

Chalklin, C.W., *The Provincial Towns of Georgian England* (Montreal: McGill–Queens University Press, 1974).

Clark, Peter, ed., *The Early Modern Town* (New York: Longmans, 1976).

Clark, Peter and Paul Slack, eds., *Crisis and Order in English Towns 1500–1700* (London: Routledge and Kegan Paul, 1972).

Clark, Peter and Paul Slack, eds., *English Towns in Transition 1500–1700* (London: Oxford University Press, 1976).

Clark, Terry N., ed., *Community Structure and Decision-Making* (San Francisco: Chandler, 1968).

Clark, Terry N., ed., *Community Power and Policy Outputs: A Review of Urban Research* (Beverly Hills: Sage Publications, 1973).

Daunton, M.J., "Towns and Economic Growth in Eighteenth Century England," in Abrams and Wrigley, 1978, 245–277.

Davis, Allen F. and Mark H. Haller, eds., *The Peoples of Philadelphia: A History of Ethnic Groups and Lower Class Life, 1790–1940* (Philadelphia: Temple University Press, 1973).

Dewey, Richard, "The Rural-Urban Continuum: Real But Relatively Unimportant," *American Journal of Sociology*, 66 (July, 1960), 60–66.

Duby, Georges, *The Early Growth of the European Economy* (Ithaca: Cornell University Press, 1974).

Duncan, Otis Dudley et al., *Metropolis and Region* (Baltimore: Johns Hopkins University Press, 1960).

Dyos, H.J., ed., *The Study of Urban History* (London: Edward Arnold, 1968).

Dyos, H.J. and Michael Wolff, eds., *The Victorian City*, 2 vols. (London: Routledge and Kegan Paul, 1973).

Eames, Edwin and Judith G. Goode, *Anthropology of the City: An Introduction to Urban Anthropology* (Englewood Cliffs: Prentice-Hall, 1977).

Everitt, Alan, ed., *Perspectives in English Urban History* (New York: Barnes and Noble, 1973).

Foster, John, *Class Struggle and the Industrial Revolution: Early Industrial Capitalism in 3 English Towns* (New York: St. Martin's Press, 1974).

Fox, Richard G., *Urban Anthropology: Cities in their Cultural Settings* (Englewood Cliffs: Prentice-Hall, 1977).

Friedl, John and Noel J. Chrisman, eds., *City Ways: A Selective Reader in Urban Anthropology* (New York: Thomas Y. Crowell, 1975).

Fustel de Coulanges, N.D., *The Ancient City* (Garden City: Anchor Books, 1955 [orig. ed., 1864]).

Geddes, Patrick, *Cities in Evolution* (London: Benn, 1968 [orig. ed., 1915]).

Gilbert, Claire W., *Community Power Structure* (Gainesville: University of Florida Press, 1972).

Gordon, David M., "Class Struggle and the Stages of American Urban Development," in Perry and Watkins, 1977, 55–82.

Gordon, David M., "Capitalist Development and the History of American Cities," in Tabb and Sawers, 1978, 25–63.

Gras, N.S.B., *An Introduction to Economic History* (New York: Harper & Bros., 1922).

Gutkind, Peter C.W., *Urban Anthropology* (Assen, Netherlands: Van Gorcum & Co., 1974).

Hadden, Jeffrey K. and Edgar F. Borgatta, *American Cities: Their Social Characteristics* (Chicago: Rand McNally, 1965).

Hauser, Philip M. and Leo F. Schnore, eds., *The Study of Urbanization* (New York: Wiley, 1965).

Herbert, D.T. and R.J. Johnston, eds., *Spatial Processes and Forms* (London: Wiley, 1976).

Hodgett, Gerald A.J., *A Social and Economic History of Medieval Europe* (London: Methuen, 1972).

Hoselfitz, Bert F., *Sociological Aspects of Economic Growth* (New York: The Free Press, 1960).

Howard, Ebenezer, *Garden Cities of Tomorrow* (London: Faber and Faber, 1955).

Jones, Victor, Richard L. Forstad, and Andrew Collver, "Economic and Social Characteristics of Cities," *The Municipal Yearbook 1963* (Chicago: International City Managers' Association, 1963), 85–157.

Knights, Peter R., *The Plain People of Boston, 1830–60* (New York: Oxford University Press, 1971).

Kraeling, Carl H. and Robert M. Adams, eds., *City Invincible: A Symposium on Urbanization and Cultural Development in the Ancient Near East* (Chicago: University of Chicago Press, 1960).

Lampard, Eric E., "Historical Contours of Contemporary Urban Society: A Comparative View," *Journal of Contemporary History*, 4 (July, 1969) 2–25.

Lefebvre, Henri, *La Révolution urbaine* (Paris: Gallimard, 1970).

Mannheim, Karl, *Man and Society in an Age of Reconstruction* (New York: Harcourt, Brace, 1940).

Mellor, J.R., *Urban Sociology in an Urbanized Society* (London: Routledge and Kegan Paul, 1977).

Mohl, Raymond A. and Neil Betten, eds., *Urban America in Historical Perspective* (New York: Weybright and Talley, 1970).

Parsons, Talcott, *The Social System* (New York: The Free Press, 1951).

Perry, David C. and Alfred J. Watkins, eds., *The Rise of the Sunbelt Cities* (Beverly Hills: Sage Publications, 1977).

Pirenne, Henri, *Medieval Cities* (Princeton: Princeton University Press, 1925).

Remy, Jean and Liliane Voyé, *La Ville et l'urbanisation: modalités d'analyse sociologique* (Brussels: Duculot, 1974).

Schnore, Leo F., ed., *The New Urban History: Quantitative Explorations by American Historians* (Princeton: Princeton University Press, 1975).

Sjoberg, Gideon, *The Pre-Industrial City: Past and Present* (New York: The Free Press, 1960).

Stanback, Thomas M. and Richard V. Knight, *The Metropolitan Economy* (New York: Columbia University Press, 1970).

Strauss, Gerald, *Nuremberg in the Sixteenth Century* (New York: Wiley, 1966).

Tabb, William K. and Larry Sawers, eds., *Marxism and the Metropolis: New Perspectives in Urban Political Economy* (New York: Oxford University Press, 1978).

Taylor, Griffith, *Urban Geography* (New York: E.P. Dutton, 1946).

Thompson, Wilbur R., *A Preface to Urban Economics* (Baltimore: Johns Hopkins University Press, 1965).

Timms, Duncan, *The Urban Mosaic: Towards a Theory of Residential Differentiation* (Cambridge: Cambridge University Press, 1971).

Wade, Richard C., *The Urban Frontier: The Rise of Western Cities 1790–1830* (Cambridge: Harvard University Press, 1959).

Walker, Mack, *German Home Towns: Community, State, and General Estate 1648–1871* (Ithaca: Cornell University Press, 1971).

Warner, Sam B. Jr., *The Private City: Philadelphia in Three Periods of Its Growth* (Philadelphia: University of Pennsylvania Press, 1968).

Weber, Max, *The City* (New York: The Free Press, 1958 [orig. ed., 1921]).

Weber, Max, *General Economic History* (New York: Collier Books, 1961 [orig. ed., 1923]).

Wiebe, Robert H., *The Search for Order, 1877–1920* (New York: Hill and Wang, 1967).

Wirth, Louis, "Urbanism as a Way of Life," *American Journal of Sociology*, 44 (July, 1938), 3–24.

11.
Perspectives on Poverty in Early American Sociology

Chaim I. Waxman

The subject of poverty played a very prominent role in the social-problems literature of the 1960s and first half of the 1970s. Two perspectives, the culturalist and the structuralist, emerged as the dominant ones both in terms of theory and social policy. Essentially, the culturalist perspective, most frequently expressed in the writings of the late anthropologist Oscar Lewis, argued that the poor manifest norms and values which are characteristically different from those of the dominant society and culture, that these unique norms and values are transmitted intergenerationally through socialization, and that they have become the subcultural determinants of the lower socioeconomic status of many of the poor in American society. The structuralists, on the other hand, argued that the behavior patterns of the poor are not internally derived as the products of a unique value system. Rather, they are situational adaptations, that is, they are normal reactions to situations in which the dominant social structure is unfavorably disposed toward and restricts the options of the lower class. The norms of the poor are, thus, not internally, but externally derived.[1]

Although they reached their prominence in the second half of the twentieth century, both the culturalist and the structuralist perspectives have their antecedents in early American sociology. This article will trace the development of both perspectives through the writings of early American sociologists up until Oscar Lewis' coinage of the term "culture of poverty" in 1959.

American sociology is one of the offspring of the American Social Science Association, whose original constitution, adopted in 1866, declared as its objectives: "to guide the public mind to the best practical means of promoting the Amendment of Laws, the Advancement of Education, the Prevention and Repression of Crime, the Reformation of Criminals, and the progress of Public Morality. . . . It will give attention to pauperism and the topics related thereto; including the responsibility of the well-endowed and successful, and the wise and educated, the honest and respectable, for the

183

failure of others. It will aim to bring together the various societies and individuals now interested in these objects, for the purpose of obtaining by discussion the real elements of Truth; by which doubts are removed, conflicting opinions harmonized, and a common ground afforded for treating wisely the great social problems of the day."[2] Thus, "pauperism and the topics related thereto" were even then of "the great social problems of the day," and the members of the association saw their concern with these problems as directed toward and necessary for "treating wisely" and alleviating the problematic conditions.

As a whole, American sociology staunchly rejected biological explanations of inequality. This definite repudiation of biological determinism is evident in the writings of one of the first American sociologists, Lester Ward. Ward saw social classes as resulting from conquest and subjugation, and he most emphatically denied any innate differences between members of different classes: "If the same individuals who constitute the intelligent class at any time or place had been surrounded from their birth by exactly the same conditions that have surrounded the lowest stratum of society, they would have inevitably found themselves in that stratum," and vice versa. "In other words, class distinctions are wholly artificial, depend entirely on environing conditions, and are in no sense due to differences in native capacity. Differences in native capacity exist and are as great as they have been pictured, but they exist in all classes alike."[3] Ward appears to be contradicting himself, at first attributing differences to the environment of the lower stratum versus that of "the intelligent class," and then maintaining that the differences are equally distributed in all classes. What he apparently means is that the potential is equally distributed, and it is the environment rather than any innate differences that results in the distinctions. The distinctions are class-linked because of environmental differences. In an essay published in the *American Journal of Sociology*, Ward makes the very important distinction between manifest intelligence and intelligence potential, and maintains that there is no correlation between the latter and class. "Their unequal intelligence has nothing to do with their capacity for intelligence. Intelligence consists in that capacity together with the supply of information for it to expand itself upon." We see therefore that both kinds of inferiority of the lower class [physical inferiority, "due entirely to conditions of existence," and intellectual inferiority — *CIW*] are extraneous.[4]

Ward was a severe critic of the doctrine of laissez faire. He staunchly advocated a welfare state, a "sociocracy," which he saw as "one form of government that is stronger than autocracy or aristocracy or democracy, or even plutocracy," and is the only form which can assure that society will "escape . . . conquest of power by the egoistic intellect."[5] Since "the welfare or happiness of mankind consists entirely in the freedom to exercize the natural faculties," and "all want is deprivation, i.e., the withholding of whatever is necessary to set the system into healthy operation,"[6] be it the withholding of material things or "the means to utilize the materials and forces of nature," he called for "the socialization of achievement"[7] and he saw sociology as providing the methods by which this might be realized. "When all human achievement is socialized . . . then civilization and progress will come to be the same, and all art will fulfill its usual function of increasing the algebraic sum of good and evil in the world. Sociology is the science which sets forth the principles and indicates the method for attaining this end."[8]

There was, however, no consensus among the early sociologists on these matters, as is evident in the thoughts on the lower classes by a contemporary antagonist of Ward, William Graham Sumner, as depicted in his best known work, *Folkways*.[9] Social class, Sumner maintains, is a function of "societal value," in terms of intellectual, moral, economic, and physical elements. While the possession of these elements is not always harmonic, some possess more of one and less of others, "nevertheless societal value is a concrete idea, especially on its negative side (paupers, tramps, social failures, and incompetents). The defective, dependent, and delinquent classes are already fully differentiated, and are the subject of statistical enumeration."[10] Further on he continues, "Every civilized society has to carry below the lowest sections of the masses a dead weight of ignorance, poverty, crime, and disease."[11] As to the possibilities of reform, Sumner asserts that "political institutions readjust and redistribute the burdens of life over a population, and they change the form of the same perhaps, but the burdens are in the condition of human life. They are always present, and political institutions never can do away with them at all."[12]

A more vivid picture of Sumner's attitudes can be found in his tract, *What Social Classes Owe to Each Other*,[13] in which he defends the doctrine of laissez faire, and sees the responsibility of the state only in guaranteeing rights, which "do not pertain to *results*, but only *chances*. They pertain to the *conditions* of the struggle for existence, not to any of the results of it; to the *pursuit* of happiness, not to the possession of it."[14] These rights being assured, no one, no group nor class is obligated to any other; rather, society must recognize the "value, as a sociological principle, of the Rule to Mind One's Own Business."[15] The weak, the poor, "are the ones through whom the productive forces of society are wasted. They constantly neutralize and destroy the finest efforts of society in all its struggles to realize any better things."[16]

But Sumner was unique; in the main, from its inception, American sociology has viewed the poor as products of their environment.

In 1909, Charles Horton Cooley wrote his famous book, *Social Organization*, wherein he devoted a chapter to a discussion of "poverty."[17] Being poor, he asserts, implies not only lack of adequate food and shelter; it "commonly implies other lacks, among which are poor early training and education, the absence of contact with elevating and inspiring personalities, a narrow outlook upon the world, and, in short, a general lack of social opportunities."[18]

Cooley maintained the impossibility of distinguishing between individual and social causes of poverty, because "everything in personality has roots in social conditions, past or present."[19] The distinction has validity only in reference to a particular individual and whether or not the social condition has become so internalized and a part of his personality so as to allow for any benefit from resocialization through a change in social influences. The great majority of the poor would respond positively to a change in their social situation; only a minority of them have "intrinsic defects of character which must always keep them poor so long as they are left in the ordinary degree of self-dependence."[20] Cooley further regarded those characteristics typically associated with poverty — laziness, shiftlessness, and vice — to be "quite as much the effect as the cause of poverty."[21]

Since the source of poverty and its results are social, "the method of elimination must also be social, namely, the reform of housing and neighborhood conditions, improvement of the schools, public teaching of trades, abolition of child-labor and the humanizing of industry."[22] And, in a statement befitting delivery before the Congress of the United States in 1973, Cooley forecasted: "If we can give the children of the poor the right start in life, they will themselves, in most cases, develop the intelligence, initiative, self control and power of organization which will enable them to look out for their own interests when they are mature. The more one thinks of these questions the more he will feel that they can only be solved by helping the weaker classes to a position where they can help themselves."[23]

Cooley argued that it is futile to attempt to explain poverty as resulting solely from internal sources (personality, etc.) because, in the final analysis, even the internal sources derive from external ones. The self is, in Cooley's words, a "looking-glass self." Thus, even if personality "deficiencies" are detected in the poor, their poverty cannot be explained by those personality characteristics because they too have been formed from external sources. As we have suggested elsewhere,[24] Cooley's insights provide the basis for an alternative that accounts for many of the deficiencies in both the cultural and structural perspective.

During the second decade of the twentieth century, American sociology, in its attempt to achieve scientific status, shifted from macrosociology to a sociology of specific institutions and a sociology heavily grounded in empirical observation. The prototype of this new trend was "the Chicago School," which included such figures as W.I. Thomas, Park, Burgesss, McKenzie, Wirth, among others, and it is this school which gave birth to the subcultural approach or perspective toward poverty, an approach which much later came to be identified with the anthropologist Oscar Lewis.

W.I. Thomas was among the first sociologists to emphasize the importance of recognizing and understanding the attitudes and values of immigrant groups as a precondition to assisting them. Toward the end of his study of *The Polish Peasant In Europe And America*[25] (with Florian Znaniecki), he has some words of criticism directed toward social workers, which set the tone for much subsequent discussion. As Morris Janowitz points out,[26] one only has to substitute the word "Negro" or "poor" for "immigrant" or "Polish" in the following passage, to find many of the contemporary issues:

> It is a mistake to suppose that a "community center" established by American social agencies can in its present form even approximately fulfill the social function of the Polish parish. It is an institution imposed from the outside instead of being freely developed by the initiative and co-operation of the people themselves and this, in addition to its racially unfamiliar character, would be enough to prevent it from exercising any deep social influence. Its managers usually know little or nothing of the traditions, attitudes, and native language of the people with whom they have to deal and therefore could not become genuine social leaders under any conditions. . . . Whatever real assistance the American social center gives to the immigrant community is the result of the "case method," which consists in dealing directly and separately with individuals and families. While this method may bring efficient temporary help to the individual it does not contribute to the social progress of the community nor does it possess much preventive influence in struggling against social disorganization. Both of these purposes can be attained only by organizing and encouraging social self-help on the co-operative basis. Finally, in their relations with immigrants the American social workers usually assume, consciously or not, the attitude of a kindly and protective superiority, occasionally, though seldom, verging on despotism.[27]

Janowitz correctly emphasizes the influence of Thomas and the subsequent "Chicago area project" as a source of "intellectual stimulation for federal programs of "community action."[28] What should also be emphasized is "the influence of Thomas on the subcultural perspective to poverty which, according to many observers, stands in opposition to the 'community action' approach."[29] Ironically, both find roots in Thomas.

Whereas Thomas was critically sympathetic toward social work, Robert Park was downright hostile.[30] He "always openly scoffed at do-gooders in conversation"[31] and to his students who wanted to join the fight for Negro rights, "Park told them flatly that the world was full of crusaders. Their role instead was to be that of the calm, detached scientist who investigates race relations with the same objectivity and detachment with which the zoologist dissects the potato bug."[32]

Park was convinced that an understanding of social problems could be derived from the study of the growth of the city and its changes. "The growth of the city involves not merely the addition of numbers, but all the incidental changes and movements that are inevitably associated with the effort of every individual to find his place in the vast complexities of urban life. The growth of new regions, the multiplication of professions and occupations, the incidental increase in land values which urban expansion brings — all are involved in the processes of city growth, and can be measured in terms of changes of position of individuals with reference to other individuals, and to the community as a whole."[33] Thus, Park, together with Ernest W. Burgess and Roderick D. McKenzie, sought to understand through detailed descriptive analyses the cultural patterns of urban life. Accordingly, they who plotted the physical and social layout of the city in terms of neighborhoods of concentric circles, with Zone I, the center, the downtown; Zone II, the "zone in transition" with its slums and ghettos; Zone III, the "zone of workingmen's homes"; Zone IV, the "residential zone"; and Zone V, the "commuter's zone."[34] They spurred numerous studies of the slums and ghettos in the outskirts of Zone I and in Zone II, which have resulted in such monographs as F.M. Thrasher, *The Gang*;[35] W.C. Reckless, *The Natural History of Vice Areas in Chicago*;[36] H.W. Zorbaugh, *The Gold Coast and the Slum*;[37] N. Anderson, *The Hobo*;[38] among many others which depict, in depth, how people in these areas live, and the extent to which the social problems are the result of their environment.

It is Park, above all others, who may be called the "father" of the subcultural approach for which Oscar Lewis was later to become famous. Many of the ingredients of the subcultural perspective are explicit in the following words of Park:

> The fact is, however, that the city is rooted in the habits and customs of the people who inhabit it. The consequence is that the city possesses a moral as well as a physical organization, and these two mutually interact in characteristic ways to mold and modify one another. It is the structure of the city which first impresses us by its visible vastness and complexity. But this structure has its basis, nevertheless, in human nature, of which it is an expression. On the other hand, *this vast organization which has arisen in response to the needs of its inhabitants, once formed, imposes itself upon them as a crude external fact, and forms them, in turn, in accordance with the design and interests which it incorporates.*[39]

What Park says explicitly, and what is implicit in many of the works which derived from the "Chicago School," is that the patterns of the neighborhood, and slum in particular, once they come into being, take on a life of their own and are, to a great extent, self-generating and self-perpetuating sources of poverty. Opponents of this perspective argue that the source of the perpetuation of poverty is not internal, but rather in the external forces of the dominant society. Poverty persists, they argue, because of the persistent restrictions placed upon the poor by the forces of the larger social structure. The roots of this perspective are found in a major statement by Robert K. Merton.

In 1938, Robert K. Merton began a new trend in the analysis of the relationship between poverty and crime, with the publication of his aforementioned essay, "Social Structure and Anomie."[40] In an attempt to discover "how some social structures *exert a definite pressure* upon certain persons in the society to engage in nonconformist rather than conformist conduct,"[41] Merton singles out for analysis two elements of the social and cultural structure, namely, cultural goals and institutional norms. Social and cultural integration can occur only when there is relative equilibrium between these two components of the structure. When there is disproportionate stress on one or the other, social and cultural malintegration results. Specifically, when "certain aspects of the social structure . . . generate countermores and antisocial behavior precisely because of differential emphases on goals and regulations," then "the integration of the society becomes tenuous and anomie ensues."[42]

Insofar as the correlation between poverty and crime with which we are concerned, poverty and "lack of opportunity" per se do not cause crime. "Poverty is not an isolated variable"[43] and "poverty as such, and consequent limitation of opportunity, are not sufficient to induce a conspicuously high rate of criminal behavior."[44] In fact, there are areas in southeastern Europe which have high poverty rates with very limited opportunities for vertical mobility, that do not have correspondingly high crime rates. So there must be something about poverty and its meaning in the United States which is the source of the high crime rates among the poor. The answer, Merton maintains, lies in certain unique characteristics of American culture.

A major aspect of American culture, says Merton, is the high premium it places on economic affluence for all. Americans are admonished to succeed, the success is defined and demonstrated in terms of pecuniary success. This success ideology pervades throughout the social structure; it is internalized by all the strata. "These goals are held to *transcend class lines*."[45] At the same time that the goal is internalized by all the strata, however, "the actual social organization is such that there exist class differentials in the accessibility of these *common* success-symbols."[46] The farther down one goes in the stratification system, the more he is confronted with restrictions in terms of the availability of legitimate means for achieving the success goal. This conflict between culture goals-success, and the institutionalized means available for achieving them leads to anomie. "Frustration and thwarted aspiration lead to the search for avenues of es-

cape from a culturally induced intolerable situation; or unrelieved ambi-
tion may eventuate in illicit attempts to acquire the dominant values."[47]
Thus, as the evidence from sections of southeastern Europe indicates, poverty and deprivation in and of themselves do not necessarily lead to crime.
The high correlation between poverty and crime in the United States is due
to the unique aspect of American culture which gives poverty a special
meaning and this induces criminal behavior. "It is only when the full configuration is considered, poverty, limited opportunity and a commonly
shared system of success symbols, that we can explain the higher association between poverty and crime in our society than in others where rigidi-
fied class structure is coupled with differential class symbols of achievement."[48]

It is at this point in the literature that much of the discussion of poverty
is intertwined with a discussion of race and ethnic relations. Because the
majority of the members of a particular racial or ethnic group may be perceived as in a state of poverty, as in the case of the black American, the
study of one necessarily involves the study of the other. A number of the
sociological studies of the black Americans of that period will, therefore,
now be examined, in an attempt to extract a perception of the poor.

Having completed his graduate work at the University of Chicago,
E. Franklin Frazier may be seen as a "chip off the old block," in the sense
that his theoretical approach and his methodology are Chicago true. In an
essay entitled "Theoretical Structure of Sociology and Sociological Research,"[49] Frazier stated his approach: "The various systems of social relationships which come into existence as the result of association are, according to our view, the proper subject matter of sociology. A social system
may consist of a family group, a labor union, or a nation. The character of
the social system depends upon such matters as the spatial distribution of
people, the division of labour, institutions, social stratification, and the nature of contacts and communication among its members."[50]

Frazier's most important book is *The Negro Family in the United
States*,[51] wherein he traces the social conditions which shaped the (patho-
logical) condition of the lower-class black family. Having been brought to
this country as slaves, and having "often been subjected to influences that
tended to destroy the significance and meaning of their African heritage,"[52] all that remained of the African heritage was "scraps of memories,
which form only an insignificant part of the growing body of traditions in
Negro families."[53] As slaves, the instability of marriage and family was assured, for "the duration of marriage as well as its inception was subject to
the whim of the masters."[54] Under such conditions, "only the bond between
the mother and her child continually resisted the disruptive effect of economic interests that were often inimical to family life among slaves. Consequently, under all conditions of slavery, the Negro mother remained the

most dependable and important figure in the family."[55] Emancipation pre-
cipitated geographic mobility and this "tore the Negro from his customary
familial attachments."[56] With many black men and women roving about
"aimlessly" or looking for adventure and a job, the South set up a vast system of laws which, for all intents and purposes, reenslaved the Negro. The
matriarchal system that resulted from the slave situation thus continued
and even extended. Following World War I, there was a mass migration of
Negroes from the South to the industrial North resulting from the demand
for labor in northern industries brought on by the war. "The sudden descent of this vast human tide upon a few northern cities constituted a
flight, replete with dramatic episodes, from medieval to modern America."[57] Most of those migrating masses settled in the four major cities which
most demanded unskilled labor: New York, Philadelphia, Chicago, and
Detroit. It was in these cities that the inpouring blacks saw their opportunity to improve their economic and social condition. Large black communities sprang up in these northern cities, and their character is the result of
social forces, and not simply "white racism." Frazier maintained that "a
close scrutiny of these communities reveals that, while race prejudice has
not been altogether a negligible factor, the general character of these Negro communities has been determined by the same economic and cultural
forces that have shaped the organization of the community as a whole."[58]
The general character of these communities, specifically, "the poverty and
disorganization of Negro family life in the urban environment,"[59] can be
understood only when one understands the social and economic forces
which determine their development. The most important characteristics of
the urban black family are family desertion by fathers, illegitimacy and
juvenile delinquency, all of which are products of rapid urbanization upon
the post-slavery condition. As Frazier concluded: "The urbanization of the
Negro population since 1900 has brought about the most momentous
change in the family life of the Negro since emancipation. This movement,
which has carried over a million Negroes to southern cities alone, has torn
the Negro loose from his cultural moorings. Thousands of these migrants
have been solitary men and women who have led a more or less lawless sex
life during their wanderings. But many more illiterate or semi-literate and
impoverished Negro families, broken or held together only by the fragile
bonds of sympathy and habit, have sought a dwelling place in the slums of
southern cities. Because of the dissolution of the rural folkways and mores,
the children in these families have helped to swell the ranks of juvenile de-
linquents."[60] The significance of Frazier's hypothesis that the rise in the
delinquency rate is due to "the dissolution of the rural folkways and
mores," will become evident shortly. Frazier continues: "Likewise, the
bonds of sympathy and community of interests that held their parents together in the rural environment have been unable to withstand the disinte-

grating forces in the city. Illegitimacy, which was more or less harmless in the country, has become a serious economic and social problem."[61] The urbanization of blacks was even more rapid during and following World War I, and the northern migration became even more significant than the earlier southern movement, because "the migration of the Negro to northern cities has forced him into a much more rigorous type of competition with whites than he has ever faced." Social workers held useless "conferences on the housing conditions of Negroes (and) they have been forced finally to face the fundamental fact of the Negro's poverty. Likewise, social and welfare agencies have been unable to stem the tide of family disorganization that has followed as a natural consequence of the impact of modern civilization upon the folkways and mores of a simple peasant folk."[62] Thus, to Frazier, urbanization has destroyed the old cultural life, or what was left of it, and this destruction of the folkways and mores in turn is the source of the social disorganization and poverty of the black community.

In 1940–41, four studies commissioned by the American Council on Education that dealt with aspects of the personality development of black youth were published. The studies are: *Children of Bondage*: *The Personality Development of Negro Youth in the Urban South*, by Allison Davis and John Dollard;[63] *Negro Youth at the Crossways*: *Their Personality Development in the Middle States*, by E. Franklin Frazier;[64] *Growing up in the Black Belt*: *Negro Youth in the Rural South*, by Charles S. Johnson;[65] and *Color and Human Nature*: *Negro Personality Development in a Northern City*, by W. Lloyd Warner, Bulford H. Junker, and Walter A. Adams.[66] Many of the basic issues and questions that divided the culturalists and structuralists during the 1960s find expression in these pioneering works.

Davis and Dollard, using the orientation of the as then yet unpublished "Yankee City" series of W. Lloyd Warner and associates and Dollard's *Caste and Class in A Southern Town*,[67] found classes differing in expectations, repressions, punishments and rewards, and types of anxiety that they produce in their youth. The black youth of the lower class, as a result of the permissiveness of their class, are able to realize their goal responses of aggression and sex, whereas middle and upperclass black youth conform to the values of their classes which repress aggression. The most important factor influencing the personality development of black adolescents is social class, with caste of only secondary importance. "The sanctions of class position, as enforced by the family, the clique, and the larger class environment, are among the most important controls in the formation of human habits."[68] And in a footnote to the above the authors remark that, "It necessarily follows, then, that these class controls are an equally important source of *resistance* to efforts by educators, social workers, or politicians to change the motivation and habits of individuals in our society."[69] Their conclusion regarding the strength of "class controls" as a source of resistance to change is precisely that which formed the crux of the culturalist perspective, of which Oscar Lewis and Walter B. Miller are usually regarded as the original proponents.

Frazier states explicitly that he was attempting "to determine what kind of a person a Negro youth is or is in the process of becoming as a result of the limitations which are placed upon his or her participation in the life of the communities of the border states."[70] After interviewing 200 youth between the ages of 9 and 23 years, Frazier classified their responses according to the socioeconomic status or class of their parents, and analyzed them in terms of differential class feelings. Lower class black youth were found to be "influenced in their conceptions of themselves as Negroes by their parents' acceptance of the belief that the Negro is inferior and that his subordination to the white man is inevitable."[71] Because of his acceptance of inferior position, and being convinced of the almost impossibility of achieving significant employment, "many lower-class youth are becoming convinced that illegal and antisocial means of making a living must be resorted to and are justified."[72] Having been isolated "by their poverty and lower level of culture,"[73] these youth in the border states are unaffected by social movements and ideologies which prevail in the large northern areas. In sum, "the *culture, traditions,* and *economic position* of the family determine not only the type of discipline to which the child is subjected but the manner in which he develops his conception of himself as a Negro. . . . Because of the limitations which make impossible free and easy participation in the larger community, his attitudes and overt behavior will show more or less the influence of the isolated social world to which he is confined."[74]

Charles S. Johnson, in his study of black youth, *Growing up in the Black Belt,* found conditions in the cotton plantations of the rural South similar to those reported in the previous studies. "Poverty and ignorance imprison the lowest economic classes in a low cultural and social world. In the lower economic group of the rural Negro population, the families are not only poor but on the whole disorganized socially."[75] Lower class black youth find greater difficulty than other youth in achieving social mobility, and as a result live a free life "that acknowledges little responsibility to accepted standards."[76] Since they cannot achieve recognition and esteem through the socially approved channels, they seek their esteem through sexual and physical prowess and through other forms of antisocial or deviant behavior. Johnson here makes a very important point, which seems to differ somewhat from the view expressed by Frazier. He states that, "this does not mean, however, that all members of this group are morally disorganized. Many of the families are merely uneconomic units which are incapable of self-support, because the number of young children, old persons, or other nonearning members is too great for the earning capacity of the breadwinners. *They may be sensitive to community values* but forced to live only as conditions permit, whether their social behavior is sanctioned or not."[77] Thus, Johnson saw the antisocial behavior of lower-class Negro youth as resulting essentially from their economic position, whereas Frazier saw it as the result of economic conditions combined with their "culture" and "traditions."

W. Lloyd Warner and his associates produced the "Yankee City" series and provided the conceptual framework within which social classes are seen as developing unique class cultures. The key to the approach is in their defintion of social class, which they see as more than simply economic position.[78] "Social class refers to levels which are recognizable in the general behavior and social attitudes of the people of the whole community where such levels exist. Although economic factors are of prime importance and are some of the principal determinants of social class, they are insufficient to account for all social-class behavior or for its presence in contemporary America."[79] Social classes are distinguishable on the basis of two sets of variables: objective factors, such as occupation and income; and subjective factors, such as values and attitudes. The objective and subjective factors taken together are what make up the "style of life" of social classes.

The general picture of the lower-lower class as reported by Warner is that it has the highest birth rate of all classes; the smallest percentage of elderly people (over 60); the greatest number of people with ethnic affiliations (blacks, Poles, Russians, Greeks, French-Canadians, and Italians); the earliest age of first marriage; the highest percentage of unskilled and semiskilled workers; the highest percentage of unemployed and part-time employed, and people on relief; the smallest number of property owners, and homes of least value; the highest rate of poor housing conditions; the highest percentage of arrests and earliest age of arrests; and a higher percentage of children at work than any other class.[80]

August B. Hollingshead, an associate of Warner, studied "The Impact of Social Classes on Adolescents," and reported his findings in *Elmtown's Youth*.[81] His research was conducted between June 1941 and December 1942, and his hypothesis was that "the social behavior of adolescents appears to be related functionally to the positions their families occupy in the social structure of the community."[82] Hollingshead found five major prestige classes, which correlate almost identically with Warner's classes.

The "cultural characteristics" of Class V, that class which "occupies the lowest-ranking stations in the prestige structure,"[83] include passivity and fatalism. "Class V persons give the impression of being resigned to a life of frustration and defeat in a community that despises them for their disregard of morals, lack of 'success' goals, and dire poverty."[84] The incomes, occupations, and housing conditions of this class are the same as reported in Warner's description of the lower-lower class, above. Hollingshead adds some more details of the family pattern. "The family pattern is unique. the husband-wife relationship is more or less an unstable one. . . . The evidence indicates that few compulsive factors, such as neighborhood solidarity, religious teachings, or ethical considerations, operate to maintain a stable marital relationship. On the contrary, *the class culture has established a family pattern where serial monogamy is the rule*. . . . Marriage occurs in the middle teens for the girls and the late teens or early twenties for the boys. Doctors, nurses, and public officials who know these families best estimate that from one-fifth to one-fourth of all births are illegitimate. . . . Another trait that marks the family complex is the large number of children. The mean is 5.6 per mother, the range, 1 to 13. There is little pre-natal or post-natal care of either mother or child. . . . Death, desertion, separation, or divorce has broken more than half the families (56 percent). The burden of child care, as well as support, falls on the mother more often than on the father when the family is broken. The mother-child relation is the strongest and most enduring tie."[85]

Among the other reported characteristics were low level of education, weak or no religious ties, almost total isolation from community activities, and a high rate of official contact with representatives of the legal system, such as police, prosecutors, and judges.

With the introduction of the notion of class culture and its effects upon its members, Warner and Hollingshead opened up a "Pandora's box," which resulted in a proliferation of studies attempting to demonstrate the relationship between social class and such variables as child-rearing, crime and delinquency, education, leisure time activities, marriage and marital stability, manifestations of types of mental illness, morality, occupation, opportunities, personality, political behavior, religion, and values, among others. During the 1940s and 1950s there were numerous studies of the "cultures" of the various social classes, and the literature is replete with references to lower-class culture, working-class culture, middle-class culture, and upper-class culture.

The stage was thereby set for anthropologist Oscar Lewis to posit a "culture of poverty" as a framework for explaining the condition of the various families which he studied. The concept was first introduced by Lewis in 1959, with the publication of his *Five Families: Mexican Case Studies in the Culture of Poverty*,[86] and Lewis elaborated on the concept in a number of his subsequent publications.[87]

Notes

1. Waxman, Chaim I., *The Stigma of Poverty: A Critique of Poverty Theories and Policies* (New York: Pergamon Press, 1977), ch. 1 & 2.
2. Bernard, L.L., and Jessie Bernard, *Origins of American Sociology* (New York: Thomas Y. Crowell Co., 1943), p. 562.

3. Ward, Lester, *Applied Sociology*, reprinted in Henry S. Commager, *Lester Ward and the Welfare State* (Indianapolis and New York: The Bobbs-Merrill Co., 1967), p. 355.
4. Ward, Lester, *American Journal of Sociology*, vol. XIII (1968), pp. 623–27; reprinted in Commager, *Lester Ward*, pp. 403–408.
5. Commager, *Lester Ward*, p. 172.
6. Ibid., p. 349.
7. Ibid., p. 428.
8. Ibid.
9. Sumner, William Graham, *Folkways* (1906; new edition, New York: Dover Publications, 1959).
10. Ibid., p. 41.
11. Ibid., p. 50.
12. Ibid., p. 267.
13. Sumner, William Graham, *What Social Classes Owe to Each Other* (1883; reprinted, Caldwell: Caxton Printers, 1966).
14. Ibid., p. 141.
15. Ibid., pp. 97–106.
16. Ibid., p. 19.
17. Cooley, Charles Horton, *Social Organization*, (1909; paperback edition, New Brunswick, N.J.: Transaction Books, 1983), pp. 290–300.
18. Ibid., p. 290.
19. Ibid., p. 291.
20. Ibid., p. 292.
21. Ibid.
22. Ibid., p. 296.
23. Ibid., p. 300.
24. Waxman, *The Stigma of Poverty*, p. 92 ff.
25. Thomas, W.I. and Florian Znaniecki, *The Polish Peasant In Europe and America* (1927; reprinted, New York: Dover Publications, 1958).
26. Thomas, W.I., *Social Organization and Social Personality*, edited with an introduction by Morris Janowitz (Chicago: University of Chicago Press,1966), p. lvi.
27. Thomas, W.I., *The Polish Peasant*, II, p. 1526–27, quoted in Janowitz, *Social Organization*, pp. lvi–lvii.
28. Ibid., p. lvii.
29. *Cf.* Warren C. Haggstrom, "The Power of the Poor," in Chaim I. Waxman (ed.), *Poverty: Power and Politics* (New York: Grosset and Dunlop, 1968), pp. 113–136.
30. Janowitz, *Social Organization*, p. lvi.
31. Faris, Robert E.L., *Chicago Sociology 1920–1932* (San Francisco: Chandler Publishing Co. 1967), p. 40.
32. Park, Robert E., *On Social Control and Collective Behavior*, edited with an introduction by Ralph H. Turner (Chicago: University of Chicago Press, 1967), p. xvi.
33. Ibid., p. 58.
34. Park, Robert E. and Ernest W. Burgess, *The City* (Chicago: University of Chicago Press, 1925), pp. 47–62.
35. Thrasher, Frederick M., *The Gang* (Chicago: University of Chicago Press, 1927).
36. Reckless, Walter C., *The Natural History of Vice Areas in Chicago* (Chicago: University of Chicago Press, 1933).

37. Zorbaugh, Harvey W., *The Gold Coast and the Slum* (Chicago: University of Chicago Press, 1921).
38. Anderson, N., *The Hobo* (Chicago: University of Chicago Press, 1923).
39. Park, Robert E., "Human Behavior in Urban Environment," in Park and Burgess, *The City*, p.4 (emphasis added).
40. Merton, Robert K., "Social Structure and Anomie," *American Sociological Review*, vol. 3 (1938), pp. 672–682.
41. Ibid., p. 672.
42. Ibid., p. 674.
43. Ibid., p. 680.
44. Ibid., p. 681.
45. Ibid., p. 680.
46. Ibid.
47. Ibid.
48. Ibid., p. 681.
49. Frazier, E. Franklin, "Theoretical Structure of Sociology and Sociological Research," *British Journal of Sociology*, Vol. 4 (1953), pp. 292–311. Reprinted in *E. Franklin Frazier on Race Relations*, edited with an introduction by G. Franklin Edwards (Chicago: University of Chicago Press, 1968), pp. 3–29.
50. Edwards, G. Franklin, Ibid., p. 4.
51. Frazier, E. Franklin, *The Negro Family in the United States* (original ed. 1939, all references are to the revised and abridged edition with new foreword by Nathan Glazer, Chicago: University of Chicago Press, 1966).
52. Ibid., p. 7.
53. Ibid., p. 15.
54. Ibid., p. 30.
55. Ibid., p. 32.
56. Ibid., p. 209.
57. Ibid., p. 225.
58. Ibid., p. 232.
59. Ibid., p. 243.
60. Ibid., p. 363.
61. Ibid.
62. Ibid., p. 364.
63. Davis, Allison and John Dollard, *Children of Bondage: The Personality Development of Negro Youth in the Urban South* (paperback edition, New York: Harper Torch Books, 1964).
64. Frazier, E. Franklin, *Negro Youth at the Crossways: Their Personality Development in the Middle States* (paperback edition with introduction by St. Clair Drake, New York: Schocken Books, 1967).
65. Johnson, Charles S., *Growing Up in the Black Belt: Negro Youth in the Rural South* (paperback edition with introduction by St. Clair Drake, New York: Schocken Books, 1967).
66. Warner, W. Lloyd et al., *Color and Human Nature: Negro Personality Development in a Northern City* (paperback edition, New York: Harper Torch Books, 1969).
67. Dollard, John, *Caste and Classes in a Southern Town* (New Haven: Yale University Press, 1937).
68. Davis and Dollard, *Children of Bondage*, p. 259.
69. Ibid.
70. Ibid., p. 261.

71. Ibid., p. 263.
72. Ibid., p. 166.
73. Ibid., p. 169.
74. Ibid., p. 268 (emphasis added).
75. Johnson, Charles S., *Growing Up in the Black Belt*, p. 98.
76. Ibid., p. 99.
77. Ibid. (emphasis added). For a similar hypothesis with respect to black street-corner men in Washington, D.C., see Elliot Liebow, *Tally's Corner* (Boston: Little, Brown, 1967), p. 222.
78. Warner, W. Lloyd, *Yankee City*, abridged edition (New Haven and London: Yale University Press, 1963). This is an abridgement of the five volume series published between 1941–59 (researched between 1930–35).
79. Ibid., p. xvi.
80. Ibid., p. 262–265.
81. Hollingshead, August B., *Elmtown's Youth: The Impact of Social Classes on Adolescents* (paperback edition, New York: John Wiley and Sons Science Editions, 1961).
82. Ibid., p. 9.
83. Ibid., p. 110.
84. Ibid., p. 111.
85. Ibid., pp. 116–117 (emphasis added).
86. Lewis, Oscar, *Five Families: Mexican Case Studies in the Culture of Poverty* (New York: Basic Books, 1959).
87. Lewis, Oscar, *The Children of Sanchez* (New York: Random House, 1961); *La Vida: A Puerto Rican Family in the Culture of Poverty — San Juan and New York* (New York: Random House, 1966). Also see Lewis' response to critiques of his concept, *Current Anthropology*, vol. 8 (1967), pp. 480–500.

12.
Pluralism and Ethnicity

Nathan Glazer

Beyond the Melting Pot was written at a rather quiet point in the history of studies of American race and ethnicity.[1] The age of mass immigration had ended long before, in 1924. Little major work on ethnic groups was going on. The sociological classics on the Northern urban Negro were already some time in the past: *Black Metropolis*, by St. Clair Drake and Horace Cayton, for example, had been published in 1945.[2] The flood of detailed historical work on American ethnic groups of the 1970s was still to come (Some of it is directly on the issues raised in *BTMP*, for example, a recent analysis of Jewish and Italian mobility in New York City. But I make no effort in this essay to refer to all the scholarly work done since 1963 that bears on the hypotheses and assertions of *BTMP*).[3] The form and timing of *BTMP* was a product of a series of historical accidents, and perhaps it would not be amiss to record them here.

I may have had thoughts about writing a book on American ethnicity in 1959, but memory is fallible and I am not sure. I had for some time been working on ethnicity in the United States, sometimes intentionally as in *American Judaism* (1957), sometimes inadvertently as in the research for a study of the membership of the American Communist party and its relationship to American social structure, in which ethnic factors turned out to be much more important than class (*The Social Basis of American Communism*, 1961).[4] I had written essays on the role of ethnicity in American life, some of which I thought of as a program for future work. But the project that resulted in *BTMP* grew out of a problem the New York *Post* encountered when it commissioned the writer Irwin Ross to write a series on the Jews of New York. He found that it required a good deal of research and background and that the normal amount of time available for newspaper writing simply would not do the job. Daniel Bell, a friend of Irwin Ross, and of James Wechsler, the editor of the *Post*, suggested a research project on the peoples of New York, funded by the New York Post Foundation, which would produce a quantity of background research material which *Post* writers could use for a series on the ethnic groups of New York City. He broached the idea to me in a

199

letter on 14 August 1959, and I responded with a memorandum outlining a project on "The Peoples of New York City" on 20 September 1959.

At the time I had no institutional affiliation. Martin Meyerson, then Professor of City Planning at Harvard and Director of the newly-founded Joint Center for Urban Studies of Harvard-M.I.T., suggested that I do the work under their auspices, and I liked the idea. A complicated contract between the New York Post Foundation and the Joint Center was then worked out in the early months of 1960, and I began work on what were to be six papers on the ethnic groups of New York City, three to be delivered in six months, three six months later, all to be completed within a year. The New York Post Foundation was to pay $30,000 for me, for assistants, and for associated costs. The New York *Post* did not like the first three on the Negroes, Jews, and Puerto Ricans, and cancelled the contract in November, 1960, after paying out less than half the $30,000 in the project. It nevertheless retained the right to reprint the book free, which it eventually did, and to share in the royalties. The *Post* therefore not only got the articles it wanted, but in the end probably got back all it put into the project from its share of the royalties.

I continued work nevertheless. The Joint Center did continue to support the project, and the writing was substantially complete in September 1961 when I left for a seven-month stay in Japan. It had always been my intention to recruit associates to write some of the specific essays. It turned out that my only collaborator was to be Daniel P. Moynihan, then at the Maxwell Graduate School of Citizenship and Public Affairs at Syracuse University. No one else with whom I had discussed collaboration responded as immediately and as empathetically to my sense of American ethnicity and its role as he did, and his chapter on the Irish, which bears all the marks of a distinguished and distinctive style and a subtle mind, fulfilled perfectly the scheme and approach I was trying to realize.

Five groups were covered; my original intention of writing an essay on German-Americans or white Anglo-Saxon Americans was given up in favor of some discussion of these groups in an introduction. When I left for Japan, the book still needed an introduction and conclusion; these were fashioned in 1962, after my return, while Moynihan and I were both working in Washington. *BTMP* is a book thus written mostly in 1960 and 1961, and published in 1963, at which point race relations in the United States were exploding, and a rather quiet period in the study of ethnicity and race was coming to a dramatic end.

BTMP suggested what was at the time a somewhat original way of looking at ethnicity in the United States. Ethnicity, from the point of view developed in the book, was not simply a survival from the age of mass immigration from Europe which had come to an end in 1924, and therefore fated to become less and less significant with the passage of time. Looking at New York City in

1959, ethnicity rather seemed remarkably strong in certain key respects thirty-five years after the end of mass immigration, in particular, in shaping politics, and in affecting the moral outlooks which were a significant part of politics. Nevertheless, it was also perfectly clear that the immigrants and their children and grandchildren had been transformed, and were no longer Italians or Poles or Irishmen who happened to be living in America—they *were* Americans. What the situation in New York City suggested was that ethnicity was a new social form that had been created in the American environment, and further that American society had been structured since the early nineteenth century so as to expect and in measure create the kinds of ethnic differences that were so prominent in New York City twenty years ago. As we wrote:

> It is striking that in 1963, almost forty years after mass immigration from Europe to this country ended, the ethnic pattern is still so strong in New York City. It is true we can point to specific causes that have served to maintain the pattern. But we know it was not created by the great new migrations of Southern Negroes and Puerto Ricans into the city; nor by the "new" immigration, which added the great new communities of East European Jews and Italians to the city; it was not even created by the great migration of Irish and Germans in the 1840's. Even in the 1830's, while the migration from Europe was still mild, and still consisted for the most part of English-speaking groups, one still finds in the politics of New York State, and of the city, the strong impress of group differentiation. In a fascinating study of the politics of the Jacksonian period in New York State, Lee Benson concludes: "At least since the 1820's, when manhood suffrage became widespread, ethnic and religious differences have tended to be *relatively* the most widespread sources of political difference" (Lee Benson, *The Concept of Jacksonian Democracy*, Princeton, New Jersey, 1961, p. 165).
>
> There were ways of making distinctions among Welshmen and Englishmen, Yorkers and New Englanders, long before people speaking strange tongues and practicing strange religions came upon the scene. The group-forming characteristics of American social life—more concretely, the general expectation among those of new and old groups that group membership is significant and formative for opinion and behavior—are as old as the city. The tendency is fixed deep in American life generally; the specific pattern of ethnic differentiation, however, in every generation is created by specific events.[5]

This was at that time a somewhat new and different way of looking at American ethnicity. I do not think that scholarship on ethnic groups in the United States, whether sociological or historical, had suggested before the possibility—I leave aside for the moment the degree to which it can be sustained—that the ethnic group in the United States was in some important sense not a survival but a form propped up, and shaped by, processes in American life. The quotation suggests political processes, and that is certainly an important part of the story. Samuel Lubell had already, in a book that influenced me greatly, shown that ethnic influences on voting survived long after the time the group in question was considered to be fully assimilated. His examples were the Germans and the old English settlers, and he explained the strong anti-interventionist stand of the Midwest and the interventionist stand of the South on World War II in terms of the German and English background of the settlers of the two regions.[6]

I did not try to develop any systematic theory of this notion of ethnic re-creation. *BTMP* suggested strongly that specific occupational concentrations, characteristic of each group because of the time of its arrival and the nature of its resources in education, money, and experience at the time of arrival, characterized each group. This supported a group fellow-feeling, and made the group an interest-group in the economic sense (and therefore susceptible to specific interest-group political appeals) as well as an interest-group in the more direct ethnic sense. In an ethnic group, one might expect to find an interest in the home country, or the maintenance of religion and culture. Economic and ethnic interests came in bundles. "Jewish," "Puerto Rican," "Italian," I argued, was not an inaccurate shorthand for certain class interests; the terms described an interest group as well as such terms as trade-union members, or unskilled workers, or welfare recipients, or shopkeepers, and perhaps the ethnic term was more meaningful, politically.

There was another aspect of *BTMP* that was, if not original, a new emphasis in the treatment of ethnicity. It was that ethnic groups were indeed different. One must recall that the spirit of 1959 was still one shaped by the aftermath of the war against Hitler, and part of our propaganda effort in that war—one in which social scientists as well as publicists and politicians were engaged—was to argue that there were no meaningful differences among groups. If these differences were ascribed to race, genetic inheritance, I agreed; but if the further argument was that all observable differences were simply the result of different degrees of prejudice and discrimination, and a different stage in the inevitable progress of acculturation and assimilation, I disagreed. Much of my early reading had been in anthropology, and while undoubtedly ethnic groups in America did not differ as much as Ruth Benedict's Kwakiutl and Hopi in culture, they did differ, and these differences helped determine their experiences. Through both the direct influence of culture as well as of historical experience shaped to some degree by culture, groups continued to be different. Genetic inheritance played no part in this; cultural inheritance did. And it was for this reason that in the discussion of each group I included a section on family and its influences, and scoured psychiatric and social-work literature, for there one had the greatest opportunity to find ways in which family style differed from group to group.

I was influenced by a line of work that is now almost forgotten, and certainly not now much followed: the studies of national and social character that had been pursued by Margaret Mead, Geoffrey Gorer, Abram Kardiner, and others. In this style of work, differences rather than similarities among ethnic and national groups were pursued, emphasized, and perhaps overemphasized. But I suspect I was also influenced by reading detailed ethnic history and by Robert E. Park, not by his well known formulation of a race-relations cycle through which groups move from conflict to assimilation, but by the fascinating concrete materials of his book, *The Immigrant Press and Its Control*, which suggested that the process of assimilation would be no simple and uniform one, but that immigrant groups could proceed on many courses and through many stages.[7]

The concerns of *BTMP* were analytical, rather than policy-oriented. In this respect, it reflected an earlier orientation in social science, rather than the one that was to become prominent in the 1970s. In 1960–61, there was little in the way of policy manifestly designed to raise the condition of one ethnic group or another. The Japanese-Americans had recovered from the World War II disaster on their own, without even thinking much of getting government compensation; American Indians were not yet gaining enormous sums in compensation for past wrongs; and black Americans were not thinking of compensation or compensatory public action, only of getting nationally the kind of protection they had against discrimination in New York and other advanced states. It was still a world in which it was expected that people and ethnic groups would advance on their own, without much in the way of solicitous concern from government.

Looking back from 1981, we see strangely enough that once again many voices argue that people should make it on their own, with the role of government limited to getting out of their way rather than directly assisting them through public action. That, at least, is the mood of the present administration. In between, of course, there has been an enormous expansion of public programs, and even the cutbacks that at this writing agitate minority leaders and representatives aim at reductions that would bring us back, at worst, to 1977, rather than 1961.

Thus one change since 1960–61 is our greater concern with public action to affect differential minority achievement. This was not much in our minds while *BTMP* was being written, though Moynihan, much more attuned to public action and the possibilities of public action because of his experience in government, began during his service in the Labor Department in Washington to demonstrate, with many ingenious proposals, what public action might do to positively affect black Americans and assist their rise.

In so doing, he undoubtedly deflected a good deal of criticism that might have been directed at *BTMP* (and indeed was), because his report on the Negro family in 1965 became the subject of an enormous national debate.[8] Moynihan in his research had gone considerably beyond *BTMP*. In particular he had discovered a striking anomaly—that the rise in female-headed families was in the early 1960s no longer directly related to the unemployment rate (as it was not to be for the next two decades, as it rose inexorably). While he pointed to the family as the source of many black problems—as did *BTMP*, owing to its emphasis on culture and social character that I have referred to above—he proposed action basically in the realm of economic opportunity. But that did not help him. The differences among groups that *BTMP* discussed in an analytic framework became dynamite when raised in a political and governmental action framework.

On this issue, *BTMP* saw little that government could do, and in this sense lacked imagination. Improvement in the economic situation, as well as in education, and in the attitudes, behavior and competence of public agencies, it argued, were all important.[9] But it came down strongest on what we can only call self-help: "Institutions organized, supported and staffed by Negroes might be much more effective than the government and private agencies that now deal with these problems."[10] And in the conclusion to the section on Negroes, once again this theme was emphasized.[11] This was, as I have pointed out, before the great increase in government efforts. We are now in the lee of that vast enterprise. It still continues, but in bureaucratic forms, formalistically, without much enthusiasm or hope. And black leaders now, only on occasion but more frequently in the past, say that if it is to be done, blacks will have to do it.

On the other great "problem" group in New York City, the Puerto Ricans, *BTMP* was overoptimistic, and this optimism was even, alas, maintained in the long introduction to the 1970 edition, when enough had happened to raise serious alarm signals. It was the simple fact that more Puerto Ricans than blacks were engaged in small business enterprise that suggested to me that they were basically on the same track as previous ethnic groups. I was wrong. Twenty years after, the Puerto Rican community suffers from severe social problems, and has not gotten much further up the rungs of economic and political advancement, though undoubtedly more second generation Puerto Ricans are to be found in professional and middle-class employment.

What went wrong? *BTMP* did not emphasize as strongly for Puerto Ricans as for blacks a distinctive social and cultural background to problems, but it did point to the problem of the family, with its system of consensual marriage and early pregnancy, and too frequent pattern of male abandonment of mother and children, in the island, and on the mainland. We have not had an explosion of controversy on the Puerto Rican family as we did on the black family, but in fact there were enough significant differences between the Caribbean family and that of European immigrants, peasant or urban, to have directed attention to its possible importance. The controversy—of a distinctly lesser sort—did accompany the publication of Oscar Lewis's *La Vida* in 1966.[12]

I do not feel that the concentration on family background, or, as the anthropologists put it "culture," the inheritance of customs, values, habits and attitudes that have been shaped in the past by distinctive experience, was overdone in *BTMP*. But it is true that one great determinant of change and opportunity was neglected: the place of New York City in the American economy, and the threat to it as a city of economic opportunity. This is not the place to detail or analyze what happened to New York in the 1970s, and what might have been foreseen in the 1960s. New York suffered from a hemorrhaging of industrial and semi-skilled jobs, the kind that had been the stepping stones upward for the European immigrants of the decades between 1880 and 1920. Simultaneously, following national policy (and continuing it through the early Nixon years under the administration of John Lindsay), New York City and New York State, under Governor Rockefeller, enormously expanded governmental expenditures for the poor, rapidly expanded programs of welfare, social service, and education, imposing a disproportionate burden of taxation on business and industry. All this was added to the disadvantages of the older Northeastern cities: location in an area that was growing more slowly, wider unionization, higher taxation, greater difficulties in acquiring land for the newly favored single-story industrial structures with plenty of open land for parking and delivery and shipment (New York's factories, clothing, printing, and others, had been uniquely and remarkably, located in high multi-story structures on crowded streets). Further, public opinion tended to be hostile to business and industry—not surprising in a city where there were far, far more tenants than landlords or home-owners.

BTMP did not explore the larger economic setting in which all groups would have to make their way in New York City, and the national economic setting within which New York might suffer disadvantage. Had we done so, we could have argued that ethnicity was still closely connected with New York City's decline. Business and industry moved not only to escape unions and taxation, but also to find more willing labor. Willing labor was not only easier to find in the Pennsylvania countryside, or even further afield, but New York's welfare and social services, so heavily expanded in response to its liberal political climate (and much of that was owing to Jewish predominance), reduced the willingness of labor to take jobs at low wages. Conceivably there were also cultural factors that made labor of different ethnic backgrounds more acceptable to employers than blacks and Puerto Ricans. Thus many elements interacted in the decline of New York: its age, geographical setting, political traditions, public policy, and the backgrounds of those who potentially were available to take poorly paid jobs. Ethnic factors were certainly important for the last three elements. How to evaluate them would be difficult to say, and they are almost impossible to quantify. But any conversation with an employer suggests they were important.

Ethnic studies have expanded greatly since *BTMP*, and possibly some small influence might be detected from the book itself.[13] There has been an enormous amount of historical work, a great deal of sociological work, even more polemical and popular work of all types. One major political trend, and some minor ones, have shaped discussion of ethnicity, and require some comment. The major political trend was the rapid rise and success, marked by major legislation, of a black and white civil rights movement, followed by more exclusively black movements, separatist and radical, at the turn of the 1960s, and succeeded by a steadier black presence, increasingly dominated by elected leaders in city halls and legislatures rather than by voluntary groups such as the NAACP and the Urban League. Parallel to this, but of lesser weight, have been similar political developments among Mexican Americans, Puerto Ricans, Asian-Americans, and American Indians. These political developments spurred the rise of ethnic studies movements concentrated on each of these groups, and the publication of a great deal of literature, and texts for teaching purposes, with varying admixtures of the popular, polemical, and scholarly represented. This complex of factors helped create a milder parallel white ethnic development, with its organizations, its efforts to affect policy, its ethnic studies interests and the like. None of this was foreseen or suggested in *BTMP*; undoubtedly much in these developments was spurred by the greater involvement of government in policies affecting ethnic and racial groups, and by its involvement even in policies directly impinging on the work of cultural maintenance that ethnic groups had once done for themselves (bilingual and bicultural programs, ethnic heritage support programs, and the like).

This has raised a number of questions that were not considered in *BTMP*. On the large questions of whether ethnicity should be maintained, strengthened, weakened, or ignored, *BTMP* took no position. It specifically asserted it was not a book of advocacy for cultural pluralism or assimilation, but, despite its occasional sprightliness, a book of analysis: what ethnicity meant, not what it should mean.[14] In other contexts, the authors have taken various stands on these matters. Nor did *BTMP* insist, as some think, that ethnicity, interpreted as attachment to language, culture, heritage, would not weaken over time. In these respects ethnicity does weaken, but it seems still to be of significance in shaping behavior, response, attitude, and it was hard then—and it is hard now—to foresee the developments that would change this. The weakening and even disappearance of original culture need not change attachment to ethnic interests, both because of the new creation of an ethnic-class interest group, and also of what can only be called emotional attachments to a people, even if its members in distant lands no longer share much in the way of culture with those who considered themselves, in the United States, the same people.

The most striking example of this is the close relationship of Jews with Israel. Israel was by 1960–61 very far from a country of East European immigrants; by 1981 it is even further, more than half consisting of Jews of African and Asian origin who never knew Yiddish, and most of the rest now Hebrew-speaking. This did little to weaken the links between American Jews and Israel, which were stronger in the 1970s than they had been in the 1950s. It was the danger to Israel that seemed to drive this relationship, not simply cultural and linguistic ties. One suspects that if Italy or Poland could possibly face the same danger of annihilation Israel did, one might see a similar response.

This kind of ethnic interest, while it might definitely ebb and flow, and one might in time find that it meant little, was already familiar to political and other analysts when *BTMP* was written. What was less familiar was the creation, within each ethnic group, of a moral outlook that was to some extent distinctive and that shaped politics. We described this moral outlook for Jews, Italians, and Irish. It is interesting that some issues most susceptible to moral responses have entered politics and have taken a much larger role since 1960–61. The abortion issue was turned into a national political issue by the Supreme Court, and one of the most bitterly fought in American politics. Interventions in the schools—busing, prayer, discipline—have all raised moral issues, and the responses to them have been shaped by the ethno-religious complex of attitudes that is distinctive to each group. One can interpret these responses in class terms, and indeed class does help explain why, for example, on the whole Jews support abortion and Italian Americans oppose it, and one can see differences by class within each group. But it would be naive to deny that the specific experience of each group, with religion, with family, with ethnic heritage, has not also shaped these responses.

Much of the argument within sociology over ethnicity has dealt with the relative weight of class factors and ethnic factors in shaping response and behavior. Mixed in with this has been a second major argument: whether blacks should be seen as another ethnic group—different from each, of course, as each is different from the other—or as quite different in American society, a group shaped by its race and by forced migration and slavery, and thus part of no continuum of ethnic groups, however diverse from one another, but a quite separate category in American life, requiring a different analysis, and different policies if it is to achieve rough equality with other groups. Mexican Americans, Puerto Ricans, Asian Americans, American Indians, can be in varying degree seen in the same light—defined differently from white European ethnic groups, either by race, or conquest, or state discrimination. The thesis of basic difference was perhaps first put forward by Robert Blauner, but Ronald Takaki and others have made the same argument, and we are indebted to all these writers for pointing up aspects of the American past and present that had been somewhat obscured in the more optimistic decade of the

1950s.[15] I argued against Blauner's first formulation of his thesis in 1971; I argued against the thesis that American society was basically closed to peoples of different racial origins, or those who had entered American society through forced slavery or conquest, in *Affirmative Discrimination*.[16] One could not disagree that the history of each group was radically different, that the oppression suffered by blacks was unique. But as to the bearing of this past on current opportunities, current policies, one could disagree.

It is inevitable that the argument will be continued, nor is it possible, by the nature of the kind of evidence history and the social sciences bring forth to bear on complex questions of this sort, that we shall ever have a clear answer on one side or the other. Presumably history itself will answer the question. It has in a sense answered it for Chinese and Japanese, and will probably answer it the same way for Koreans, Asian Indians, and Vietnamese. Some peoples of different race "make it" in America, despite an early history of serious discriminatory law and practice. But what of the others, the groups that now clamor for better jobs, higher income, greater representation in high positions of the economy and polity? What explains their situation today, and what policies are thereby suggested?

BTMP, in an earlier day, referred to social background, distinctive history, the nature of the city, and the time of arrival. All analysts engaged in the dispute today agree on the significance of these factors. All participants also agree on the weight and significance of past discriminatory practices in determining the position of each group. Where they disagree is in two other respects: the weight of present discriminatory behavior, and perhaps most important, the weight of present social structure and culture, regardless of its origins. It is understandable that around these issues the dispute should be fierce. If present discrimination is at fault, even stronger measures to fight it than those I criticized in *Affirmative Discrimination* are necessary. If social structure and culture play a substantial role, then one is given pause as to what government can do directly. How does government deal with the 40 percent female-headed family rate among blacks, which brings black income down severely, and which undoubtedly affects in some way to their detriment the children raised in such families?

BTMP, following on the anthropologists who had studied group differences and traced them to family and child-rearing patterns, and influenced by the culture-shaping effects of history, applied a culturally-biased analysis to American ethnic groups. Little enough dispute was created when this was used to explain the differences between Jews and Italians: in time, the Italians did well enough. Fierce controversy broke out when the same analysis was used to explain even in part the differences between blacks and others. Indeed, an effort to do so meant the subject was submerged for fifteen years. One senses it cannot be submerged for much longer, at which point *BTMP* may take on a surprising contemporaneity.[17]

NOTES

1. Nathan Glazer and Daniel P. Moynihan, *Beyond the Melting Pot: The Negroes, Puerto Ricans, Jews, Italians, and Irish of New York City* (Cambridge, Mass. 1963, 2d ed., with a new introduction, 1970); referred to henceforth as *BTMP*.
2. St. Clair Drake and Horace R. Cayton, *Black Metropolis: A Study of Negro Life in a Northern City* (New York, 1945).
3. The two major scholarly publications on ethnic groups in New York City in recent years are Thomas Kessner, *The Golden Door: Italian and Jewish Immigrant Mobility in New York City 1880–1915* (New York, 1977); and Ronald H. Bayor, *Neighbors in Conflict: The Irish, Germans, Jews and Italians of New York City, 1929–1941* (Baltimore, 1978).
4. Nathan Glazer, *American Judaism* (Chicago, 1957); and *The Social Basis of American Communism* (New York, 1961).
5. Glazer and Moynihan, *BTMP*, p. 291.
6. Samuel Lubell, *The Future of American Politics* (New York, 1952).
7. Robert Park, *The Immigrant Press and Its Control* (New York, 1921).
8. Daniel P. Moynihan, "The Negro Family: The Case for National Action," in *The Moynihan Report and the Politics of Controversy*, Lee Rainwater and William C. Yancey (Cambridge, Mass., 1967).
9. Glazer and Moynihan, *BTMP*, p. 43.
10. Ibid., p. 53.
11. Ibid., pp. 84–85.
12. Oscar Lewis, *La Vida: A Puerto Rican Family in the Culture of Poverty—San Juan and New York* (New York, 1966).
13. It has sold widely for a book of this type: almost 300,000 copies in hard cover and paperback. It has also been cited more than 380 times in the *Science Citation Index* and the *Social Sciences Citation Index*—see *Current Contents: Social and Behavioral Sciences*, where it is a "Citation Classic," 7 January 1980.
14. Glazer and Moynihan, *BTMP*, pp. 21–22.
15. Robert Blauner, *Racial Oppression in America* (New York, 1972); Ronald Takaki, *Iron Cages: Race and Culture in Nineteenth-Century America* (New York, 1979).
16. Nathan Glazer, "Blacks and Ethnic Groups: The Difference, and the Political Difference It Makes," *Social Problems* 18 (1971): 444–461; and *Affirmative Discrimination: Ethnic Inequality and Public Policy* (New York, 1975).
17. I have reviewed a number of recent books relevant to this controversy in *The New Republic* (July 4 and 11, 1981): Edna Bonacich and John Modell, *The Economic Basis of Ethnic Solidarity: Small Business in the Japanese American Community* (Berkeley, Ca., 1980). Stanley Lieberson, *A Piece of the Pie: Blacks and White Immigrants since 1880* (Berkeley, Ca., 1980); and Stephen Steinberg, *The Ethnic Myth: Race, Ethnicity, and Class in America* (New York, 1981).

This article originally appeared in the *Journal of American History*, Vol. 1, No. 1 (Fall 1981), pp. 43-55.

13.
Moral Development, Authoritarian Distemper, and the Democratic Persuasion

Irving Louis Horowitz

The problem of moral development is inherent in the coupling of the two words. Few would dispute that there is such a thing as morals, and fewer still that there is another entity called development. Whether they fit together conceptually in a neat, two-tiered package becomes a large question. The present disarray of moral philosophy has not helped. Ethicists are as polarized as can be. One sense of moral development is that it is a historical, evolutionary, and soiological concept of expanding rights. Relativists like Richard Brandt[1] and Abraham Edel[2] have argued this thesis. There is a diametrically opposite view of moral development, advocated by people such as Leo Strauss[3] and Richard Flathman,[4] claiming a normative, natural law foundation to human behavior; the assumption being that social obligations are analogous to mathematical axioms: deduced from a set of first principles.

Relativists and Normativists

Underlying this debate between relativists and normativists is an assumption of the degrees to which options and choices in the world exist. For the relativists, choices are limited only by circumstances, and hence decision making about political issues are historically conditioned searches for rights. For normativists, the world is far less permissive, sometimes even predetermined, and hence the real search ought to be for the foundations of obligations. What is at stake are a series of choices that people make based on fundamental, underlying premises of the rights and wrongs of behavior. For the relativists, morals are constantly evolving in a wide-open universe; whereas for the normativists, choices are made within well understood, or at least well defined social structures. At the risk of turning a drastic oversimplification into caricature: what is good and what is evil for relativists constanty shifts, often according to community norms and changing external pressures. What is good and evil for normativists stays the same, while people do the shifting, achieving higher levels of ethical purification in the process.

A basic form of reconciliation of these two long-standing positions is now in order. Many efforts in this direction are underway. The rise of both the social sciences and policy research may offer some clues as to these new directions. I would propose a retention of the normativist *framework*: what is good and what is evil remains essentially the same now as it did in the world of ancient Athens. But add to this the relativistic *perspective*: what changes drastically are the consequences of choices. At this evel, both political sociology and political psychology can shed light on the subject of moral development.

In the past, we tended to think of homocide as an evil under most circumstances. But we have also viewed terminating life arbitrarily as basically a one-to-one relationship: one person destroying another person. In the twentieth century, the situation is more like one nation destroying another nation. The magnitudes, technically conditioned and depersonalized, so profoundly alter the consequences of behavior that the same moral choices have hugely differing outcomes. There are qualitative leaps in technology that make decisions about life and death critical for large numbers. Social experimentation may permit a reconciliation of natural rights and historical evolution, but only if the evaluative criteria are clearly spelled out and publicly debated.

Several caveats are in order. First, if we mean by moral development a set of goals determined and defined by political leadership for society as good, and departures from those pretested, preset norms as evil, then the phrase simply is a clever disguise for totalitarian temptations. For moral development in this sense means nothing short of the total unification of a society along a certain path, road, or model. In this sense, moral development is but an Orwellian device disguising political repression. Second, and contrariwise, if moral development is viewed in a pluralistic context, as expanding possibilities for making meaningful choices, serving both personal, particular, general, and universal goods, then the phrase "moral development" can be infused with democratic meaning because we are then raising the prospect of development as a moral sensibility which is an attribute of individuals — that is, the ability to place oneself in another individual's position, rather than moral development as an attribute of a social system as a whole. At such a level, moral development is related to cognitive prerequisites rather than collective wills.

Both collective and individual standpoints must be reckoned with. Those societies that have put forth eugenic theories of moral development, such as the Nazi view of the biologically healthy individual, are clearly willing to sacrifice the individual self to the organic whole. Such moral development leads to fantacism and ultimately outlaws all choices and decisions as an attribute of unsponsored individuals. On the other hand, if the development of morals represents a statement of how each individual is ultimately responsible for, and is a repository of, both personal and general goods, then the spirit of democratic interpretation is preserved. Certainly, whether it be John Locke in the British constitutional tradition, or Mohandas K. Gandhi within the Hindi tradition of nonviolent resistance to tyranny, such a view of a morally-centered polity — in which individuals determine their fate — has been of great significance with both the East and West in the evolution of societies.

Moral Strategies and Intellectual Standpoints

Moral development can be viewed epistemologically. The processes of cognition by which citizens learn to distinguish what constitutes right from wrong, or good from evil is a learning situation. In this sense, moral development is a process of socialization. The literature on political socialization is by and large concerned with describing how such concepts are applied to the body politics. Studies of children's reactions to the assassinations of President John F. Kennedy or Martin Luther King, Jr., represent empirical studies on the process of becoming socialized into things political. The work of scholars like Dawson[5] and Zeigler[6] typify such orientations, and can properly be said to constitute a special sort of theory of moral development — one based on experiential adaptation, rather than a didactic set of ritualized commitments.

From the standpoint of political sociology, moral developments can be considered as those kinds of moral postures that come about as a result of class, ethnic, or racial factors. Within such a social framework, moral development refers to the growth of isomorphism between human consciousness and socioeconomic interests. Specifically, moral development is viewed as representing a coalescence of factors between actual stakes in a social order and perceived sorts of political and ideological responses. This aspect of moral development is considerably different from political socialization, for political sociology assumes a correlation between interests and behavior. The work of Marx,[7] and Mannheim,[8] and Scheler,[9] among many others, suggests a special vision of moral development: the development of a set of moral postures based on class positioning and its effects on such "superstructural" features as religion, culture, or race and other ascriptive features.

A third notion of moral development, evolving from the Kantian tradition of transcendental apriorism, and perhaps Platonic sources as well, considers the question of moral development axiomatically, as a process of learning to distinguish truth from falsity. In this way it is assumed that the person comes closer to identifying with the true nature of a political system as he or she accepts the structure of such a system. Politics in this sense represents an axiomatic vision of the moral order. Becoming political is like becoming mathematically adroit, i.e., learning about those axiomatic foundations determines the logical structure of the State (in the case of Plato) or World Order (in the case of Kant).

The psychoanalytic tradition has contributed a fourth perspective on moral development. Even if we ignore the obvious "moralistic" biases of Freudian psychoanalytic theory,[10] Freud — at the conscious level at least — eschewed a moral grounding for mental health or illness. This is not the case with the new Freudians; the views of Erikson on the "ages of man" provide a clear-cut prolegomena to a psychoanalytic theory of moral development.[11] The ages (or better stages) are: oral, anal, phallic, oedipal, latency, and puberty. Without arguing the presumed "intuitive righteousness" of Erikson's ages, as some have, the position of Erikson on theological or political figures like Luther and Gandhi[12] indicates that the postpuberty stage — extending from roughly fourteen to death — involves a powerful moral component of responsibility for behavior not carried or anticipated in the earlier adolescent period.[13]

This notion of anticipatory development, or more inclusive identities, certainly implies a fusion of rational prognosis and moral rightness, or at least the absence of dogmatism, and sensitivity to the diversity and complexity of the human personality. But whether such broad categories can be operationalized, or prevent the arbitrary and capricious rendering of moral acts, is a problem not only faced by Erikson, the veritable father of human development, but by the psychoanalytic tradition as a whole. For while the stages of development in adolescents are essentially behavioral, and by implication not easily subject to adult criteria of morals, just how that moral self penetrates human behavior remains cloudy.

Freud saw in morality a transliteration of superego and censor mechanisms, but how do good works become working good? Civilization and its Discontents describe antagonistic mechanisms of work and sexuality, but not how moral components infuse such broad ranging biosocial categories.[14] There is a commonsensical definition of moral development that is all too easily overlooked among sophisticated analysts. That is the notion of moral development as rendering instruction to the needy — a sort of gerontological vision of advice from the elderly or established to the youthful or needy. More than one wing in the current revival of interest in this subject of moral development has as its hidden agenda a concept of instruction in right morals.[15] In contrast to this, is a briefer, but I daresay equally honorable, tradition in which moral education has to do with the ability to absorb new information without hierarchical or traditional impediments otherwise known as learning.[16] The learning concept is less taken up with status considerations of who does or does not have the right to offer instruction. Learning is a process far more difficult than teaching, since it involves a far more complex art of listening rather than speaking.

If these varieties of moral development can be kept clear of each other, many problems would dissolve along with the linguistic ambiguity and confusions created by overlaping conceptual frameworks. But not only are these standpoints on moral development not properly distinguished, they are further saddled by a world of social psychology in which phrases like human development are viewed as isomorphic with moral development; and more pertinent, in which correlates of cognition and judgment, description and prescription, are muddled beyond belief. As if the situation inherited from the past is not a severe enough handicap, educators have thrown in an additional phrase for good measure: moral education in contrast to affective education.[17] Here we turn full circle, with a strong tendency to equate "fundamental" as normative. Hence, pedagogical conservatives speak of moral education and the political order as an intertwined behavioral process summed up in the restoration of civics and civil behavior.[18] Deficiencies in education rather than inequalities in society are held to strict account for the current "breakdown" and "malaise" presumably characteristic of our times.

The language of breakdown and fragmentation replaces that of social structure and political conflict as crucial explanatory devices. As a consequence, and without too much elaboration, one can see that the ebb and flow of interest in moral development, far from being self-explanatory and transparent, is actually comprised of a series of distinctive policy frameworks: some of which offer the potential for new linkages between events and ethics, others that offer little else but further intellectual disputation, or worse, an end to disputation in order to disguise the paucity of naturalistic solutions to long-standing human problems.

Democratic Persuasions and Authoritarian Distempers

The fusion of moral development, political style, and democratic persuasion takes us from Deweyan to Meadian premises; from pragmatism as a theory of education to symbolic interaction as a theory of politics. Mead understood democracy to mean the ability to absorb information from others; to listen before forming judgments, to take the role of the generalized other as a precondition to action.[19] In this sense, moral education for democracy entails the ability to learn how to absorb alien information about other peoples with different sentiments, values, and interests. This naturalistic vision is the diametrical opposite of a notion that moral education is a matter of "us" teaching "them" right values. Democracy always has had, and will continue to be plagued by a certain ambiguity, an indecisiveness. That is because not knowing everything apriori is a characteristic of the democratic polity.[20] The tentativeness which permits breakdown also is that which makes possible a theory of moral development based on learning new information, rather than instructing others about the virtues of old information.

A democratic theory of politics must take the clear differentiation between moral development and the development of morals. Such a distinction takes on distinctive practical meaning, because it is primarily in the context of statist repression (or permission) that either notion (moral development in contrast to the development of morals) has ultimate significance. Moral development as a brute fact, derived from commonsensical attitudes toward order and civility, is handmaiden to a panoply of authoritarian ideologies. The forms of such an ideology might be thoroughly benign, even genteel, but ultimately the notion of moral development rests on the imposition of behavior through methods of authority or divinity for their realization. At the same time, the notion of the development of morals, in its nature, assumes a plurality and even a plethora of moral standards and standpoints; hence the development of any one set of morals signifies the sorts of codification a society considers essential for its growth and survival.

The democratic persuasion is not an argument claiming the unlimited nature of moral possibilities or the impossibility of assessing relative advantages or disadvantages of one ethical framework against another. It is an assertion that moral choices are not ultimate or revealed verities that deductively or cosmologically flow from the nature of the state. Ethics can be measured by the consequences they yield to the person and the society rather than by the initial goals set for the person or society. Contrariwise, activities of a routine sort can be measured by ethical standards deemed operationally satisfactory, even necessary in specific societal contexts. The democratic position is now back in a world of discourse where the quest is for certitude rather than experience. Certitude blocks out possible lines of enquiry, and hence limits the range of experiences, while experiences tend to produce yet newer experiences, and hence create the grounds for ever-increasing doubt and uncertainty. The choice is by no means an easy one to make, but the consequences have a great bearing on what citizens in a republic expect from their polity.

Quite apart from the need to disaggregate normative and empirical frameworks to examine issues of moral development, it has become evident that the situation in theory basically mirrors conditions in world affairs. It can be said without much fear of contradiction that the twentieth century bears witness to powerful demands for life-giving egalitarianism, in both intimate and international relations. At the same time, it has exposed an underbelly of genocide and impersonal mass murder that has transformed moral issues into engineering issues: i.e., the questions of punishment, execution, burial, etc., are reduced to matters of cost efficiency and double-entry accountancy.[21] In the European nations where the strongest tendencies toward egalitarianism were formerly manifest (for example, socialism in Germany and communism in Russia), there one often found forms of genocide raised to the highest levels of science. Of course, traditional forms of genocide can be found where one might expect: in places such as Paraguay and Uganda. In these latter instances, genocide serves to prevent contact with the developing world. But one must be cautious about offering general theories: forms of democracy are found in unanticipated places, just as genocide takes place in equally unexpected nations.

Genocide is imperfect. After all, the Japanese did survive as a nation despite atomic attacks, and Jews did survive as a people despite mass exterminations. But so too is democracy imperfect. One can easily criticize even the best of the democratic societies with relative ease: from its tolerance of waste to its indecisions on basic human issues. This only points up the need to firmly establish a naturalistic set of criteria for considering moral development, however absolutist we may hold the concept itself. The process of perfecting, rather than a belief in the perfect, is the hallmark of such a view of moral development.

Too often, ideas of the perfect have led to intense fanaticism, to what Arendt[22] and Talmon[23] in different ways have described in terms of totalitarian democracy and political messianism. The process of perfecting is admittedly infuriatingly vague. But it provides the intellectual space that permits free people to operate effectively, if inefficiently. Holding firm to the inefficiencies of such an open-end notion of moral development is a costly affair in economic terms, inviting a certain amount of waste. But to achieve moral development at the price of the political democracy is an unholy trade-off that only assures bureaucratic efficiency in the long run.

Several years ago, Harold Lasswell shrewdly observed that there is a linkage between personality systems and demands for severity. By extension, I think there is also a relationship between demands for moral development as some sort of metaphysical given, and the extensive network of international punishment in the form of global warfare and genocidal conflict. It is worthwhile to appreciate the degree to which concepts such as moral development are little else than disguised choices for sanctioning norms. The warrant for such behavior deserves to be explained by social and behavioral scientists, but not necessarily rationalized. The claims of a society to impose suffering as an end in itself usually carries within itself a further compounded belief that such suffering is warranted for the maintenance of order and the establishment of first principles. But such claims can scarcely withstand anthropological scrutiny. Comparative studies between cultures reveal the relative nature of most — if not all — universal claims. This does not imply that a society should avoid choices, or that some moral systems are superior to others against alien factors and forces.

The danger inheres in the belief that somehow social science can properly sanction what thousands of years of theological edicts and constraints have failed to achieve: a finely tuned theory of moral development. Again, we can scarcely find a better mentor than Lasswell in determining the limits of social science as an agenda-setting network for moral develment.

> We cannot look to the behavioral scientists in their professional capacity to shoulder our individual responsibility for deciding what manner of individuality to seek in ourselves or to permit in our children, or in others whom we influence. But the growth of knowledge will expose the total consequences of conformity as well as of originality or deviation. The crude initial studies of the costs of difference will be supplemented — as indeed they are being supplemented — by studies at the costs of stereotyping and conformity. Already there are indications of the latent problems that arise when talents and propensities are suppressed or repressed out of deference to the steamroller of conformity. These are the issues that rise to plague and embitter the later years of life with a sense of estrangement from experience and a haunting sense of chagrin and guilt for a lifetime of timidity and cowardice. We are engaged in a vast reconstruction of our cultural inheritance in the light of the behavioral sciences. Our conclusion is that the impact upon primary and sanctioning norms has been to bring the practices of our civilization into somewhat closer harmony with the basic ideals of human dignity.[24]

If the democratic persuasion involves choices, then a notion of moral development needs to be enlarged. Helen Merrell Lynd, paraphrasing Guyau, writes: "Not 'I must, therefore I can,' but 'I can, therefore I must.'" Lynd amplifies her view by noting that the scientific temper of discovery poses issues not in terms of morality and immorality, but among conflicting moralities. Writing in the maelstrom of McCarthyism, she put forward that fusion of the democratic temper and scientific credo which offers a solution to the dangerous quest for certainty on one hand and the complete relativizing of values on the other. "Entering fully into the nature of contemporary conflicts calls upon one to make choices beyond coping with difficulties to gain security: beyond the polarity of good on one side, evil on the other; in terms of multiple possibilities. . . . Acting in the faith that there may be ranges of individual and social development as yet unknown requires ability to live with ambiguity and varied probabilities and possibilities."[25] It would be difficult to find a better prolegomenon for democratic policy making, and at the same time, a surer grounding for core principles from which can be derived a democratic vision of morals in development.

Rights, Obligations, and Moral Development

Getting beyond prolegomena and resolving ambiguities becomes the next, and by far the most difficult step in evolving a meaningful statement about moral development. To do this, to take this next giant step, we must return to the classical statements on democratic political theory from Locke to Rawls, since the essence of that classic tradition is, in fact, the linkage of politics to ethics. The fundamental debate over the relationship of personal rights to social obligations is what moral development is about, and the highest form of such development is to maintain the balance, the tension, between rights and obligations. This tension — the antithesis rather than the synthesis — is precisely what justice is about, and moral development is the wisdom to engage in the conduct of justice. To "resolve" the argument over rights and obligations in some arbitrary, ultimate way is to either surrender the society to the Anarch, or, at the other extreme, to the Behemoth.[26] And such a resolution can only be bought at the price of democratic community.

Theories that account for political obligation in terms of the consent of the governed are highly amibiguous and confusing. It is rarely clear whether laws are justified by the fact that they are "willed" by those subject to them, or by the justice of what is enacted. In Locke two quite different arguments are inextricably interwoven. His aims were to defend the obligation to obey legitimate authority (i.e., authority based on consent) and to defend the right to resist coercive force in the absence of legitimate authority. He based authority on contractual consent, but behind the contract are the laws of nature and ultimately the standard is the "good of the community."[27] Since man in the state of nature has only as much power over others as he needs to preserve his own life, liberty, and security of possessions, this degree of power is all he can properly be asked to surrender to the state.

> Man being by Nature, all free, equal and independent, no one can be put out of his estate, and subjected to the Political Power of another, without his own Consent. The only way whereby any one divests himself of his Natural Liberty, and puts on the bonds of Civil Society, is by agreeing with other Men to join and unite into a Community. When any number of Men have so consented to make one Community or Government, they are thereby presently incorporated, and make one Body Politick, wherein the Majority have a Right to act and conclude the rest.[28]

Locke used the term consent broadly. At first he insisted that it was only consent, in the sense of voluntary agreement undertaken by people who knew what they were committing themselves to, which made authority legitimate; he later argued that a man, when he inherits property, gives consent to the state recognized by his father. In fact, consent is given tacitly whenever a man travels on the roads, takes lodging for a week, and so on. Locke's argument, that by remaining within the state and accepting its benefits, we tacitly consent to its legitimacy and acknowledge an obligation of obedience to its laws, is fraught with difficulties.[29] For one thing, it removes any distinction between legitimacy and coercion. Locke could be accused of forgetting one of his primary tasks: the moral justification of the right of revolution. He avoided this dilemma by making obligation dependent on the nature of government. Men enter society with the intention of better preserving themselves, their liberty, and their property; the power of the government they establish can never extend further than the preservation of the common good.

It is one thing to show that people have a right not to have a government thrust upon them before a government has been founded, and quite another to argue that no one is required to obey an established government unless they have agreed to do so. Benn and Peters suggest that "if consent is a necessary condition for political obligation, it would deny a government any rightful authority over anyone who dissented from the basic principles of the constitution."[30] People who rejected the basic assumptions of the goals of government could not be morally obliged to obey laws, for the laws would not be their laws. On the other hand, if consent is taken as a sufficient condition for obligation, it implies that, having once submitted, one is bound to accept the consequences thereafter. This argument is not very appealing to the person who conceives of moral development as accepting postulated goals and ideals of government, but disapproving of the practices of a particular government in straying from one's perception of these goals.

In order to overcome these difficulties between rights and obligations, Locke was forced to find ways to prove that men have agreed to obey, even when they have not in fact done so. In the end he virtually makes obedience imply consent. Locke failed to distinguish between how political authority arises and what makes it legitimate. As Plamenatz correctly notes: "political authority is always limited by the ends it ought to serve, so that, where those who have this authority do not serve those ends, their subjects have a right to resist them or get rid of them."[31] Obligation depends, therefore, not on moral development but on whether the government is such that one ought to consent, whether its actions are in accord with the authority a hypothetical group of rational men in a state of nature would give to any government they were founding.

If it could be established that a given set of political arrangements deserved our consent, would this not make moral development irrelevant to political obligation? A distinguished line of political philosophers have taken this position. T.H. Green, for example, stated that his purpose was "to consider the moral function or object served by law . . . and in so doing to discover the true ground or justification for obedience to law." Society's claim to exercise powers over the individual rested on the fact that "these powers are necessary to the fulfillment of man's vocation as a moral being, to an effectual self-devotion to the work of developing the perfect character in himself and others."[32] Thus, laws are morally justified only to the extent that they promote the self-realization of the individual, but moral development is meaningful only if it obeys laws. This circular reasoning was no monopoly of the conservatives; liberals and socialists developed their own variations on this theme.

Laski followed Green in arguing that politics was an acivity in which men worked through the state as an instrument of social organization to achieve personal and social fulfillment. Laski defined the state as "an organization for enabling the mass of men to realize social good on the largest possible scale." The social good is "such an ordering of our personality that we are driven to search for things it is worthwhile to obtain, that, thereby, we may enrich the great fellowship we serve."[33] Accordingly, it must be recognized that the moral development of the individual cannot be abstracted from the general good of other people. In this way, socialism incorporated utilitarian doctrine with startling simplicity.

Explanations that sugggest that the grounds of political obligation lie in the nature and purposes of government can be criticized on the grounds that it is impossible, and not necessarily desirable, to find general criteria to justify political obligation. Necessary and sufficient conditions of good government and political obligation can never be known. Only in totalitarian regimes can the aims of the state be reduced to one overriding purpose. Concepts such as the social good or the general welfare should not be conceived as something determinate. Nor should it be assumed that moral development means agreement about ultimate ends. In a sphere of activity such as politics, there can never be complete agreement about what counts as right, as there can be in other spheres of rule-governed activity. What reasons can be given for believing that a given state represents the "rational will" or the "common good," and by what criteria are we to be guided in deciding whether particular states or institutions conform to these requirements.

Rawls' vision of justice contains a doctrine of moral development that overcomes some weaknesses of the classical arguments, but not others. Obligations are defined by the principle of fairness. They are related to institutions or practices that can be judged by principles of justice for institutions. Obligations are thus tied to the nature and ends of government. This construct is based on a variant of contract theory, which, according to Rawls, overcomes the pitfalls of the classical theories of Locke and Rousseau. This is so because the principles of justice are those that would be chosen by rational men, acting in their own self-interest, in an initial position of equality. However, the actual adoption of these principles is purely hypothetical; all that is needed for the purposes of the theory is that there are the principles which would be adopted by fully moral persons. Confusion over the questions of how authority arises and what makes it legitimate is conveniently avoided.

Rawls maintains that "a person's obligations and duties presuppose a moral conception of institutions and therefore that the content of just institutions must be defined before the requirements for individuals can be set out." The choice of principles for individuals is simplified by the fact that the principles of justice for institutions have already been adopted. Rawls uses what he called "the principle of fairness" to account for all requirements that are obligations as distinct from natural duties.

> A person is required to do his part as defined by the rules of an institution when two conditions are met: first, the institution is just (or fair), that is, it satisfied the two principles of justice; and second, one has voluntarily accepted the benefits of the arrangement or taken advantage of the opportunities it offers to further one's interests.[34]

There are no political obligations for people generally, since obligations arise as a result of voluntary moral acts, which are either express or tacit undertakings, or simply accepting benefits. The first part of the principle of fairness formulates the conditions necessary if these voluntary acts are to give rise to obligations, since the content of obligations is defined by Rawls as an institution the rules of which specify requirements for action. It also implies that it is not possible to be bound to unjust institutions, or to institutions that exceed the limits of tolerable injustices.

The principle of fairness is related to what Hart calls mutuality of restrictions. In this vision, moral development is defined as follows:

> A number of persons engage in a mutually advantageous cooperative venture according to rules, and thus restrict their liberty in ways necessary to yield advantages for all; those who have submitted to these restrictions have a right to a similar acquiescence on the part of those who have benefited from their submission.[35]

The moral obligation to obey rules is thus a function of cooperation. People who accept legislative enactments serve to consecrate standards of behavior. This moral reason for obeying the law is distinct from other moral reasons in terms of good consequences or the principle of fairness. Further, acceptance of the law does not imply that there will be no circumstances where disobedience is justified. The obligation to obey the law on these grounds is based on rights. The law arises between members of a particular political society out of their mutual relationship. Again, for Hart as for

Rawls, moral development is a societal balancing act preventing either the Anarch or the Behemoth from triumph.

The principle of fairness binds only those who assume public office or state power. Those individuals who possess the most advantages in society are those likely to accept the obligations of the state. There is a difference between institutions that apply to us because of ascriptive factors of birth, and those that apply because individuals have done certain things as a way of advancing the ends of achievement. Thus there is a natural duty to comply with the constitution, and an obligation to carry out the duties of an office. Obligation is therefore a term reserved by Rawls for moral requirements that derive from the principle of fairness, while all other requirements are called natural duties.

Rawls implies that we are bound to obey the law simply because it exists. He insists that "as citizens our legal duties and obligations are settled by what the law is." This is certainly true as a statement of fact. However, to fall back upon the obligatory character of law is surely to avoid the problem of moral consent. It does not solve the problem of why the presence of legitimate authority provides a ground for acting in the manner required by this authority. What the law demands and what justice requires are distinct questions, even if the two principles of justice are used by the courts to interpret and apply the law. There are two principal ways in which injustice may arise: first, current arrangements may depart from the publicly accepted standard of justice; and second, arrangements may conform to a state's conception of justice, but this conception itself may be unjust. Rawls maintains, however, that "when the basic structure of society is reasonably just, we are to recognize unjust laws as binding provided that they do not exceed certain limits of injustice."[36] This is so because when we submit to democratic authority, we submit to the extent necessary to share equitably in the inevitable imperfections of a constitutional system.

This argument is also beyond democracy. It was made earlier in sociology by MacIver. The notion was that tradition of loyalty include the assumption that we should extend our law-abidingness beyond the limits of immediate approbation.[37] There is a danger that this line of reasoning could be carried to the extreme where virtually no right of resistance remains, and moral development is reduced to blatant violations only, rather than ethical decision-making as a rule.

It is just too dangerous and limiting to reduce moral development to how one defines "equal liberty" and "fair equality of opportunity." There may be numerous occasions when resistance is justified, despite the duty "not to invoke too readily the faults of social arrangements." Civil disobedience is an appeal to the conscience of the larger society, and may be justified if the established authority is acting inconsistently with its own established standards. In this sense, moral development is not equivalent to rampant individualism or disobedience of the law on the grounds that it conflicts with personal standards or principles. Resistance is justified by reference to social principles, i.e., the two principles of justice, but not by appeals to conscience. On the other hand, some element of individualism is critical if moral development is not to be reduced simply to reasons of state or appeals to people.

> In morals every man must be his own legislator and rely in the end on his own judgment. . . . A duty can be a moral duty, then, only if it can be shown to serve a greater good or avert a greater wrong. It is therefore a conditional, not an absolute duty, and must depend on the use to which authority is put. And this implies that though we may have an obligation to act on someone else's judgement, we have no duty to suspend judgment.[38]

Part of any adequate definition of moral development is that a person cannot be deprived of the right to form his or her own judgment. As Pitkin has said: "The capacity for awareness and intention is a precondition for being fully obligated."[39] It follows that one is not really obligated unless one empirically recognizes and morally acquiesces in that obligation.[40] However, obligation does not consist only of inner awareness and itentions, it also has a long-range aspect. It is concerned with the social consequences of action. In the public realm, we are confronted with official interpreters and institutions who judge actions. At times of resistance or revolution these authorities are called into question. The question then arises, who is to decide what times are normal and which are not, or when resistance is justified or even obligatory? If we say that each individual must decide for himself, then we deny the morally binding character of law and authority, or if we say the majority must decide we are unable to cope with a situation where the majority is being challenged. Herein lies the limits of moral development.

There is no final answer to the problem of moral development, since we cannot hope to specify a set of necessary and sufficient conditions of political obligations for all eternity. If society is faced with an indefinite set of vaguely shifting criteria, differing for different times and circumstances, then it may often, if not nearly always, be necessary to scrutinize political relations to see whether individuals are on any particular occasion justified in giving or withholding support to a measure or a government. But in doing so, we resurrect a pure theory of political rights. Again, moral development is the decision-making process whereby the balance-wheel of rights and obligations is maintained. If such a balance-wheel becomes impossible, then the problem of moral development becomes moot, since the choice is made on the basis of raw power — and for decision making in the absence of choice one needs counter power, not moral standards.

Notes

1. Richard B. Brandt, *Freedom and Morality* (Lawrence: University of Kansas Press, 1976); *Ethical Theory: The Problems of Normative and Critical Ethics* (Englewood Cliffs, N.J.: Prentice-Hall, 1959).
2. Abraham Edel, *Ethical Judgment: The Use of Science in Ethics* (Glencoe, Ill.: The Free Press, 1955); and *Method in Ethical Theory* (Indianapolis: Bobbs-Merrill, 1963).
3. Leo Strauss, *Natural Right and History* (Chicago: University of Chicago Press, 1953); *What is Political Philosophy?* (Glencoe, Ill.; The Free Press, 1959).
4. Richard E. Flathman, *Political Obligation* (New York: Atheneum, 1972).
5. Richard E. Dawson and Kenneth Prewitt, *Political Socialization: An Analytic Study* (Boston: Little, Brown & Co. 1977, second edition).
6. L. Harmon Zeigler, *Interest Groups in American Society* (Englewood Cliffs, N.J.: Prentice-Hall, 1964); and *The Political Life of American Teachers* (Englewood Cliffs, N.J.: Prentice-Hall, 1967).
7. Karl Marx and Frederick Engels, *The German Ideology* (London: Lawrence and Wishart, 1970).
8. Karl Mannheim, *Ideology and Utopia: An Introduction to the Sociology of Knowledge* (New York: Harcourt, Brace & World, 1968).
9. Max F. Scheler, *Formalism in Ethics and Non-Formal Ethics of Values: A New Attempt Toward the Foundation of an Ethical Personality* (Evanston: Northwestern University Press, 1973, 5th revised edition.)
10. Philip Rieff, *Freud: The Mind of the Moralist* (Garden City, N.Y.: Doubleday, 1961).
11. David Elkind, "Erik Erikson's Eight Ages of Man," in *Readings in Human Development: Contemporary Perspectives*, edited by David Elkind and Donna C. Metzel (New York: Harper & Row Publishers, 1977), pp. 3–11.
12. Erik M. Erikson, *Young Man Luther: A Study of Psychoanalysis and History* (New York: Norton Publishers, 1958); and *Gandhi's Truth; On the Origins of Militant Nonviolence* (New York: Norton Publishers, 1969).
13. Erik N. Erikson, *Childhood and Society* (New York: Norton Publishers, 1963, second edition.)
14. Sigmund Freud, *Civilization and Its Discontents*, translated by James Strachey (New York: W.W. Norton, 1962).
15. Robert L. Ebel, "What are Schools For?," in *Readings in Human Development: Contemporary Perspectives*, edited by David Elkind and Donna C. Metzel (New York: Harper & Row Publishers, 1977), pp. 12–16.
16. John Dewey, *Democracy and Education: An Introduction to the Philosophy of Education* (New York: Macmillan Co., 1917).
17. Lawrence Kohlberg, "Development of Moral Character and Moral Ideology," *Review of Child Development Research*, edited by Martin and Lois Hoffman (New York: Russell Sage Foundation 1964), pp. 398–401.
18. For a behavioristic summary of the "cognitive" standpoint on moral development, see Lawrence A. Kurdek, "Perspective Taking As the Cognitive Basis of Children's Moral Development," *Merrill-Palmer Quarterly*, Vol. 24, No. 1 (January 1978), pp. 3–28.
19. George Herbert Mead, *Mind, Self and Society: From the Standpoint of a Social Behaviorist*, edited by Charles W. Morris et al. (Chicago: The University of Chicago Press, 1934); see also, *On Social Psychology: Selected Papers*, edited by Anselm Strauss (Chicago: University of Chicago Press, 1964).

20. Ralph Barton Perry, *General Theory of Value* (Cambridge: Harvard University Press, 1926), pp. 115–19; and his *Puritanism and Democracy* (New York: Vanguard Press, 1944), pp. 589–609.
21. Irving Louis Horowitz, *Genocide: State Power and Mass Murder* (New Brunswick, N.J.: Transaction Books, 1977, second edition.)
22. Hannah Arendt, *The Origins of Totalitarianism* (New York: Harcourt, Brace & World, 1966, revised edition.)
23. Jacob L. Talmon, *The Origins of Totalitarian Democracy* (London: Secker & Warburg, 1952); and *Political Messianism* (New York: Praeger Publishers, 1960).
24. Harold D. Lasswell, "The Choice of Sanctioning Norms," in *On Political Sociology*, edited by Dwaine Marvick (Chicago: The University of Chicago Press, 1977), pp. 348–365.
25. Helen Merrell Lynd, *On Shame and the Search for Identity* (New York: Science Editions Inc., 1961), pp. 224–26.
26. Irving Louis Horowitz, *Foundations of Political Sociology* (New York and London: Harper & Row, Publishers), 1972.
27. John Locke, *Two Treatises of Government* (Cambridge: Cambridge University Press, 1960), section 163, p. 394.
28. John Locke, *Two Treatises of Government* (Cambridge: Cambridge University Press, 1960), sections 95, 119, pp. 348, 366.
29. David Hume, "Of the Original Contract," in *Social Contract* (New York and London: Oxford University Press, 1946), pp. 221–22.
30. S.I. Benn and R.S. Peters, *Social Principles and the Democratic State* (London: George Allen & Unwin, 1959), p. 322.
31. John Plamenatz, *Consent, Freedom and Political Obligation* (New York and London: Oxford University Press, 1968), pp. 230–31.
32. T.H. Green, *Lectures on the Principles of Political Obligation* (London: Longmans, 1895), pp. 29–41.
33. Harold Laski, *A Grammar of Politics* (London: Allen & Unwin, 1970), p. 25.
34. John Rawls, *A Theory of Justice* (Cambridge, Mass.: Harvard University Press, 1972), pp. 110–12.
35. H.L.A. Hart, "Are There Any Natural Rights?" in *Political Philosophy*, edited by Anthony Quinton (New York and London: Oxford University Press, 1968), pp. 61–62.
36. John Rawls, *A Theory of Justice* (Cambridge, Mass.: Harvard University Press, 1972), pp. 349, 351.
37. Robert M. MacIver, *The Modern State* (New York and London: Oxford University Press, 1926), p. 154.
38. S.I. Benn and R.S. Peters, *Social Principles and the Democratic State* (London: George Allen & Unwin, 1959), p. 326–27.
39. Hannah Pitkin, "Obligation and Consent" in *Obligation and Dissent*, edited by Donald W. Hanson and Robert B. Fowler (Boston: Little, Brown & Co., 1971), pp. 41–44.
40. Burton Zwiebach, *Civility and Disobedience* (New York: Cambridge University Press, 1975), pp. 169–200.

14.
Social and Communal Acculturation of German-Jewish Immigrants of the Nazi Period in the United States*

Herbert A. Strauss

I.

The migration of Jewish and political victims of the regime from Nazi Germany was a world-historic event comparable to few other migratory movements in its immediate and long-range impact on the cultures and societies receiving the émigrés.

This impact rested on a "successful" integration, and is one of its indices. Such integration includes persons whose impact was entirely oppositional and a stimulant to "countercultures" or to movements claiming to reject the "integrative systems" of present industrial societies. The late Herbert Marcuse had his short fling at world-historic significance, although his integration rested on the preaching of nonintegration. Henry Kissinger had his impact on world politics as a social and political conservative representing a nonideological foreign policy under Kennedy and Johnson. The pacifist-socialist Einstein signed a letter to President Franklin D. Roosevelt that began the process that led to the construction of the first atomic bomb. With Jacob Burckhardt, one is tempted to place "Glueck" or "Unglueck" — success or failure — in integration into an ironic perspective.

The work accomplished so far in the scholarly assessment of this unique migration has been properly concentrated on the elites in public life, literature, the arts, the sciences. The *International Biographical Dictionary of Central-European Émigrés, 1933–1945*, which owes its existence to the steadfast support of the *Deutsche Forschungsgeneinschaft* especially during its first hesitant years of development, will, or should, advance research in several disciplines. The archives, on which the dictionary is based, contains about 25,000 worldwide émigré biographies. It will, or should, reveal

"Glueck" and "Unglueck" in terms of research, deflected creative lives, the ravages of poverty, alienation, uprooting, and despair. The next phase of research in migration history for this group and period should introduce the breadth of vision necessary to deal with the impact of the group in worldwide terms. It should deal with integration in terms broader than the momentary self-understanding of writers or public figures caught in the immediacies of the psychological and political insecurities of expulsion and homelessness. A combination of intellectual and social history methods might lead beyond present disciplinary limitations.

The concentration on intellectual elites and public figures in research has dominated the "image" of the émigré of the Nazi period, at least in German-language research. Relatively little attention has been given to the large numbers of nonelite Nazi victims in research conducted since the end of World War II. This is especially true for the Jewish migrant from Germany and Austria. They may have numbered about 300,000 for Germany, and an additional 125,000 for Austria alone. In Jewish and non-German social science priorities, the migrant of the Nazi period was replaced by the problems of the holocaust, of the camp survivor, and of Israel. The Leo Baeck Institute, which had not included research on these contemporary Jewish subjects on its agenda, concentrated on research in German-Jewish history since 1750. For this institute, the end of the German-Jewish "symbiosis" in 1933 also denotes the limits of its historic perimeter. This is not the place to consider the several motives that produced this self-imposed limitation in research interests.

German *Exilforscher* appear not to have made major contributions to the study of the Jewish émigré. Generally, the Jewish emigration has been dubbed "Juedische Massenemigration." I do not know the origin of the term, and cannot judge clearly any longer whether it implies the usual snobbery tinged with ignorance that the term "Masse" used to imply in political thought since LeBon or Ortega y Gasset. Unless the term denotes only the uprooting of large numbers of people for the anonymous reason of their Jewish ancestry, and their subsequent large-scale immigration to countries of refuge and resettlement, it is singularly inappropriate by the standards of international migration history. German-Jews — the group to which these remarks will be restricted from here on — were probably the single group of expellees in world history with the most differentiated internal structure. One is tempted to compare them with Huguenots or white Russians in social or intellectual diversity. In American immigration history, it is fair to say that no single group since the gentlemen-planter generation or the German "1848ers" (a probable total of 3,000 for the latter group!) was as diversified in whatever structural terms one chooses to apply.

The research situation on the proper comparative and worldwide scale for the Jewish immigrant from Nazi Germany has improved greatly since I began to draw attention to this field of study in 1969. I was unaware, at the time, of the *Exilliteratur* interest dominant in Germany, or the political research done in the German Democratic Republic. By 1969, scholars and writers had analyzed the immigration policies of different countries, and, since we began our work, other scholars have done work in several countries on the German Jewish immigrant. On another level, work also has begun on the relationship between the pattern of persecution in Nazi Germany and the flow of emigration (see my forthcoming "Nazi persecution and the pattern of Jewish emigration, 1933–1945" in the next two issues of the *Year Book, Leo Baeck Institute*, for references to literature). Still, neither the Research Foundation for Jewish Immigration, New York, nor the Council of Jews from Germany (London) have progressed far enough in their work to make a comparative approach feasible. The preparation of basic tools, including the massive work on the *International Biographical Dictionary*, have taken an inordinate amount of our time and energy. For this reason, I propose to restrict these remarks to the Jewish immigrant in the United States.

Another possible reason for the pale (and probably pejorative) term *Massenemigration* derives from the difficulties of perceiving the diversity of the Jewish group in Germany. To deal with this, I propose to call Jews in Germany an ethnic core group, whose basic ethnicity was not recognized, for good political and cultural reasons, even by its own major spokesmen. The cultural center of this group was religious, while its customs, language, education, economic and social structures were part of German culture, but remained influenced by Jewish ethnic tradition in two ways. First, the traditionalist origins of German-Jewish life were still represented by the rural *Gemeinden* in South and West Germany, by the orthodox communities, and by Silesian and Posen Jews where Jewish settlement had reached the "critical mass" that made a "folk culture," separate from German or Polish folk cultures, possible into the late nineteenth century. Second influence was the presence of a demographic frontier in Eastern Europe. About one-fifth of all German Jews, about 100,000 of 500,000 in 1933, were of foreign, mainly Eastern European nationality, and were linked more closely to Jewish folk ethnicity of the Eastern-Jewish settlement type than to German Jewish settlement pattern.

Having postulated this "core ethnicity" as a corrective in the image of the German Jew implies no value judgment about the role of Jews in German culture and society prior to the advent of Nazism. If German nationalism, as represented by its major ideologues, had had room for cultural diversity or ethnic pluralism, i.e., if *Staatsnation* and *Kulturnation* concepts had been accepted as a basis for cultural pluralism, a consensus about the role of Jews in German society might have developed along less self-

conscious lines. It would have had room for the entire spectrum of acculturation and modernization that structured the German Jewish group.
Nazi persecution turned about 870,000 persons in Germany into a "group"
(if persons of Jewish descent but not of the Jewish religion are counted as
persecutees under the racial laws of the Third Reich) which by any standard of social analysis was not a "group." The analysis of the group in its
migration and resettlement should not be based on the literary sources produced by only one segment of the German-Jewish acculturation continuum.

The following remarks, in sum, are meant to add a dimension to literary
and intellectual elite analysis. They concentrate on Jews of the Jewish religion, affiliated in one way or another with the Jewish community in
Germany and/or during their emigration, resettlement, and acculturation
in the United States. The *Ansatz* is derived from the attempt to understand
the acculturation history of this Jewish group as that of an ethnic group of
both German and Jewish character in the context of American immigration history.

II.

The Jewish émigré from Germany did not see himself as an exile but as
an émigré/immigrant in the overwhelming majority and as a matter of
public Jewish policy, wherever he found refuge from persecution. It is possible that German Jews failed to develop a coherent *Faschismusbegriff*,
and, for that reason alone, were unable to engage in the sophisticated political analysis that would have permitted them to discount the realities of
their persecution and expulsion experiences for a future Utopia that, after
all, never came for most of their politically-minded fellow sufferers. In this
attitude, they may well have revealed that they were "part of their time" as
a German ethnic minority whose deep roots had been severed, as had the
roots of émigrés from Germany before them, by the persecution, exploitation and defamation visited upon them by the *dankbare Vaterland* with
whose liberal-democratic potential they had been identified, as a whole,
since the beginning of their emancipation in the mid-eighteenth century.
By 1938, it had become a matter of personal pride and *Charakter* not to
ask for acceptance,, equality, or love while all German power centers, the
churches, the universities, the *Beamtentum*, remained silent or ineffective
in the face of Nazi anti-Jewish measures. The policies of all Jewish organizations, the latest by 1935, recognized emigration, not exile, as the only
means available to the powerless and isolated Jewish group. Across the
country, especially in rural areas and smaller towns, local persecution
joined with Reich level measures to stress the end of Jewish life in
Germany. Jewish publicity, in full awareness of its responsibility, stressed

Auswanderung and *Einordnung*. The *Hilfsverein der Juden in Deutschland*, the major organization aiding émigrés, had admonished potential radicalism that might endanger the chance of those still waiting to emigrate by giving support to restrictionist forces in countries of settlement. Persecution had reactivated Jewish group understanding. By whatever intellectual constructs German Jewry under persecution accounted for its being German, *Auswanderung* became soon the *only* constructive response to discrimination. The efforts of Jewish organizations in Germany were bent on occupational training and retraining for resettlement abroad. The *Kristallnacht* of November 1938 destroyed much more than houses of worship. The about 30,000 men interned in concentration camps suffered shock deepened by the total irrationality of their internment. It was shared by those lucky enough to escape such internment. For the middle-class Jew, unable to rationalize his persecution in other than Jewish-historical terms, it followed from his self-understanding as a citizen that the break had become final.

III.

Jewish emigration was typically a family migration including, where possible, two, often three, generations of the immediate family, and a migration without capital since German *Devisengesetze* stripped all but the very rich of whatever they possessed before emigration. Arriving in the United States, significant numbers of newcomers became beneficiaries of the vast voluntary welfare system that had sprung up in the Jewish — and non-Jewish — community to aid the refugee. Meeting the social worker became the immigrant's introduction to the social pattern perceived as typical for the immigrant situation. The immediate need was to get the immigrant back on his economic feet in the traditional "entry" job.

The economic integration of the immigrant, which began with this step, has not yet been studied systematically over the entire range of the period. If the observation is correct that the recovery in job and business conditions that began with the late 1930s allowed the immigrant to move to levels of earnings roughly corresponding to pre-emigration levels in the postwar period, it has to be tempered by a consideration of what this pre-emigration socioeconomic condition was actually like: immigrants to the United States, for historic reasons, came in large numbers from south and southwest Germany (and from Berlin, as descendants of migrants from Posen and Silesia), and belonged, in the majority, to the small to middling *Buergertum* whose economic independence had frequently masked marginal economic positions and poverty induced by the economic depression of the early 1930s and the economic dislocations of the Nazi period. A considerable segment of immigrants remained in low-level employees' and workers' jobs during their working life, and did not reach middle-income levels.

That this immigrant group succeeded in avoiding the social pathology of unemployment and appeared to have had no significantly larger incidence of mental sickess than expected as a result of persecution and uprooting must also be ascribed to the work ethics typical of the Jewish community in Germany — as it was typical of German immigrants before and after them.

Economic integration, economic necessity, and the desire to continue the upward mobility had been characteristic of Jews in Germany. They were intertwined in a knot that is hard to disentangle in the interview material from which these tentative findings are extracted.

In any event, perceiving himself as an immigrant and thrown into the labor and economic market by necessity, the urge to succeed provided the first stimulus for a functional acculturation. All but menial work demanded language proficiency, behavioral changes, and changes in attitudes in economic group contacts. The educational preparation of the immigrant for learning a new language, his self-understanding as an immigrant rather than an exile — deepened by war-induced attitudes, the war-service of the younger groups, and information about the holocaust — made such functional acculturation typical for the first generation itself. In this respect, this immigrant group may have differed from earlier and differently structured immigrant groups in the United States in the speed with which acculturation proceeded. This corresponded to their urban and middle-class structure and values. A comparison with twentieth century German groups may show fairly close parallels on this functional integration level.

The process of economic integration (which cannot be presented in detail in this article) exhibited considerable variations in the difficulties which had to be overcome in entering the labor market. These difficulties were objective enough — finding and holding a job, moving to new and higher positions, combining jobs with education or study, etc. They were also subjective — the conflict between the status-system and the self-perception of persons uprooted from an accustomed career, and the apparently status-minimizing egalitarianism of economic and job interactions; conflicts between class-specific social behavior of native worker and immigrant; language difficulties induced in part by class- and the class-specific dialects, etc.

Few immigrant biographies lack references to initial menial jobs, regardless of previous occupation of respondents. For commercial employees, retraining in a craft was often the only way to secure a position, and the refugee services set up training centers in several American cities. The literature of the 1940s abounds with descriptions of "new industries" introduced by immigrants, mainly in the food, consumer, and luxury goods fields. Economically significant were private banks, brokerage partnership or firms, international metal trading, export/import companies and a variety of manufacturing companies, retail outlets or chains, tool and dye manufacturing companies and the substantial group of management, industrial or engineering executives in government-directed or private industries. They were, of course, dwarfed by giant American companies.

Most printed information — and thus most studies based on the self-evaluation of the writers, often uncritically — reflects the psychological and ideological course of the professional groups among immigrants — a total of 7.3 percent of gainfully employed immigrants. H.A. Walter's recent reflections on the political developments of the *Aufbau* takes this weekly's claim seriously that it spoke for the Jewish immigrant community. This claim needs to be qualified in important respects, and conclusions based on this assumption remain subject to corrections, since the editorial board and the small group of men with whom Manfred George had to work out his editorial policy were not truly representative of the social and economic orientation of the silent majority that read the paper. Manfred George was atypical in nearly every way, his ideological course reflected, in my opinion, the judgments of New York left-wing sentiments and the American-Jewish left wing. This differed from the apolitical reactions of the German-Jewish immigrant intelligentsia of the 1930s and 1940s. Contemporary and retrospective studies show that the professional group experienced considerable economic and psychological difficulties in adapting its German social status self-evaluation or expectations as educated elites to the realities of the roles they were forced to play in traditional American immigration terms, as they entered the labor market in un- and semi-skilled levels. For the professional group it is possible to speak of successful and unsuccessful integration if success is defined as the ability to regain a professional role commensurate with the role played prior to arrival, or, where persecution had interrupted careers, to take up a similar career following immigration. Many lawyers' careers were rebuilt only when German *Wiedergutmachung* permitted them to use their German legal training in an immigrant setting. Physicians met with the traditional anti-Semitism of the American medical profession, which had imposed quotas on the admission of Jewish students to medical schools until the 1950s. They faced a variety of professional and licensing problems in getting reestablished. Many engineers, university teachers, industry scientists, performing artists, and other groups of professionals, while facing similar occupational and social obstacles, appear to have reintegrated with success — as defined in the above terms — in the American professional structure after a shorter or longer period.

No conclusive and systematic study of the factors that account for the "success" or "failure" of professionals in objective or subjective terms is available. The material in the archives of the IBD should ultimately form a sufficient basis for such a study. Some of the major factors, besides psychological factors, time of emigration, specialization, level of preparation, family connection and background, were probably age, American education or retraining, the influence of service in the U.S. Army and study under the "GI bill of rights," and the little explored process by which American intellectual conditions favored or hindered the acceptance of the scholarly, humanistic, or scientific traditions brought along by immigrant intellectuals. The analysis of individual biographies in terms of the "Atlantic civilization" and the "brain drain" (which preceded and followed the emigration of the intellectuals from Germany!) — i.e., in terms of *Wissen-schaftsgeschichte* and the migration of ideas — may offer new clues for a better understanding of the integration process.

In any event, findings for the professional group among immigrants do not apply to the 90 percent nonprofessionals among them. There is enough evidence in the files of Jewish immigrant self-help agencies in New York to suggest that even under the boom conditions characterizing the American war and postwar economy, a considerable number of émigrés, especially white and blue collar workers, beginning to age in terms of the American labor market, did not enjoy middle income levels long enough to accumulate adequate reserves for retirement incomes typical for their counterparts in American society. Without the considerable economic aid derived from German *Bundesrepublik, Rueckerstattung, Wiedergutmachung*, and pension laws for Nazi victims, the bulk of the older-generation immigrant community would most likely have faced near-poverty levels of existence in their declining years.

This observation should be applied to the much-discussed problem of class and status among the Jewish immigrant community for which we also have no systematic longitudinal study. The image of status anxiety and of the impact of the image of a more egalitarian American class system that emerges from the written accounts of professionals no doubt reflects a basic change in the immigrants' self-evaluation. It also reflects the true kindness and understanding the refugee's fate met among practically all American social groups in personal contacts. This helped the refugee to rationalize the transition from his rigid ascriptive system to the flexible and segmented American social structure system during his learning period. In reality, however, subjective status images and objective class status, especially for immigrants unable to communicate adequately in English, clashed for a considerable period following arrival. The immigrant had more than one reference group for his status and class self-perception, including the immigrant community, his (often menial) job community, the generalized image of American class structures, the Eastern-Western Jewish "ethclass" differences, and the remembered community from which he emigrated.

Objectively, the self-evaluation of the immigrant and his place in American society clashed, especially where education was stressed as a factor in class ascription in reference to job or social (peer) community. This clash provided an additional stimulus for speedy, first-generation acculturation (compensation for low status).

For New York City, where immigrants settled in large numbers (estimated at 70,000), geographic mobility analysis suggests upward mobility. Preliminary analysis shows that immigrants moved from a part of Manhattan (Washington Heights) to areas of the borough of Queens characteristic of middle-income groups, especially young couples with children. Additional movement occurred to single-dwelling suburbs — moves characteristic of comparable American groups moving upward on the social and income scale.

IV.

Of somewhat greater than functional significance are the changes brought about by acculturation in the family. Jewish migration was, to a large extent, family migration, independent of country of resettlement. The social circumstances of expulsion and resettlement reaffirmed, once again, one of the roots of traditional Jewish family cohesion: the primary social group, based on trust and mutual aid, provided the primary economic group, the key psychological forum for changes between the generations and between the marriage partners, and a center for information on all aspects of the integration and acculturation process.

U.S. immigration law, in fact, stressed blood relationship between an immigrant and his American sponsors; guarantees that the prospective immigrant would not become "a public charge" had greater force if they came from relatives of the immigrant. As a result, significant numbers of quota-immigrants of the Nazi period originated in South, South-West, and West Germany, as well as Berlin (where descendants of nineteenth century Jewish immigrants to America from Poznan and Silesia had moved as part of the Jewish urbanization movement and *Binnenwanderung*). Immigrants had to locate descendants of a nineteenth century émigré-relative willing to provide the guarantees needed to obtain a visa. It appears, however, that family relations following arrival of the immigrant became strained: immigrants expected the mutual aid characteristic, especially, of rural-Jewish traditions in Germany, while American relatives expected the immigrant to repeat the "traditional immigrant experience" and start "from the bottom," i.e., be self-sufficient. Conflicts arising from these differences were especially pronounced in cases where previous persecution or internment in camps had created a pattern of dependency and expectation of support in view of past sufferings.

The family as a social unit appears to have maintained stability, i.e., observation suggests that the incidence of divorce was low in the older immigrant generation as a whole but rose significantly in the younger generation, e.g., among persons listed in the forthcoming second volume of the *International Biographical Dictionary* (Science and Arts). Frictions appeared to have occurred especially in families migrating with three generations, as grandparents and grandchildren confronted each other over education, manners, the use of leisure time, dating, etc., while both parents were at work. (The first immigrant-established "residence home for the elderly" in New York was designed to alleviate problems of this nature.) Major changes occurred in the immigrant family's pattern of authority and the position of the wife and mother. Women appeared to have been more adaptable to changed labor conditions, and took menial jobs earlier and without apparent psychological difficulties. Many women had retrained for such jobs prior to emigration, or used traditional skills acquired prior to marriage and withdrawal to the middle-class role of housewife and mother. Women also appear to have been less concerned with using their as yet faulty English than men. During wartime, wives found war-work in factories or volunteered for war-related social or medical activities, some directed the business of their husbands while the men served in the armed forces. (At the end of the war-created production boom, women were among the first to be dismissed, however.)

As a result of this changed role of women, and the major burden borne by women as breadwinners *and* housewives, husband and wife appear to have gained a more equal view of each other, i.e., traditional authority patterns appear to have relaxed. Naturally, age at immigration was a crucial factor in this change, but an in-depth study (R. Neubauer) suggests that changes occurred in orthodox-Jewish as well as nonorthodox and nonaffiliated families. In the postwar period, advancing age, the leaving of grown-up children; increased income from husband's work or *Wiedergutmachungs*-payments, being widowed, the availability of voluntary social services on the pattern of American-Jewish life, were additional factors influencing women's roles.

Age at immigration was perhaps the major factor affecting differences in depth and speed of acculturation. This difference as it appears, e.g., in the *International Biographical Dictionary* (which includes all foreign-born eligibles, in line with U.S. census practice), is crucial for the understanding of the integration and acculturation of the German-trained older-generation émigré. To date, no comprehensive study has been done on younger immigrants from Nazi Germany, their career patterns, education, marriage patterns or attitudes. However, data on the children of immigrant families suggest some tentative observations: families with children were forced to relate to American education and peer-group pressures for conformity among their children. There were incentives to use at least two languages in the home. Children experienced considerable parental pressures to excel in schools, and college education was considered an avenue of economic and occupational advance to the professions, corresponding both to the original German-Jewish and to American-Jewish patterns. Pressures increased where parents expressed low opinions of the American educational system. (The data contained in the archives of the *International Biographical Dictionary* suggest that this educational concern led large numbers of younger immigrants into academic and professional occupations). Different from some earlier (and less literate) immigrant groups, the German-Jewish younger and second generations appear not to have experienced the social pathologies associated with their "alienation" from the parents' culture *anomie*, criminality, violence. Among immigrant groups, the Jewish-orthodox appear to have maintained more cultural continuity between parent and child generations than other Jewish immigrants. Since new ethnic awareness became widely accepted by American college groups in the 1960s, traces of a sense of alienation found by investigators in second- and third-generation Jewish immigrant children may be presumed to have been lessened (Neubauer, Sanua).

However these observations and findings may be changed by systematic longitudinal research. The integration and acculturation of the younger and second-generation (i.e., American-born) immigrant, his geographic and social mobility, his final rooting in American society and culture provided basic stimuli for family-centered Jewish immigrants not to consider returning to the homeland a viable personal option.

V.

If the changes in economic and social status, the family, sex and age roles could be described without being *consistently* related to the concrete historic events in the United States, in Germany, in the Jewish world, and in World War II (which formed their ever-present background), the group formation among Jewish immigrants from Germany in the United States grew as much out of the immediately felt needs of the immigrant community as it was affected by the historic developments before, during, and after World War II. The continued existence of this group structure into the late 1970s permits not only observations by this writer as a participant, but permits observations transcending the periodization generally observed among *Exilforscher*: for the latter, *Exil* ends at the latest with full *Freizuegigkeit* of the exile back to his homeland, i.e., with the foundation of the Federal Republic of Germany and the German Democratic Republic under Allied occupation status; for the immigrant, acculturation remains a continued process opening into the future by generational changes.

The German-Jewish group arrived in the United States with all elements of a community. Persecution had driven out community leaders and followers alike. After November 1938, all income groups and occupations had taken flight. The lay and secular leadership of German Jewry was forced out of Germany, except for those who would or could not leave and became martyrs to duty. Where refugees congregated in larger numbers, primarily in the major cities in the United States, they formed a "critical mass" and became a new community. In New York City alone, as many as 70,000 of the about 132,000 immigrants from Germany may have settled permanently. Up to 40,000 of these may have been affiliated with religious congregations (10,000 family memberships) or had been in contact with the network of organizations established by immigrants. The New York group and its equivalents in major centers of resettlement on the East coast, the Mid- and Far West, in organizing itself, thus followed what amounts to age-old precedents characteristic of Jewish migrants and of American immigration history. These precedents offer clues to the analysis of the social and cultural roles played by these organizations, and suggest some comparisons.

In social and occupational composition, the network of immigrant organizations included most groups with the important exception of academic teachers, political exiles, literary figures, most artists, and the majority of persons whose relationship to groups were structured more by professional and occupational than ethnic influences, and had already been structured in this fashion in Germany prior to emigration. Further study may show whether or not members of this group had moved closer to viewing themselves as members of the Jewish group under the impact of persecution, holocaust, the foundation of the state of Israel, and, significantly, the pattern of sociability and group stereotyping they may have met with in the United States (space forbids pursuing this line of thought further). Among those affiliated, however, and with the limitations mentioned, the social classes characteristic of Jews in Germany were reproduced in the structure of the immigrant group with some approximation (Davie, Strauss). Within the organizational structure there existed in fact the system of ethnic classes — "ethclass" — observed among similar immigrant structures.

The models for the organizations established by German Jews derived from several German Jewish prototypes. Students organizations (American-Kartell-Convent Fraternity), sports associations (Bar Kochba, Maccabi), the Jewish War Veterans Organization (former members of the *Reichbund juedischer Frontsoldaten*, the German-Jewish *Frontkaempfer* of World War I), and some welfare organizations (Blue Card, Inc., based on the *Blaue Karte*, a broad-based welfare and aid organization established by Jews in Germany) were patterned as "successor" or "tradition" organizations often continung the original names of homeland groups. More significantly, religious organizations followed regional or subdenominational lines established in Germany. One entire community, the *Gemeinde* of orthodox Jews of Frankfurt, led by their rabbi (Joseph Breuer) transplanted itself to New York's Washington Heights, attracted other orthodox Jews from Germany, and established an entire network of religious service organizations (schools, teacher-training seminary, *yeshivoth*, a ritual-slaughter supervisory system, a burial society etc.). Most of the about 30 religious congregations established in New York alone by 1941 were set up by rabbis or teachers attracting the adherents from their hometowns in South- and South-West Germany, and represented basically middle to lower-middle class groups (Nuernberg, Wuerzburg, Muenchen, and rural towns and districts). A third type of congregation was represented by a Gemeinde (*Habonim*), whose founders, led by the rabbi of Essen and former national-Jewish leaders in Germany, aspired to becoming representative of advanced Jewish religious thought and attracted a citywide (ethclass) upper-middle class and professional membership in addition to ideologically sympathetic middle-class followers. In line with Jewish custom, most congregations acquired a burial ground soon after being founded. In cities where too few German-Jewish immigrants had resettled to form a congregation, or where no religious leader was available, German Jews founded burial societies (*chevrah kadisha*) to provide the services to the dead they had been accustomed to prior to emigration. The numerous social groups, both formal and informal, paralleled models of *Frauenvereine*, lodges, occupational groups, and other *Vereine* and offered popular entertainment and sociability. The American Federation of Jews from Central Europe was patterned after the *Reichsvertretung der Juden in Deutschland* established in 1933, and founded, in part, by the same people as its predecessor in Germany. The mutual aid organization Selfhelp of Émigrés from Central Europe (New York, Chicago, Los Angeles) continued the voluntarism and nonprofessionalism of *Stiftungen*, the *Gemeinde* labor exchanges, and *Wanderfuersorge* of German-Jewish life (it had been founded by New School professors to help colleagues in need abroad in 1936). The New World Club (originally German-Jewish Club), although, founded in 1924 by earlier immigrants from Germany, combined several German-Jewish models in its wide range of activities: *Volkshochschule*, hiking club, social service, newspaper publisher, youth and sports *Verein*, political *Honoratiorenverein* (the club launched Senator Javits on his congressional career in Washington Heights in 1947), etc. The research groups incorporated after World War II (Leo Baeck Institute, Research Foundation for Jewish Immigration) also had their precedents in German-Jewish history (*Akademie fuer Wissenschaft des Judentums, Verein fuer Geschichte und Literatur der Juden, Gesellschaft fuer juedische Familienforschung*, etc.).

The initial impetus for founding this network often came from a transplanted immigrant community leader reproducing the models of the homeland and creating a needed position for himself. The success of his venture rested on the changing needs an organization served under immigration and acculturation conditions. As acculturation proceeded and needs changed, organizations unable to respond to changing needs atrophied as the founders retired or died.

Religious organizations repeated Protestant, Catholic, as well as Jewish precedent by creating a "sacred ethnicity" (Strauss 1976) — not primarily in using German as the language of the sermon, as had nineteenth century German-Jewish congregations like Temple Emanuel in New York — but by continuing the often minutely different local ritual, prayer, and cantorial and communal music which, already in Germany, had become canonized. Burial societies often grew out of the dislike caused in German-Jewish immigrants by the commercialized "American way of dying," like embalming, costly coffins, and other practices used by American undertakers. In addition, religious grouping served important emotional needs. They created a community of persons undergoing similar experiences as immigrants, offered informal contacts and information on economic opportunities, allowed for cultural and identificational continuity during the period of first integration, and provided "ethclass" roles for immigrants affected by status loss. Such needs were served, in similar fashion, by the social clubs and organizations founded in most immigrant communities; the New World Club was the largest of these groupings and transcended their functions in the several ways pointed out above. The major function of Selfhelp of Emigrés from Central Europe and its affiliated and related organizations was to provide job placement, organize summer camps for the young and indigent unable to leave the city for short periods of recreation, and to provide supplemental income to impoverished immigrants and above the welfare rates established by Jewish organizations or municipal welfare departments. Blue Card, Inc., similarly provided (and provides) supplemental welfare aid to indigents. In this, Selfhelp and Blue Card followed German precedent: German *Wohlfahrtsaemter* had provided aid to Jewish indigents on an equal footing with non-Jews until November 1938 (cut-off *Erlass* effective January 1, 1939). An *Erlass des Reichsinnenministers* had regulated the upper limit for supplemental aid by Jewish organizations beyond which German public assistance to Jews would be curtailed (*Reichsvertretung* etc., *Arbeitsberichte*, 1935, p. 45; Adler-Rudel). The American Federation of Jews from Central Europe was established in 1941 to coordinate the defense of the immigrant community (and its organizations) against encroachments of their civil rights as enemy aliens, and to fight for liberalized immigration laws. Soon after, legal and political publicity and lobbying for German reparations to Nazi victims was added to this list. In 1962, the American Federation established, as its community chest, the Jewish Philanthropic Fund of 1933. This fund has received donations mainly from legacies. It has provided the seed capital for the nursing home for refugees built in New York (see below), and allocated each year funds in support of major social and cultural activities. It has received no *Wiedergutmachungs*-funds and is entirely carried by former immigrants from Germany. Its board includes several generations of immigrants and their children.

VI.

The history of the Jewish community bears out the thesis current in U.S. immigration history that immigrant organizations serve also as stimulants to acculturation (see Strauss, 1976, note 4, p. 121 for references). Although immigration from countries of intermediate settlement and the reuniting of German-Jewish families continued after the end of World War II (mainly from South America and England), basic organizational structures were not changed by the most recent immigrants. Such modifications and additions as occurred were caused by internal rather than external factors, or by changes in the political environment and its impact on organizational functions. With the end of major new immigration, the acculturation function appeared more strongly than before.

In most general terms, organizational policy toward a return to Germany or, correspondingly, integration in American life had been decided by the impact of the war, the holocaust, and the struggle for the establishment of the state of Israel in 1948. The German-Jewish immigrant community reflected in its attitudes American-Jewish policies, whether or not organizations had formally affiliated with the major national Jewish coordinating agencies. No independent policy on either Israel or postwar Jewish life in Germany emerged among immigrant organizations and differences in attitudes among German Jews did not come to the surface. The younger generation, having served in the U.S. armed forces, made its impact felt in congregations, social agencies, and clubs across the country. Like American-Jewish congregations, immigrant congregations displayed the American and the Israeli flag in synagogues and temples.

This reflected, to some extent, the intellectually eclectic influence of the American-Jewish environment: like the Irish, Italians, or Germans before them, American Jews understood their concern with the home-country's fate in terms of traditional liberal American foreign policy, and identified the success of stable democracy in Israel with American national interest. Israel became the major item on the Jewish (including the German-Jewish) political agenda in the United States. Whatever reservations German Jews may have retained toward nationalism or with respect to the Arab question did not surface effectively.

The same eclectic influence led also to a shift in emphasis in most organizations, especially the religious congregations. Generally, organizations stressed social and communal activities over intellectual pursuits. In one congregation (*Habonim*), the attempt to transplant the *Lehrhaus* concept failed. Neoromantic religious concepts were smothered by the all-pervasive liberalism of the Jewish equivalent of the "social gospel." (The German *Lehrhaus* movement of the 1920s had owed its existence precisely to neo-irrational influences.) The orthodox community in Washington Heights maintained its German-Jewish character much longer than other congregations, but it, too, expanded its social and communal activities, and saw itself forced to participate in New York politics to preserve its neighborhood against population changes threatening its security. By 1945, English had become the dominant language. It was used in education from the start. Practically all organizations felt compelled to add social service branches like brotherhoods, sisterhoods, or youth groups, to their table of organization, and organize fundraising, social service or "interfaith" activities. This too, corresponded to the agenda of American-Jewish organizations. Some of these changes were reflected in the power- and decision-making structures of organizations. Control by elected lay boards diminished, but did not entirely erase the traditional control by *Honoratioren*, as new activities encouraged wider "democratic" participation, and younger members applied their communal experiences and education to their parents' organizations.

For social service organizations, the original need of assisting new immigrants to find jobs declined. The economic prosperity of the war and postwar years had permitted immigrants to become self-sufficient as workers, employees, independents, or professionals. Instead, care for the aged emerged as the main social problem of the German-Jewish immigrant group. German *Wiedergutmachung* payments in the form of restitution, indemnification, widows' pensions, compensation for damages to health or careers, or social security provided significant assistance for numerous marginally integrated persons. A new organization (United Restitution Organization) was founded to assist Nazi victims to submit *Wiedergutmachung* claims under the laws of the German Federal Republic. The American Federation of Jews from Central Europe became the recognized spokesman for the legal and political interests of the immigrant community vis-à-vis the governments of the United States and the German Federal Republic. Its activities on behalf of *Wiedergutmachung* constituted a unique chapter in the history of forced emigration: no government had ever attempted to indemnify the victims of its predecessor governments on this scale, or had sought ties with the victims amounting to material as well as moral indemnification. Close cooperation with American as well as German executive and legal branches in this area, and international cooperation with other government and private agencies raised representative immigrant organizations to a level of communal activities unknown to previous U.S. immigration history. (As yet, no study of the impact of *Wiedergutmachung* on the immigrant community is in preparation.)

Wiedergutmachung also affected the activities of immigrant social agencies turning their attention to the new social problems posed by the aging of the first-generation immigrant, the impoverished Austrian-Jewish immigrant left out of *Wiedergutmachung*, and the "displaced person" primarily the concentration camp survivor of Eastern-European background. Another new agency (United Help, Inc.) was established in 1954 to distribute collective *Wiedergutmachung* funds to immigrant welfare groups in major centers of German-Jewish settlement in the United States (similar arrangements were followed in other countries). These funds helped to build two large apartment house complexes for elderly immigrants in New York. (A third such complex, not funded by *Wiedergutmachung* any longer, is under construction.) United Help supported old age homes in Chicago, Los Angeles, San Francisco, and Houston, and set up a scholarship fund (1958) to assist students who were children of Nazi victims — all Nazi victims, independent of national origin or place of persecution. Still another group of agencies founded in the 1960s (New York Foundation for Nursing Homes, Kew Gardens Nursing Home Company) erected a nonprofit nursing home in Queens, New York, once again without the help of *Wiedergutmachung* funds. This home houses 120 elderly clients. In New York, too, Selfhelp developed from a storefront volunteer agency founded in 1936 into the largest social service agency in New York City providing home care and other programs for the elderly, while continuing its (considerably smaller) aid to needy Nazi victims, primarily the elderly. Its pioneering contribution to social services in the United States has been widely recognized. It remains controlled by a board of directors composed of Jewish immigrants from Germany and Austria and their children.

In contrast to this pattern of culture changes, other types of immigrant organizations remained bound up with the *Landsmannschaft*-character of their origins and atrophied or ceased functioning as their clientele faded away. This is true of all social and popular culture groups whose offerings were little appreciated by potentially new members beyond the nostalgia circuit of the founders. It is, to some extent, also true of organizations whose work was tied in with the German language. (The special case of the German language *Aufbau* and its post-George development will be omitted here for lack of space.) Most mutual aid organizations designed for special groups (jurists, physicians, war veterans, nurses, rabbis, etc.) disappeared with the end of the immigration emergency that had created them. Religious congregations established by *Landsmannschaften* were affected not only by the limits to which "sacred ethnicity" can be maintained through generational change in a metropolis, but also by the move of younger and upwardly mobile generations from first-settlement neighborhoods to other parts of the cities, and the suburbs. In addition, the changes in the racial composition of former "German-Jewish" neighborhoods caused by the arrival of black and Hispanic minorities created security problems, especially for the elderly, and affected immigrant congregations. As a result of these and similar factors, such congregations have declined in number and have lost younger members. Their educational services were frequently discontinued for lack of children, and the quality and education of rabbis they attracted to their congregations changed. To maintain their viability, congregations joined with other local groups to stem the decline in neighborhoods, or to open up communications with black and Hispanic community groups. (Some congregations participated in setting up car patrols to deter potential street crimes committed often by juveniles.) In spite of such efforts, however, the demographic decline of such congregations was inevitable. (A detailed neighborhood study documenting these observations further is yet to be undertaken, as are studies of organizations not touched upon in the foregoing remarks.)

VII.

For the topic of this essay — acculturation — enough detail has been compiled not only to show the need for further research but also to attempt some generalizations and comparisons. Clearly, one group of organizations had reached the limits of its acculturation because of its social composition, cultural orientation, and demographic-ecological position. For these and similar groups, joining on *landsmannschaftliche* principles provided a basis for social interactions in which German, Jewish, and American traits in behavior and culture fused in changing mixtures depending on personal and historical factors. This social interaction structured the immigrant's response to the demands made on him by the then (i.e., in the 1940s and 1950s) prevailing ideology of "Americanization" by creating a communal frame of reference. This contributed to saving him from social isolation without limiting economic or occupational integration. Where organizations had joined national organizations (B'nai B'rith, the congregational coordinating agencies, etc.) and adopted programs conceived on national scales for local affiliates, links to American-Jewish patterns were strengthened for the immigrant membership as well.

For a second group of organizations, the unique constellation of government actions involved in Allied and Federal German Republic *Wiedergutmachung* presented stimuli for organizational action (legal, social welfare, political, international coordination) which, in effect, drew persons into immigrant activities whose professional or intellectual expertise had been well established outside the immigrant community. Acting as lobbies, pressure groups, legal aid societies, or social service agencies, organizations responded to needs and engaged in activities in typically German, Jewish, immigrant, American, and international contexts. This area resembled, as it were, a subculture of its own.

A third group of organizations similarly retained their organizational framework and their German-Jewish immigrant leadership but extended their activities by circumstances or policies beyond their original clienteles or memberships. Some religious congregations led by American-trained (if German-born) rabbis adopted a policy of slowly changing the composition of their membership and lessening congregational identification with German-Jewish traditions or rituals. Their programs generally followed directives developed by national synagogue federations. One major orthodox congregation, whose members appear to have had more children than would have been expected from their social composition and the Jewish birth rate in the United States, underwent functional changes in organizational cooperation with its national body while drawing on the children and grandchildren of the original founders for membership. Its intellectual and personal influence on American-Jewish orthodoxy remained substantial. (Members of its circle also established another major old-age and residence home for orthodox immigrants in the New York area.)

Social agencies like United Help or Selfhelp represented still another level of acculturation. When President Johnson's "Great Society" program made large government funds available for social purposes, and when state mortgages became available to nonprofit agencies for building programs, these immigrant agencies qualified for government funds very quickly, helped by their conservative "German" accounting and financing practices. The resulting expansion reflected a broad trend in American charitable work linking volunteer agencies with government programs designed to solve the massive social problems recognized in the 1960s. Cooperation between government and private social agencies, however, changed traditionally sectarian volunteer social work: government grants were tied to nondiscriminatory clauses demanding service for *all* eligible persons, including racial or ethnic minorities like blacks or Hispanic-speaking groups whose poverty had made them primary clients of social services. Thus, immigrant agencies repeated, in a few years, the history of other immigrant- or Jewish-founded hospitals, health services, or funds: they became general service agencies although still controlled by immigrant boards while retaining priority services for needy German- or Austrian-Jewish immigrants and for Nazi victims generally. (In 1979–80, a new "Fund for Survivors" being established in New York was to serve all kinds of victims of persecution ultimately independent of religion or national origin.)

The acculturation of the Jewish immigrant from Germany consists not of one, but many social and communal patterns even if differences in attitudes among individuals or social groups and the psychological background of their reactions to the major events of Nazi and postwar history are disregarded. Focussing research on immigrant attitudes toward Germany, or using one newspaper as the only source for the reactions of the community appears to narrow down a polymorphous, even fragmented, history. Organizational histories, sermons, memoirs, letters, oral history, the organizational press and mimeographed materials, organization programs and other materials offer basic documentation still to be collected and classified. Identificational acculturation — the changes in consciousness and stereotyped perception of emotional symbols like Germany, Nazism, the United States, Israel, in positive or negative terms — rests on changes in social and political realities. This article has shown how much information still needs to be synthesized if a balanced social and intellectual history of the Jewish immigrant of the Nazi period is to emerge.

VIII.

This chapter points to many questions that still have to be answered by precise and controlled studies. To point this out was, in fact, one of the purposes of this article.

In spite of this, however, the article made clear that the social, economic, and communal history of the German-Jewish immigrant must form the frame of reference within which the self-evaluations and ideological developments must be understood that are available in the written and unwritten sources of the period. The attempt to stress the contribution social history can make to the understanding of immigrant acculturation in an article of this length, i.e., the *Ansatz* of these remarks in group history and social change, has removed this article to some extent from the ebb and flow of concrete historic events. We expect to correct this methodological shortcoming in a full-length history.

Whether integration and acculturation may be pronounced successes or failures will depend on the values the participants in the process and later observers will bring to bear on the issue. German Jews were ill-prepared for the test historic forces, dimly understood, thrust upon them. Uprooting and re-integration left many lives permanently diverted from the self-fulfilling achievements that would have been within their grasp. The best of Jewish thought in religion, Jewish politics, or social thought was submerged in the determined *re-embourgeoisement* of the group, or in the eclectic intellectual environment they faced in their new homeland. Such issues remained the concern of a few isolated individuals. German Jews, as a group, made few if any contributions to issues of social equality — racial and ethnic minorities, urban plight, educational reform, civil rights, etc.

They played no role in American politics, and shunned the intellectual insecurities that afflict those who prefer to judge the present by the future. Comparative history may show that, in this, they shared the limitations of past German immigration waves to the United States more than the intellectual and political history of past Jewish immigrants. Like their German forerunners, through their work-orientation, they preferred concrete responses to the crises imposed on them. In this, they remained true to the social and intellectual qualities that formed the basic continuities — and such "success" in their own terms — in the process of culture change. Their very success was a condition of their failures.

References

* This article is based on a position paper prepared for the Directors of the Research Foundation for Jewish Immigration, New York. It was designed to review research directions of potential concern to the Foundation. The author gratefully acknowledges his debt to projects financed by the National Endowment for the Humanities, Deutsche Forschungsgemeinschaft, City University of New York Research Foundation, and the Research Foundation for Jewish Immigration and its sponsors.
The term "ethclass" denotes the system of class and status accepted *within* an ethnic minority or immigrant group. Its usage conforms to the terminology of American immigration history and the current analysis of American ethnic minorities.

S. Adler-Rudel, *Juedische Selbsthilfe unter dem Naziregime 1933–1939 im Spiegell der Berichte der Reichsvertretung der Juden in Deutschland* (Schriftenreihe Wiss. Abh. des Leo Baeck Institutes, 29, Mohr, Tuebingen, 1974).

C.J. Child, *The German-American in Politics 1914–1927* (University of Wisconsin Press, Madison, 1939).

D. Cunz, *The Maryland Germans. A History* (Princeton University Press, 1948).

M. Dobkowski, "The Fourth Reich — German-Jewish Religious Life in America Today" in *Judaism*, No. 27, 1 (Winter 1978), pp. 80–95.

M.R. Davie, *Refugees in America* (Harper Books, New York, 1947).

Ph. Gleason, *The Conservative Reformers. German-American Catholics and the Social Order* (Notre Dame University, Notre Dame-London, 1968).

J. Goldstein, I.J. Lukoff, and H.A. Strauss, "An Analysis of Autobiographical Accounts of Concentration Camp Experience of Hungarian Jewish Survivors," project MH 213, Grad. Fac., New School for Soc. Research, New York 1951, 147 pp. (mimeograph).

J.A. Hawgood, *The Tragedy of German-America* (sic) (Putnam's, New York-London, 1940).

D. Kent, *The Refugee Intellectual. The Americanization of the Immigrant of 1933–1945* (Columbia University, New York, 1953).

R. Neubauer, "Differential Adjustment of Adult Immigrants and their Children to American groups (The Americanization of a Selected group of Jewish Immigrants of 1933–1942)." Ed. D. Thesis, Columbia University, New York 1955 (ms.).

Research Foundation for Jewish Immigration, New York, *The Jewish Immigrant of the Nazi Period in the U.S.A.*, ed. Herbert A. Strauss (K.G. Saur Publishing Co., New York, 1979) — vol. I: H.W. Siegel, comp., *Archival Resources*, 1979; II: J. Wasserman, H. Braun, D. Gardner, et al., comp., *Classified and annotated bibliography*, 1980; vol. III–1: J. Lessing, comp., *Descriptive list: Oral History Holdings of the RFJI*, 1980; vol. III–2: *Classified list of articles on emigration and resettlement in the German-Jewish Press, 1933–1938 (1941)* (in preparation).

Research Foundation for Jewish Immigration, New York, M. Dobkowski and H.A. Strauss, "A Social and Intellectual History of the German-Jewish Immigrant of the Nazi Period in the U.S.A.," forthcoming.

Research Foundation for Jewish Immigration: Oral History Collection, 1972–date
D. Schneider, "Aufbau-Reconstruction and the Americanization of German-Jewish Immigrants 1934–1944." Thesis, History Department, Amherst University, Amherst, Mass. 1975 (ms.).

V.P. Sanua, "Differences in Personality Adjustment among Different Generations of American Jews and Non-Jews." Ph.D. thesis, University Michigan, Ann Arbor, Michigan, 1956 (ms.).

H.A. Strauss, "The Immigration and Acculturation of the German Jew in the United States of America," In *Year Book, Baeck Institute* XVI, 1971, pp. 63–94.

H.A. Strauss, "Resources and Research Directions in the History of the Emigré from Germany (1933–1945)." Paper, Georgetown University History Forum, Sept. 1975. 15 pp. (ms.).

H.A. Strauss, "Changing Images of the Immigrant in the U.S.A." In *Amerikastudien* No. 21, 1 (1976), pp. 119–138.

H.A. Strauss, "Nazi Persecution and Jewish Emigration from Germany 1933–1941." (Scheduled to appear in *Year Book, Leo Baeck Institute*, XXIV and XXV, 215 pp. (ms.).

C. Wittke, *German-Americans and the World War (with special emphasis on Ohio's German-language Press)* (Ohio State Archaeology and History Society, Columbus, 1936).

H.A. Walter, *Deutsche Exilliteratur 1933–1950* (Band 4, Exilpresse, Metzler, Stuttgart, 1978), pp. 543–678: "Aufbau."

15.

The Politics of American Jews: An Example of Ethnic Group Analysis

William Spinrad

"Ethnic politics" has been one of the most appealing subjects within the general domain of American ethnic group analysis. Analyses of the politics of American Jews have been especially popular, partly because, whatever the other manifestations, it is uniquely categorizable by one encompassing designation, "liberalism."[1] Recently, however, some commentators have noted a Jewish turn toward "conservatism."[2] Among the indications offered are the positions of many Jews on specific controversial issues of the past decade and a half, the vote in particular elections, the prominence of individual Jews among the spokesmen for "neoconservatism," and the anti-Israel postures of some "leftists."

Arguments about the subject naturally involve some attention to empirical data, with varying emphases and interpretations. But, they also typically depend upon specific definitions of "liberalism," assumptions about the dynamics of political attitude formation, notions about the political impact of ethnicity, and, above all, explanations for the observed long-time American Jewish political predilections. Put another way, one's expectation about continued Jewish liberalism or its decline is closely related to interpretations of what it is, how and why it came about and prevailed for so long.[3] Our own account will cover all these items in some manner, starting with an effort at clarification of the concept "liberalism," and an attempt at discerning whether it still describes the dominating political perspective of American Jews.

Liberalism and American Jews Today

What Is "Liberalism"?

Many discussions about "liberalism," especially those related to the specific subject of "Jewish liberalism," suffer from two opposed analytical fallacies. They either emphasize some very specific discrete issue or event or, at the other extreme, some generic, encompassing philosophical orientation to politics — both outlooks oddly joined by a presumed belief in a *real* essence called liberalism.[4] The more seminal approaches refer to a group of political values, manifested in a constellation of attitudes on issues, vote choices, etc. Since these values tend to be correlated, i.e., they go together in people's perceptions and judgments, the inclusive category, "liberal," is appropriate and useful. However, what is frequently missed is that the correlations, both among the values and clusters and within them, are not inherent or inevitable. They may all be logically consistent, but not logically unassailable, that is, other correlations and clusters are logically possible. One very pertinent current example, not immediately relevant to our subject matter, might properly indicate the intent of this conceptualization. Both political rhetoric and popular attitudes have recently stressed the twin demands for reduced inflation and tax cuts as parts of an intimately-related program, even though, in terms of orthodox Keynesian logic, they are inherently contradictory. In other words, all observed connections among attitudes and values are not universal inherent relations, but products of concrete historical experiences.

From that vantage point, the *liberalism* we should be talking about is a constellation of three general political thrusts that became significantly correlated in American political discourse and popular perceptions by the 1930s: a demand for an active role of the government in relation to the economy, particularly as related to welfare state concerns; a drive toward equality, including the legal provisions subsumed under the concept of civil rights; a quest for individual freedom from coercion in those areas which are exclusively individual, legally manifested in protection of civil liberties. Most variants of "left radicalism" emerge, at least initially, from similar value emphases, even though the politics thus developed may sometimes turn into something directly opposed to the original tenets, (e.g., the anti-civil libertarian tendencies of official communism). The general "socialist" orientation, which we will dwell on at several points, includes a wide variety of principles and proposals; for our operational purposes, it is simply perceived as akin to contemporary liberalism, only more so. "Internationalism" is commonly added as another crucial value emphasis, especially since it seems to fit in with the assumed liberal "essence." As will be later illustrated, the attitudes included under this heading are uniquely historically-specific and are peripheral to our analysis.

The Continuation of Jewish Liberalism?

From the vantage point of these definitions, let us look at some of the publicized events supposedly exemplifying the decline of Jewish liberalism — the confrontation between the largely Jewish local of the United Federation of Teachers and a black community school board in Ocean Hill-Brownsville in Brooklyn, the opposition of Jewish residents in Forest Hills to low cost public housing, the heavy Jewish vote for "law and order" local candidates and against presumably "liberal" spokesmen, widespread Jewish hostility to the American Civil Liberties Union after it defended the right of Nazis to march in Skokie, Illinois, the opposition of Jewish organizations to minimal "quotas" for black medical school applicants under the Affirmative Action formula in the Bakke case. Many more could easily be added. In actuality, these illustrate some of the special tensions confronting the liberal position in recent times, in fact the divisions within the typical liberal coalition. But, they were internal tensions because they posed such a dilemma within the general continuing direction of orientation, and Jews were heavily represented on the other side, for instance among the members of the Civil Liberties Union and those who supported the idea of quotas in the Bakke case. In summary, none of these situations seems to represent a significant widespread diminution of the general political value-thrusts listed.

More importantly, the evidence for continuing American Jewish liberalism is powerful. Voting for national Democratic candidates is considered one useful index. Even in 1972, when George McGovern was regarded as a captive of the New Left and Nixon as a friend of Israel, McGovern received, according to poll data, about 65 percent of the Jewish vote, compared to 38 percent in the nation.[5] Carter got about 70 percent of the Jewish vote in 1976, about 51 percent nationally. (It should be unnecessary to describe the similar findings for earlier presidential elections.) In the absence of extensive data, it is reasonable to suggest that similar findings are likely for most congressional, senatorial, and gubernatorial elections, except when the Republican candidate assumed the liberal mantle or when other unique candidate features were important.[6]

However, the Jewish retreat from liberalism was supposedly most marked in local elections, when the "newer issues" were most relevant and when traditional allegiances had less of a bearing. Others have carefully appraised these situations; it is unnecessary to review them all, but in all cases those candidates popularly defined as liberal (itself a controversial designation) did much better among Jewish voters than among any other nonblack, non-Hispanic group.[7] True, the Jewish vote for such candidates was less than typical, and in one election, that in Philadelphia in 1971, the strident "law and order" candidate, Mayor Rizzo, did get about half the Jewish vote. Some saw these instances as revealing an obvious trend, but it would be best to perceive them as responses to immediate situations of tension, not as inherently continuing phenomena, as illustrated by subsequent elections. In Los Angeles, for instance, victorious black mayorality candidate, Bradley, received 60 percent of the Jewish vote in 1973; he got 55 percent in his unsuccessful bid four years earlier, after a scurrulous campaign by incumbent Mayor Yorty.[8] (By the late 1970s, voting in municipal elections, so heavily influenced by fiscal crisis anxieties, typically assumed too confusing a pattern for any meaningful analysis along these lines).

Perhaps the best indicators of continuing Jewish liberalism, in terms of all three dimensions listed, is provided by responses to survey questions. Whatever is recently available indicates strong Jewish adherence to liberal tenets on such issues as government health insurance, programs for jobs, tax reform, help for the poor, postures toward unions and big business, support for black aspirations.[9] Similar responses show up on the advertized "social issues" — civil disobedience, amnesty, abortion, marijuana. According to one analyst, the difference between Jewish "liberalism scores" and those of the rest of the population was about the same as in the 1950s, and, furthermore, the data suggests that Jews were actually more liberal on most issues than "they were twenty years ago."[10] Of additional significance is the observed predominance of liberalism among younger Jews on all issues, regardless of amount of education or family income.[11]

Of course, exceptions and deviations, divergences among Jews, etc., can readily be noted, but the overall tendency remains decisive.[12] Despite persistent reports of, and frequent fervent hopes in some quarters for, a Jewish "shift to the right," especially in the current context of supposed "growing conservatism," the predominant liberalism of American Jews, down to this day, should be accepted as a given datum. The purpose of this article is, then, to appraise various explanations for this phenomenon, and to place it within the framework of analyses of ethnic politics generally, with some attention to recent developments.

Explanations for American Jewish Liberalism

All the varied explanations for the persistence of American Jewish liberalism can be usefully grouped under the headings of social structure, culture, and communication.

Social Structure — Social Positions and Interests

The most obvious, and probably the most common type of explanation is some variant of the stress on the typical "outsider" position of Jews — prejudice and discrimination (for which the code word "anti-Semitism" is usually applied), marginality, status-insecurity. All "out ethnic groups" tend to have special political vantage points in all countries, varying with the specific characteristics of each group and the relevant historical background, often with a marked "right" or "left" component.[13] For American Jews this has typically meant support of liberal politics and liberal politicians, most likely in the Democratic party since the 1930s, because they were mostly associated with liberal political positions deemed beneficial to Jewish interests.[14] Why should this be so, why should such politics be seen as "pro Jewish," especially since the liberal economic program, and that of the leading democratic figures, has been, according to popular impressions, inimical to the economic interests of better-off Jews, and few conservatives and Republicans have been expressly anti-Jewish? Certainly, although there are arguments about the continued liberal-Democratic allegiance of high-status members of the other out-ethnic groups, their loyalty has hardly been as marked as that of high-status Jews.[15]

One frequent answer dwells on the continuation of a tradition that developed in Europe with the modern era.[16] The protagonists for the Enlightenment included Jewish emancipation in their political agenda. The French Revolution accented the same type of sentiment, and, throughout later European history, the liberal forces were the ones most likely to proclaim and defend Jewish rights, and Jews were often prominent in their ranks. In the extreme version of the scenario, the generic universalistic ethos implicit in political liberalism becomes, essentially, an ideological legitimation for the enhancement of Jewish interests.[17] Perhaps the ultimate expression of such an historical coincidence hypothesis is Halpern's assertion that Jewish liberalism was a "functional equivalent," in an historically appropriate time, for the traditional conservatism of Jewish communities in the "pre-liberal" era.[18] As an illustration of his observation that such liberalism was neither inherent nor universal, he points out that many Jews remained loyal to "protecting" monarchal rulers, as in Holland. Cohn, writing in the mid-1950s, when anxieties about "populist" thrusts were so prevalent among American intellectuals, further perceives Jewish liberalism as part of the continuing collective effort at protection from mob anti-Semitism by an always marginal social group.[19]

Cultural Continuity

The foregoing does involve some notion of cultural continuity from recent European experiences, appropriately activated in terms of recent and current social positions. Another type of popular analysis, which does not ignore the contemporary social-position features, emphasizes more long-range Jewish cultural traditions, after going back to the ideas of the Bible and Talmud. Above all, such depictions are presented as a way of accounting for the liberalism of higher-status American Jews. The most quoted example is that of Fuchs, some twenty-five years ago, who accented three central ingredients of the tradition most hospitable to contemporary liberalism:[20]

1. "Zedekah" — the concept of justice rather than charity in dealing with the deprived and unfortunate.

2. Intellectuality — a passion for nonutilitarian learning.
3. Nonasceticism — a belief that the good life is possible for all.

In terms of their relevance for liberalism, intellectuality would be associated with civil libertarian doctrines, such as autonomy from authoritarian controls, Zedekah with the principle of community, i.e., governmental responsibility for citizen welfare, nonasceticism with the belief in the possibility of obtaining such a general welfare. Fuchs admits that many Christian theologians have proclaimed similar doctrines, but too many have been offered contrary philosophies.

Elazar presented a later, rather fanciful interpretation, admittedly largely speculative.[21] To him, prevailing American Jewish political perspectives represent both a facile adaptation to American traditional values and a realization of Judaic political tenets unique in Jewish diaspora history. His constituent elements are the following: tradition, as opposed to ideology; agrarianism, as opposed to urbanism; federalism, as opposed to central government; messianism. The "agrarian" notion is certainly opposed to most appraisals of the Jewish tradition, but he seems to assume that the rustic virtues, so extolled by the prophets, have continued to offer direction through all the centuries of urban residence; in turn, the rural *Gemeinschaft* ethos is translated into concerns about moral justice in contemporary urbanized America. The American federalist scheme is considered akin to the Judaic vision of government by covenant. However, the obvious demand for a greater role by central government in recent liberalism is seen as a reflection of another tenet of Judaic politics, brought into the discussion ad hoc, the "monarchal" principle, in the classic Greek sense — the goal of a "positive government." Elazar adds one other observation: Judaic tradition shares the Yankee moralistic culture, including the drive for politics as moral action, an assessment in contrast to Fuchs' portrayal of the Yankee Puritan morality as being, at least in some versions, antithetical to the notion of Zedekah. In addition, Elazar does admit that some aspects of the Judaic tradition are alien to American liberalism — something typically ignored by most analysts: the demand for the suppression of "error" and the somewhat related national and religious intolerance.

Several have described how various aspects of the tradition — intellectuality, universality, justice — help make American Jews more "internationalist."[22] Others pinpoint the individual political figures, who were so heavily supported by Jews, as exemplars of the desired cultural traits; Franklin Roosevelt is thus defined as a latter-day prophet, proclaiming the need to help the downtrodden; Adlai Stevenson as a fitting replica of the man devoted to ideas.[23] Such contentions will be later appraised, but it is appropriate to indicate, at this point, that these two interpretations represent cogent examples of the type of superficial, casual statements so common in political-social analysis.

One other culturological explanation also appears frequently, the socialist or "radical" aspect conspicuous in American Jewish political history. Since this is a major feature of my own analysis, and the nature of the impact is usually insufficiently spelled-out, further consideraion is reserved for later discussion. However, its appropriateness is related to a recent comment by Fuchs that some current manifestations of Jewish liberalism may be partly a result of "visceral attachments to the political symbols and associations of the past."[24] In its bald form, this would imply that political perspectives may be little but collective memory traces, but it does suggest the viability of past responses as anchoring points for present outlooks.

Communal Organization and Communication

Jewish American communities have been uniquely internally-cohesive and well organized, both formally and informally.[25] Such an observation is hardly open to refutation. Although definitely representing an example of historical continuity, based on both the collective Jewish social position and cultural values, its meaning for the American scene, where the "joining habit" has always been extolled, is especially pertinent. Among other things, such considerations accent an appreciation of the fact that political attitudes, values, etc., like any others, are not merely a product of individual reactions but are also, to a large extent, developed in communication with others, a truism which is often slighted. In addition, the specific thrust of so many Jewish communal organizations may be specifically significant. More than those of other groups, they have been oriented, especially in the United States, toward various forms of "help" for community members in accord with the noncondescending Zedekah principle, often with a very institutionalized style. Litt offers the imaginative possibility that this added up to a "welfare state in miniature," thus making Jews very susceptible to the idea of extending the scheme to the entire society.[26]

Appraising the Explanations

Position-Interests

Each of these approaches, as a general type and as a set of specific assertions, will be briefly appraised in turn, with some attention to their connection with ethnic group politics in general. It should be unnecessary to belabor the point that the various "outsider" interpretations have much relevance. Still, they have to account for the continuing liberalism when Jews have so improved their positions in American society, individually and collectively. This is not merely a matter of economics; it also covers questions of status, power, and acceptability. The argument about continuing anti-Semitism is too glib, for it can explain anything one chooses. Of course, many commentators have predicted that increasing Jewish conservatism would result. As has been pointed out, specific Jewish "interests" may sometimes foster attitudes in violation of the traditional pattern, but, overall, the possible "trend to conservatism" has been grossly exaggerated.

The "outsider" emphasis comes up against another caution, as proposed by Litt.[27] He insists that the more insecure, marginal American Jews have the fearful vista of the "submerged," evident in the lack of tolerance and absence of political activism, further implying the kind of anomie so frequent among similar types everywhere which is most likely to assume a nonliberal political direction. According to Litt, the liberal Jew possesses a more "positive self" from "positive Jewish identity," which emerges from the specific American Jewish subculture and communal life.[28] In other words, the cultural and communal-communication aspects must be a salient part of any analysis. An interesting reflection of the juxtaposition of these elements is seen in some developments of recent times — the situation where interests come into conflict with ideologies, as in arguments over affirmative action and the problem of Jewish "New Leftists," faced with the dilemma of supporting their political colleagues' condemnations of Israel and their propensity for loyalty to the Jewish state.[29]

The position-interest aspects are thus very complex, especially their relation to liberalism. Outsiders, for instance are obviously not always liberal on civil liberties and civil rights questions. In this instance, because of the explanations offered by Litt and the specific political-cultural heritage, this feature of the liberal perspective remains strong, even for those who are hardly outsiders any longer.[30] The experience of discrimination and denial is not merely individual. The knowledge of what has happened to so many others, pervasively communicated in the subculture from the cradle on, steers one toward, in the context of other elements of the subculture, a liberal tolerant orientation, even for those who have had little personal contact with those affected.

The welfare state component of contemporary liberalism still has to be further related to current positional-interest considerations. Is this persistent Jewish orientation mostly a matter of cultural continuity, a longstanding ideological answer to national problems not directly appropriate to any particular spots in the social schema for the large proportion of Jews who have long since left the lower rungs of the economic ladder? This would still constitute a powerful impetus for that kind of politics, and is probably a major part of the explanation. But, a closer examination of current American Jewish occupational composition, apparently not available in sufficient detail, suggests another explanation for their economic liberalism in terms of current positions. The upward mobility from the world of their fathers has, apparently, been mostly to either entrepreneurial or managerial positions, in small and medium-sized businesses, or to professions.

The characteristic political tendencies of small businessmen vary widely with historical and personal circumstances, but are often associated with economic liberalism.[31] In some cases, it may also turn toward super patriotism, radical right politics, or even fascism; for many reasons which need not be here detailed, the latter is unlikely among Jewish small businessmen. The other occupational classifications may be too gross, being insufficiently attentive to specific work situations. Thus, the most politically alert and active American Jews, the "opinion leaders" of the community, are likely to be found among what several have called the "New Class," wherever they would fit under more conventional terminology.[32] These include teachers, social workers, health providers, scientific and technical researchers, policymakers and planners, those in some branch of the communications industry. Many live both off and for ideas, thus both continuing the Jewish tradition of intellectuality and, more important for our purposes, placing them in the interpersonal milieu of other American intellectuals whose dominant political ethos is liberalism, at least along the dimensions we have emphasized. As a more specific stimulus for the welfare state posture, a large proportion are involved in, help determine, or at least require government programs and government expenditures for their work. Thus, New Class people involved in the New Politics behind McGovern's nomination in 1972 and those working for the Committee for a Democratic Majority which sought Henry Jackson's nomination, opposed to each other on many questions, particularly on foreign policy, generally agreed on welfare state items. It is also appropos that Jews form a significant part of the membership and leadership of the fastest growing unions, those representing teachers and government workers, both containing a sizeable proportion of New Class types. Occupational changes have thus not all resulted in alterations in Jewish social positions which make any aspect of liberalism less appealing.

Cultural Continuity

Among the culturological explanations, many of the ideas mentioned are facile, enchanting intellectual tidbits, difficult to refute or support, ultimately of little value heuristically. To take Elazar's quaint formulation, for instance, messianism may have something to do with the optimism of American Jewish liberalism, after all the twentieth century cataclysms.[33] But, adopting the canon of parsimony, it is hardly necessary for any sound analysis. More easily dismissed is the portrayal of specific American political leaders, such as Franklin D. Roosevelt and Stevenson, as symbolic expressions of the Jewish ethos. The first national political hero for Jews was probably Al Smith, a plebian politician rather than a replica of the prophets. Stevenson's Jewish vote was lower than that of most Democratic presidential candidates; the vote for Lyndon Johnson, the crude school teacher from Texas turned master politician, was similar to that for Franklin Roosevelt.[34]

The more challenging culturological schema, best exemplified by Fuchs' formula, looks for a very long term influence, grounded in the ancient religious tenets.[35] In the extreme form presented, it bears the mark of a belief in a transcendental folk *Geist*. The influence of religious doctrines and practices, traditional or more recent, upon the typical politics of any group is related to the specific historical-societal context for which it is relevant, whether the explanation is sought in terms of immediate group interests and/or as a reflection of a continuing political culture. Thus, Fuchs himself describes how American Southern Jews, pre-Civil War and under the Confederacy, tended to be loyal to the Slavocrat position, regardless of whether they were slave owners themselves. Examining the larger Jewish historical perspective, the notion of an inherent, liberal-type political ethos, grounded in universalism, justice, learning, etc., becomes even more suspect. All religious traditions are many-faceted.[36] Elazar appropriately notes the intolerant and xenophobic elements that often cropped up in the Jewish tradition.[37] While Jews may have tended to be internationalists in the modern era, many, as pointed out by Halpern, became chauvinistic nationalists of their respective countries, symbolized by, of all people, Alfred Dreyfus.[38]

Without implying anything resembling a comprehensive review of Jewish world history, it is easy enough to note examples of social and cultural styles associated with a "conservative" vista, using the derogatory implications emphasized by opponents — authoritarianism, intolerance, parochialism, obscurantism, disdain for the underdog, and, in the current context, less than enthusiastic support for welfare state principles. One recent commentator even offers the proclamation that "the alternative to liberalism is Judaism."[39] While this bizarre formula can be appropriately dismissed, representations of many of these attributes easily suggest themselves for the premodern era, i.e., before Jews were much involved in the politics of the larger society.[40] Since then, the pattern has not been all in one general political direction. Even the Jewish adherents of Enlightenment were varied in their political outlooks. For instance, the early nineteenth century Haskalah of Central and Eastern Europe, so dedicated to having Jews absorb all the new learning of the Western world, frequently admonished the poor for their laziness and lack of diligence in language as abrasive and pontifical of the extreme exemplars of the Puritan Ethic.[41] Hassidism, with all its spiritual-communal uplift quality, has frequently exhibited all the "antiliberal" attributes of any other tightly-unified and self-contained charismatic sect, very evident in the United States today.[42] A large part of the world Jewish population, those living in North Africa and the non-Israeli Near East, apparently so ignored by historians until recently, seem to have had societies and cultures with many of the nonliberal features listed.[43] Certainly, the political role of the immigrants from these areas in Israel has been sufficiently noted, including their inclination to vote for the Herut Party, the local spokesmen for conservatism in all contemporary meanings of the term.[44] When they helped elect Begin as prime minister, they illustrated that certain types of Jews in certain types of situations are disposed toward the politics of a political leader, who, at the time of his election at least, represented an Israeli equivalent of a Ronald Reagan or a Barry Goldwater.

Finally, accounts of the supposed liberalism of American Jews up to the latter part of the nineteenth century indicate another instance of poorly operationalized concepts. Largely of German heritage, they may have brought with them the hopes of the ill-fated 1848 revolution in that country.[45] Translated into contemporary American terms, this included opposition to slavery (but little sympathy with abolitionist movements), ultimately to identification with the Republican party and its dominant philosophy — commitment to rapid economic expansion under a system of laissez-faire capitalism dominated by industrial and financial tycoons. Some, more socially conscious Jews, did adhere to the progressive wing of the party, whose orientation toward the deprived contained, according to many historians, a large element of aristocratic noblesse oblige rather than the Zedekah concept of universal justice.[46]

Community-Communication

So many discussions of "group factors" in politics, particularly those about ethnic groups, ignore such aspects. Implicitly, they seem to assume that each person develops his political attitudes, values, perspectives, etc., by himself. As indicated, several analyses of American Jewish politics do dwell on this feature. Jews influence other Jews, and several elements of their subcommunity situation make such mutual impact especially effective. The likelihood that their interpersonal contacts will be so dominantly with other Jews, even for the most "accepted" and least isolated, means a pervasive milieu for any political inclinations prevalent among Jews, such as contemporary liberalism. Of course, the numerous formal organizations also provide an effective arena for such dissemination. However, it is my contention that explanations of Jewish liberalism in terms of both cultural continuity and communication, and, to some extent, social-structural factors, require one additional ingredient, an appreciation of the importance of the socialist heritage.

The Socialist Heritage

The characteristic political style of the twentieth century American

Jews did not emerge until the mass immigration from Eastern Europe. The politics the immigrations brought with them, and further developed in the American scene — socialism and kindred political doctrines — was the major cultural influence on all later American Jewish perspectives. Socialism seemed to have had little appeal for the German Jewish population in the United States, even though non-Jewish Germans provided one of the two ethnic sources of American socialist strength up to World War I.[47] The other, of course, was the population of the urban ghettos that stemmed from Eastern Europe. As Jews in those countries became interested and involved in secular politics, socialist ideas and organizations became their appropriate vehicle.[48] Traditional liberals had done little to change authoritarian systems and, accordingly, to ease Jewish emancipation. The socialists, of all tendencies, most clearly expounded the goals of freedom and equality, had prominent intellectual spokesmen and the potentiality of mass organization. Socialist movements provided the best liaison between Jews and gentile political forces, and, on the other hand, supplied, in the Jewish Socialist Bund, a unique mechanism for maintaining national and cultural identity. One other feature demands reiteration. So much of the Jewish population was poor — proletarians, artisans, petty shopkeepers. To them, socialism meant more than justice in the abstract sense, but a concrete vision of a satisfying economic existence. (Incidentally, there seems so little recent recognition of the fact that much of the dynamic spirit and creative leadership responsible for Israel sprang from similar roots).

Those who did not bring their socialism with them to America picked it up, or some offshoot thereof, in their immediate environment, so dominantly Jewish, and from the continuing immersion in poverty for considerable numbers, especially the shopworkers. Enough writers have described the vigorous, many faceted, large-scale involvement in socialist and labor organizations, and the educational and cultural activities with which they were associated, all so closely tied in with Yiddishism, the expression of the culture of Eastern Europe Jewish masses.[49] Very symbolically, the socialist *Forward* was the single most influential publication. As the most politically-informed sector of the Jewish communities in the larger cities, the socialists, or at least socialistically-inclined, had considerable influence over the ideas of their nonsocialist relatives, friends, coworkers, and neighbors, even among many religious-minded Jews who were alienated by the agnosticism, sometimes outspoken atheism, of some socialist spokesmen. What is additionally important is that most other Jews completely accepted the socialists personally, i.e., they were not regarded as pariahs or strange deviants, but as colleagues and comrades, often as opinion leaders.

Of course, socialist movements declined and so many Jews moved into higher-status occupations and more comfortable economic circumstances, but the heritage remained. Sometimes it took the form of a renewed interest in socialism, as during the 1930s depression, when Jews, often the descendents of the earlier socialists,, were again prominent among the leaders and members of the revived socialist movements.[50] (The growing communist movement of those days, which was, in so many ways, alien to the tenets of the American Jewish political tradition, had a special appeal for many American Jews because it developed out of the same origins.) Similarly, when the New Left developed in the 1960s, with its own peculiar and hazy socialist directions, Jews, often with similar family antecedents, were again a conspicuous part.[51] Current emerging socialist groupings, obviously small but with a meaningful potential following, also probably contain a conspicuous Jewish presence, if not as prominent proportionally as previously.

The major influence for most Jews has been in the direction of ready acceptance, and even forceful proclamation, of the idea of a welfare state, the belief in a "positive" government role vis-à-vis the economy, especially when such a perspective was a viable part of the national political agenda, as in the 1930s. New Dealism was obviously a reaction to the calamities of that decade, but its ideological origins can be traced to a combination of sources of which socialism was one significant part, alongside, among other things, the Populist and Progressive traditions and the plebian-based politics of the municipal machines.

Yes, the socialism of most American Jews has been only a lingering memory, their own or of their parents or grandparents. Sometimes it would come to life again under specific historical circumstances. More often it supplied a useful guide for viewing contemporary American politics, providing a meaningful and appropriate orientation to the problems of the times, readily reinforced and reinvigorated by personal contacts and the legitimacy of their position in the general political culture. Thus, New Deal liberalism, and its later derivatives, became the current equivalents of the earlier politics. Accounts of the loss of dedication and passion are besides the point. This is how the political attitudes of these concrete human beings were steered, whatever the intensity of their commitment. The unique strains of any moment, and the current disputes which pose questions not so neatly in line with the traditional politics, must still be viewed within the general context of that heritage, regardless of the present individual or collective social positions of American Jews.

All that has been said includes many references to the impact of interpersonal communication, a subject further developed later.

Ethnic Politics

Our analysis still has to be put into some conceptualization of the twentieth century American Jewish political perspective within a model of explanation for ethnic politics generally, including some attention to recent complications. Let us probe once more the second half of the concept — politics. For our purpose, we have emphasized that the principal attitudes and values of the modern "liberal" perspective were classifiable under the headings of civil liberties, civil rights, and the positive economic role of government-welfare state cluster. These three can, obviously, fit together, but there is no inherent logical reason why they have to be universally correlated under a generic *Weltanschauung* called "liberalism." Certainly, the typical liberalism of nineteenth century Europe attests to the opposite possibility. They are, similarly, not an intrinsic part of a universal Jewish historical tradition, originating in the Bible and Talmud, although themes in accord with those attitudes and values can certainly be found and may have had some cultural influence. By now, any historical interpretation that concentrates only on persistent ideological themes should be suspect.

Through a combination of historical coincidences, readily explainable, these three dimensions became intimately associated in political policy, rhetoric, personages, organizations. Their relative "outsider" positions and the Jewish experience in modern Europe made most American Jews, initially, adherents of civil liberties and civil rights, in watever form these appeared on the agenda in those days. But, this had little to do with the economic policy aspects of later liberalism. That became part of the prevalent politics of American Jews through the socialism of Eastern European immigrants, initially transformed into an approval of the mild, plebian social reform program of an Al Smith in the 1920s, later stimulating ready acceptance of New Dealism when its policy thrusts became cogently relevant. That, in some form, is the major ingredient of the political perspectives of the overwhelming majority of American Jews to this day.

Note, I have generally left out of the discussion two publicized and obviously meaningful aspects of American Jewish political orientation — the "internationalist" outlook and the significance of Israel, or, for that matter, Zionist ideology. Taking the latter first, Zionism undoubtedly had a transcendental meaning for many American Jews, and almost all have been passionately devoted both to the protection of Israel and to its further development. They have therefore tried to influence American policy accordingly. But, this had had little to do with American political disputes, for there has been an amazing consensus on national policy toward Israel, whatever the disagreement on very specific questions, both in the positions advanced by most politicians and in popular opinions.[52] (Whether this could change in the future is much too speculative to consider.)

The "internationalist" idea is much more complicated. Surely, the Jewish experience tended to encourage internationalist outlooks; despite frequent contrary examples, Jews have too often suffered from nationalistic chauvinisms and conflicts, have typically gained more by peace than war. But the positions usually included under the heading in discussions about the United States are historically-specific, often in a historically-special relation to the various elements of the liberal political perspective. It is usually forgotten that, in the early part of the twentieth century, intervention in foreign affairs was often associated with the strident belligerence of right-wing nationalists, isolationism with American radicalism, perhaps best symbolized by Senator Robert LaFollete, Sr. The Socialist party vigorously opposed the nation's participation in World War I, for which Debs and others went to prison. It was only in the period before World War II that the interventionist-isolationist debate developed its connection with the struggle against fascism, thus obviously important to Jewish interests and values. On the other hand, the right wing-isolationist cohorts began to coalesce, although never as completely as assumed in usual interpretations, providing for the ready inclusion of interventionism, the code word for internationalism at this time, within the complex of liberal values, a coincidental concomitance which analysts have since exaggerated.

The postwar period continued this line-up, almost as an appropriately simple and convenient way for alignment inherited from the recent past. For Jews, the development of the United Nations further presented a conceivable protection for their colleagues everywhere and particularly for the state of Israel, officially created by the U.N. In this instance, position-interest considerations moved American Jews toward an "internationalist" position. But, this stance did not prevent Jewish hostility toward the U.N. for its later many anti-Israel acts, from the condemnation of the Sinai invasion in 1956 to the resolutions attacking Israel in various U.N. bodies. Finally, the foreign policy issues of the 1960s and 1970s, especially those most divisive, cannot, in any useful sense, be defined in terms of the old labels — Viet Nam War, détente with Russia, etc. In fact, former "internationalists" are likely to be the most vociferous proponents of reductions in American military commitments abroad. For American Jews specifically, neither interests nor values suggest any continuing ideological categorizations on that score.

I have also given little attention to the question of "identity," which looms so large in many discussions of ethnicity. The reason should become evident in my attempt to spell out a version of at least one type of ethnic politics as a phenomenon, pointedly reflected in the dominant politics of American Jews. The usage of the concept of "ethnic group" is as varied as references to any other "group." In the more limited, and more consequential personal meaning, a "group" implies a collectivity of individuals with some interaction among its members and, in Giddings' classic language, some "consciousness of kind." Many ethnic group analysts emphasize this formulation, particularly when talking about ethnic politics — that is, it is based upon recognition, by a sizable number of objectively-located "ethnics," of their group's boundaries from other groups, with whom they conflict, ally, bargain, etc., by formal and informal mechanisms.[53] In political terms, this is what identity actually adds up to.[54]

The importance of this phenomenon should obviously be recognized in many historical examples of ethnic politics. But, it is not a crucial element of many analyses of such politics and is, by the canon of parsimony, almost unnecessary for most of my depiction, and those of others, of the bases for the prevalent American Jewish political ethos. In other words, noting the incidence of group identity is helpful for understanding some specific features at particular times, but is not essential for our overall analysis.

It is sufficient to define ethnic groups as "socially-relevant categories," an analytically primitive version of a "social group." To start with, let us assume that ethnicity, of any type — race, religion, nationality background, etc., or some combination thereof — is, initially, only an objective attribute noted by an observer. However, suppose he further notes a statistical correlation between that attribute and, for want of a better inclusive term, some mental manifestations. Political examples would include such things as: vote choice, attitudes revealed by a variety of techniques, clusters of attitudes indicating more general value orientations, etc. Of course, such statistical associations may be spurious for several technical reasons, may explain little, or may reveal something analytically important. By whatever method the finding is deemed meaningful and valuable, some more generic explanation is ultimately presented, using other systematic data or in casual ad hoc fashion. The attribute is thus shown to be politically-relevant, which, to repeat, does not involve any necessary assumption of subjective identity. The relevance simply results from one or more of the following:

1. Those in politically-relevant social categories are likely to have had, and still have, similar positions in the social-political system which affects their views of "what's good for them."
2. Those in similar categories are likely to have had similar experiences, including absorption of something resembling a "subculture," which affects their evaluation of the various political ideas proclaimed in the political arena.
3. Those who are in similar categories are likely to be, and have been, recipients of similar interpersonal communication, including frequent communication with each other.

The use of the term "likely" accents the probabilistic nature of all observations, with accompanying recognition of the fact that all individuals have, among other things, many social attributes, have each had varied experiences, communications, etc. — a truism that, somehow, always has to be repeated.[55]

This paradigm is, obviously, in precise accord with our categories of explanations for prevalent American Jewish politics, which also included little reference to questions of subjective identity. The outsider social position aspect most likely implies some self-identity, but is still comprehensible without any such emphasis. That is, it did not take any profound mental effort to realize that being Jewish brought inherent problems, no need for "consciousness-raising" about their "groupness" to reveal their difficulties, or, for that matter, to suggest solutions, which, for the thrust of this essay, were mostly along the lines of a set of general American political tenets. In addition, the occupational and income situation also facilitated such tenets, as did the economically insecure positional situations of the depression era and, perhaps, the New Class occupational situs of recent times. While we have critiqued any universalistic culturological explanation, the more immediate cultural antecedents, originally in modernizing Western Europe and, later and more importantly, among the Eastern European immigrants, reinforced and expanded in the American setting, has been extensively discussed.

The "communication" feature was noted at various points, but warrants further explanation. The personal milieu of so many of the Eastern European Jews and their descendents, with socialist ideas so much a part of the atmosphere, was dominantly Jewish. Even nonsocialists, as already explained, were under the constant personal influence of those immersed in that setting, who were probably often the political opinion leaders of their circles. For the early shop workers, their non-Jewish acquaintances were likely to be occupational colleagues or other plebian neighbors. The mutually-reinforcing communication was further intensified in the many formal organizations, and the receptivity to other communication, such as that from the mass media, was undoubtedly "selectively" steered by the political perspectives learned in interpersonal contacts. In obviously modified form, we can extend this formula to this day. As a summary proposition, it can be reasonably stated that American Jews have tended to be placed in interpersonal networks in which liberalism has been the dominant political strain whenever politics is discussed. Even those, who, by position and other social contacts, should be expected to have different views, are likely to have a large circle of interpersonal contacts with people who express the liberal creed, and who, so frequently, are most informed, involved, and persuasive.

Ethnic politics need not be a matter of structured ethnic groups, as has been suggested.[56] As explained by Samuel Lubell some twenty years ago, "their influence is exerted through common group consciousness, through the effect of common antecedents and cultural traditions which enable them to view developing issues from a common point of view."[57] Thus, ethnic politics does not require any definitive ethnic posture or "celebration."

While such expressions can intensify the impact of ethnicity on politics, they are not only unnecessary for exploring the dominant politics of American Jews; the search for their manifestations can be analytically misleading. Nevertheless, under certain circumstances, they may assume a special importance, at least as episodic phenomena. This has been, to some extent, true recently, as will be later considered.

Conclusion

One can view ethnic politics as representing a series of relations among groups, composed of people who clearly define themselves as members of such groups, involving an array of interests, conflicts, and, hopefully, accommodations. The historic prototype is the old-style municipal political machine, with its allotments of patronage and other favors to each group, its balanced electoral tickets, and so on. Writing from the vista of the late 1960s, Litt questions how the "stability of pluralistic politics," upon which ethnic bargaining takes place, will be able to survive the severe strains from more comprehensive black demands, requiring policies beyond the realm of any municipality.[58] He ignores the other picture of ethnic politics which I have emphasized — distinctive ethnic styles developing from specific ethnic subcultures, transmitted and reinforced in communication networks, oriented toward *national* political policies. Although group interests are important, both as impetus for accepting such policies and applying them in specific instances, the proposed programs are likely to be presented as answers to common problems rather than as solutions for purely parochial needs.

In the past decade or so, many commentators have either noted or proclaimed the need for the first type of ethnic politics, based upon the defense or enhancement of clearly observable group interests for American Jews, which could, conceivably, diminish the generic liberalism related to the second type. The inspiration for such observations came, to a large extent, from the apparent strained relations between Jews and blacks, whose problems and concerns had been, and should continue to be, of prime importance to those who uphold liberal doctrines. In many situations involving such questions as control of schools, neighborhood changes, police and judicial policy, Jews have not only been pitted against blacks, but this has been the major contest. More recently, in the application of job and educational affirmative action programs, Jewish and black organizations have sometimes been the leading contenders. Furthermore, well publicized organizations, like the Jewish Defense League, have obtained some following with no other goal but that of "Jewish interests," as they define them, with announced advocacy of "illiberal" methods.

Yet, the data earlier described indicate that all this has had little apparent effect on the general liberal political orientation of most American Jews, whatever their views in specific situations. As mentioned, Jews have even been prominent in presenting the officially "non-Jewish" side of the affirmative action debate, and, despite their differences on precise applications of this type of policy, major Jewish and black organizations typically maintain close collaborative relations in pressing for their many common programs.[59] Let us add one more apparently antiliberal trend. In the absence of much definitive data, one can assume that Jews have joined other Americans in their adherence to reduced government spending and tax reduction as *the* solutions to national and personal economic problems.

The inordinate attention to all of these, and to occasional other-type incidents involving possible anti-Semitism among varied groups, illustrates a common danger in many political analyses, a failure to make appropriate distinctions between the episodic-ephemeral and the lasting-endemic, sometimes casually assuming that the former will automatically be persistent and historically consequential. That is why, for instance, so many discussions about the 1960s now sound so stale, especially coming from those who still seem to talk as though those turbulent days were still with us. Emphasizing the historically continuous, the liberal approach has been an effort to answer the problems posed by modern American capitalist society, with its many, if limited, democratic features. It has provided a framework, which does not necessarily mean it has genuinely solved those problems or that it supplies an easy answer on every issue that arises. But, for those who adhere to it, it seems to have been sufficiently satisfying and thus not easily destroyed. That is why it has remained the predominant guide for the politics of American Jews, seen as both the proper direction for their group's collective fate and for the nation of which they are a part. Whether it will still be capable of giving the acceptable answers is another question.

For several years now, the preponderant political mood of the nation has been one of alienation from major institutions and diffuse *resentment*. For one thing, the economic problems are unique, and no conventional answers seem to work. To some observers, much of the tension is a result of "system overload"; too many people are asking for too many things for which they believe they are "entitled."[60] Both contemporary capitalism and contemporary liberalism have encouraged such feelings. For instance, whatever the supposed "conservative mood" and the prevailing rhetoric, polls indicate that most people want a great deal from government. Most importantly, the economic system, which has suggested the easy availability of affluence since World War II, has found it increasingly difficult to find jobs and careers for the young, minority ethnic group members, and the many women encouraged to aspire for better careers. That is why affirmative action disputes have been so serious.

What all this will do to the position of Jews in America and to the viability of liberal political perspectives is difficult to foresee at this point. My own contention is that, if liberalism does not pick up a strong element of socialism, it may not provide the necessary solutions. Speculations about alternative political tendencies are beyond the scope of this essay. However, if significant socialist movements do emerge as one response, American Jews, reinvigorating that heritage which remains as a potent substratum of their political thinking, will definitely constitute a significantly observable element.

Notes

1. Earlier analyses include the following: Werner Cohn, "The Politics of American Jews," in Marshall Sklare, ed., *The Jews: Social Patterns of an American Group* (Glencoe, Ill., The Free Press, 1958), pp. 614–625; Edgar Litt, "Status, Ethnicity, and Patterns of Jewish Voting Behavior in Baltimore," *Jewish Social Studies*, 22, pp. 159–164; Edgar Litt, "Jewish Ethno-Religious Involvement and Political Liberalism," *Social Forces*, 40, pp. 328–332; Lawrence Fuchs, *The Political Behaviour of American Jews* (Glencoe, Ill., The Free Press, 1956), Nathan Glazer & Daniel Moynihan, *Beyond the Melting Pot* (Cambridge, MIT Press, 1963), pp. 137–189; Lucy S. Dawidowicz & Leon S. Goldstein, "The American Jewish Liberal Tradition," in Marshall Sklare, ed., *The Jewish Community in America* (New York, Behrman House, 1974), pp. 285–300.

   More recent examples include: William Schneider, Martin D. Berman, & Mark Schultz, "Bloc Voting Reconsidered: Is There a Jewish Vote," *Ethnicity*, 1, pp. 345–392; Edgar Litt, *Beyond Pluralism — Ethnic Politics in America* (Glenview, Ill., Scott, Foresman, 1970), pp. 113–126; Daniel J. Elazar, "American Political Theory and the Political Notions of American Jews," in Peter I. Rose, ed., *The Ghetto and Beyond: Essays on Jewish Life in America* (New York, Random House, 1969), pp. 203–223; Lawrence H. Fuchs, "Introduction," *American Jewish Historical Quarterly*, 66, pp. 181–189; Alan S. Miller, "Class Factors in the Jewish Vote," *Jewish Social Studies*, 39, pp. 37–52; Henry L. Feingold, "The Jewish Contribution to American Politics," *Judaism*, 25, pp. 312–319; William Day Heitzman, *American Jewish Voting Behaviour: A History and Analysis* (San Francisco, R & E Associates, 1975); Milton Himmelfarb, "The Case for Jewish Liberalism," in Seymour M. Lipset, ed., *Emerging Coalitions in American Politics* (San Francisco, Institute for Contemporary Studies, 1978), pp. 297–305; Bernard Rosenberg & Irving Howe, "Are American Jews Turning to the Right," in Lewis A. Coser & Irving Howe, eds., *The New Conservatives: A Critique from the Left* (New York, Quadrangle, 1973), pp. 64–89; Alan Fischer, "Continuity and Erosion of Jewish Liberalism," *American Jewish Historical Quarterly*, 66, pp. 322–348.

2. Seymour Siegel, "An Anatomy of Liberalism: A Conservative View," *Judaism*, 21, pp. 24–31; Himmelfarb, "The Case for Jewish Liberalism"; Rosenberg & Howe, "Are American Jews Turning to the Right."

3. See, for instance, the varied justifications for future predictions in "Judaism and Liberalism — Marriage or Divorce: A Symposium," *Judaism*, 21, pp. 6–50.

4. The literature on this subject is much too vast and varied to list.
5. Fischer, "Continuity and Erosion"; Himmelfarb, "The Case for Jewish Liberalism."
6. Siegel, "An Anatomy of Liberalism"; Schneider, et al., "Bloc Voting Reconsidered."
7. Fischer, "Continuity and Erosion"; Miller, "Class Factors"; Rosenberg & Howe, "Are American Jews Turning to the Right."
8. Fischer, "Continuity and Erosion."
9. Most of these findings are well summarized in Ibid. Also see material in Andrew M. Greeley, "Catholics and Coalitions," Lipset, *Emerging Coalitions*, pp. 271–295. The findings are, admittedly, mostly from the early 1970s. Details on more recent Jewish opinions are not readily available, but the data at hand suggest no appreciable change. See, for instance, the results of a New York Times-CBS 1978 election day poll ("Voting Jews Remain Liberal," *New York Times*, November 12, 1978).

   As an ad hoc addendum to their imaginative study of Jewish voting in the Boston area, Schneider et al. assert that, while Jews tend to identify themselves as "liberals," they are becoming "operational conservatives." The evidence: one New York City study that revealed Jews to be against "quotas" and in favor of the assumed "illiberal" side in several famous local controversies. This type of claim is a fitting example of the misplaced concreteness so common in such analyses. (Schneider, et al., "Bloc Voting Reconsidered.)
10. Fischer, "Continuity and Erosion."
11. Ibid.
12. For instance, class differences in voting among Jews have been noted; the general interpretation is that lower status Jews are less likely to vote for the more "liberal" candidates, as popularly defined, especially in municipal elections (see Fischer, "Continuity and Erosion; Miller, "Class Factors"). Similarly, some age differences also show up. A very elaborate investigation in the Boston area also examined differences among Jewish voters by city-suburban residence and type of "Jewish commitment," as well as utilizing the age and class variable. The most interesting finding was that, when the "liberal" candidate is a Republican, upper status Jews are likely to support him, while lower status Jews are more likely to emphasize their Democratic allegiance. (See Schneider, et al., "Bloc Voting Reconsidered.) All of these findings, although valuable, offer no significant challenge to the assessment of general continuing Jewish liberalism.
13. Seymour M. Lipset, *Political Man: The Social Bases of Politics* (Anchor edition, Garden City, New York, Doubleday, 1963), pp. 249–261.
14. It should be unnecessary, at this juncture, to document this assertion. Sufficient evidence can be readily located in most of the references under note 1.
15. Of course, the allegiance of more obviously "outsider" groups, such as blacks, is more pronounced.
16. Cohn, "The Politics of American Jews"; Ben Halpern, "The Roots of American Jewish Liberalism," *American Jewish Historical Quarterly*, 66, pp. 190–214.
17. Fuchs, "Introduction," *The Political Behaviour*; Halpern, "The Roots."
18. Halpern, "The Roots," p. 203.
19. Cohn, "The Politics of American Jews."
20. Fuchs, *The Political Behaviour.*
21. Elazar, "American Political Theory."

22. *Ibid*; Fuchs, *The Political Behaviour*.
23. Fuchs, *The Political Behaviour*, p. 187; Davidowicz & Goldstein, "The American Jewish Liberal Tradition," p. 299.
24. Fuchs, "Introduction," *The Political Behaviour*, p. 189.
25. Litt, *Beyond Pluralism*.
26. Ibid.
27. Ibid, p. 118–119.
28. Ibid, p. 119.
29. Mordecai Chertoff, ed. *The New Left and the Jews* (New York, Putnam, 1971); Nathan Glazer, "The New Left and the Jews," *Jewish Journal of Sociology*, 11, pp. 121–132.
30. Litt, *Beyond Pluralism*.
31. Lipset, *Political Man*, pp. 126–173.
32. Among the many discussions of the subject, with varying interpretations of the term, see Michael Harrington, *Toward a Democratic Left* (New York, MacMillan, 1968); Joseph Bensman & Arthur Vidich, *The New American Society: The Revolution of the Middle Class* (Chicago, Quadrangle, 1971); Alvin W. Gouldner, "The New Class Project, Part I," *Theory and Society*, 6, pp. 153–203.
33. Elazar, "American Political Theory."
34. For Jewish support of Smith, see Dawidowicz & Goldstein, "The American Jewish Liberal Tradition," pp. 295–297; Stevenson received about 75 percent of the Jewish vote in both 1952 and 1956, Johnson about 90 percent in 1964.
35. Fuchs, *The Political Behaviour*.
36. See the varied interpretations of the Judaic tradition in accord with personal political predilections in "Judaism and Liberalism" (note 3).
37. Elazar, "American Political Theory."
38. Halpern, "The Roots."
39. Robert Lowenberg, "The Theft of Liberalism — a Jewish Problem," *Midstream*, 28, p. 33.
40. Note the long history of intolerance against "heresies" in Moishe Carmelly-Weinberger, *Censorship and Freedom of Expression in Jewish History* (New York, Sepler-Herman Press with Yeshiva University Press, 1977).
41. Raphael Mahler, "The Social and Political Aspects of the Haskalah in Galicia," *Yivo Annual of Jewish Social Science*, 1, pp. 64–85.
42. Efraim Schmiali, "The Appeal of Hassidism," *The Jewish Journal of Sociology*, 11, pp. 5–27; Solomon Pool, *The Hassidic Community of Williamsburg* (Glencoe, Ill., The Free Press, 1962).
43. Shelomo Dov Golein, "Portrait of a Yemenite Weavers Village," *Jewish Social Studies*, 17, pp. 3–26; Jacob R. Landau, *Jews in Nineteenth Century Egypt* (New York, New York University Press, 1969).
44. Seymour M. Lipset, "How Labor Lost," *Israel Horizons*, 26, pp. 17–20.
45. Fuchs, *The Political Behaviour*.
46. Richard Hofstadter, *The Age of Reform* (New York, Vintage, 1955); Robert Wiebe, *The Search for Order: 1877–1920* (New York, Hill and Wang, 1967).
47. Little information is available on the possible appeal of socialism to Jews in Germany in early nineteenth Century. For one thing there was hardly any genuine socialist movement. One can, at most, point to the number of Jews, or at least those of Jewish origin, among the prominent spokesmen. Therefore, neither their German background or the America to which they migrated provided much of a basis for socialism among German Jewish immigrants.

Michels, however, did note a later appeal of socialism to many Jews in Germany. (Robert Michels, *Political Parties*, Glencoe, Ill., The Free Press, 1949, pp. 261–262.) For much later evidence of Jewish socialist voting in a "German" country, see Walter B. Simon, "The Jewish Vote in Vienna," *Jewish Social Studies*, 23, pp. 38–48. On the German-American support of socialism, particularly in the city of Milwaukee, see David A. Shannon, *The Socialist Party in America* (New York, MacMillan, 1955), p. 23.

48. The number of accounts is voluminous. A crisp summary can be found in Lucy S. Dawidowicz, "Introduction — The World of East European Jewry," in Lucy S. Dawidowicz, ed., *The Golden Tradition: Jewish Life and Thought in Eastern Europe* (New York, Holt-Rinehart-Winston, 1969), pp. 5–89.

   Many writers have dwelt on the anti-Semitism of some socialist leaders, particularly in the earliest days. Whether this phenomenon was significant for later developments is irrelevant for our analysis. Enough Jews found socialism and socialist movements in line with their needs and aspirations.

49. One of the best descriptions of the entire milieu is Irving Howe's *World of Our Fathers* (New York, Harcourt-Brace-Jovanovich, 1976). Some recent, crisp descriptive statements include Arthur Liebman, "The Ties that Bind," *American Jewish Historical Quarterly*, 66, pp. 285–321; Henry L. Feingold, "The Jewish Radical in His American Habitat," *Judaism*, 22, pp. 92–105; Louis Ruchames, "Jewish Radicalism in the United States," in Rose, ed., *The Ghetto and Beyond*, pp. 228–251.

50. See *Ibid.*, pp. 245–247; Nathan Glazer, *The Social Basis of American Communism* (Westport, Conn., Greenwood Press, 1961), pp. 130–168. Both deal more with the Communists but make some reference to the renewed appeal of the Socialist party for Jews. Also see Feingold, "The Jewish Contribution," p. 96.

51. Chertoff, *The New Left and the Jews*; Glazer, "The New Left and the Jews."

52. Although the findings are complex, opinion polls have generally indicated a predominant pro-Israeli sentiment among Americans. See Seymour M. Lipset, "The Polls on the Middle East," *Middle East Review*, 9, pp. 24–30.

53. For an elaborate development of this approach, see Martin Plax, "Towards a Redefinition of Ethnic Politics," *Ethnicity*, 3, pp. 19–33.

54. Probably the most discussed import of "identity" in political matters concerns the area of "class consciousness." Whatever one might say about this complex subject, attempts to consider "ethnic consciousness" as, in any way, similar, are misleading. Beyond the fact they both represent "group" phenomenon, they are typologically too discordant for any precise analogies.

55. As Fuchs puts it, "like all of us, Jews relate to many reference groups." For instance, a Jewish doctor may adhere to the norms of the AMA or to "Jewish norms." (Fuchs, *The Political Behaviour*, p. 199.)

56. Note Plax, "Towards a Redefinition"; Litt, *Beyond Pluralism*. A similar emphasis is part of the basis for all those who see, predict, or hope for a diminution of traditional American Jewish liberalism because of the need to defend "Jewish interests" in contest with other, frequently unnamed, groups. A similar scenario is involved in the counterposition of "particularistic" vs. "universalistic" interests. For those who so inappropriately apply Talcott Parson's typology, it is well to point out that most groups adopt some versions of the 1950s slogan: "What is good for General Motors is good for the nation."

57. Samuel Lubell, "Political Behaviour of Ethnic Groups," paper delivered at the Conference on Group Life in America under auspices of the American

Jewish Committee at Arden House, November 9–12, 1956, cited by Glazer and Moynihan, *Beyond the Melting Pot*, p. 338.

58. Litt, *Beyond Pluralism*, pp. 155–168.
59. See, for instance, "Many Rights Groups Press for Unity," New York, *Amsterdam News*, November 9, 1977.
60. Amitai Etzioni, "Societal Overload: Sources, Components and Corrections," *Political Science Quarterly*, 92, pp. 607–631; Daniel Bell, *The Cultural Contradictions of Capitalism* (New York, Basic Books, 1976).

16.

The Demography of Asian and African Jews in Israel

Calvin Goldscheider

Introduction

Ethnic pluralism is a conspicuous feature of Israeli society and few if any social processes are unaffected by ethnic diversity. Yet, etnicity in Israel has changed dramatically over the last several decades, while at the same time new forms of ethnic group identification have emerged. The coincidence of ethnicity and socioeconomic status, of ethnic group origin and social-economic-political-cultural power, shapes the nature of intergroup relations between and within the Jewish and Arab populations. The ubiquitousness of ethnicity, the transformation of ethnic group identification, and the centrality of the ethnic factor in social differentiation and stratification are the defining qualities of Israel's dynamic structural and cultural pluralism.

The evolving ethnic mosaic in Israeli society is the result of a complex set of sociohistorical, political, and ideological factors. The perpetuation of ethnic diversity remains a central axis around which revolve fundamental political, social, economic, and cultural issues. Demographic processes have played a significant role in the evolution, transformation, and perpetuation of the ethnic factor in Israel. Among the most imortant demographic processes associated with ethnicity in Israel are: (1) the volume and timing of immigration from diverse, heterogeneous countries of origin; (2) the dramatic changes in mortality and fertility among immigrants from Asian and African countries and the convergence patterns among ethnic groups in these patterns; (3) patterns of ethnic urbanization and residential segregation; (4) the changing size of Israel's Jewish population relative to Israel's Arab minority and to the size of world Jewish population; and (5) the changing ethnic composition of the Jewish and Arab populations of Israel.

This article presents an overview of some of the major demographic aspects of ethnic diversity and change for the Asian-African Jewish population in Israel. The argument in its simplest form will be that demographic processes are fundamental to the analyses of the determinants and consequences of ethnic continuity and change. The focus will be on the Asian-African ethnic population who have experienced the most extensive transformation in sociodemograhic processes in a short period of time and, hence, highlight in extreme form the issues, problems, and dilemmas of ethnicity in Israel.[1]

Immigration and Ethnic Composition

The political-ideological struggles to establish a Jewish state and the evolution of Israeli society are intimately tied to immigration patterns and policies.[2] We begin, therefore, by asking: What have been the patterns of Asian and African immigration to Palestine and Israel? Between 1914 and 1977 over two million immigrants arrived in Palestine and Israel; of these over 800,000 were from Asian and African countries — 39 percent of the total.[3] The immigration from Asian and African countries was not distributed evenly over this period. Between 1914 until the establishment of the state of Israel in 1948 only 10 percent of the 450,000 immigrants were from Asian-African countries and most of those were from Asian countries, particularly Yemen, Iraq and Turkey.

In the three decades following the establishment of the state (1948–77), over 1.5 million immigrants arrived, 47 percent from Asian-African countries. Again, neither the pattern of total immigration nor the distribution by ethnicity was evenly spread (Table 16.1). In the period of mass immigration (1948–51) almost 700,000 immigrants arrived in the new state, 48 percent of whom were from Asian-African countries. The number of immigrants from Asian countries was significantly greater than from African countries during this period and both groups tended to arrive later when compared to European immigrants. While 14 percent of the immigrants in 1948 were from Asian-African countries, the proportion increased to 47 percent in 1949, 50 percent in 1950, and to 71 percent in 1951.

The proportion of immigrants from African Countries was high in the post mass-immigration period, particularly 1952–57 and again in the early 1960s. Since the Six-Day War in 1967, the overwhelming majority of immigrants to Israel have been from European-American countries, largely reflecting the depletion of Jewish populations in Asian-African countries.

The essential facts of immigration emerging from these data are: (1) the great volume of immigration from Asian-African countries in the first several years following the establishment of the state of Israel in absolute terms and relative to the population in Israel and the Jewish population in Asian and African countries; (2) the later arrival of African compared to Asian immigrants; (3) the greater concentration in time of immigrants ar-

TABLE 16.1
**Number of Immigrants to Palestine and Israel and Percent Born in
Asia and Africa, 1919–77**

	Total Number of Immigrants (thousands)	Average Annual Number (thousands)	Percent From Asia	Percent From Africa***
1919–23	35.1	7.0	3.9	0.8
1924–31	81.6	10.2	11.6	0.7
1932–38	197.2	28.2	8.4	0.6
1939–45	81.8	11.7	17.0	1.3
1946–48*	56.6	22.6	2.3	1.7
1948**	101.8	203.6	5.1	9.0
1949	239.6	239.6	30.8	16.7
1950	170.2	170.2	34.4	15.2
1951	175.1	175.1	59.2	11.6
1952–54	54.1	18.0	25.2	50.6
1955–57	164.9	55.0	6.1	62.1
1958–60	75.5	25.2	17.9	18.0
1961–64	228.0	57.0	8.8	51.8
1965–67	60.8	20.3	17.6	20.2
1968–73	247.8	41.3	12.9	13.9
1974–77	93.2	23.3	4.7	3.2

*Until May 15, 1948. Annual Immigration was calculated on the basis of 2.5 for
this period.
**After May 15, 1948. Annual Immigration for this period was doubled for consistency
with other periods.
***Excluding South Africa

Source: Adapted from D. Friedlander and C. Goldscheider, The Population of Israel,
Columbia University Press,1979, Tables 2.8 and 2.11 with additional data from the
Statistical Yearbooks of Israel, 1975–78.

riving from Asian Countries; and (4) the later arrival of both Asian and
African immigrant groups compared to the bulk of European immigrants.
Perhaps of greatest importance for understanding the sociodemographic

development of Israeli society is the fact that immigrants from Asian-African countries were entering an entirely different type of society along almost every social, economic, political, and cultural dimension compared to their country of origin. Oriental immigrants came to a society that in large part was settled, controlled and dominated — politically, socially, economically, culturally, and demographically — by previous waves of European immigrants.

The timing of immigrant arrival is critical in understanding the societal conditions that immigrants found upon initial entrance. The socioeconomic background of the migrants helped shape the extent to which they were able to adjust to the new society and fit into and take advantage of the social and economic opportunity structure. The subsequent development of the ethnic mosaic in Israel was therefore a result of the volume and timing of ethnic immigration, the social origins/background that immigrants brought with them, and the subsequent experiences of ethnic groups in Israeli society.

In the present context, Asian and African immigrants to Israel were doubly disadvantaged relative to Europeans. First, they came from societies and communities where social, economic, and demographic conditions were far less developed than in European societies. Their background characteristics included lower levels of education and occupational skills, extended family structure and lower status of women, large family size, and traditional Jewish religious culture. Second, the concentration of immigration during the early period of statehood — later in time than Europeans — not only created severe socioeconomic hardships but resulted in the absence of initial optimum conditions for socio-economic integration.

Ethnic Heterogeneity

Part of the differential patterns of Asian and African developments in Israel relates to the differential timing of arrival of these two broad groups defined in terms of continent of birth. Yet it is clearly a sociological error to treat the Asian and African populations as homogeneous units. Within both groups there is as much ethnic-cultural heterogeneity as there are differences in the timing and volume of immigration.

A clue to the ethnic diversity of the Oriental population in Israeli society may be found in the distribution of Asians and Africans by specific countries of birth and for the Israeli born by country of father's origin (Table 16.2). Data for 1977 show that no one specific ethnic group dominates among Asians. Over one-third of the Asians are Iraqis, 23 percent are from Yemen, 15 percent are from Iran, and the remainder are from Turkey, India, and Pakistan. Among the "other" Asians (totaling about 52,000 in 1977), the majority are from Syria (about 30,000), with about 15,000

TABLE 16.2
Jewish Population by Country of Birth and Ethnic Origin for Asians
and Africans in Israel, 1977 (percentages)

	Foreign Born	Israel* Born	Total**	Percent Israel Born
Asia	100.0	100.0	100.0	57.5
Iraq	35.6	37.6	36.7	58.8
Yemen	17.9	26.7	22.9	66.9
Iran	17.0	13.9	15.2	52.5
Turkey	15.0	11.4	12.9	50.7
India-Pakistan	6.5	3.4	4.7	41.7
Other	7.6	7.1	7.3	55.9
Number (thousands)	302.8	410.1	712.9	--
Africa***	100.0	100.0	100.0	51.6
Morocco-Tangier	65.4	59.8	62.5	49.4
Algeria-Tunisia	15.6	16.8	16.2	53.6
Libya	8.3	13.3	10.9	63.0
Egypt-Sudan	9.3	9.5	9.4	52.1
Other	0.4	0.5	0.4	58.0
Number (thousands)	337.1	359.8	696.9	--

*For Israel born, ethnic origin is father's place of birth.

**Total includes only foreign born and native born of foreign born parents; Excluded are 362,000 Israeli born Jews where the father was also born in Israel.

***Excluding South Africa

Source: Israel, Statistical Abstract, 1978, Table 2/23

equally divided between Afghanistan and Lebanon. Hence, in focusing on Israelis of Asian origin or birth there is a considerable ethnic range in terms of social origin, time of arrival, and subsequent change.

Among African Jewish ethnics, the spread of heterogeneity is much less pronounced. Fully 63 percent of the African first and second generations in Israel are from Morocco and an additional 16 percent are from Algeria and Tunisia. The remainder are largely from Libya and Egypt.

The ethnic heterogeneity within Asian and African populations varies somewhat for the first and second generations, reflecting in large part the differential timing and volume of immigration. For example, about two-thirds of the Yemenites are second generation compared to less than 42 percent of the Indian-Pakistani group. This clearly reflects the earlier immigration of Jews from Yemen.

On the whole, the African ethnics are more concentrated among the foreign born than among the Israeli born when compared to the Asian ethnics. For the majority group among the Africans — the Moroccans — slightly less than half are Israeli born; in contrast over 60 percent of the Iraqis and Yemenites (who make up about 60 percent of the Asians) are Israeli born.

Clearly an analysis of the cultural patterns of these subgroups would require much greater detail focusing on specific places of origin — communities — among particular ethnic groups.[4] Nevertheless, the category "Asian-African" is not without sociological meaning or symbolic significance. Sociodemographic processes characterizing specific ethnic groups in Israel and the transformations experienced by ethnic immigrant groups and their children vary more in terms of structural features than cultural traits specific to ethnic groups. Length of exposure to Israeli society, timing of immigration, and socioeconomic characteristics of ethnic groups seem to be the most critical dimensions of variation within ethnic subpopulations.

In addition, there appears to be greater convergence in sociodemographic characteristics and behavior among ethnics within the broad category Asian-African (and European) than between Asian-African and European. More generally, it may be argued that one consequence of integration processes in Israeli society has been the development of new forms of ethnicity. The ethnicity patterns that seem to be emerging are less in terms of specific cultural group and more in terms of broader categories of "Oriental," i.e., Asian-African, and "European" ethnics. Out of the diverse and heterogeneous immigrant ethnic subpopulations within Asian, African and European groups two new ethnic categories have evolved and are Israeli created products. This seems to be more true of second than first generation ethnics and will probably increasingly characterize the emerging third generation. It is interesting to note that such new forms of ethnic identification parallel processes of ethnic formation in other pluralistic societies.[5]

The Demographic Dominance of Asian-Africans

The volume and timing of Asian-African Jewish immigration combined with their higher levels of fertility have resulted in the growing demograhic dominance of the Oriental segment of the Jewish population. In the 30 years subsequent to statehood, the small Oriental demographic minority has become the dominant ethnic group within the Jewish population.

As of December 1977, there were over three million Jews in Israel. Of these, 47 percent was foreign born (first generation Israelis), 42 percent was born in Israel of foreign-born fathers (second generation), and the remaining 11.8 percent was at least third generation, i.e., they and their fathers were Israeli born. Among first generation Israelis, those born in Asian and African countries accounted for 45 percent; among the second generation, the Israeli born of Asian-African origins accounted for the overwhelming majority (60 percent).

Details on the ethnic origins of third generation Israelis are not readily available but some evidence suggests that the proportion of European origins is declining (although they remain a majority), while the proportion of Asian-African origins is increasing. In the five-year period 1972–76, for example, the proportion of third generation children below the age of ten whose grandfather was born in Asia-Africa increased by 90 percent, accounting for over one-fourth of all third generation children. During this same period, the proportion of third generation Israeli children of European origins declined to 58 percent.[6]

A clearer picture of the demographic dominance of the Oriental ethnics emerges when we focus on the first and second generations (i.e., 88 percent of the total Jewish population). The Oriental population was a demographic majority of first and second generation Israelis in 1977 — 52 percent (Table 16.3). Although the growing demographic dominance of Asian-Africans is the result of differential immigration and fertility patterns, the recent increases and growth are a direct result of their higher fertility rates. In the decade since 1969, only 20 percent of the Jewish immigrants to Israel were from Asian or African countries.

Even more revealing in reflecting past patterns and shaping the thrust of future patterns is the age structure of the various ethnic segments. Data for 1976, for example, show that there were over one million second generation Israeli Jews below age 30, representing over one-third of the total Jewish population. Fully 65 percent of these second generation Jews were of Asian-African origins. Of the second generation Jews below age 14, 71 percent were of Asian-African origins. In sharp contrast, almost three-fourths of the second generation over age 30 were of European origins.[7]

The changing numerical dominance of the Asian-African population must be viewed against the background of changes over the last several decades. In 1948, for example, about two-thirds of the Jewish population was foreign born and less than 15 percent of the foreign born was from Asian-African countries. Three decades later, in 1977, about half of the Jewish population was foreign born and almost 45 percent was born in Asian and African countries.

TABLE 16.3
Foreign-Born and Israeli-Born of Foreign-Born Parents by Ethnic Origin,
Jewish Population of Israel, 1977 (percentages)

Ethnic Origin	Foreign Born	Israel Born	Total*
Asia	21.1	32.1	26.3
Africa	23.7	28.3	25.9
Europe	55.2	39.6	47.9
Total %	100.0	100.0	100.0
Number (thousands)	1,438	1,277	2,715

*Total equals foreign born and Israel born of foreign born parents; excludes Israel born of Israel born parents.

Source: Israel, Statistical ABSTRACT, 1978, table 2/21.

More significantly from the point of view of the future is the changing relative balance of ethnic groups among the Israeli born. At the time of Israel's first full-scaled census in 1961, 46 percent of the Israeli born Jewish population was of European origins compared to less than 40 percent of Asian-African origins; the remaining portion was at least third generation. By 1977, the proportion of European origins declined from 46 percent to 31 percent, while the proportion of Asian-African origins increased from 40 percent to 47 percent. Eliminating the third generation group where ethnic origin is unknown, comparisons can be made between Israeli-born Jews of European and Asian-African origins for the period 1961–77. This comparison reveals clearly the growing demographic dominance of the Asian-Africans that will determine the future ethnic composition of Israeli society as a whole. In 1961, 54 percent of the second generation Israelis were of European origins and 46 percent were of Asian-African origins. Both ethnic subgroups increased in size during 1961–77. The Israelis of European origins increased by over 50 percent from 335,000 to 506,000; in the same period, the Israelis of Oriental origins increased from 289,000 to 771,000 or by 167 percent in 17 years — three times the growth rate of the European-origin Israelis. Thus, by 1977 over six out of ten Israeli-born Jews were of Asian and African origins.

The demographic dominance of Asian-Africans among the Jewish population of Israel does not imply social, political, and cultural dominance or control over economic resources. Indeed, the growing numerical majority of the Asian-Africans has not been accompanied by an equivalent growth in power and influence. The heterogeneity of the Asian-African ethnic group, their socioeconomic characteristics, and residential dispersal, and the interests of the Europeans in preserving their position of status and power prevent an easy conversion of demographic power into sociopolitical dominance and economic control. Indeed, it is the tension between demographic change and social stratification that often generates ethnic conflict in Israel.[8]

The Vital Revolution and Demographic Assimilation

Perhaps there is no clearer indication of the revolutionary changes experienced by the Asian and African immigrants than changes in mortality and fertility. The vital revolution or the demographic transition involved very rapid changes in mortality and fertility in a short period of time for Asian and African ethnics. These changes resulted, most importantly, in demographic convergences among ethnic groups within the Asian and African categories, between the Asian and African groups, and between Asian-Africans and Europeans. The closing of the demographic gap in mortality levels and the convergences in fertility may be viewed as forms of ethnic demographic assimilation in Israeli society. The persistence of some fertility differentials by ethnicity, however, illustrates the continuity of ethnic factors and more particularly the socioeconomic status–ethnicity connection.

Ethnic differences in mortality are almost nonexistent within the Jewish population. To the extent that differential mortality is reflective of, or related to, social inequalities, the evidence seems to suggest that some types of ethnic inequalities have diminished or disappeared entirely. Thus, in contrast to estimated high infant mortality levels of immigrants from Yemen (376), North Africa (273), and Iraq (141) before arrival in Israel, by 1952 the range was between 30–36 per 1,000. For the 1960–63 period, infant mortality levels of Asian-African Jews were 27 per 1,000, only slightly higher than the rate among European origin Israelis.[9] By the 1970s, ethnic differences in mortality within the Jewish population of Israel have probably been eliminated entirely.

Issues associated with fertility changes are much more complex. Nevertheless, fertility reductions among Asian-Africans have been dramatic and the fertility gap between Asian-Africans and Europeans has narrowed considerably. Reductions in Asian-African fertility have been compressed in time, without government intervention, with the retention of relatively high fertility ideals, and the general absence of modern contraception.

A review of period fertility rates shows the enormous decline for Asian-African born women.[10] In the quarter of a century following 1951 the gross reproduction rate[11] fell steadily and continuously by 46 percent — from 3.1 in 1951 to 1.7 in 1977. Similarly, the total fertility rate declined by about one child each decade — from 5.7 in 1955 to 4.6 in 1965 to 3.8 in 1975. The detailed period fertility data show the very rapid reduction in fertility and, in turn, the convergence of fertility between Asian-African and European born women. Nevertheless, the fertility convergence does not imply that all differences by ethnicity have been eliminated. In 1977, for example, the total fertility rate of Asian-African-born women was 3.4 compared to 2.8 among European-born women. An examination of the parity distribution of births in 1977 reinforces this point. Of the 71,809 Jewish births, 3,923 or 5.5 percent were of the sixth or higher birth order. Asian-African born women accounted for 72 percent of these higher order births while accounting for about 30 percent of all births. Viewed in another way, 12.5 percent of all births to Asian-African born women in 1977 were higher parity births compared to 3.5 percent of the births to European women.

A detailed study of cohort fertility patterns among Israel's Jewish ethnic subpopulations allowed for the examination of retrospective reproductive histories of Asian and African women of the first and second generations.[12] These data document clearly the sharp decline in fertility for cohorts of women from Asian and African countries. For Asian migrants, for example, fertility fell by 50 percent for cohorts marrying 25 years apart — from 6.5 births to just over 3 births. This decline occurred 10–15 years later for Asian women who immigrated after 1948 when compared to those who immigrated before the establishment of the state. After 20 years of marriage, 75 percent of the Asian women from the marriage cohort 1930–34 had 5 or more births; only 17 percent of the women marrying 1950–54 had 5 or more births. Identical patterns characterize African-born women. Differences between African and Asian women are in the intitial levels of fertility, which are higher for African women, and the timing of immigration (later for African women). However, when length of exposure to Israeli society is examined, African fertility levels declined in precisely the same way as Asian fertility levels.

The remarkable "fit" between exposure to Israel and fertility decline has resulted in clear convergence in the fertility patterns between Asian and African women and between Asian-African women and those born in Europe (both West and East). These convergence patterns are already evident for foreign-born women and reinforced among the second generation. Israeli-born women of Asian-African origins have lower fertility rates than their foreign-born mothers, while second generation European origin women have higher fertility rates than their first generation European-born mothers. Fertility convergence between second generation Israelis of Asian-African and European origins is, therefore, the result of generational declines for Asian-African women and generational increases for European women.

Further clarification of these fertility convergences may be obtained by examining fertility norms.[13] Among older marriage cohorts of Asian and African women, family size desires tend to be lower than actual family size — i.e., fertility levels exceeded fertility desires. Among more recent cohorts there is a congruence between family size desires and expectations. The data indicate that over time family size norms among Asian and African women have changed downward and family size expectations have been reduced to fit into family size desires. In sharp contrast, both first and second generation European women have moved family size expectations upward to fit into desires that in the past have exceeded actual family size. Hence, the high fertility of Asian and African women of older cohorts was higher than they desired and higher than they considered ideal for the average Israeli family. With exposure to Israeli society their reproductive norms and their fertility behavior changed in conjunction with the social and economic conditions and toward lower levels. Among second generation Israelis, fertility expectations and desires are only slightly higher for those of Asian-African origins than those of European origins.

It should be noted that family size and income levels are inversely related and a continuation of large family size among selected ethnic segments reflects socioeconomic factors. Of greater importance is the fact that large family size tends to perpetuate the cycle of ethnic poverty and reinforce the relationship between ethnic origin and socioeconomic differentiation.

The Persistence of the Ethnic Factor

The evidence on demographic assimilation, particularly the lack of mortality differentials by ethnicity and the clear convergence trends in ethnic fertility differentials, raises the question about the future of ethnic differentiation at least in terms of sociodemographic processes. There is some evidence that suggests the growing importance of alternative anchors of identity among Jews in Israel and the diminishing importance of the ethnic factor among the Israeli born.[14]

It is clearly premature, on the basis of the evidence available and the relatively short length of time ethnic groups have been exposed to Isreali society, to gauge the future of ethnicity in Israel. Theoretical models based on other pluralistic societies are not directly applicable, nor is there any general consensus as to the future of ethnic differentiation.[15] Nevertheless, three major contexts are central to evaluating changes in ethnic convergences and divergences within the Jewish population and are of particular importance in sociodemographic processes. These include: (1) ethnic residential segregation; (2) marital endogamy; and (3) social mobility.

The Israeli-Jewish population as a whole and the ethnic subpopulations within it are remarkably concentrated in urban settlements. Over 90 percent of the Jewish population was concentrated in urban settlements in 1977, about the same level as at the time of the 1972 census and only slightly higher than at the time of the 1961 census (85 percent). The high level of concentration in urban areas has been a conspicuous feature of Jewish populations outside of Israel for over a century. It is remarkable, however, in the context of the Zionist idelogical emphasis on rural type settlements.[16]

Within urban and rural areas the census distinguishes between "veteran" and "new" settlements based on the date of settling: before or after the establishment of the state in 1948.[17] In 1972, 79 percent of the Jewish population in urban areas was in localities settled before 1948; 43 percent of the Jewish population in rural areas was in localities settled before 1948 (Table 16.4). An examination of these data for the ethnic Jewish subpopulations provides clues to the residential dimension of ethnic continuity.

For all the Jewish ethnic groups, the proportion in urban areas is very high with well over 90 percent of all foreign-born ethnics and only a slightly lower proportion of native-born groups in urban areas. Although there is some variation in this proportion, no significant ethnic pattern emerges. The critical ethnic distinctions emerge not for overall levels of urban concentration but rather in the proportion of urban residents who live in areas settled before 1948 (veteran settlements). A much lower proportion of Asian and Africans are located in veteran urban settlements than are Europeans; this characterizes both first and second generations and holds within periods of immigrant arrival in Israel. Overall, 87 percent of the foreign-born Europeans living in urban areas are located in veteran settlements compared to 78 percent of the Asian and 53 percent of the African foreign born, respectively.

Part of the overall ethnic difference in veteran urban area concentration reflects the timing of immigration but it is clearly not the sole or major factor. Without exception, the higher proportion of Europeans concentrated in veteran urban settlements and the lower concentration of Africans in these areas holds within periods of immigration. For example, among those who immigrated to Israel in 1948–54, 89 percent of the Europeans were in veteran urban settlements as of the 1972 census, compared to 79 percent of

TABLE 16.4
Proportion in Urban Settlements and Proportion in Veteran Settlements of Urban and Rural Areas by Place of Birth and Time of Immigration, Jewish Population of Israel, 1972

	Proportion in Urban Settlement	Proportion of Urban in Veteran Settlements	Proportion of Rural in Veteran Settlements
Total	90.5	78.5	42.6
Foreign Born			
Asia Immigrated	93.5	78.4	17.8
Before 1948	96.4	96.7	54.8
1948–54	92.0	79.4	13.3
1955–60	93.2	68.9	17.7
1961–64	97.5	66.2	26.2
1965 +	97.5	62.6	41.6
Africa Immigrated	92.6	53.3	16.9
Before 1948	95.1	88.8	39.4
1948–54	89.2	69.3	13.4
1955–60	90.2	46.1	10.8
1961–64	96.8	41.7	30.2
1965 +	95.8	55.1	41.9
Europe Immigrated	91.9	86.9	61.9
Before 1948	88.3	97.0	81.9
1948–54	93.4	89.2	42.8
1955–60	93.2	81.5	42.7
1961–64	95.6	73.0	46.0
1965 +	92.3	74.8	54.9
Israel Born			
Total	88.3	80.6	42.6
Father Born			
Asia	90.0	80.0	18.5
Africa	88.7	56.4	13.6
Europe	86.8	89.9	61.6
Israel	88.2	92.9	64.8

Source: Israel, Central Bureau of Statistics, Demographic Characteristics of the Population, Part II, Population and Housing Census 1972 Series, Jerusalem, 1976,Table 16

the Asians and 69 percent of the Africans. The same is true of other periods as well. Indeed, these patterns characterize not only the first generation and have persisted through the 1970s — a quarter of a century after immigration for some groups — but persists among the second generation. Over 80 percent of Israeli-born Jews living in urban areas are in veteran settlements, but this varies by ethnic group in the same way as for first generation ethnics. Only 56 percent of the second generation Israelis of African origins are in veteran urban settlements compared to 80 percent of the Asians and 90 percent of the Europeans. While these ethnic differences are related in part to age structural differences between ethnic groups, the same patterns emerge when age differences are standardized.

These Oriental-European differences are even more pronounced among rural settlements. Among the foreign-born, 62 percent of Europeans in rural areas are located in veteran settlements compared to about 17 percent of the Asians and Africans. The same difference characterizes the second generation and holds within periods of immigrant arrival in Israel.

The differential settlement patterns of ethnic groups may have two types of consequences. First such settlements may reinforce ethnic community institutions and distinctive ethnic consciousness and behavior. Residential concentration of ethnic groups clearly maintains the visibility of ethnic identification for the ethnic group as well as for others. Most importantly, residence in areas of relatively high ethnic density may have a major impact on ethnic socialization, interaction, marriage, and mobility patterns. Indeed, ethnic residential concentration has been viewed as one of the major mechanisms for the continuity and survival of ethnic communities.[18]

The data reviewed above and other direct evidence on ethnic group residential segregation[19] suggest that ethnic groups in Israel will continue to be differentiated residentially over the next period of time. Annual rates of intercommunity migration support this conclusion. In 1977, for example, internal migration rates are significantly higher for European than Asian-African ethnics even within life cycle (age) and period of immigration controls.[20] To the extent that Asian-Africans are located in new towns and nonmetropolitan urban areas, such lower migration rates imply continued sociocultural segregation.

Settlement patterns and ethnic residential concentration are part of the structural, ecological, and demographic conditions that shape the persistence of ethnic group identification. There is a basis for continuity in ethnic differentiation despite evidence of convergence in a variety of demographic and sociological dimensions.

Another context for evaluating the persistence of ethnicity is the question of interethnic marriages. In 1955, less than 12 percent of the marriages taking place in Israel were between persons from Oriental origins to persons from European origins. In the subsequent two decades the level increased to 19 percent. An index used to measure the extent of endogamy fell from 0.81 to 0.64, 1955 to 1975.

This increase in ethnic intermarriage within the Jewish population of Israel is clearly a conservative indicator of the total range of ethnic intermarriages. The ethnic unit (continent of origin) is much too broad; marriages between Asians and Africans and between those of specific ethnic origins within both groups are not included. Nor are distinctions between generations made in these marriage registraion data. Census data (from 1961) clearly show the increase in intermarriage levels by generational status.[21] Nor is it clear what are the social characteristics of the ethnic intermarried or their ethnic identity. And the interpretation of increases in ethnic intermarriages is problematic since such increases may reflect patterns of integration, assimilation, or issues associated with the unavailability of marriage partners from the same ethnic group, limitations in ethnic marriage markets, or marriage squeezes.

Nevertheless, whatever the determinants of such intermarriage across ethnic lines, two facts are beyond dispute: (1) the level of ethnic intermarriages, however defined, is increasing, and (2) there are implications of ethnic intermarriages for the strength of ethnic identity and the continuity of ethnic patterns for future generations. As the third generation native Israelis move into the marriage market, the choices made in terms of ethnic endogamy will have major implications for the struture and change of ethnic groups.

The significance of the ethnic factor as a basis of social differentiation rests with the connections between ethnic origins and social inequality. Studies over the past several years have demonstrated the very strong and persistent relationship between country of birth, generation in Israel, and a wide range of measures of socioeconomic status and social mobility.[22]

In comparing the diffferential educational attainment and occupational achievement of Asian-Africans and Europeans it becomes clear that current differences are a function of two complex processes: (1) the differential social origins of these ethnic populations — i.e., the educational-occupational distributions of their parents; (2) the differential changes experienced in Israel. Ethnicity impinges therefore on initial stratification differentials as well as on subsequent behavior.

The results of the first national mobility survey in Israel suggests that intergenerational mobility has for the most part not closed the educational or occupational gap between ethnic groups. On the one hand, every ethnic group has been characterized by social mobility patterns between generations. On the other hand, such mobility has not diminished the gap between ethnics and often the socioeconomic gap has increased. Thus, even when there is rapid development and growth, the opening up of new opportunities within a relatively open stratification system, the salience of the ethnic factor has persisted.[23] The ethnicity-stratification connection appears to be reinforced when additional residential location-ecological considerations are taken into account.[24]

The continuing residential segregation by ethnicity, changing marital patterns, and the persistence of the ethnic-stratification connection suggests that the ethnic factor in Israel will continue to be salient at least for the next generation. And the dominant factors involved are structural. For the Asian-African ethnics, these structural dimensions imply continuing tension and conflict between demographic dominance and assimilation, on the one hand, and sociopolitical subordination and socioeconomic inequalities, on the other. The ways in which such tensions and conflicts are managed in Israel will have major implications for the emerging ethnic pluralism in Israeli society.

Notes

1. The use of Asian-African rather than Sephardim is based on two considerations. First, Sephardim is a much more heterogeneous and less well defined category. Second, all the data are available by country of origin rather than some broader ethnic category. Cf. R. Patai, "Western and Oriental Culture in Israel," in M. Curtis and M. Chertoff, (eds.) *Israel: Social Structure and Change* (New Brunswick, N.J.: Transaction Books, 1973).
2. A detailed analysis of immigration patterns and policies in Palestine and Israel is presented in Dov Friedlander and Calvin Goldscheider, *The Population of Israel* (New York: Columbia University Press, 1979).
3. Unless otherwise indicated the data presented are from Israel, Central Bureau of Statistics, *Statistical Abstract of Israel*, 1978.
4. See Judah Matras, '*On Changing Matchmaking, Marriage and Fertility in Israel*," *American Journal of Sociology* 79 (Sept. 1973), pp. 364–88; Harvey Goldberg, "Culture and Ethnicity in the Study of Israeli Society," *Ethnic Groups* 1 (1977), pp. 163–86.
5. Cf. William Yancey, et al., "Emergent Ethnicity: A Review and Reformulation," *American Sociological Review* 41 (June 1976), pp. 391–402. F. Kobrin and C. Goldscheider, *The Ethnic Factor in Family Structure and Mobility* (Cambridge: Ballinger, 1978).
6. Israel, Central Bureau of Statistics, *The Demographic Characteristics of the Population in Israel*, 1972–76, Special Series, No. 562, Jerusalem, 1978, Table 18.
7. Ibid. table 9. On the importance of age structure for the future ethnic composition see Friedlander and Goldscheider, *The Population of Israel*, chapter 7.
8. See the articles on ethnic relations and power in Curtis and Chertoff, *Israel: Social Structure and Change*, pp. 281–378.
9. See Dov Friedlander, "The Fertility of Three Oriental Migration Groups in Israel," in U.O. Schmelz, et al., *Papers in Jewish Demography*, 1969 (Institute of Contemporary Jewry, The Hebrew University, Jerusalem, 1973), pp. 131–141; E. Peritz and B. Adler, "Linkage Data on Infant Mortality in the Jewish Population of Israel" in E. Peritz and U.O. Schmelz (eds.), *Late Fetal Deaths and Infant Mortality 1948–72* (Israel, Central Bureau of Statistics,

Special Series No. 453, Jerusalem, 1974); E. Peritz, et al., *Mortality of Adult Jews in Israel* (Israel, Central Bureau of Statistics, Special Series No. 409, Jerusalem, 1973).

10. For details see Calvin Goldscheider and Dov Friedlander, "Patterns of Jewish Fertility in Israel," in Paul Ritterband (ed.), *Modern Jewish Fertility* (Leiden: Brill, 1980).
11. The gross reproduction rate measures the number of daughters that would be born to women passing through their reproductive years, assuming the continuation of current age-specific birth rates.
12. On cohort Jewish fertility changes in Israel see Dov Friedlander and Calvin Goldscheider, "Immigration, Social Change and Cohort Fertility in Israel," *Population Studies* 32 (July 1978), pp. 299–312.
13. Calvin Goldscheider and Dov Friedlander, "Fertility Expectations, Desires, and Ideals Among Jewish Women in Israel," in *Papers in Jewish Demography* (Institute of Contemporary Jewry, The Hebrew University, 1980).
14. Cf. Calvin Goldscheider and Dov Friedlander, "Religiosity Patterns in Israel," forthcoming, 1980.
15. Cf. N. Glazer and D. Moynihan (eds.), *Ethnicity: Theory and Experience* (Harvard Unviversity Press, 1975); Kobrin and Goldscheider, *The Ethnic Factor in Family Structure and Mobility*, chapters 1 and 11.
16. Erik Cohen, "The City in the Zionist Ideology," *The Jerusalem Quarterly* 4 (Summer 1974), pp. 126–44.
17. See Israel, Central Bureau of Statistics, *Demographic Characteristics of the Population*, Part II (Population and Housing Census 1972 Series, No. 10, Jerusalem, 1976), pp. IX–XIV.
18. See Kobrin and Goldscheider, *The Ethnic Factor in Family Structure and Mobility*, chapter 4 and references cited.
19. V. Klaff, "Ethnic Segregation in Urban Israel," *Demograhy* 10 (May 1973), pp. 161–84; V. Klaff, "Residence and Integration in Israel," *Ethnicity* 4 (1977). See also A. Berler, *New Towns in Israel* (Israel Universities Press, Jerusalem, 1970).
20. Israel, Central Bureau of Statistics, *Monthly Bulletin of Statistics, Supplement* 30 (August 1979), p. 56, table 5.
21. Cf. Matras *"On Changing Matchmaking, Marriage and Fertility in Israel,"* table 2.
22. See the several studies reported in Curtis and Chertoff (eds.), *Israel: Social Structure and Change*, chapters 12, 13, and 22.
23. Judah Matras and G. Noam, "International Educational Mobility in Israel — An Overview," Working Paper No. 1 (Brookdale Institute, Jerusalem, April, 1976); Judah Matras and Dov Weintraub, "Ethnic and Other Primordial Differentials in Intergenerational Mobility in Israel," paper read at ISA Stratification and Mobility Seminar, Jerusalem, April, 1976; Judah Matras, "Ethnic and Social Origin 'Dominance' in Occupational Attainment in Israel," paper read at American Sociological Association meetings, Chicago, September 1977.
24. V. Kraus and D. Weintraub, "Social Differentiation and Locality of Residence: Spatial Distribution, Composition, and Stratification in Israel," paper presented at ISA committee meeting on Social Stratification and Mobility, Dublin, April, 1977; S. Spilerman and J. Habib, "Development Towns in Israel," *American Journal of Sociology* 81 (January 1976), pp. 781–812; J. Matras, "Israel's New Frontier: The Urban Periphery," in Curtis and Chertoff (eds.), *Israel: Social Structure and Change*, chapter 1.

Partitioning and the Search for Core-Boundary Equilibrium: The Case Study of Israel

Saul B. Cohen and Emmanuel Maier

Introduction

The political partitioning of the Holy Land is a phenomenon as old as the geopolitical concept of this ancient land itself. Abram and Lot, returning from Egypt, found the resource base of Canaan inadequate to support their combined sheep and cattle holdings. As compromise, they agreed upon partition, Lot selecting the irrigable Jordan Valley and Abram retaining the grassy Canaanite hills. Since then the land has rarely been unified, be its division between Philistia and Canaan, the Israelite and the Judean Kingdoms, or among the various provinces of the Arab and Ottoman periods. The purpose of this article is not to review the history of 4,000 years of Holy Land partition, or to examine partitioning during the last half century as an isolated phenomenon. Instead, focus is upon how, in recent times national boundary delimitation has reflected the process of core establishment and development. If the past is to serve as a meaningful guide to future partitioning, we must be mindful of how demographic, economic, and ideological conditions combine to create, expand, and recreate core areas. These cores in turn shape the development in the national periphery in general terms, and the boundaries of this periphery specifically. These boundaries of the periphery are the boundaries of the national state.

The development of most national core areas takes place as a consequence of internal forces. Occasionally, external pressures create, abort, or even eliminate a national core. Rarely has sustained conflict shaped core/ boundary relationships in so profound a way as the Arab-Israeli clash. In the Holy Land, trends in growth of the Israelis' core are a better long-term test of the durability of boundaries than are fleeting military victories or ideological dogma.

Cores

The concept of core derives from a view that treats the state as an organism built around a single nucleus (in rare cases a state may have multiple nuclei). The relationship between core and periphery varies: (1) sometimes interaction is one-way, or exploitative, with the core feeding off the periphery by drawing upon the latter's natural or human resources without making adequate compensation; (2) at other times the core may have to support all or a portion of the periphery so that the core experiences a net loss of resources; and (3) still at other times the relationship between core and periphery is two-way, or interdependent.

Neither the core nor periphery are fixed in space. Generally, the core expands into the periphery, incorporating some portions of the latter in a process of accretion. Occasionally, however, parts of the core may become peripheral, for example, through population diminution or exhaustion of material resources. There are also instances within the life of a nation state, when an overwhelming shift of the locus of population and economic/political power causes the core to become part of the periphery, a new core springing up elsewhere. Finally, concern of core leadership with securing the frontier may create a core-periphery-derived core spatial model, in which frontier zones that have been built up by substantial investment of the core's manpower, capital, and political energy become forward zones quite separate from the intervening periphery. These derived cores may continue to mirror the values of the primary core, or they may adopt a stance that more nearly reflects the values of the periphery.

Significance of core as a spatial concept emerged during the period when land was the major resource from which wealth was accumulated and the economy was developed. Land tenure was the overriding societal-organizing instrument and political mechanism by which people competed for power. Core areas were those most favorably endowed in terms of soil and other physical variables which differentiate land. When labor became more important than land as the major resource in the means of production, the core concept retained its utility, but often with a different geographic locus, as areas with greater concentrations of manpower attained economic and political primary. The value of the core in a military context also applies for these two periods, central space offering strategic advantages for maneuver and providing a base for applying manpower resources from which to dominate the periphery.

It is only with the advent of the postindustrial, automated, and highly-managed service age that the concept of the spatial core, especially the single, dominant core apt to lose its utility in a strategic sense. Moreover, as an example of cultural lag, national psychology and attitudes appreciate the significance of this technological change much more slowly. But for most of the world this is a matter of future contemplation. The United States may emerge as the first example of a society with a widely diffused network based upon a grid that connects a number of political and economic power-generating nodes. For the present, the concept of the territorial core is "alive and well" in nearly all national states. Certainly the dynamism of the Israeli core(s) is pertinent to an understanding of the Israeli-Arab geopolitical scene, including territorial partitioning and anticipated boundary adjustments.

The Precore Area

During the past one hundred years of the Zionist return the modern Jewish (Israeli) parts of Palestine have known several core areas (see Figure 17.1). The first may more appropriately be described as *pre-core*, since it failed to generate Zionist ideological dynamism and values that could be transmitted throughout the area of Jewish settlement. This pre-core area was located on the coastal plain north and south of Jaffa, from Hadera to Gedera. Here was the locus of the agricultural-settling activities of the First Aliya (Immigration Wave) — the Jewish private farmers/plantation owners who were drawn to Palestine with the emergence of the moshava in 1878. The cultural ideological underpinnings of this wave of settlers, whose primary concern was with individual economic gain rather than with national pioneering tasks, and who had a traditional and almost colonial mentality, limited the role that the First Aliya's geographical base played in shaping the outlines of the new Jewish national territory.

Still, compared to Jerusalem which was then the core of the religious "Old Yishuv" (the Jewish population) the coastal plain's specialized farming villages of the late nineteenth century did serve as the base for important Zionist economic and political territory-wide institutional seeds. The first centralized Jewish national colonization efforts took up headquarters locations in Jaffa, when, in 1909, Arthur Ruppin set up the Palestine Office there. Ruppin's office housed the Zionist Organization and its various institutions, such as the Jewish National Fund, the Palestine Land Development Corporation, and the Palestine Real Estate Company, strengthening Jaffa's role at the center for the colonies of the "New Yishuv" that were located both on the coastal plain and in the Galilee.[1]

The North as Nuclear Core

The nuclear core area for the Zionist state was the North: The fringes of the Galilee, the Upper Jordan Valley, the Valley of Jezreel. Nuclear core is used to describe the historic core area from which the state-idea is derived. While it may be argued that Jerusalem, the ancient capital and pre-Zionist center for the religious "Old Yishuv" is a type of nuclear core, traditional religious values did not form the basis of modern Zionist ideology. For a

FIGURE 17.1
Political Cores of Israel

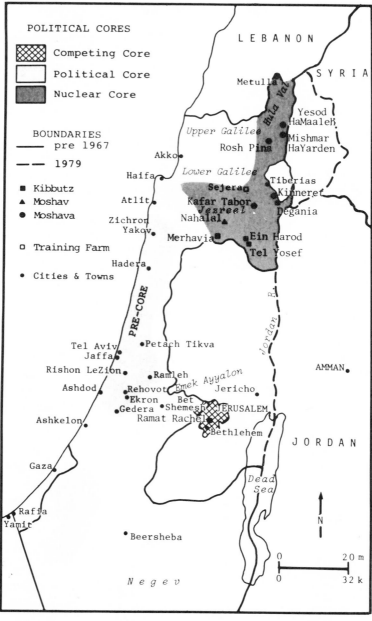

variety of reasons early Socialist-Zionist immigration waves were attracted to the north, and the region became the central stage for the collective and cooperative agricultural pioneering movement. The Second (1904–1914) and Third (1919–1923) Aliyot were immigration waves dominated by those committed to the concept of conquest of the land. These "founding fathers" eventually created the labor parties and organizations that articulated the ideological values, fashioned the national myths, staffed the bureaucracy, and shaped the Zionist state. In the north emerged the values that permeated the entire national territory. These values influence public allocation of resources, foreign orientation, and defense.

Both myth and geopolitical reality directed the attention northward. There the pioneers first came to search for a landscape with some resemblance to the open, humid, grassy southern and forested western Russian rural milieu, rejecting the noise and squalor of Arab Jaffa, and the paternalism that characterized their relations with Jewish farm owners in the coastal Jewish colonies.[2] Geopolitical considerations also strongly influenced this pull to the north, because the north was the source for most of the water resources of Palestine.[3] It should be noted that in Solomonic times, part of the Litani River and the Jordan's headwaters were included within the Jewish kingdom (see Figure 17.2).

Chief among the values of the Jewish pioneers of the north were Jewish labor, self-defense, self-sufficiency, self-labor, and cooperation. In 1907 and 1908, the non-Zionist ICA (Jewish Colonization Association) farm at Sejera was organized by placing management of the farm in the hands of a workers' committee. In the fall of 1909, the Palestine Office signed a contract with disgruntled workers at the private farm colony of Kinneret, permitting them to farm the land of Um Juni cooperatively. A year later, the workers renamed the settlement Degania, and established it as the first fullblown collective — a kvutza.[4]

Also in 1907, the base of operations of Bar Giora, the secret defense society and forerunner of Hashomer, was established in the Galilee at Sejera.[5] In 1909, in the Jewish lower Galilean village of Meshca (Kfar Tabor) the decision was taken by Bar Giora leaders, joined by the collective at Sejera and by the leaders of the Russian Jewish self-defense movement who had just arrived in Palestine, to reorganize in the form of a broadened, more open self-defense force, Hashomer. Members of Hashomer, in turn, participated in establishment of Degania. Finally, in 1911, a federation of agricultural workers of the Galilee was established in the same year that a Judean agricultural workers federation was organized in Petach Tikvah. These became major bases for the later development of the Histadrut — the Federation of Jewish Workers in Eretz Israel. From these locally tested values emerged broader Zionist concepts that were to shape

FIGURE 17.2
The Different Palestines

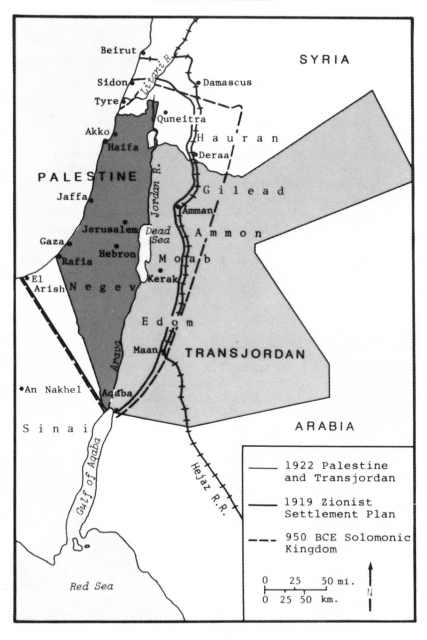

the state: Jewish national self-sufficiency independent of indigenous Arab
and mandatory forces; ingathering of the exiles; a popular defense army;
and a Workers' Commonwealth. A decade later in 1921, the north, in
which were concentrated 28 of the country's 57 Jewish agricultural settlements, was to give rise to the Gdud HaAvoda (the Legion of Labor), the
Hagana (Defense Force), and the Histadrut. These institutions were not
destined to remain based in the region, however.

The Center as Core Area

While the north served as the nuclear core, it was the center, the coastal
plain area from Hadera to Rehovot with its focus on Tel Aviv, and where
the first modern Jewish colonies had been established, which began to
emerge in the 1920s as the dominant core for Jewish Palestine. Heralding
the shift from the north was the establishment of the first all Jewish city,
Tel Aviv, as the headquarters for the Yishuv's three most important political institutions, the United Labor Party (Achdut HaAvoda, 1919), the
Histadrut (1920), and the Hagana (1920). Through them the pioneering
ideology of the north was transplanted to the population and economic
base of the coastal plain.

The large scale immigration waves of the 1920s and 1930s, especially
the Fourth Aliya of 1924–1928 from Poland, and the Fifth Aliya of
1932–1935, brought overwhelming concentration of population and economic activity to the coastal plain. Tel Aviv became the country's largest
and only all-Jewish city, eclipsing the mandatory capital Jerusalem in size,
when its population grew to 135,000 in 1935. Industry expanded rapidly,
especially during 1933–35. These were years of great prosperity for Palestine, with foreign trade increasing by 50 percent over the previous base,
and major economic and financial institutions, public, private, and cooperative, being established.

As the political and economic core (the "ecumene") clearly became
rooted around Tel Aviv, control of its political destinies was more firmly
gathered up by the leaders of the second and third pioneering immigration
waves. The ruling élite, now located in Tel Aviv, included many who retained formal membership in the northern or coastal plain communal and
cooperative settlements in which they had labored. They brought their central concerns for agricultural pioneering and the development of a national
Jewish infrastructure (roads, buildings, ports) to the forefront of the
Yishuv's national values.[6] Thus, the nuclear core of the north and the more
urbanized ecumene of the central coastal plain became ideologically and
economically united.

From statehood until 1967, the coastal plain center increasingly built up
its primacy. This was in spite of vigorous efforts by the Israeli government
to disperse population and economic activities throughout the periphery by

establishing new development towns and cooperative villages. But the combination of the natural attraction of the coastal plain for manufacturing and the Ben Gurion étatist philosophy of "mamlachtiut" (state-building), in which primacy of the state was asserted over sectoral institutions, tended to centralize matters within the core more than ever. This was especially the case because the largest public institutions, the Defense Ministry, the headquarters of the Israeli Armed Forces, and the Histadrut did not move from Tel Aviv to Jerusalem when the latter became Israel's capital in 1950.

Jerusalem as New Competing Core

Since 1967, the primacy of the coastal plain core has been challenged by the emergence of Jerusalem, its derived core, as a competing core. Political unification of Jerusalem and unprecedented growth and development there have shifted a good deal of the national political energy to this upland capital. Thus, Jerusalem, the major Jewish urban center until the twentieth century, but a city that had become part of the periphery from 1949 to 1967, has begun to reassert some of its traditional leadership role.

It is premature to suggest that Israel's political core is shifting to Jerusalem, or that the center has expanded physically to embrace Jerusalem. However, not only has Jerusalem grown in size and attracted much of national energy, it has come to symbolize the particular values held by large sectors of the national population. These are new/old values. They have to do with settlement and defense policies, with the issue of frontiers and territorial annexation, and with general attitudes toward the return of the occupied territories. If Jerusalem is not yet Israel's major core area, it is also no longer in the periphery of the state.

As Israel's new competing core, Jerusalem is at least as accessible to the periphery as is Tel Aviv, and is more directly involved in Arab-Jewish conflict and accommodation owing to its ethnically-mixed and frontier city status. As lines have hardened in Israel between "doves" and "hawks" over the return of administered territories, it should be remembered that the strength of the "doves," largely in the Labor party, the recently-split Democratic movement of the center, and in factions and parties to the Left, is in the Tel Aviv and Haifa areas. The periphery, on the other hand, has been more "hawkish." Much of the strength of the religious "Gush Emunim" group that has spearheaded the most recent settlement efforts in the West Bank, comes from supporters in Jerusalem. Moreover, support for settlement in the Golan Heights and opposition to withdrawal from North Sinai has come strongly from collective and cooperative villages in Israel's northern and southern periphery. In the debate within Israel over the future of the territories, groups based in Jerusalem have played a particularly strong role in arguing for Jewish settlement of the West Bank.[7]

The Boundaries of Partition

The partitioning of the Holy Land in modern times, even though the immediate result of military struggle or of a political decision by an external power(s), has been directly related to the establishment, shift, and expansion of the core areas of the Jewish population. This analysis of the partitioning process covers the events of the past sixty years.

The First Stage of Partition

A major consequence of World War I was the reorganization of many national boundaries so as to be *subsequent* to either concentration of settlements of ethnic groups, or of particular expressions of power. Whereas, previously, national boundaries had often been vaguely drawn, sometimes as zones rather than lines, the pressure at Versailles was for detailed and precise lines on well-known ground. In Palestine, where Arabs and Jews had competing claims emerging out of the historic presence of the two peoples and their World War I roles in support of the Allied powers, the boundary-making process followed the general principles of being subsequent to settlement and power, and of being precisely marked. The boundary changes also reflected attempts to find compromise in the conflict that has engulfed the Palestinian scene from the beginning of this period.

The first territorial compromise between the contending peoples culminated with the partition of Palestine in 1922 (see Figure 17.2). At that time, the Cairo Conference affirmed the Churchill White Paper's establishment of Transjordan. Formally confirmed as an emirate in 1925, the land east of the Jordan was closed to Jewish settlement. Transjordan represented 76 percent of the total land area of the Palestine Mandate. The land that retained the name Palestine was now approximately one-third of biblical Palestine.

In fact, Zionist leaders never seriously entertained the notion of settling in all of what was to become Transjordan. In 1919, Zionists presented a settlement plan that was based upon the lines of the Israelite settlement of Solomon's kingdom.[8] The Zionist plan contained much of biblical Edom, Moab, and Ammon, including the hot steppe climatic region (over 200 mm. annual rainfall) of modern-day Jordan, as well as the Dead Sea-Arava reaches. Its eastern boundary lay just west of the Hejaz railway, on which were situated Amman, Deraa, and Maan. As in the Solomonic kingdom, the Golan Heights, Mount Hermon, and the Lower Litani River were included in the plan. So were Philistia (Jaffa to Gaza) and the Northern Palestinian coast (Tyre to Akko), over which Solomon never succeeded in gaining control (see Figures 17.2 and 17.3).

Meinhertzhagen, in 1919, had proposed substantially the same area for Palestine, save for a northern boundary that followed the northern bank of

FIGURE 17.3
Palestine's Boundaries Early Twentieth Century

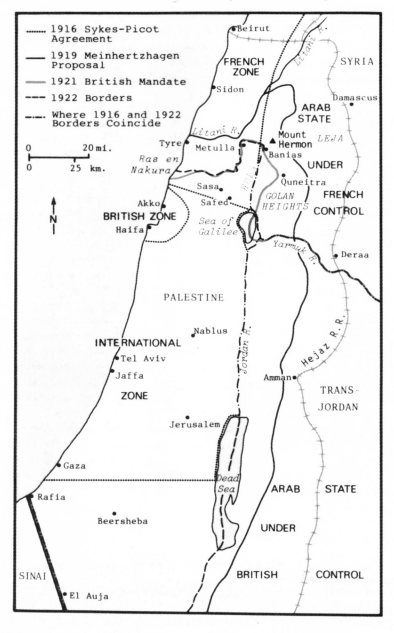

the Lower Litani (rather than including the entire basin almost to Sidon).⁹ By suggesting a boundary that included both banks of the Litani up to the Litani gorges, and then including those of the Hermon waters which flow into the Litani or Jordan basins, Meinhertzhagen sought to assure Palestine of control of its essential water sources — a matter of vital concern to the Zionists. Southeast of the Dead Sea, he suggested a slightly narrower strip of land to the Gulf of Aqaba just east of the town of Aqaba.

The northern boundary of Palestine proved a point of considerable contention between the British and the French (see figure 17.3). The French wished to base the boundary on the Sykes-Picot Agreement of 1916, continuing east beyond the Sea of Galilee across the Yarmuk Valley to Deraa. The British sought a line that followed the Lower Litani thalweg to the bend of the river and then east to Banias, and the western end of the Leja region. After several years of negotiation and change, the line was fixed in 1923. It extended east from Ras en Nakura, then turned north to Metulla, east to Banias and south to include the Jordan headwaters as they flow through the Hula Basin. The western part of the Golan Heights, treated as part of Palestine in the French-British agreement of 1920, was detached, while the French gave up their claim to the Hula Basin and to a small area along the northern frontier, north of Sasa.

The Second Stage of Partition

The second stage of territorial compromise began with a series of partition plans formally or informally put forward as early as 1932. It was brought to a head by the United Nations Palestine Partition Plan of November 27, 1947, and culminated in the armistice agreements with Egypt, Lebanon, Jordan, and Syria of February-July, 1949 (see Figure 17.4).¹⁰ The various partition proposals and the UNSCOP plan recommended boundaries that for the most part were *subsequent* to the settlement distribution pattern (the Negev being the exception). On the other hand, the 1949 armistice boundaries laid down new lines that were in accord with Israeli military power, but were in advance of Israeli settlement. Thus the boundaries at the end of the second stage of partition had become *antecedent* boundaries: active immigration then stabilized these lines and obliterated some of the characteristics of the antecedent boundary. Roads and settlements, and the development of an infrastructure produced a more mature political landscape. As a result of the process of negotiation, war, and renegotiation, the Jewish territorial base at the end of this second stage included approximately 20 percent of the total land area of the original Palestine Mandate, and 40 percent of the territory to which Zionist leaders had hoped the Balfour Declaration would apply. On the other hand, the new state now had a total of 26,000 square kilometers, or about one and one-half times the area allotted to the Jewish state in the United

Nations plan. The area now controlled by Israel was remarkably similar to a plan advanced by the Jewish Agency in 1946, except for the division of Jerusalem, and the loss to the Arabs of the area north-west of the Dead Sea.[11]

The Third Stage of Partition — The On-Going Process

This stage can be described as the search for "defensible" boundaries. Continued Arab hostility toward Israel marked by terrorist attacks and Egypt's 1956 blockade of the Suez Canal and the Gulf of Aqaba, brought on the 1956 Sinai War. Israel's victory at that time and subsequent yielding of the captured Sinai did not bring a halt to guerilla infiltration or to Egyptian-Syrian military pressures and blockades. The result of these further Arab hostile actions was Israel's preemptive war of 1967. Israel's 1967 occupation of the West Bank and Gaza, all of the Sinai, and the Golan Heights marked the beginning of the third stage of partition. Several years later, again in the wake of war, came modest Israeli withdrawals in Sinai and the Golan.

This third partition period has already been marked by three wars: the Six Day War of 1967, the War of Attrition of 1969–70, and the Yom Kippur War of 1973 — and by Israel's invasion of southern Lebanon. This stage is also characterized by: global diplomatic struggles in such agencies as the United Nations, UNESCO, and the I.L.O.; economic boycotts (OPEC pressures against those nations allied with Israel, and the Arab boycott against firms and individuals that do business with Israel); conflict in adjoining territories (the Palestinian Liberation Organization-Jordanian hostilities of 1970, the Lebanese War of 1975–78); international terror and Palestinian guerilla actions within Israel, and Israeli counterstrikes; and formal negotiations such as the first and second Sinai agreements between Israel and Egypt of January 18, 1974 and September 1, 1975, and the Israeli-Syrian agreement along the Golan Heights in May 31, 1974 (see Figure 17.5). The Israeli-Egyptian agreement of March 26, 1979 calls for return of all Sinai to Egypt at the end of three years. The first subphase, Israeli withdrawal from the North Sinai coast to El Arish was completed in May of 1979. The treaty called for Israeli withdrawal east of a line from El Arish to Ras Muhammed by the end of 1979, thus evacuating two-thirds of the Sinai, and full withdrawal by April 25, 1982.

The process is still going on, and it is inexorable. The Israeli-Egyptian Peace Treaty that derived from the Camp David agreements among Israel, Egypt, and the United States has hastened the time when a new territorial partition will be drawn up as a compromise between the boundaries of 1949 and those of 1967. This treaty deals not only with the Sinai; it is linked to negotiations on Palestinian self-rule in the West Bank and the Gaza Strip. It, therefore, represents another stage in the ultimate determi-

FIGURE 17.4
UNSCOP Partition Plan and 1949 Armistice Line of Israel

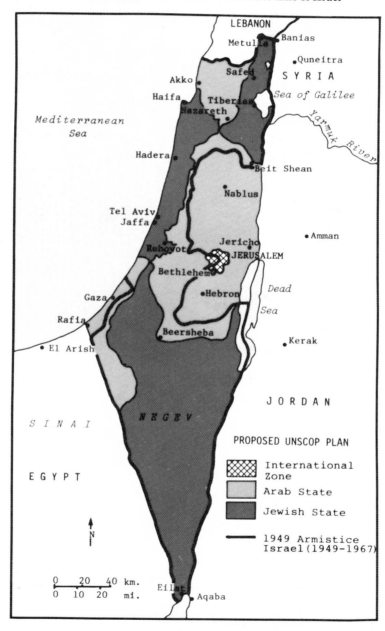

FIGURE 17.5
Israel and the Administered Territories (1973–79)

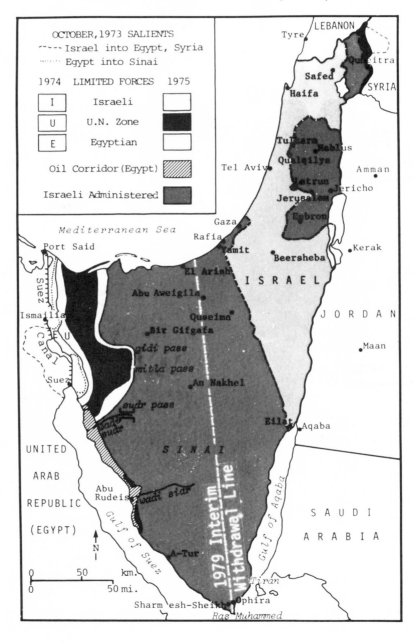

OCTOBER, 1973 SALIENTS
---- Israel into Egypt, Syria
······ Egypt into Sinai

1974   LIMITED FORCES   1975

I	Israeli
U	U.N. Zone
E	Egyptian

Oil Corridor (Egypt)

Israeli Administered

LEBANON

Tyre

Quneitra

Safed

Haifa

SYRIA

Tulkarm

Nablus

Qualqilya

Tel Aviv

Amman

Latrun

Jericho

Jerusalem

Hebron

Mediterranean Sea

Gaza

Rafia

Beersheba

Kerak

Port Said

Yamit

El Arish

I S R A E L

Abu Aweigila

Ismailia

Quseima

J O R D A N

E U

Bir Gifgafa

gidi pass

mitla pass

Maan

Suez

An Nakhel

sudr pass

Eilat

Aqaba

wadi sudr

S I N A I

UNITED

1979 Interim Withdrawal Line

ARAB

Gulf of Aqaba

REPUBLIC

Abu Rudeis

wadi sidr

S A U D I

(EGYPT)

Gulf of Suez

A R A B I A

N

A-Tur

0   50   km.

0   50 mi.

Tiran

Ophira

Sharm esh-Sheikh

Ras Muhammed

nation of boundaries between Israel and its Arab neighbors. While some obvious forces — comparative military might, superpower intercession, the nature of the specific agreement (cease-fire, nonbelligerency, or peace) — will determine the location of the line, other less predictable forces will also play a role. These include the ultimate outcome of the Lebanese conflict (whether status-quo-ante, partition into Christian and Muslim states, or de facto control by Syria); the strength and durability of the efforts to forge a Syrian-Jordanian alliance; and the role of Saudi Arabia in supporting Egypt's peace-making efforts. Whatever the outcome, then, of this third partition stage, it will not be the last one in territorial rearrangement unless it has as its quid-pro-quo a formal peace between all the Arabs and the Israelis that includes direct participation by the Palestinian Arabs in the resolution of the Palestinian problem.

Core and Outer Boundaries

In the decade that Jerusalem has emerged as Israel's competing core, the major coastal plain core has also expanded. In the north, Hadera has grown rapidly; in the southeast, Ramleh has developed as Israel's major aircraft manufacturing center; in the south, the new industrial port of Ashdod and the adjoining residential center of Ashkelon have extended the center's limits. Population density in the center averages 500 persons per square kilometer, with more than ten times this density in the Tel Aviv district.

Israel's future population will be reflected in continued expansion of the core, given the population's projected increase from 3.5 million to 5 million over the next two decades (see Figure 17.6). In all likelihood the center will link up with Jerusalem via Ramleh, Emek Ayyalon, Bet Shemesh, and the Jerusalem Corridor. The Jerusalem district's population density is already over 500 persons per square kilometer, or the average for the center. In the north, prospects are for the Haifa district, whose density is also over 500 persons per square kilometer, to be joined to the core, too. Northeast from Hadera expansion will embrace the Vale of Irron (Wadi Ara), the corridor that connects the coastal plain to the Valley of Jezreel. The direction of the southward extension of the core is more speculative. But with continued growth of Beersheba, the core will probably envelop the Gaza Strip, extending from Ashkelon southeast to Beersheba and then westward in the direction of the Mediterranean toward the Rafia Approaches. The latter, the North Sinai Israeli wedge between the Gaza Strip and Sinai, is a region that has been developed by agriculture and the urban center of Yamit. With the North Sinai wedge's return to Egypt as a consequence of the Camp David agreement, the pressures on Israel to develop areas in Israeli territory immediately to the east of North Sinai will increase. The Hevel

FIGURE 17.6
Expansion of Israel's Ecumene

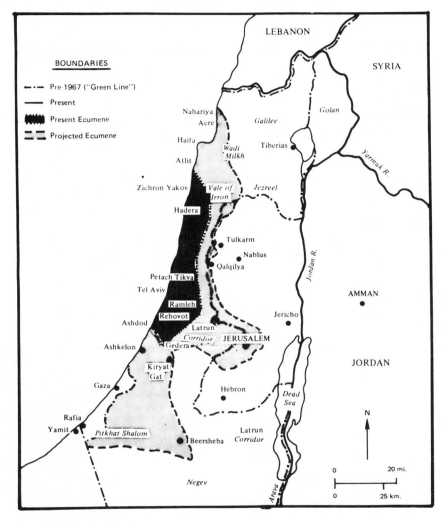

Eshkol area that abuts the Rafia wedge has received considerable settlement activity since the Israeli-Egyptian treaty signing.

Expansion of Core

Prospect of the center's expansion has significant implication for any lasting partition, for the location of the core sets limits on Israel's political and strategic abilities to compromise on its outer, national boundaries. A unified Jerusalem is not likely to be relinquished through diplomatic processes. Moreover, where the Israeli core adjoins the West Bank and Gaza, lack of periphery to provide defensive depth makes demilitarization of any Arab entity that might emerge a sine qua non for Israel. The Upper Jordan Valley, although in the Israeli periphery, is also part of the country's nuclear core. The area, therefore, has greater political influence upon the government than would normally be expected of a peripheral area. Because of this, Israel is, at a minimum, likely to insist upon demilitarization of the western half of the Golan Heights in any ultimate formal accommodation with Syria and control of the headwaters of the Jordan and all lands immediately to the east of the Sea of Galilee, so as to secure the lake effectively.

Relationship to the West Bank

Territorial development of Israel's core and changing configurations of its outer boundaries have made a strong impact upon the West Bank's potential for territorial cohesiveness. Israeli Jerusalem separates Samaria from Judea, and Israel's Negev and Southern Coastal Plain isolate Gaza. Any emerging Palestinian West Bank entity would be truncated, organized around three isolated "corelets" — the Nablus district, the Hebron district, and the northern end of the Gaza strip. Israeli objections to emergence of an independent Palestinian West Bank state (Israeli leaders often refer to it as a potential "rump" state) have referred to its lack of viability, as well as to the danger of its becoming a Soviet-backed terrorist base. Absence of a strong Palestinian Arab core area in the West Bank is certainly a major liability for separate statehood. Under normalized political conditions, the size and dynamism of Greater Amman would make it the logical core area for a combined Jordanian-West Bank state. But Israel is not likely to jeopardize its security by foregoing demilitarization of the West Bank. Moreover, a sovereign Jordanian-Palestinian (or Palestinian-Jordanian) entity can hardly be expected to agree to demilitarization of a major part of its national territory. As an interim measure, therefore, a West Bank entity, truncated, demilitarized and discontiguous (not unlike the European feudal state) is a more logical political option. In the long run, Prime Minister Begin's agreement to concede local autonomy for the Palestinian Arabs of the West Bank may well have to lead to a Palestinian self-determination that will embrace statehood.

In the discussions over the future of the territories that began at Camp

David, Israel has adopted a firm "no negotiations" posture on the issue of Jerusalem. There is little doubt that ultimately Jerusalem will prove the greatest bone of territorial contention between Israel and the Arabs, and be the greatest obstacle to Arab-Israeli formal agreement on the West Bank. Paradoxically, however, a unified Israeli Jerusalem could, in the long run, help secure enduring peace by serving to link Israel and a Palestinian state of the West Bank in geopolitically functional terms.[12] In a peaceful setting, Jerusalem would then become the natural urbanized core for a large city-region, with only vestigial national boundaries.

Arenas of Conflict and Defensible Boundaries

This may be better understood by viewing the Arab-Israeli conflict as taking place at two geographical levels: local (Jews versus Palestinian and other Arabs nearby) and regional (Jews versus the Arab states). The conflict within Israel, the West Bank, and what was "Fatah-land" in Southern Lebanon is essentially guerrilla activity and a small-scale military response that occurs in or near heavily populated Jewish areas. The setting of the regional or external conflict, in which are arrayed massed armed forces, are border reaches more removed from major Jewish centers of population — the eastern end of the Golan Heights, the Jordan River Valley, and in Sinai. Prior to the 1967 war, the two forms of contention took place within Palestine in the same geographical arenas; now they are spatially separated, even though linked politically and ideologically.

Various arguments over what territorial concessions Israel can afford to make often fail to distinguish clearly between the two different levels of contention. But the strategic implications to Israel of yielding territory in the Sinai and in much of the Golan are considerably different from the implications of abandoning military and settlement presences — within the "Green Line" that is the border of the West Bank, surrounding Gaza, in Jerusalem, or along the Lebanese-Syrian border.

With respect to its regional, Arab-state geopolitical relations, Israel may well be able to work out accommodations with Egypt, Syria, Jordan, and in Lebanon. Her viability as a state would not be threatened if mutual concessions were made, linking territorial compromises to a political declaration of recognition and nonbelligerency; to limitations of armaments and disposition of armed forces; to the establishment of demilitarized zones; to assurance of international water passageways; and to outside power guarantees of the status quo. It is in the local arena that Israel must enroll its map of territorial compromise. The outlines of Labor's territorial policy have been succinctly summarized by Haim Bar-Lev, Labor's defense minister-designate: the Jordan Valley, southern Gaza, Jerusalem, the Etzion Bloc, and minor border adjustments. This, in effect, is Labor's interpretation of U.N. Resolution 242. One of the problems with so brief a policy statement is that it focuses, wittingly or unwittingly, on the narrower aspects of Israel's security problems — military defensive positions against most attacks from east of the Jordan or from Sinai, tactical surveillance over the West Bank, and tactical defenses in the vicinity of the "Green Line."

The annexation by Israel of land in Samaria, Judea, Gaza, and the Golan, or the designating of special areas, security zones, and corridors for long-term use by Israel should, however, be considered more broadly. This is because the strategic relationship between territory and security has economic and demographic, as well as military dimensions. For Israel, territorial adjustments must include four categorical needs: (1) water control; (2) surveillance points, marshalling areas, and corridors; (3) defensive depth; and (4) population growth space. These are not mutually exclusive, although generally one category holds greater salience over the others in any given piece of geographical space.

Water Control

Water control in the north was the basis for Zionist settlement policy going back to the early part of the twentieth century. The boundaries between Palestine and Syria that were drawn by the French and the British in 1923 were the result of these Jewish settlement activities, of Haganah actions, and of Zionist political pressures. The same issue of water control was a major cause for hostilities between Israel and Syria prior to 1967. In the north, the Syrians sought to divert the Banias headwater of the Jordan, they disputed Israel's right to farm land in the demilitarized lands west of the Jordan in the Bnot Yakov bridge and they threatened Israel's unrestricted use of Lake Tiberias, harassing fishermen and other lake users from that part of the Golan Heights that overlooked the northeastern quadrant of the lake. There the Syrian boundary extended only ten meters from the water's edge. Future territorial adjustments that will secure Israel's water supply require that Israeli sovereignty be exercised over the Har Dov-Banias headwaters region (e.g., the Israeli settlement of Naveh Atib), the Golan slopes east of the upper Jordan (e.g., the urban center of Katzrin several kilometers east of the Bnot Yakov bridge), and the Golan Heights that overlook Lake Tiberias. In this latter area, a ring of settlements has been established three to seven kilometers from the 1967 border, from Mavo Hama overlooking the Yarmuk River, through Afik and the regional center of Bnai Yehuda, to Ramot and Maale Gamla.

To the south, Jordanian seizure of the northwestern quadrant of the Dead Sea limited Israel's access to Sdom via a single route east from Arad. More generally, Israel's restriction to the southwest quadrant of the sea between 1948 and 1967 created political impediments to economic develop-

FIGURE 17.7A
Proposed Territorial Adjustments — Samaria and Judea

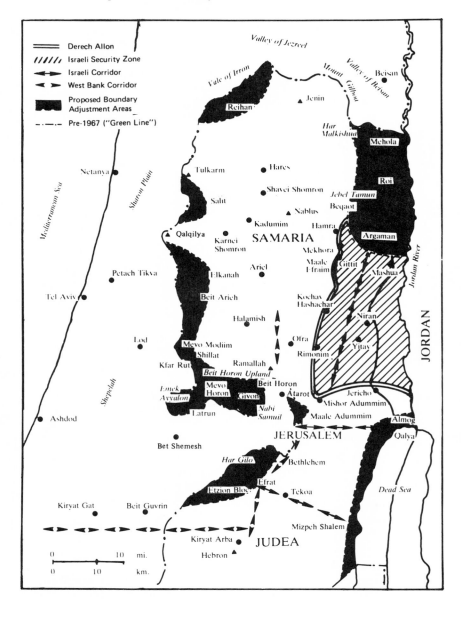

FIGURE 17.7B
Proposed Territorial Adjustments — General

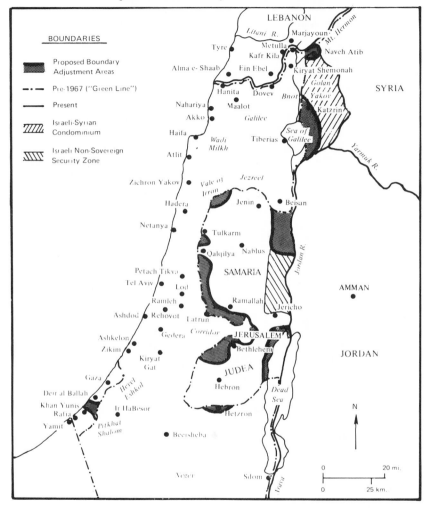

ment and tourism. These have now been obviated, as Israel has developed
the northwest shore from Almog and Qalya to Mitzpe Shalem. Sharing the
delta of the Jordan and controlling the entire western half of the sea se-
cures Israel's claim to joint mineral and development rights, and broadens
Israel political-geographical options with respect to building of the pro-

posed Mediterranean-Dead Sea Canal which will impact on the water level
of the sea in its entirety.

Surveillance Points, Marshalling Areas and Corridors

There are two types of surveillance requirements, one against terrorism
within the West Bank, and the other against attack by massed armies. The
first presents tactical and the second strategic problems. To command the
West Bank tactically, a limited number of fixed points and marshalling
areas, supplemented by mobile patrols over designated security zones
would suffice. Certain territorial adjustments need to be made to include
under Israeli sovereignty areas which overlook key Arab West Bank centers or which can interdict hostile traffic. On the southern edge of Judea,
the highland area of Southern Har Hebron (Yattir in the Dhahiriya-
Eshtemoa area) is a base from which both Beersheba can be protected and
Hebron monitored. Surveillance over Hebron from the north can be maintained from the Etzion Bloc and the proposed urban center of Efrat. Territorial adjustment that includes the Judean Mountain area across the
"Green Line" from Beit Guvrin to the Etzion Bloc and then northward to
the heights of Beit Jala (Har Gilo), drawn so as to exclude Bethlehem and
Beit Jala, would protect the southern flank of Jerusalem and widen the
Jerusalem Corridor at its southern entrance to the Holy City.

A unified Jerusalem under Israeli sovereignty whose heights command
the Judean desert to the east, and provide a major surveillance base for activities across the Jordan, dominates Ramallah and Southern Samaria, and
effectively interdicts hostile linkup between the West Bank portions of
Samaria and Judea. On the northeastern edge of Samaria, the annexation
to Israel of the southern extension of the Gilboa Mountains from Har
Malkishua to Jebel Tamun would protect the Valley of Beisan from infiltration, dominate Jenin to the west and Wadi Fara to the south, and could
threaten Jenin-Nablus movement. These heights also provide surveillance
across the Jordan Valley over to northern Jordan from the Yarmuk to
Jerash (Mehola, Argaman).

The strategic problem of having distant early warning points against
massed attack from the eastern front is a matter of a different order. It requires long-term Israeli military control and an Israeli settlement presence, though not necessarily legal sovereignty (the phasing might be from
military occupation to a long-term lease). The Allon Plan called for annexation of the strip that includes both the terraces of the Jordan Valley and
the eastern slope of Samaria. In response to this strategy, two strings of
settlements have been developed, the lower one from Yitav and Niran
north of Jericho to Mashua overlooking the Damiya Crossing of the Jordan
(Gesher Adam). The upper string of settlements connected by the 48 kilometer Derech Allon, extends from Adumim on the Jerusalem-Jericho road

to Michmash to Kokhav HaShachar, to the proposed urban center Maale Efraim and Gittit, to Mekhora and Hamra overlooking Wadi Fara. This "watch on the Jordan" is what Israel expects to keep under Israeli control as one of the "defined security zones" mentioned in the Camp David agreement.

In any peace agreement with the Palestinians, especially if the West Bank should become federated with Jordan, it is unlikely that the Jordan Valley could become sovereign Israeli territory. For its part, Israel must maintain its military presence in these Samarian wastelands and Jordan terraces that overlook the river to monitor the threat of arms infiltration or mass attack from Syrian or Jordanian territory. The Jewish settlements are also crucial because they are a paramilitary system whose very existence forges a corridor between northern Israel and the Dead Sea. These settlements could constitute a nonsovereign "Jewish Pale" located at the edge of West Bank territory over which Israel would maintain long-term military control. For their part, the Arabs of Samaria and Judea would require a highway link east of Jerusalem and a land corridor through Israeli territory to the Gaza Strip over which they could expect to have full economic and political freedom of movement. In the same way, Maale Adumim, now being developed as an urban site a few kilometers east of Jerusalem's city boundary, could be the hinge to a security corridor for Israel from Mount Scopus to the northern end of the Dead Sea, and Efrat could hinge a security corridor from Tekoa to the Dead Sea.

There has been previous discussion of the need for Israel to annex politically the western fringes of the Golan for the tactical purposes of securing Israel's water supply and assuring the defense of the Upper Jordan Valley settlements. However, there is the strategic issue as well — the need to have a marshalling area and distant early warning points against attack by Syrian armor.

When Israel withdrew from the eastern edge of the plateau up to Kuneitra in 1975, it eased its offensive threat against Damascus. But the central and major part of the Golan (1,250 square kilometers), if returned to Syria even under conditions of demilitarization and United Nations surveillance, could be remilitarized by the Syrians in a matter of hours. Only the actual presence of Israeli tanks and heavy weapons can guarantee that the Central Golan will not become a base for massed tank attack against Israel's vital north. The Israeli settlements that adjoin Kuneitra (from Har Oden to Zivan), and those to the southeast, from Keshet to Ramat Magshimim to Nov and Eli Al have a function similar to the Jordan Valley settlements. They constitute a security zone that has to be controlled militarily by Israel whatever the Syrian position may be.

The Syrians insist that their major quarrel with Israel is not over the Golan now, but over the West Bank. Should there be a West Bank solution, a short-term compromise on the Central Golan might be to convert the area into an autonomous Druze region, whose non-Jewish residents could opt either for Syrian or Israeli citizenship and which would be militarily manned by Israeli forces and some international force. The Druze have been a majority in the Golan Heights and have connections with kinsmen in both Syria and Israel. A form of condominium could be exercised, with Syria responsible for civil government and Israel for military control.

The southern end of the Gaza Strip could be treated as strategic territory to be used as a buffer against Egyptian forces in Sinai. On the other hand, the accommodations between Israel and Egypt through the demilitarized zones in Sinai that border the Negev, peacekeeping forces, and the redeployment of the Israeli military to the Negev represent Israel's major strategic defenses in the south. An Israeli foothold in Gaza is, then, more tactical in nature. It would separate the Palestinian Arabs from the Egyptians, making more difficult the passage of arms and men from North Sinai to possible Gaza-based terrorist activities.

Because of Gaza's tactical importance, Israel is likely to seek to annex the South Gaza area of Israeli settlement between Khan Yunis and Deir al Ballah. This narrow wedge (from Netzer Hazzani to Kfar Darom) is several kilometers wide and constitutes a corridor between the Mediterranean and Pitkhat Shalom.

Whether the corridor should become the western terminus for the Med-Dead Tunnel Canal as has been proposed by the Begin Government, or whether the canal should originate at Zikim just south of Ashkelon, has become a focus for major debate in Israel. The canal's direct purposes of generating electricity, raising the level of the Dead Sea, and providing reservoirs for recreation, fishing, or possible nuclear power station sites are augmented by its ideological potential to serve as a nation-mobilizing effort.

Choosing the site before negotiations is, however, untimely. If the choice were to be made as part of the negotiations, it might be possible to have the canal extend through a zone which would contain alongside it the Gaza-Judea land corridor for the Palestinian West Bank entity. Choice of the Southern Gaza or Zikim terminal points could be made on rational economic grounds. Indeed, locating the canal in a corridor that contains the Arab land passageway might make it possible for Jordan to accept the Med-Dean Canal as a joint venture. This would anticipate and minimize tensions over regulation of the Dead Sea level that are bound to occur if the canal was operated by Israel on a unilateral basis.

Defensive Depth

It is obvious that the narrowness of the Sharon coastal plain and the intrusion of the Latrun salient at the conjunction of the Shephela and the western edge of the Jerusalem Corridor are strategic liabilities that require boundary adjustment. Another aspect of this problem has to do with those sections of the "Green Line" where Israeli Arab villages adjoin the West Bank and have a potential for destabilization. How to provide for territorial adjustments and still provide for a West Bank entity that has rational territorial limits is a complex question. Certainly a boundary that follows Gush Emunim settlements on the ridgetops of Samaria ten to fifteen kilometers east of the "Green Line" would leave little territorial integrity to a West Bank entity. On the other hand, modest territorial adjustments several kilometers eastward into the Samarian piedmont are needed for Israel's security.

This includes the following areas: the northwest corner of Samaria, where the hills west of Jenin and Emek Dotan overlook densely-populated Israeli Arab villages in Wadi Ara (Reihan, Shaked); a small area between Tulkarm and Qalqilya that adjoins the Arab villages of Taiba and Tireh (Salit); and the western approaches to the Jerusalem Corridor. It is especially important to incorporate the Latrun wedge, including the former demilitarized zone opposite Lod. The core here is Emek Ayyalon and the Israeli settlements that have been established to its north (Shillat, Kfar Rut), and on the Horon Upland to the east (Beit Horon, Mevo Horon). Extending from this western sector, the corridor has to be widened all along the north so that Jerusalem will not be dependent on one major road for its lifeline. The proposed highway link runs from Lod through Emeq Ayyalon and along the ridge tops from the Beit Horon upland to Nabi Samuel and Givon, together with settlements in the Beit Horon area on the west and Givon on the east. A security zone on the northern side of the corridor, around which a subsequent boundary could be delimited, is anticipated to be developed.

Broadening the corridor in the south via the Etzion Bloc has already been discussed. This would permit another highway link to Jerusalem starting at Kiryat Gat to Beit Guvrin to Efrat and north to the city.

With all of these changes, the corridor at its eastern end would run from Atarot and Givon in the north to Har Gilo and Gush Etzion in the south, a distance of 25 kilometers. All told, the annexed territories would provide the corridor with the optimal defensive depth that can be expected.

Population Growth Space

Long-term security provisions for the state include space for population growth and dispersal in the years ahead. For Israel to accommodate a population of five million in the next decade and a half, its current population and economic core (the ecumene) will have to expand its current coastal plain borders from Zichron Yakov in the north to Gedera in the south, to Lod and Ramleh in the east. Such an expansion may be anticipated northward to Haifa, Wadi Ara, Nahariya, and the slopes of the Western Galilee; eastward through the Jerusalem Corridor to include Jerusalem; southeastward to Kiryat Gat and beyond Beersheba, and then westward to include Pitkhat Shalom up to Gaza-North Sinai.

The piedmont southeast of Qalqilya and on a line opposite Kfar Saba-Petach Tikva (Elkanah) represents an important expansion area for urban residence and industry. This is also the case for the higher sections of the piedmont east of the Petach Tikva-Lod line (Beit Arieh), which are particularly well adapted for light, high-technology industry. The western Jerusalem Corridor area already discussed also falls into this boundary change category.

In general, Israeli population growth will need space anywhere from fifteen to twenty kilometers from the coast. We envisage a dense, high-rise urban settlement in these annexed Samarian foothills. Hopefully, the environmentally-injurious trend of blocking the coast with high-rise apartments tapering off with low-density urban sprawl several kilometers from the coast can be reversed. Ideally, the density profile should have shown a low point at the coast (to provide spaces for recreation, port facilities, industry, and free air movement) and increased in the interior. The past cannot be reversed, but at least the new high densities can be concentrated on the piedmont and create a new pattern.

There are no boundary changes that seem necessary or justified along the Lebanese border to enhance Israel's security. The current border follows defensible natural features. The turmoil in Lebanon, which has prevented its government from maintaining peace and stability in the south, has justified Israel's support of the Haddad Christian ministate as a buffer against the PLO. Only if Syria were to absorb all of Lebanon, liquidating the Christian Maronite stronghold in the center, would there be need for Israel to occupy Southern Lebanon up to the Litani River — a zone 25 to 30 kilometers deep. Even such a move would be justified in the form of long-term military occupation only, rather than as permanent territorial annexation.

An alternative to such a drastic move could be the change in status of the current Christian ministate to that of a security zone such as has been proposed for the Central Golan. This region could have condominium status, under Lebanese control for civil matters and Israeli control for military affairs. The Christian and Shiite Muslim residents of the zone could opt for Lebanese or Israeli citizenship. In such an eventuality, the remaining area north to the Litani would have to be cleared of PLO and operated as a demilitarized region.

Jerusalem

Three of the four criteria that have been discussed — surveillance points, marshalling areas and corridors, defensive depth, and populative growth space — apply to Jerusalem. Thus, over and above Israel's historic and spiritual claims to a unified Holy City, there are compelling geopolitical grounds for maintaining its unity under Israeli sovereignty. The boundary extensions that were made in 1967, which expanded the city's area two and one-half fold, had a strategic purpose, of course. But urban land annexation is also a significant land use planning tool. One of the ills of modern urbanization is the dichotomy between city and suburb, and the attendant political atomization of local government. A unitary rather than a metropolitan framework obviates many of these ills.

Modest extensions in the current boundary would provide a firmer base both strategically and for planning purposes. Adding the Givon and Nabi Samuil areas to the northwest, and Har Gilo to the southwest will complete the widening of the Jerusalem Corridor, accommodating the additional highways from the coast that will be needed by a city whose population could reach 600,000 by the year 2000. This expansion will also provide additional tactical surveillance capabilities over southern Samaria from Nabi Samuil. Eastward extension of the municipal boundary would supply additional defense marshalling areas and enhance surveillance capacity over the Judean desert and across the Jordan. When the Maale Adumim developments were initially conceived, they were to have occupied sites midway between Jerusalem and Jericho. The decision to construct the urban settlement closer to Jerusalem, indeed, only three kilometers east of the present boundary, makes the city's boundary extension to include this area to the east geographically feasible.

To maintain the geopolitical unity of the city with modest expansions of its political boundaries will require a quid pro quo for the Arabs. These must go beyond such steps as are envisaged in various suggestions for a borough system, and the granting of extraterritorial status to Old City's Muslim and Christian holy sites and even to the residential quarters in their entirety. For in addition to what takes place within the city to provide maximum local autonomy to the Arabs at the neighborhood and borough levels, two new geopolitical entities need to be developed: Metropolitan Jerusalem and the Jerusalem regions.

The former is the geographically smaller of the two, extending from Beir Zeit and Ramallah on the north, to Latrun on the west, to near Beit Guvrin on the southwest, to the Etzion bloc on the south, to Herodion and Nabi Musia on the east. Its population is about 600,000. The city-region adds the Hebron and all of the Ramallah and Bethlehem districts, thus extending to Kfar Malik and Lubba on the north, Dhahiriya on the south, and the northwest quadrant of the Dead Sea on the east. The population reaches nearly 700,000. What is politically important to the Arabs is that they would represent half of the population of each of these regions. The regions would not be comprehensive units of government. Rather each would be the setting for a number of individual administrative functional authorities serving Jerusalem and its surrounding environments. Within metropolitan Jerusalem, the various authorities could include transportation, waste disposal, recreation, urban housing, and markets. Within the Jerusalem city-region, these authorities could include electricity and water planning, tourism, agriculture, labor exchanges, and industrial development.

Conclusion

Israel's ability not only to withdraw from the Golan Heights and Sinai, but to permit the emergence of a West Bank entity, depends very much on its succeeding in making the kinds of adjustments to the pre–1967 boundaries that have been discussed. Certainly a West Bank entity, be it localy autonomous, federated with Jordan or ultimately independent, will not emerge without formal Palestinian recognition of Israel, renunciation of terrorism, mutual freedom of movement and limited settlement across boundaries for both sides. Initially subject to Israeli military supervision, such a Palestinian entity would eventually have to be demilitarized, and treaty violations would be grounds for renewal of conflict.

Diplomatic and public debate over the rights of Israel to establish settlements in territories captured from the Arabs in 1967 have obfuscated the main issue. Settlements are a means, and only one means to an end. The end is establishment of sovereignty by Israel over strategically-important territory gained as a result of wars that have been forced upon it.

Control of territory to enhance security is a legitimate national objective. Since World War II, this objective has been attained by a number of states, noteworthy among them the U.S.S.R., Poland, and China. The legitimacy of territorial annexation has been recognized by most of the world's nations, including the United States. It is, therefore, important that the debate be shifted from such themes as historic rights and/or the illegitimacy of settlements to the subject of territorial readjustments dictated by security needs. These adjustments in the local arena have to be negotiated now, and not left to follow broad agreements in principle.

If the issue of secure borders is not squarely faced, peace agreements will not be permanent. Any general set of peace principles agreed upon by Israel and Egypt, and whether or not they also include Jordan, will be undermined if the issue of territorial-adjustments is not treated now. Defensible boundaries are a prerequisite to peace. Once such peace becomes a pattern of political and economic life, then these boundaries will achieve a higher level of functional development, in which they will lose their barrier-like functions, and become permeable lines that possess more of a socio-cultural character than the political-military one which the earlier stage required.

The concept of defensible boundaries has been applied to an analysis of Israel's core and periphery. In the current political context, the concept is especially germane to a consideration of the Jerusalem city-region and corridor. Jerusalem is the strategic fulcrum for Israeli-Palestinian Arab relations in the West Bank as a whole. Outside powers trying to advance negotiations for a Middle Eastern peace should keep in mind the lack of symmetry between the strategic significance to Israel of Sinai and the eastern Golan, and the strategic significance to Israel of a united, expanded Jerusalem region. There can be no peace without self-determination for West Bank Palestinians, either in independent fashion or linked to a broader Arab entity. But there also can be no peace without Israel's securing Jerusalem as a strategic hedge against the possibility of a demilitarized West Bank political entity being transformed into a serious military threat.

Notes

1. Ruppin cited a number of reasons for choosing Jaffa: (1) it was already head office for the Anglo-Palestinian company (founded in 1903 as the first Jewish bank in Palestine), the Odessa Committee of the Hovevei Zion, and the Geulah land development corporation; (2) it was centrally located among the largest Jewish agricultural settlements; and most important, (3) it contained the greater part of the "New Yishuv." Jaffa's Jews then numbered 8,000 out of the total of about 20,000 Jewish colonists living in Palestine after thirty years of pioneering efforts. See *Arthur Ruppin: Memoirs, Diaries, Letters*, edited by Alex Bein, translated from the German by Karen Gershon (Jerusalem: Weidenfeld and Nicholson, 1971), pp. 88–90.

2. On moving to Sejera in 1908, the young immigrant David Ben Gurion said: "The constant work with the hoe (in a coastal plain colony) did not entirely satisfy me. There was the scent of workshops in this dull, unceasing thud of the hoe. I yearned for spacious fields, for waving corn, for the scent of herbage and the song of the ploughman; and so it was that I resolved to go to the Galilee. Here in Sejera I found that Homeland for which I longed so greatly. . . . There was opportunity to think and envision and dream." See Yehuda Erez, ed., *David Ben Gurion — A Pictorial Record* (Tel Aviv: Ayanot Publishing House, 1953), p. 8.

3. "It is necessary that the water sources, upon which the future of the Land depends, should not be outside the borders of the future Jewish homeland. . . . For this reason we have always demanded that the Land of Israel include the southern banks of the Litani River, the headwaters of the Jordan, and the Hauran Region from the El Adja spring south of Damascus. All the rivers run from east to west or from north to south. This explains the importance of the Upper Galilee and the Hauran for the entire country. The most important rivers of the Land of Israel are the Jordan, the Litani and the Yarmuk. The Land needs this water. Moreover, the development of industry depends on water power for the generation of electricity." See David Ben Gurion, *Zichronot (Memories)*, Hebrew, Vol. I (Tel Aviv: Am Oved, 1973), p. 164. Col. Richard Meinhertzhagen, the English soldier and diplomat, had made the same argument in a letter to Lord Curzon in 1919. See Col. Richard Meinhertzhagen, *Middle East Diary, 1917–1956*, pp. 61–63.

4. *Arthur Ruppin: Memoirs, Diaries, Letters*, pp. 101–105.
5. Yigel Allon, *Shield of David* (Jerusalem: Weidenfeld and Nicolson, 1970), pp. 17–31.
6. Ibid., pp. 70–72 and Walter Laqueur, *A History of Zionism* (New York: Holt, Rinehart and Winston, 1972), pp. 287–295.
7. Saul B. Cohen, *Jerusalem — Bridging the Four Walls* (New York: Herzl Press, 1977), pp. 96–100.
8. The Zionist Organization submitted a territorial plan for Palestine to the Paris Peace Conference in February 1919 that was rejected. What promoted this initiative was the Sykes-Picot agreement of May 1916 (also abandoned at the Paris Peace Conference), which gave the French control of the area from a line north of Acre to the northern end of the Sea of Galilee, and reserved the Negev (a line from south of Gaza to the Dead Sea) for an Arab state under British protection. The Sykes-Picot plan proposed Palestine's organization as international (a condominium), with an undefined role for Russia and direct control of the Acre and Gaza ports by Britain.
9. Meinhertzhagen, *Middle East Diary, 1917–1956*, pp. 51–53.
10. Official Records of the Second Session of the General Assembly, Supplement No. 11, *United Nations Special Committee on Palestine — Report to the General Assembly* (Lake Success, New York: A/364, September 3, 1947), Volume I, 65 pp., and A/364, Add. 1, September 9, 1947, Volume II, 64 pp. and maps. the Israel-Arab Armistice Agreements were signed at Rhodes: The Israel-Egypt Agreement on February 24, 1949, the Israel-Lebanon Agreement on March 23, the Israel-Jordan Agreement on April 3, and the Israel-Syrian Agreement on July 20. These are documented in S/1264/Rev. 1, Security Council, Official Records, Fourth Year: Special Supplement No. 3: General Armistice Agreement between Egypt and Israel (Lake Success, December 13, 1949). Special Supplement No. 4: General Armistice Agreement between Lebanon and Israel (Lake Success, April 8, 1949). Special Supplement No. 1: General Armistice Agreement between Jordan and Israel (Lake Success, June 20, 1949), and Special Supplement No. 2: General Armistice Agreement between Syria and Israel (Lake Success, June 20, 1949). Iraq, Saudi Arabia and Yemen, which had also been involved in the invasion of Palestine, refused to sign armistice agreements. The Iraqis, who played a substantial military role in the war, declined to sign on the grounds that they had no common frontier with Israel.
11. For reviews of various partition plans, see H. Eugene Bovis, *The Jerusalem Question, 1917–1960* (Stanford: Hoover Institution Press, 1971), pp. 21–44; Ben Halpern, *The Idea of the Jewish State* (Cambridge: Harvard University Press, 1961), pp. 344–375; and Cohen, *Jerusalem — Bridging the Four Walls*, pp. 188–199.
12. Saul B. Cohen, *Geopolitical Bares for the Integration of Jerusalem, Orbis, A Journal of World Affairs*, Vol. 20, No. 2 (Summer 1976), pp. 287–313.

Selected Bibliography of Werner J. Cahnman

Books

1959   (with Jean Comfaire): *How Cities Grew: The Historical Sociology of Cities* (Madison, N.H.: Florham Park Press).

1963   Ed.: *Intermarriage and Jewish Life: A Symposium* (New York: The Herzl Press and the Jewish Reconstructionist Press).

1964   Co-ed. (with Alvin Boskoff): *Sociology and History: Theory and Research* (New York: The Free Press).

1971   Co-ed. (with Rudolf Heberle): *Ferdinand Toennies on Sociology: Pure, Applied, and Empirical* (Chicago: University of Chicago Press).

1973   Ed.: *Ferdinand Toennies: A New Evaluation* (Leiden: E.J. Brill).

Articles

1937
"Warum hebräisch lernen?" in *Frankfurter Israelitisches Gemeindeblatt* (March 1937).

1941
"The Decline of the Munich Jewish Community 1933–38," in *Jewish Social Studies* Vol. III, No. 3 (1941), p. 285.

1942
"Jewish Morale in Our Time," in *Social Forces*, Vol. 20, No. 4 (May 1942), pp. 491–496.

"Methods of Geopolitics," in *Social Forces*, Vol. 21, No. 2 (December 1941), pp. 147–154.

"Stefan Zweig in Salzburg," in *The Menonah Journal*, Vol. XXX, No. 2, pp. 195–198.

1943
"An Ethical Will and A Memorial Tribute," in *The Reconstructionist*, Vol. IX, No. 10 (June 25, 1943), pp. 29–32.

"Concepts of Geopolitics," in *American Sociological Review*, Vol. VIII, No. 1 (Feb. 1943), pp. 55–59.

"The Mediterranean and Caribbean Regions — A Comparison in Race and Culture Contacts," in *Social Forces*, Vol. 22, No. 2 (Dec. 1943), pp. 209–214.

"A New Learning," by Franz Rosenzweig, in *The Chicago Jewish Forum*, Vol. 1, No. 3 (Spring 1943), pp. 55–61.

"Reflections on the Sociology of the Jews," in *Jewish Frontier*, Vol. X, No. 4 (99) (April 1943), pp. 13–17.

"A Regional Approach to German Jewish History," in *Jewish Social Studies*, Vol. V, No. 3, pp. 211–224.

"Two Maps on German-Jewish History," in *The Chicago Jewish Forum*, Vol. 2, No. 1 (Fall 1943), pp. 58–65.

1944
"An American Dilemma," in *The Chicago Jewish Forum*, Vol. 3, No. 2 (Winter 1944–45), pp. 92–96.

"The Concept of *Raum* and the Theory of Regionalism," in *American Sociological Review*, Vol. IX, No. 5. (Oct. 1944), pp. 455–462.

"Ethiopia and Palestine," in *Jewish Frontier*, Vol. XI, No. 9 (116) (Sept. 1944), pp. 12–16.

(with Wayland J. Hayes) "Foreign Area Study (ASTP) as an Educational Experiment in the Social Sciences," in *Social Forces*, Vol, 23, No. 2 (Dec. 1944), pp. 160–164.

1945
"Conflict Patterns in the Near East," in *The Chicago Jewish Forum*, Vol. 4, No. 2 (Winter 1945–46), pp. 81–85.

"France in Algeria," in *The Review of Politics*, Vol. 7, No. 3 (July 1945), pp. 343–357.

"Negroes and Jews," in *Youth and Nation*, Vol. XIII, No. 9 (June 1945), pp. 11–13.

1946
"The Arabs and Zionist Policy," in *Youth and Nation*, Vol. XIV, No. 7 (May 1946), pp. 6–8.

"Ein Deutscher Jude an einer Neger-Universität," in *Aufbau* (April 19, 1946), pp. 19–20.

"The Emergence of Negro Consciousness," in *Jewish Frontier*, Vol. XIII, No. 4 (134) (April 1946), pp. 14–17.

"The Italians in America," in *Jewish Frontier*, Vol. XIII, No. 2 (132) (Feb. 1946), pp. 8–10.

"Life History of the Norwegian Americans," in *Jewish Frontier*, Vol. XIII, No. 1 (131) (Jan. 1946), pp. 16–19.

1948

"Communication and Opinion," in *American Sociological Review*, Vol. XIII, No. 1 (Feb. 1948), p. 96.

"Intercultural Education and Jewish Content" in *The Reconstructionist*, Vol. XIV, No. 6 (April 29, 1948), pp. 9–15.

"Outline of a Theory of Area Studies," in *Annals of The Association of American Geographers*, Vol. XXXVIII, No. 4 (Dec. 1948), pp. 233–243.

"Principles for Jewish Centers," in *The Chicago Jewish Forum*, Vol. 7, No. 1 (Fall 1948), pp. 43–47.

1949

"Attitudes of Minority Youth: A Methodological Introduction," in *American Sociological Review*, Vol. XIV, No. 4 (Aug. 1949), pp. 543–548.

"Frontiers Between East and West in Europe," in *Georgraphical Society*, Vol. XXXIX, No. 4 (1949), pp. 605–624. (Reprinted in the Bobbs-Merrill *Reprint Series in Geography*.)

"Theories of Anti-Semitism" in *The Chicago Jewish Forum*, Vol. 8, No. 1 (Fall 1949), pp. 50–53.

1950

"The Jewish Scene in the United States," in *Midwest Journal*, Vol. 3, No. 1 (Winter 1950–51), pp. 24–30.

1952

(with H. Mendelsohn) "Communist Broadcasts to Italy," in *Public Opinion Quarterly*, Vol. 16, No. 4 (Winter 1952–53), pp. 671–680.

1953

"The MacIver Report Recommendations and Philosophy," in *The Chicago Jewish Forum*, Vol. 11, No. 1 (Fall 1953), pp. 1–5.

1954

(with Alice Taylor) "Spain" in *Focus*, Vol. V, No. 3 (Nov. 1954), pp. 1–6.

1955

"The Story of North Africa," in *The Chicago Jewish Forum*, Vol. 14, No. 1 (Fall 1955), pp. 37–39.

"Suspended Alienation and Apathetic Identification, in *Conference on Jewish Social Studies*, Vol. XVII, No. 3, pp. 223–228.

"The Tercentenary Conference on American Jewish Sociology," in *The Reconstructionist*, Vol. XX, No. 19 (Jan. 21, 1955), pp. 24–28.

"The UN Territory in Jerusalem: A Proposal" in *Congress Weekly*, Vol. 25, No. 18 (Nov. 24).

1956

"Religion in Israel" in *The Reconstructionist*, Vol. XXI, No. 18 (Jan. 13, 1956), pp. 17–22.

"The Wiener Library," in *The Chicago Jewish Forum*, Vol. 14, No. 4 (Summer 1956), pp. 235–237.

1957

"Socio-Economic Causes of Antisemitism," in *Social Problems*, Vol. V, No. 1 (July 1957), pp. 21–29.

1958

"A Program for the Refugees," in *The New Outlook*, Vol. II, No. 3–4 (Nov./Dec. 1958), pp. 17–22.

"The Frustrated Escapist," in *The Reconstructionist*, Vol. XXIV, No. 2 (March 7, 1958), pp. 15–20.

"Scholar and Visionary," in *Herzl Year Book*, Vol. I, ed. Raphael Patai (Herzl Press, New York, 1958), pp. 165–179.

1959

"Adolph Fischhof and his Jewish Followers," in *Year Book IV of the Leo Baeck Institute of Jews From Germany* (London, 1959), pp. 111–139.

"Reconstruction in the Wirondacks," in *The Reconstructionist*, Vol. XXV, No. 17 (Dec. 25, 1959), pp. 12–14.

1960

"Race-Individual and Collective Behavior," in *The Chicago Jewish Forum*, Vol. 18, No. 3 (Spring 1960), pp. 229–232.

1962

"Culture, Civilization, and Social Change," in *The Sociological Quarterly*, Vol. III, No. 2 (April 1962), pp. 93–106.

1964

"In The Dachau Concentration Camp," in *The Chicago Jewish Forum*, Vol. 23, No. 1 (Fall 1964), pp. 18–23.

"The Life of Clementine Kraemer," in *Year Book IX of the Leo Baeck Institute* London, 1964), pp. 267–292.

1965

"Attitudes of German Youth," in *The Reconstructionist*, Vol. XXXI, No. 5 (April 16, 1965), pp. 14–17.

"Ideal Type Theory: Max Weber's Concept and Some of Its Derivations," in *Sociological Quarterly*, Vol. 6 (Summer 1965), pp. 268–280.

"Martin Buber: A Reminiscence," in *The Reconstructionist*, Vol. XXXI, No. 12 (Oct. 15, 1965), pp. 7–11.

"Role and Significance of the Jewish Artisan Class," in *Jewish Journal of Sociology*, Vol. VII, No. 2 (Dec. 1965), pp. 207–220.

1966

"The Historical Sociology of Cities: A Critical Review," in *Social Forces*, Vol. 45, No. 2 (Dec. 1966), pp. 156–162.

1967

"Ghetto," in *Encyclopedia Britanica* (1967), p. 389.

"The Interracial Jewish Children," in *The Reconstructionist*, Vol. XXXIII, No. 8 (June 9, 1967), pp. 7–11.

"New Intermarriage Studies: A Critical Survey," in *The Reconstructionist*, Vol. XXXIII, No. 2 (March 17, 1967), pp. 7–12.

1968

"The Stigma of Obesity," in *Sociological Quarterly*, Vol. 9, No. 3 (Summer 1968), pp. 283–299.

1969

"A Comment on My Son the Doctor," in *American Sociological Review*, Vol. 34, No. 6 (Dec. 1969), pp. 935–936.

1970

"Germany in 1970," in *The Reconstructionist*, Vol. XXXVI, No. 13 (Dec. 25, 1970), pp. 14–18.

"Tönnies and Durkheim: Eine dokumentarische Gegenüberstellung," in *ARSP* Vol. 1970, LVI/2, pp. 189–208.

1971

"Eine Geschichte der Soziologie," in *ARSP*, Vol. 1971, LVII/1, pp. 129–138.

"Sociology," in *Encyclopedia Judaica*, Vol. 15, SM–UN, columns 62–69.

1972

"Adolf Fischhof's jüdische Persönlichkeit," in *Zeitschrift für Religionswissenschaft und Theologie* (Neue Folge, XIV, Jahrgang 1972), pp. 110–120.

"Rolle und Bedeutung der Jüdischen Handwerkerklasse," in *Archiv. Europ. Sociology*, Vol. XIII (1972), pp. 111–125.

"Soziologie und Geschichte," in Hans-Ulrich Weber, ed. (Kiepenheiner & Witsch, Köln, 1972), pp. 157–186.

1973

"Jews and Blacks: An Overview," in *The Reconstructionist*, Vol. XXXVIII, No. 10 (Jan. 1973), pp. 7–14.

"Werner Cahnman at Seventy," in *The Reconstructionist*, Vol. XXXIX, No. 5 (June 1973), pp. 24–32.

1974

"Adolf Fischhof als Verfechter der Nationalität und seine Auswirkung auf das jüdisch — politische Denken in Österreich," in *Studia Judaica Austriaca* (Wien, 1974), pp. 78–91.

"Der Dorf und Kleinstadtjude als Typus," in *Zeitschrift für Volkskunde*, Vol. II (1974), pp. 169–193.

"Friedrich Wilhelm Schelling über die Judenemanzipation," in *Zeitschrift für bayerische Landesgeschichte* (Bd. 37, Heft 2, 1974), pp. 615–625.

"Der Pariah und der Fremde: Eine begriffliche Klärung," in *Archiv. Europ. Sociology*, Vol. XV (1974), pp. 166–167.

"Pariahs, Strangers, and Court-Jews: A Conceptual Clarification," in *Sociological Analysis*, Vol. 35, No. 3 (Fall 1974), pp. 155–166.

"Village and Small Town Jews in Germany: A Typological Study," in *Year Book XIX of the Leo Baeck Institute* (London, 1974), pp. 107–130.

1976

"Historical Sociology: What It Is and What It Is Not," in Baydia N. Varma, *The New Social Sciences* (Westport, Conn., Greenwood Press, 1976), pp. 107–122.

"Tönnies, Durkheim and Weber," in *Social Science Information*, Vol. 15, No. 6 (1976), pp. 839–853.

"Vico and Historical Sociology," in *Social Research*, Vol. 43, No. 4 (Winter 1976), pp. 826–836.

1977

"Agenda für das Studieren des Landjudentums," in *Vereinigte Zeitschriften über Israel und Judentum* (Heft Nr. 5–6, 1977), pp. 5–10.

"Tönnies in America," in *History and Theory*, Vol. XVI, No. 2 (1977), pp. 147–167.

1979

"Adolph Fischhof and the Problem of the Reconciliation of Nationalities," in *East European Quarterly*, Vol. XII, No. 1 (1979), pp. 43–56.

(with C.M. Schmitt) "The Concept of Social Policy," in *Journal of Social Policy*, Vol. 8, Part 1 (Jan. 1979), pp. 47–59.

1980

"Nature and Vanities of Ethnicity," in Parmatma Saran and Edwin Eames, eds. *The New Ethics: Asian Indians in the United States* (New York: Praeger, 1980), pp. 5–28.

REVIEWS

1943

Baron, *The Jewish Community*. Reviewed in *Social Forces*, Vol. 22, No. 1 (October 1943), pp. 111–113.

Dropalen, Andreas, *The World of General Haushofer: Geopolitics in Action* (New York: Farrar & Rinehart, Inc., 1942). Reviewed in *The Journal of Political Economy*, Vol. LI, No. 3 (June 1943), pp. 268–272.

Weigert, H.W., *Generals and Geography: The Twilight of Geopolitics* (New York: Oxford University Press, 1942). Reviewed in *The Journal of Political Economy*, Vol. LI, No. 3 (June 1943), pp. 268–272.

Whittlesey, Derwent, with collaboration of Colby, C.C. and Hartshorne, R., *German Strategy of World Conquest* (New York: Farrar & Rinehart, Inc., 1942). Reviewed in *The Journal of Political Economy*, Vol. LI, No. 3 (June 1943), pp. 268–272.

1944

Elbogen, Ismer, *A Century of Jewish Life*, translated from the German by Moses Hadas, with an appreciation of the author by Prof. Alexander Marx (Philadelphia: The Jewish Publication Society of America, 1944). Reviewed in *Social Forces*, Vol 23, No. 2 (October 1944), pp. 229–230.

Johnson, Charles S. and associates, *To Stem This Tide: A Survey of Racial Tension Areas* (Boston and Chicago: Pilgrim Press, 1943). Reviewed in *Jewish Social Studies*, Vol. VI, No. 3 (July 1944), pp. 286–288.

Kulischer, *The Displacement of Population in Europe*. Reviewed in *Social Forces*, Vol. 22, No. 4 (May 1944), pp. 457–458.

1945

Bienfeld, F.R. *The Germans and the Jews*, translated by Herdman Pender (New York: Frederick Ungar, 1939). Reviewed in *Jewish Social Studies*, Vol. VII, No. 2 (April 1945), pp. 161–164.

1946

Nathan, R., Gass, O., Creamer, D. *Palestine, Problem and Promise: An Economic Study* (Washington,, D.C.: Public Affairs Press, American Council on Public Relation, 1946). Reviewed in *Social Forces*, Vol. 25, No. 2 (December 1946), pp. 230–231.

1948

Hugelmann, K.G., Boehm, M.H., Hasselblatt, W., eds., "Volksehre und Nationalitaetenrecht in Geschichte und Gegenwart," Ser. 3, Vol. I (Essen: Essener Verlagsanstalt, 1940). Reviewed in *The American Journal of Sociology*, Vol. LIII, No. 4 (July 1947 – May, 1948), pp. 309–311.

Kloss, Heinz, *Das Volksgruppenrecht in den Vereinigten Staaten von Amerika*, Erster Band: *Die Erstsiedlergruppen* ("The Right of Ethnic Groups in the U.S.A., Vol. 1: "The First Settlers"). Reviewed in *The American Journal of Sociology*, Liii, No. 4 (July 1947 – May 1948), pp. 309–311.

Roth, Cecil, *The History of the Jews of Italy* (Philadelphia 5706–1946: The Jewish Publication Society of America). Reviewed in *The Menorah Journal*, Vol. XXXVI, No. 1 (Winter 1948), pp. 102–114.

Simey, T.S., *Welfare and Planning in the West Indies* (Oxford: Clarendon Press, 1946). Reviewed in *The American Journal of Sociology*, Vol. LIII, No. 4 (July 1947 – May 1948), pp. 309–311.

1949

Linton, Ralph, ed., *Most of the World: The Peoples of Africa, Latin America and the East Today* (New York: Columbia University Press, 1949). Reviewed in *The American Journal of Sociology*, Vol. LV, No. 1 (July 1949), pp. 106–108.

1952

Chonraqui, André, *La Condition Juridique de l'Israélite Marocain* (Paris: Alliance Israélite Universelle: Presses du Livre Français, 1950). Reviewed in *Jewish Social Studies*, Vol. XVI, No. 3 (July 1954), pp. 275–276.

Chonraqui, André, *Marche vers l'Occident—Les Juifs d'Afrique du Nord* (Paris: Presses Universitaires de France, 1952). Reviewed in *Jewish Social Studies*, Vol. XVI, No. 3 (July 1954), pp. 275–276.

Chouraqui, André, *The Social and Legal Status of the Jews of French Morocco* (New York: The American Jewish Committee, 1952). Reviewed in *Jewish Social Studies*, Vol. XVI, No. 3 (July 1954), pp. 275–276.

Zborowski, Mark and Herzog, Elizabeth, *Life Is With People: The Jewish Little-Town of Eastern Europe* (New York: Internaional Universities

Press Inc., 1952). Reviewed in *American Sociology Review*, Vol. 17, No. 5 (October 1952), pp. 655–656.

1954
Mead, M. and Metraux, R., eds., *The Study of Culture at a Distance* (Chicago: The University of Chicago Press, 1953). Reviewed in *American Sociological Review*, Vol. 19, No. 6 (December 1954), pp. 792–793.

Sraffa, *The Works and Correspondence of David Ricardo*. Reviewed in *Social Forces*, Vol. 32, No. 4 (May 1954), pp. 379–380.

1957
Eisenstadt, S.N., *The Absorption of Immigrants: A Comparative Study Based Mainly on the Jewish Community in Palestine and the State of Israel* (Glencoe, Ill.: The Free Press 1955). Reviewed in *Jewish Social Studies*, Vol. XIX, No. 3–4 (July – October 1957), pp. 156–157.

Hughes, E.C. and Hughes, H.M., *Where People Meet: Racial and Ethnical Frontiers* (Glencoe: The Free Press, 1952). Reviewed in *Jewish Social Studies*, Vol. XVII No. 1 (January 1955), pp. 74–75.

1958
Zwiedinek, Otto von, *Mensch und Wirtschaft*: *Aufsaetze und Abhandlungen zur Wirtschaftstheorie und Wirtschaftspolitik* ("Man and Economy: Essays and Discussions of the Economy Theory and Policy") (Berlin: Duncker and Humblot, 1955). Reviewed in *The American Journal of Sociology*, Vol. LXIV (July 1958 – May 1959), pp. 329–331.

1960
Antoni, Carlos, *From History to Sociology: The Transition in German Historical Thinking*, translated by Hayden V. White (Detroit: Wayne State University Press, 1959). Reviewed in *American Sociological Review*, Vol. 25, No. 1 (February 1960), pp. 120–121.

1961
Siddur, de Sola Pool, *The Traditional Prayerbook for Sabbath and Festivals*, ed. and translated by David de Sola Pool (New Hyde Park: New York University Books, 1960). Reviewed in *Social Forces*, Vol. 39, No. 4 (May 1961), p. 356.

1966
Schwarz, Stefan, *Die Juden in Bayern im Wandel der Zeiten* (München und Wien: Gunter Olsog Verlag, 1963). Reviewed in *Jewish Social Studies*, Vol. XXVIII, No. 1 (January 1966), pp. 43–46.

1968
Ringer, B., Vol. II: *The Edge of Friendliness: A Study of Jewish-Gentile*

Relations (New York and London, 1967). Reviewed in *American Jewish Historical Quarterly*, Vol. LVIII, No. 2 (December 1968), pp. 287–291.

Sklare, M. and Greenblum, J., *The Lakeville Studies: Vol. I: Jewish Identity on the Suburban Frontier. A Study of Group Survival in the Open Society*. Reviewed in *Americn Jewish Historical Quarterly*, Vol. LVIII, No. 2 (December 1968), pp. 287–291.

1969

Glock, Charles Y. and Stark, Rodney, *Christian Beliefs and Anti-Semitism*. Reviewed in *Social Forces*, Vol. 47, No. 3 (March 1969), pp. 349–350.

Symmons-Symonolewicz, Konstantin, *Modern Nationalism: Towards a Consensus in Theory* (New York: The Polish Institute of Arts and Sciences in America, 1968). Reviewed in *Journal of Social History*, Vol. 2, No. 4 (1969), pp. 280–282.

Weber, Max, *Economy and Society*, ed. Gunter Roth and Claus Wittich. Reviewed in *Social Forces*, Vol. 48, No. 2 (December 1969), pp. 269–270.

1970

Aron, Raymond, Main Currents in Sociological Thought, Vol. 1: *Montesquieu, Comte, Marx, Tocqueville, The Sociologists and the Revolution of 1848* (New York: Basic Books, 1965). Reviewed in *Journal of the History of the Behavioral Sciences*, Vol. VI, No. 4 (October 1970), pp. 368–370.

Aron, Raymond, Main Currents in Sociological Thought, Vol. II: *Durkheim, Pareto, Weber* (New York: Basic Books, 1967). Reviewed in *Journal of the History of the Behavioral Sciences*, Vol. VI, No. 4 (October 1979), pp. 368–370.

Erikson, Kai T., *Wayward Puritans: A Study in The Sociology of Deviance* (New York: John Wiley & Sons, 1966). Reviewed in *Journal of the History of the Behavioral Sciences*, Vol. VI, No. 4 (October 1970), pp. 367–368.

Lipset, S.M. and Hofstadter, R., eds., *Sociology and History: Methods* (New York: Basic Books, 1968). Reviewed in *Journal of the History of the Behavioral Sciences* Vol. VI, No. 4 (October 1970), pp. 373–375.

Mitzan, Arthur, *The Iron Cage: An Historical Interpretation of Max Weber* (New York: Alfred A. Knopf, 1970). Reviewed in *Journal of the History of the Behavioral Sciences*, Vol. VI, No. 4 (October 1970), pp. 373–375.

Nisbet, R.A., *Social Change and History: Aspects of the Western Theory of Development* (New York: Oxford University Press, 1969). Reviewed in *Journal of Social History*, Vol. 4, No. 2 (Winter 1970–71), pp. 190–192.

1971

Banton, Michael, *Race Relations* (New York: Basic Books, 1967). Reviewed in *Journal of the History of the Behavioral Sciences*, Vol. VII, No. 1 (January 1971), pp. 109–111.

1972

Ben-Sasson, H.H. and Ettinger, S., *Jewish Society Through the Ages* (New York: Schocken Books, 1972). Reviewed in *American Jewish Historical Quarterly*, Vol. LXII, No. 2 (December 1972), pp. 220–222.

Itzkoff, Seymour, *Ernst Cassier: Scientific Knowledge and the Concept of Man* (Notre Dame/London: University of Notre Dame Press, 1971). Reviewed in *ISIS* 63, 3, 218 (1972), pp. 425–427.

1973

Hummell, H.J. and Opp, K.D., *Die Reduzierbarkeit von Soziologie auf Psychologie: Eine These, ihr Test und ihre Theoretische Bedeutung* (Braunschweig: Friedrich Vieweg & Sohn, 1971). Reviewed in *The American Journal of Sociology*, Vol. 78, No. 6 (May 1973), pp. 1559–63.

Pollack, Herman, *Jewish Folkways in Germanic Lands (1648–1806): Studies in Aspects of Daily Life* (Cambridge, Mass.: The M.I.T. Press, 1971). Reviewed in *Journal of Social History* (Fall 1973), pp. 104–105.

1975

Medick, Hans, *Naturzustand und Naturgeschichte der bürgerlichen Gesellschaft: Die Ursprünge der bürgerlichen Sozialtheorie als Geschichtsphilosophie und Sozialwissenschaft bei Samuel Pufendorf, John Locke und Adam Smith* (Kritische Studien zur Rupprecht, Göttingen, 1973). Reviewed in *Archiv für Rechts und Sozialphilosophie*, Bd. LXI, 1 (1975), pp. 151–154.

Contributors

Karl M. Bolte is professor of sociology at University of Munich.

Alvin Boskoff is professor of sociology at Emory University.

Karl Bosl is professor emeritus of history at University of Munich.

Saul B. Cohen is president of Queens College–City University of New York.

Louis Dumont is directeur d'etudes at the Ecole des Hautes Etudes en Sciences Sociales in Paris.

Lewis S. Feuer is professor of sociology at the University of Virginia.

Nathan Glazer is professor of education and sociology at Harvard University.

Calvin Goldscheider is chairman of the Department of Demography at The Hebrew University.

Irving Louis Horowitz is Hannah Arendt professor of political science and sociology at Rutgers University.

Edmund Leites is associate professor of philosophy at Queens College–City University of New York.

Andrew P. Lyons and *Harriet Lyons* are associate professors of anthropology at Wilfried Laurier University.

Emmanuel Maier is professor of geography at Bridgewater State College.

Joseph B. Maier is professor emeritus of sociology at Rutgers University.

William Spinrad is professor of sociology at Adelphi University.

The late *Lester Singer* was dean and professor of sociology at The New School for Social Research.

Herbert A. Strauss is professor emeritus of history at The City College–City University of New York, and professor of modern history and director, Center for Anti-Semitism Research, Technical University, Berlin.

Chaim I. Waxman is associate professor of sociology at Rutgers University.

Index

Abelard, 35
Abrahams, I., 117, 119
Abrams, P., 163, 167, 178
Abravanel, S., 106
acculturation:
 of German-Jewish immigrants,
 227–248
Achad Haam, 3
Adams, R.M., 163, 178, 180
Adams, W.A., 192
Addams, J., 160
Adler, B., 288
Adler, F., 149
Adler-Rudel, S., 247
Adorno, T.W., 37, 61
Agassiz, L., 142
Agus, I., 99, 110, 118, 121
Alcalay, R., 117
Alexander the Great, 132, 134
Anderson, N., 197
Apion, 95
Arendt, H., 217, 226
Aristotle, 112, 122, 132, 144
Arnold of Brescia, 35
Arzt, M., 117, 118
Askowith, D., 102, 119
Aszod, J., 108, 109
Atticus, 133
Averroes, 104, 105
Attias, A., 83
Attias, G., 83, 91
Aufbau, 233, 243
Aufbruch, 30ff.
Augustin, 32, 82
authority:
 parental and political, 61–78

authoritarian distemper, 211–226
Axelrod, J., 108
Axtell, J., 62, 78
Azurara, G.E. de, 145

Bacci, M.L., 122
Bacharach, M.S., 96
Bachman, J., 142
Baeck, L., 3, 92, 228f.
Baer, Y., 104, 120
Baeyer, A. von, 108
Banks, J., 62
Barany, R., 108
Bar-Ilan, M., 108
Barker, E., 17, 25
Bar-Lev, H., 308
Baron, S.W., 7, 8, 91, 92, 98, 102,
 106, 117, 118, 119
Barzilay, I.E., 91
Baskerville, B.C., 120
Bateson, W., 112, 121
Bauer, Y., 119
Baugh, D.A., 169, 178
Bautier, R.H., 163, 178
Bayor, R.H., 209
Beer-Hofmann, R., 3
Begin, M., 259
Bein, A., 120
Bell, D., 199, 272
Benedict, R., 133, 144, 202
Ben Gurion, D., 319
Benjamin of Tudela, 110, 111,
 121
Benn, S.I., 220, 226
Ben-Sasson, H.H., 120
Ben Sira, 95, 97

Landsteiner, K., 108, 121
Las Casas, B. de, 137, 138
Laski, H., 221, 226
Laslett, P., 77
Laswell, H., 217, 218, 226
Lazzarino del Grosso, A., 38
Lea, H.C., 122
Leach, E.R., 143
Le Bon, G., 228
Leclerc, G.L., 141
Lederberg, J., 108
Leeuwenhoek, A. van, 141
Lefebvre, H., 180
Lenk, H., 59
Le Play, F., 10
Lewis, O., 183, 187, 188, 193,
    195, 198, 204, 209
liberalism, 249ff.
Liebman, A., 271
Lieberson, S., 209
Liebow, E., 198
Light, R.E., 146
Lindsay, J., 205
Linnaeus, C., 141
Lippmann, G., 108
Lipset, S.M., 268, 269, 270, 271
Litani, D., 118
Litt, E., 255, 256, 266, 270, 271,
    272
Livermore, H., 122
Locke, J., 59, 61–78, 213, 219,
    220, 226
Loewi, O., 108
Loomis, C., 10
Lowenberg, R., 270
Lowth, R., 83
Lubell, S., 209, 265, 271
Luis de Miranda, 114
Lukoff, I.J., 247
Luria, S., 108
Lwoff, A., 108
Lynd, H.M., 218, 226
Lyons, A.P., 161, 162

Machiavelli, N., 156
MacIver, R.M., 223, 226
Magnes, J., 5
Mahler, R., 270
Maier, J., 9, 91
Maimon, S., 96, 97, 98, 105, 118,
    120
Maimonides, M., 85, 91, 95, 99
Malefijt, A. de W., 146
Mandel, D., 121
Mandeville, B., 145
Mannheim, K., 178, 180, 213, 225
Manselli, R., 39
Marcuse, H., 43, 61, 227
Margulies, S., 108
Markus, H., 60
Marvick, D., 226
Marx, K., 87, 105, 139, 175, 213,
    225
Mason, T., 28
Masuoka, J., 144
Mather, C., 78
Matras, J., 288, 289
Mayer, T., 37
Mazzochi, A.S., 83
McGovern, G., 251, 257
McKenzie, R.D., 186, 188
Mead, G.H., 160, 215, 225
Mead, M., 146, 203
medieval historiography, 27ff.
Medini, H., 108
Meinecke, F., 22
Meinhertzhagen, R., 299, 301,
    319, 320
Melamed, S.W., 156, 162
Mellor, J.R., 163, 180
Mendelssohn, A., 105
Mendelssohn-Bartholdy, F., 105
Mendelssohn, M., 2, 105
Mendlowitz, S., 108
Merton, R.K., 189-190, 197
Metchnikoff, E., 108
Meyerhof, O., 108

Walter, H.A., 248
Ward, L., 184–185, 196
Warburg, O., 108
Warner, W.L., 192, 194, 195, 198
Warner, S.B., 169, 181
Watkins, A.J., 180
Waugh, M., 77
Waxman, C.I., 195, 196
Weardale, Lord, 149, 150, 159
Weber, M., 10, 27, 28, 32, 59,
    139, 156, 167, 181
Wechsler, J., 199
Wehler, H.U., 37
Weinreich, M., 160
Weintraub, D., 289
Werner, E., 38, 39
Weyl, N., 93, 94, 117
White, C., 142
Wiebe, R.H., 175, 181, 270
Wiener, N., 93, 94, 117
Wiesenthal, S., 119
Willey, G.R., 163, 178
Wilstaetter, R., 108
Wirth, L., 7, 169, 181, 186

Wischnitzer, M., 8
Wischnitzer, R., 8
Wittke, C., 248
Wolf, L., 154, 161
Wolff, M., 169, 179
Worsthorne, P., 143
Wrigley, E.A., 163, 167, 178

Yancey, W., 288
Yerushalmi, Y.H., 91

Zangwill, I., 150, 157, 158, 162
Zborowski, M., 117, 118, 119
Zeigler, L.H., 213, 225
Zeitlin, H., 108
Zionism, 4–8, 262ff.
Znaniecki, F., 143, 187
Zorbaugh, H.W., 197
Zubaida, S., 143
Zuns, L., 91
Zweig, S., 8
Zwiebach, B., 226
Zwiedineck-Suedenhorst, H., 3,5